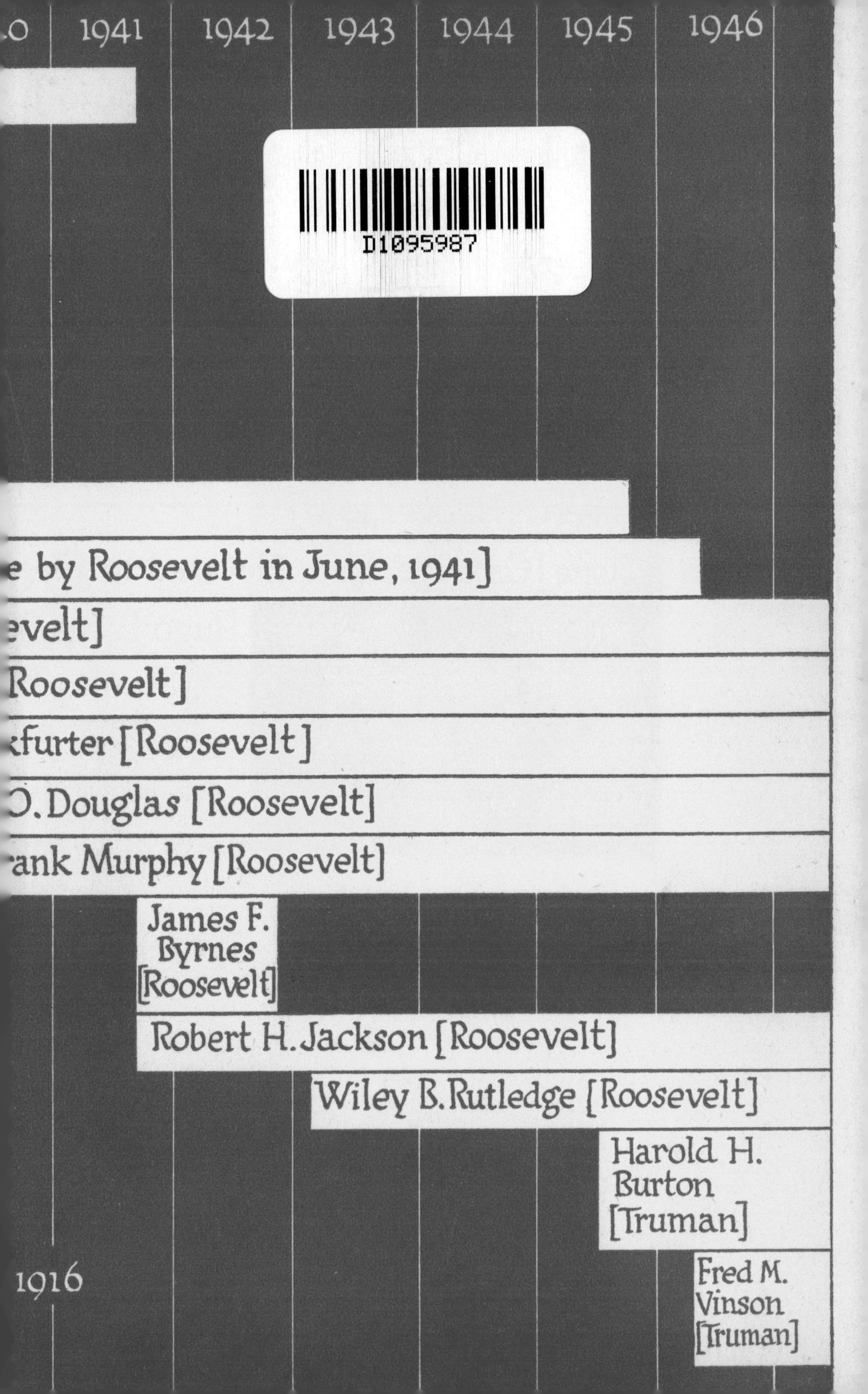
.0
1941
1942
1943
1944
1945
1946
D1095987
e by Roosevelt in June, 1941]
evelt]
Roosevelt]
kfurter [Roosevelt]
O. Douglas [Roosevelt]
rank Murphy [Roosevelt]
James F. Byrnes [Roosevelt]
Robert H. Jackson [Roosevelt]
Wiley B. Rutledge [Roosevelt]
Harold H. Burton [Truman]
1916
Fred M. Vinson [Truman]

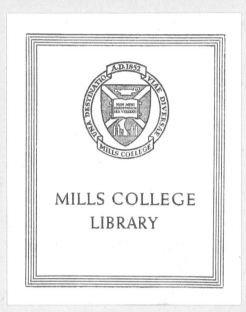

THE NINE YOUNG MEN

THE NINE YOUNG MEN

BY

WESLEY McCUNE

AUTHOR OF "THE FARM BLOC"

HARPER & BROTHERS · PUBLISHERS

NEW YORK · LONDON

5-7

THE NINE YOUNG MEN

PRINTED IN THE UNITED STATES OF AMERICA

FIRST EDITION

D-W

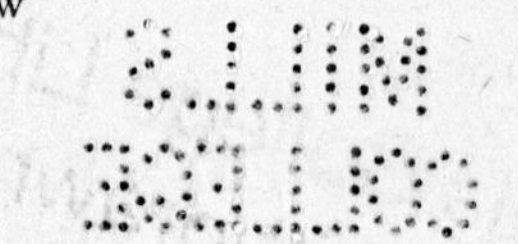

CONTENTS

Prefatory Note

TEN YEARS have passed since Franklin D. Roosevelt split the Washington air with his plan to reorganize the United States Supreme Court, better known as a plan to "pack" the Court.

A decade of judicial revolution is not easy to compress into one book, be it for lawyers or laymen. A member of the Court once told me that if the Court's opinions could be capsulized he supposed the justices would write them that way themselves. A learned lawyer, trying to be helpful, handed me a ninety-eight-page law review article he had written on *one* Supreme Court decision. It contained 458 footnotes and it is not mentioned in this book.

To break up the heavier legal subjects I have inserted profiles of the justices as alternating chapters, a sort of judicial sandwich which can also be justified as symbolic of the extent to which mortals naturally mix personal with legal opinions. Besides—in the language of the sports arena—you can't enjoy the game without the name and number of each and every player.

There could be no better illustration of this fact than the ignorance with which Justice Jackson's feud with Justice Black was received by the public. The issues raised by Jackson were newsworthy, but the real story had little to do with Black's refusal to disqualify himself from a case brought by his former law partner. The real story goes to the roots of the judicial process.

Criticism of the Court which has undoubtedly found its way into this book is meant constructively and appears as a by-product of the main task—a journalistic account of what has been going on recently at the top of the nation's judiciary.

As Justice David J. Brewer commented many years ago, "It is a mistake to suppose that the Supreme Court is either honored or helped by being spoken of as beyond criticism. On the contrary, the life and character of its justices should be the objects of constant watchfulness by all, and its judgments subject to the freest criticism. The time is past in the history of the world when any living man or body of men can be set on a pedestal and decorated with a halo. True, many criticisms may be, like their authors, devoid of good taste, but better all sorts of criticism than no criticism at all."

Two justices now on the Court, Frankfurter and Jackson, have quoted this 1898 belief with approval. In 1946 another justice, Rutledge, made a blunter statement which is pertinent. In a freedom of the press case he wrote: "There is perhaps no area of news more inaccurately reported factually, on the whole, though with some notable exceptions, than legal news."

I have accepted both the Brewer invitation to throw rocks at the Court and the Rutledge challenge of responsibility for doing so objectively.

The next generation may look at the title of this book, snort contemptuously and wonder how that bunch of old fogies could ever have been thought of as young. In fact, it may happen in my time. However, my job is to capture contemporary history of the Court, not to disclose the eternal verities or square the circle.

The nine men now on the nation's highest bench are young in years and in vitality, but to stop there would be to infer something wrong about being old, an inference of which I want no part. The justices should be in step with the times which create the litigation they settle, but age alone is too artificial to be a valid test. To avoid having to apologize to men like Brandeis and Holmes, who did some of their best work after most men retire, let us say that the phrase "Nine Young Men" is neither better nor worse than it was to label the preceding justices as "The Nine Old Men."

WASHINGTON, D. C. WESLEY McCUNE

THE NINE YOUNG MEN

CHAPTER I

One First Avenue, Northeast

THERE are many reasons for the hush which automatically comes over visitors to the Greek temple, Corinthian order, that houses the Supreme Court of the United States of America. Of course reverence is due any institution that has survived 157 years of national wear and tear, and the domicile of any institution is the physical catchall for whatever bows, genuflections and burnt offerings are intended for the spirits that inhabit it.

However, Americans not being a nation of ancestor worshipers—in the usual sense, at least—there must be more earthy reasons for their respect to the High Tribunal, the Court of Last Resort.

For one thing, the nine mortals on exhibit there put on one of the best shows in Washington, a city of highly specialized shows. There is nothing in the capital city to compare with the drama enacted about eighty times each year in the magnificent Court chamber when the gavel raps, the chief justice of the United States parts the rich red drapes behind the long mahogany bar, the eight black-robed associate justices appear from their hiding places, and all nine take positions carefully governed by years of custom.

"Oyez, Oyez, Oyez! All persons having business before the Honorable, the Supreme Court of the United States are admonished to draw near and give their attention, for the Court is now sitting. God save the United States and this Honorable Court," intones the marshal in carefully groomed syllables.

As the gavel falls again and knickered page boys scamper to adjust the chair for each justice, one is tempted to borrow a minstrel show phrase to make the ceremony complete: "Gentlemen, be seated!" It's a good show. One quarter of a million people, many of whom have waited in long queues in the severe white corridors outside, come to see it each year, even in wartime.

But if the Court is not in session visitors huddle around the open chamber door in the same hushed reverence. With the actors gone they look over the stage, the more historically minded of them recalling famous lines of the judicial theater, the others merely ohing and ahing.

There is enough in the theater building alone to make the pilgrimage worth while. The $3,000,000 worth of marble that was brought from Vermont, Alabama, Italy and Spain for the Court's new $10,000,000 home has been arranged in dignity but with as much warmth as marble offers.

As a symbol of "the national ideal of justice in the highest sphere of activity," it stands across a beautiful park from the Capitol, where for seventy-five years, up to 1935, the Court occupied a dingy room smaller than some congressional committees now have to themselves. The planners who wanted a building that would symbolize the independence of the judiciary certainly got it.

And those who wanted permanence built into the Court's home need only describe its roof: cream-colored Roman tile set on bronze strips over lead-coated copper and all resting on a slab of watertight concrete. The Court might succumb to a political storm, but it will never be driven out by any other kind of inclement weather.

This same deliberate massiveness is effected at the entrance by thirty-two tall columns and numerous wide steps of gleaming white marble. That lowly starlings, unschooled in the laws, insist on living high in the columns and fouling the pristine entrance or that the gleaming steps are dangerous when icy do not interfere materially with the Court's functions. Worldly board steps and rails are dragged out in the winter and the starlings are frightened away daily or—during the stress of war—left to their own devices.

It also seems unimportant that the chamber in which the nine justices convene to hear arguments and announce decisions is too small to seat much of the public. When the Court moved across the street from its sardine can in the Capitol to its Taj Mahal, the chamber space was increased only 60 per cent, making room on churchlike benches and extra chairs for a total of 316 people.

But small matter—the chamber is beautiful. One notices first the great yardage of rich red velour drapes, then the massive mahogany bar and the forty-four-foot ceiling with its modern indirect lighting.

Visitors who have no interest in the legalism of the proceedings cannot write letters or doze off—a roving bailiff enforces Court rules against both. However, there is no rule against admiring panels of art on the four walls above the twenty-four columns, including "Divine Inspiration," "Powers of Evil," "Defense of Virtue" and "Harmony." Or visitors may study a muralist's conception of ancient lawmakers, such as Mohammed and Confucius; but most prefer to study their nine contemporaries and watch the quick page boys fetch water or documents for Their Honors.

The building blends artfully the old and the new. A medallion of Hammurabi, promulgator in 2000 B.C. of the oldest known written code, is balanced with air conditioning and metal Venetian shades. The two library rooms upstairs—one resembling a room in an old castle, the other a room in an old cathedral—are offset by a pneumatic tube system for dispatching press copy from the chamber. The archaic system of introducing applicants for admission to practice before the Court is in sharp contrast to the basement traffic light system for the justices' cars.

The only place science fell down in designing the building was in the accoustics department. Spectators can hardly pick up the weighty pronouncements that fall from bench and bar a few feet away.

It is in oak-paneled offices arranged in a U-shape around the formal chamber that the wheels of justice actually do their grinding. Along this private corridor each member of the Court has a suite of three comfortable rooms: one for his own meditation, one for his female secretary and her records and one for his clerk, traditionally an honor graduate of the previous year's class from each justice's favored law school. Each suite includes a fireplace and ultramodern bath with glass-doored shower stall, yet the tone of each is dignified simplicity.

A typical day for a justice starts in midmorning, usually after some reading has been done at home, both after breakfast and into the night before. There are no liveried chauffeurs in the Court's ritual or expense account; the justices drive ordinary cars, walk or ride streetcars to work. The routine from October through May is divided into fortnightly periods. For two weeks the Court sits to hear oral arguments, then for two weeks it drafts and redrafts opinions. Results are announced only on three Monday noons of each month, dubbed "judgment days."

When the Court is in public session, the official work day starts a few minutes before noon, when the justices gather in their inner sanctum, formally known as the "conference room." Here they chat until time to pass into the adjoining robing room, an oversized closet where a Negro attendant helps each jurist with the black faille robe which he had tailored when he was appointed. Nowhere is the Court's system of seniority better symbolized than here. Along one of the oak-paneled walls are nine oak lockers for as many robes, the door of each labeled with a brass name plate in the order of service on the Court.

By exactly high noon—and that means *exactly* high noon—the nine justices have crossed a white marble corridor, where they stand in place behind dark red curtains until the chief justice parts the center curtains dramatically and each takes his place to stand until the Oyez ritual is finished. Before each robed justice is a reading light, a small calendar, a black leather loose-leaf copy of the official docket and assorted pencils. Beside most of them is an old-fashioned spittoon, should nature interfere with justice momentarily, and each is seated in a chair of his own selection—high-backed, black leather swivel chairs which can and do lean far back. Each party to the dispute at hand distributes its legal briefs, printed in large type by order of previous eye-weary justices.

If it is an opinion Monday, or judgment day, the Court's decision is read or given orally in essence, followed by any dissents. No matter what day it may be, if the Court is in session at all it adjourns promptly at two o'clock for a thirty-minute lunch period in the justices' private dining room upstairs. There they have a refrigerator large enough to hold a horse, but more than likely it will be found harboring a lonely can of beans. Some of the justices bring their own lunches from home.

From two-thirty until four oral arguments are resumed, with questions freely hurled or needled in from the high bench. Rare is the lawyer who has been given much more than sixty minutes for his case, which allows him time to do little more than refer to important sections of the printed brief that each justice will have to read anyway.

Saturdays are also oral argument days, but of a different kind—the nine justices argue among themselves in the privacy of their conference room. Here they sit more comfortably, around a huge table covered with black felt, and enjoy freedom from the ban on smoking which prevails on the bench. Beside each is a small table for books and other paraphernalia; in front of each is a small drawer for which he has his own key. The inevitable brass name plate is on each high black chair, and a dazzling crystal chandelier hangs over the table's center. Other light streams through three floor-to-ceiling windows, hung with blue-and-gold figured drapes. A short stepladder is handy for any justice who wants a tome from the uppermost of many shelves around the room.

As he presides, from one end of the table, the chief justice faces an old-fashioned gold clock on the mantel opposite him, above which is the only picture in the room, that of Salmon P. Chase, chief justice from 1864 to 1873.

When each justice arrives in this setting he has studied the week's grist of cases and is ready to hash over each until it appears that the time is ripe for the final vote. The freshman member is put on the hot spot by being required to vote first, followed by his less green colleagues and on up to the chief justice, who frequently is also on a hot spot by having to break a tie. Later, the chief justice assigns the job of writing majority opinions. Old-timers usually get the most important opinions, while the thankless, highly technical tax opinions are tossed to the freshman to bore himself with. The minority opinion is assigned by the senior dissenter.

Each justice returns to his office to give his law clerk the bad news and start him gathering material and technical citations. Drafts of opinions are passed up and down the corridors for comment and approval before printing.

From oral argument to announcement may have taken two weeks or it may have taken two years, but the wheels of justice have ground. The grindings fill 328 volumes of official reports on lawyers' and librarians' shelves all over the country.

One might suppose that an institution that puts everything on record—has to explain everything it does—would be the best understood of all. In the instance of the Supreme Court, however, understanding seems to run in inverse ratio to the number of pages of printed opinions. Add to the futility of reading all the Court's decisions, its various trappings and the exclusiveness of those who do business with it and you have what makes John Q. Public turn off his motor when he draws near to the Court. It is mystery—mystery of the plain, old-fashioned kind. Look at the symbolism of the Court, for example. Rare are the laymen and few are the lawyers who can explain what Grotius is doing high on the south wall of the Court's chamber. Add Hammurabi, Lycurgus and Octavius and you have a last remnant of ancestor worship in modern American government.

Or look at the Court's opening ceremony and try to find a counterpart in either of the other two divisions of government. The first thing after the Oyez, old members of the Supreme Court bar lead newcomers up to the bar one at a time, mumble a few words about each applicant's qualifications and steer him toward the clerk's desk to be sworn in with the group. This time-wasting ceremony actually boils down to window dressing for a system whereby out-of-town lawyers can tell clients they have been presented to the highest court of the land and hang a certificate to that effect on their office walls. Any lawyer who has practiced three years before the highest court of his state and can raise twenty-five dollars can go through the ordeal.

The nonsense takes an equivalent of about one work week out of the justices' lives each term, yet nothing has been done for years to trim it down to reasonableness and make way for more cases. In fact, Court observers will never forget the importance one chief justice placed on the ceremony. A congressman who was putting up for membership a lawyer friend whose unbuttoned coat disclosed no vest was told by Chief Justice Taft: "Return with your candidate when he is properly dressed."

Then there's the matter of judicial costume. Though the President and his diplomats have practically discarded the top hat, and though congressmen almost never wear their hair long or sport string bow ties any more, the Supreme Court keeps its black robes. Its marshal and clerk conform with cutaways.

But of course these are the superficialities of the mystery. More fundamental is the fact that very few laymen know what goes on in the temple of justice. Even if accoustics were brought up to the hearing point, visitors would seldom be able to tell which way a case was being decided. Even lawyers are often confused until the last word—usually "reversed" or "affirmed"—is spoken. So the public looks at the Court as a curiosity, rubbernecks at its huge pillars in much the same way as a depositor admires the supersolid façade of his bank. Few besides lawyers and justices know what is actually going on inside.

With this lack of understanding it is all the more amazing that the Court holds such high prestige year after year. Especially is this true in view of the fact that individuals need not fear their Court in the sense that citizens of past centuries had to fear theirs. That is, they are never physically hauled up before it and sentenced. The Supreme Court of the United States sometimes hears an actual defendant or plaintiff in a case, but no individual need fear the Court in the way that a child would fear a parent armed with a birch rod. Yet he is awestruck in the Court's presence. And when he emerges from the Court building on a sunny day, he is almost struck blind by the intense glare of the severe white plaza in front of the building.

The phenomenon is symbolic. The man whose plan for reorganizing the Supreme Court was to be so bitterly received as to class it with slavery and the League of Nations in the history of American debate laid not one finger on this physical picture. He may have rested a thumb on the scales of justice, but he knew better than to deface the temple. The trouble was to be that Congress and the public could see no distinction between the two.

CHAPTER II

'Tain't Legal

IT IS hard now to realize that only a short time ago, as lives of nations are reckoned, presidents were unable to find men to take jobs now so coveted. Among those who declined appointment to the first Court, two preferred to stay in the South Carolina legislature. Both Alexander Hamilton and Patrick Henry turned down the chief justiceship, and the man who first took it, John Jay, might almost as well have declined it—he ran for governor of New York twice and negotiated a treaty while holding the highest judicial post of the nation.

This early lack of interest in the Court is understandable; it must be understood for a proper perspective of the new Court which started taking shape in 1937. By 1800 the new capital city had been established on the Potomac with quarters for the executive and legislative departments, but the Supreme Court had not been considered in the elaborate plans.

In 1796 a House committee had recommended a building for the Court, but nothing was done about it until 1935. Meanwhile, the third branch of the American government met in such out-of-the-way places that historians are hardly sure of their locations. John Marshall, the nation's fourth chief justice, finally found a small committee room in the Capitol for occasional Court sessions.

The deep imprint of politics on all early Court appointments heaped more disrespect on the institution, if indeed it could be called an institution; and the arduous duties of each justice in riding the rugged circuits periodically added no dignity. John Marshall suffered a broken collarbone in one of the stagecoach accidents, which led Gouverneur Morris to remark that the "agility of a postboy," not legal learning, was the chief qualification for a job on the Supreme Court.

These judicial hardships were not mere parts of a pioneer life marked by lack of running water and other signs of civilization—they were, rather, strictly a matter of indifference to one of the theoretically co-ordinate branches of the government. However, at the beginning of the nineteenth century the judiciary left the realm of indifference to enter a more severe period, a stage of outright hostility from Congress, the President and the voters. For as the nation grew, under its brand-new Constitution, an issue arose which was to be renewed many years later—the issue of judicial supremacy over Congress and the Executive.

The melodrama out of which this issue arose might have been lifted from *Alice in Wonderland.* Even when abbreviated it is one of the great thrillers of judicial history. At the very beginning of 1801, the young nation was engrossed in a political debate between the Federalists, who wanted the country bound together firmly as one unit, and the Republicans, who wanted no more than a loose band of states, each tolerating only as much federal government as was absolutely necessary. The preceding November elections had swept John Adams and his Federalist administration out of office in favor of the dynamic Republican leader, Thomas Jefferson.

In the months before Jefferson's inaugural last volleys were being fired frantically at the Jeffersonians, one of the most ruthless shots being a law by Congress which relieved Supreme Court justices of their circuit duties and installed in their places sixteen new circuit judges. Every new job was filled with Federalists and, since the Supreme Court was already that way, the Federalists who wanted strong central government had the judiciary tied up for the lifetime of the incumbents.

Moreover, just before he was pushed out of the White House, John Adams was favored by a vacancy in the chief justiceship. Promptly, he plucked the plum for his Federalist secretary of state, John Marshall. Also, the day before moving out, Adams appointed a number of justices of the peace for the District of Columbia, the papers being shuffled so fast that four of the commissions were signed and sealed but not delivered.

When Jefferson, on March 4, 1801, rose to take the oath of office, it was administered by John Marshall, the brand-new chief justice. This was irony enough, but soon thereafter an obscure man named William Marbury called on the new secretary of state, James Madison, to pick up the piece of paper that would have made him justice of the peace had not Madison tossed all Federalist documents in the wastebasket. Madison refused to commission Marbury and the disappointed office seeker filed in the Supreme Court a suit which was to make his name immortal in judicial lore.

The wily John Marshall ordered Madison to show cause why the commission should not be issued; the equally wily Republicans refused and sat back to enjoy Marshall's apparently futile position. The Supreme Court proceeded to hear the case[1] on its merits to decide whether to issue a writ of mandamus, ordering Madison to perform the commissioning.

On February 12, 1803, after much argument all around the real issue and after Marbury had lost active interest in having the job, Chief Justice Marshall handed down one of the most famous of all judicial opinions—in favor of Jefferson. Marshall lectured Jefferson's secretary of state for illegally refusing to commission Marbury, denouncing him roundly; but Marshall would not issue the mandamus. It was his reason for refusal that made the decision immortal.

Marbury's lawyers had based his case on a section of the Judiciary Act of 1789 which gave the Supreme Court power to issue writs of mandamus "in cases warranted by the principles and usages of law, to any courts appointed or persons holding office, under the authority of the United States." But Marshall held that the Constitution, which created the Supreme Court as an appellate tribunal (except for cases not involved here), did not allow the Court to have mandamus power of this kind. Congress had violated the Constitution and John Marshall's Supreme Court had set the statute aside as null and void—for the first time in the fourteen years of the Court's existence.

Jefferson had indeed won a hollow victory; Marbury was out of his hair, but the Federalists had set aside a law of Congress. That day, February 12, 1803, had marked the first breath of a powerfully independent third branch of the government and the beginning of a national dispute which would rage, on and off, for many, many years. Jefferson's problem was to be inherited by Franklin D. Roosevelt 134 years, less one week, later.

It is not a digression to note here three twists of fate that figured in the case of *Marbury* v. *Madison,* for they illustrate the system of mortal checks and balances which operate even in the sacred grounds of constitutional law. First, the secretary of state who precipiated the case by getting the appointment papers of Marbury and others mixed up at the last hour was none other than John Marshall. Second, the author of the clause that Marshall found defective was one Oliver Ellsworth, who became chief justice after writing the law and whose departure from the Court created the vacancy into which Adams rushed Marshall. Third, had Ellsworth kept his job one more month, when Jefferson would have had the vacancy to fill, historians agree that the job would have gone to Spencer Roane, of Virginia, a man of opposite views. Thus, the law is only one part of the story of the Supreme Court.

The impact of *Marbury* v. *Madison,* though bitter, was conclusive. True, some subsequent nullifications were to be set aside by historical events, but the *principle* of judicial review stuck. Not for fifty-four years afterward did the Court exercise its self-asserted power to nullify federal legislation; then it handed down the famous Dred Scott decision[2] that was to be reversed only by the Civil War and two constitutional amendments thereafter.

In 1870 the Court invalidated the Civil War law making greenbacks legal money,[3] but the decision was reversed a year later,[4] after two members had been added to the Court. Then, in 1895, the Court declared that Congress had no power to pass an income tax law,[5] a decision that was reversed by the people in the 16th amendment.

These were only the highlights in the exercise of judicial veto, however. All together the Court nullified federal statutes sixty-one times before it started chopping down New Deal legislation. This may not appear to be many knockouts when considered along with the facts that Congress had passed about 25,000 laws and the Court had handed down about 40,000 decisions. However, a number of the nullifications struck down vital statutes.

All this time the states were suffering about the same fate with their legislation. Several hundred state laws were struck down, 232 of them under the 14th amendment alone and many of them involving not mere technicalities but broad social legislation.

But these were comparatively quiet times. Harding's "return to normalcy," Coolidge's private brand of prosperity and Hoover's rugged individualism left few concerned with controversial issues. What efforts were made toward social legislation represented a minority breaking over the majority line just long enough to pass a few laws. Court decisions negating laws met with little acrimony.

The depression shattered these halcyon days by building up a huge new majority in favor of meeting emergency conditions with drastic legislation. By the time Franklin D. Roosevelt had been President for one hundred days, the statute books were full of strange and wonderful laws, generated by the philosophy of "do *something*—but do it quickly!"

The old saying that the wheels of justice grind slowly held good for this period. While Congress and the new administration worked overtime, the Supreme Court went blithely on its way—until January 7, 1935. On that day it struck down for the first time one of the New Deal statutes upon which the nation had staked its hopes for bringing order out of economic chaos.

In June of 1933, Congress had passed the National Industrial Recovery Act, throwing over the country a blanket of codes designed to increase wages and prices and to balance production with consumption. Section 9 (c) of the act, for example, authorized the President "to prohibit the transportation in interstate . . . commerce of petroleum . . . produced or withdrawn from storage in excess of the amount permitted . . . by any State law." A company which wanted to ship out more oil than was allowed under administrative orders attacked the constitutionality of the act. In what has become known as the "hot oil" case, a company which had been penalized for shipping too much oil attacked the clause as an illegal delegation of legislative power to the executive branch.[6]

The Supreme Court agreed in an eight-to-one opinion, including this sentence: "If section 9 (c) were held valid, it would be idle to pretend that anything would be left of limitations upon the power of the Congress to delegate its lawmaking function."

Six weeks later the Court upheld only one half of the congressional cancellation of all clauses in contracts that called for repayment in gold. As to contracts between private parties the power of Congress was upheld; but as to the government's own debts the Court held, five to four: "To say that the Congress may withdraw or ignore that pledge is to assume that the Constitution contemplates a vain promise. . . ."[7]

In May of that year, 1935, the cemetery for dead New Deal statutes had many new graves dug in it. First, the Railroad Retirement Act of 1934, establishing a compulsory retirement and pension system operated as a pool of funds contributed by employees and employers, was invalidated—five to four, again. The majority found that taking contributions from one carrier to be used, through the pool, for another carrier was a deprivation of property without due process of law, forbidden by the 5th amendment. Furthermore, it was found that the act was not, as purported, a regulation of interstate commerce. "It is an attempt for social ends to impose by sheer fiat noncontractual incidents upon the relation of employer and employee. . . ."[8]

Two weeks later the Court took on and whipped, six to three, Senator Guffey's Coal Conservation Act, an elaborate system to stabilize the industry by taxing coal production, then returning the taxes of producers who complied with regulatory features. The Court was angry: "The power conferred upon the majority is in effect the power to regulate the affairs of an unwilling minority. This is legislative delegation in its most obnoxious form. . . ." Besides, snapped the Court, the *mining* of coal is local business, though marketing of it may be interstate commerce.[9]

A week after that blow, the Court took on two larger pillars of the New Deal program. It sharply limited congressional power to relieve the distress of the huge number of bankrupts,[10] then turned a unanimous-vote flame thrower on the body of the NRA.[11]

In its sprawling system of codes for regulating hours of work, scales of wages, methods of competition, etc., within industry, the National Recovery Administration ran afoul, one might say, of the stubborn Schecter Poultry Corporation, a small New York firm which was cracked down on for marketing allegedly ill poultry. What happened when the Schecters hauled the United States into the Supreme Court on the constitutional issue has gone into history unpoetically as the "sick chicken" case.

First, the Court considered the delegation of legislative power: "Section 3 of the Recovery Act is without precedent. It supplies no standards for any trade, industry, or activity. . . . Instead . . . it authorizes the making of codes to prescribe them."

Then, in language considered so broad as to knock out the entire act, the Court examined the interstate commerce question: "The persons employed in slaughtering and selling in local trade are not employed in interstate commerce. Their hours and wages have no direct relations to interstate commerce."

The NRA's famous Blue Eagle emblem moved over in history, replaced by a sick chicken.

The trend of judicial nullification continued in the next term of the Court. Bitterly divided, five to four, the Court knocked down a New York statute regulating minimum wages for women employees.[12] The due process clause had been violated again, intoned the Court, refusing to budge from its 1923 holding in *Adkins* v. *Children's Hospital*[13] that freedom of contract had been impaired.

Official Washington had no more than recovered from the festivities of New Year's Day, in 1936, when the Supreme Court handed down a stinging blow to one of the earliest New Deal measures, the Agricultural Adjustment Act, cornerstone of the farm program.[14] In this, another sweeping statute, farm production was to be balanced with consumption of farm commodities. An incident to the plan was a tax to be collected at the processing level of distribution—flour mills, for example.

In a 6-to-3 decision the Court held that the processing tax took money from one group of citizens for the benefit of another and did not fall within congressional power to tax "for the general welfare." More important, however, the Court hinged the case on another principle of the Constitution. The act, it said, "invades the reserved rights of the states." Thus, broad regulation of agriculture was placed out of reach of the federal government.

By this time it was not only predictable that a majority of the Court would stand against new laws, but it could be predicted with considerable accuracy just which way each member of the Court would vote in a split. There were three groups of justices.

In the first group were four elder jurists as immutable as dried concrete: George Sutherland, Willis Van Devanter, James C. McReynolds and Pierce Butler. This phalanx against experimental legislation was more than just immutable, however; it was bitterly so. Opinions delivered by any of these veterans were likely to be rasped at the waiting courtroom. Whether right or wrong, these bitter-enders displayed all the symptoms of hardened arteries.

Solidly against this rock wall stood three equally determined colleagues, Harlan Fiske Stone, Louis Dembitz Brandeis and Benjamin Nathan Cardozo. Stone came from roughly the same background as the immutables; but he believed that the Court should exercise more self-restraint in passing on the acts of 531 congressmen who, like the justices, had sworn to uphold the Constitution. Brandeis and Cardozo shared this view of the Court's function but came from backgrounds that made it quite plain that they believed as well in the rightness of the laws their conservative brethren were striking down.

Before joining the Court, Brandeis had developed a method of throwing at courts not only legal citations but also page after page of economic facts justifying the legal position he pleaded. His opinions on the Court, usually dissents, retained the technique of economic analysis which even today is known as "the Brandeis brief." Lawyers for the New Deal economic strategists, from 1933 on, used practically no other approach.

Cardozo had deservedly been appointed by President Herbert Hoover in 1932 to fill the seat of Oliver Wendell Holmes, "the Great Dissenter." Holmes had a low regard for most social legislation, but could subordinate his own feelings.

"I do not think," he once said, "the country would come to an end if we lost our power to declare an act of Congress void."

The third category of justices, the "swing" men, was composed of Chief Justice Charles Evans Hughes and Owen J. Roberts. Roberts usually voted with the conservatives; Hughes sometimes threw in his lot with the liberals, as the two groups became known popularly.

From 1933 through 1936 this Court stood so firm against change and had grown so advanced in age (average at the end of 1936: seventy-one) that its collective silk topper had attracted a lot of snowballs. There was no penalty attached to hurling brickbats at the Court, so nearly everyone got into the game. Soon the Supreme Court of the United States was better known by the reasonably accurate tag of *The Nine Old Men*, and a book with that title, by Washington columnists Drew Pearson and Robert S. Allen, became a best seller.

When the Court, in 1935, moved to its glistening new quarters it only became a better target.

But still the Court's vote didn't change. All that changed was that people started reading the impassioned dissents instead of the repetitious majority opinions. It was small consolation, but something had to snap.

CHAPTER III

The Case of the Overworked Chambermaid

IF PRESIDENT ROOSEVELT, on February 5, 1937, had announced invention of the atomic bomb he would have startled Washington and the nation no more than he did by suddenly announcing his now famous plan for reorganizing the judiciary. The later impact of his Court plan can't be compared with the later impact of splitting the atom, but the disclosures of both were electrical and stupefying. Anything new in the judicial realm is likely to be startling, but this was flabbergasting.

Maybe it shouldn't have been, but it was. Actually, Roosevelt had started laying plans for bold action several months before the surprise package was opened. Also, he had publicly criticized the Court long before then.

In 1932 he had tossed into a Baltimore speech a remark that the Court was an annex of the Republican party. On January 6, 1937, he was applauded by Congress for sentences like this in his "state of the union" address: "Means must be found to adapt our legal forms and our judicial interpretation to the actual present national needs of the largest progressive democracy in the modern world."

And the President had attacked specific decisions of the Nine Old Men. Four days after judicial euthanasia had been applied to his NRA, Roosevelt told a press conference that the Court was back in the horse-and-buggy days. It was pertaining to the New York minimum wage case that he accused the Court of trying to create "a no man's land of government" between state and federal powers.

Why, then, was the unveiling of a concrete plan so shocking? Broadly speaking, it was because of the back-room technique employed by the President to spring a plan that affected the personnel of an independent branch of the government rather than calling for a change in the Constitution in a regularly established way.

Franklin D. Roosevelt had hardly finished hearing returns on the landslide election of 1936 before he summoned his sagacious attorney general, Homer S. Cummings, for a progress report on plans in the works. The alternatives before them were something like this: An amendment to the Constitution, granting Congress power to do what the Court had denied it, could have been introduced; but the process would have been very slow. Or, the Court's jurisdiction could have been limited by an act of Congress; but this action, if too far-reaching, might have been struck down by the Court itself, as final arbiter. Or, Congress might have required more than a majority vote of the Court to nullify legislation, a measure which had been introduced but was also of doubtful legality. Finally, the President might have appointed enough new justices to outvote the bitter-enders.

"Packing" the Court, as the latter alternative was bound to be called, had an obviously dark future in congressional and popular appeal, where it had long been regarded as a blow below the belt. However, it had the distinct merit of going to what Roosevelt had decided was the root of the trouble—the personnel of the Court. In his bold and often personalized administration, Roosevelt was accused of many things; but he never tried to rewrite the document that occupies a place alongside the Bible in American homes.

Homer Cummings, who had long cherished a healthy desire to reform the process of justice by making it speedier and less expensive for the 140,000,000 people it supposedly serves, sat in his fancy office one day pondering the alternatives for the umpteenth time. Suddenly the plan that was later to be adopted dawned on him, a plan to make old age of the justices the basis for bringing new blood to the Court. From a book which he and a colleague had written a short while before, *Federal Justice*, Cummings reread that two of his predecessors had proposed an even firmer plan for retiring aged jurists. One of these plans, though it dealt with all courts except the highest one, particularly attracted his eye. It was that of James C. McReynolds, proposed while the associate justice was attorney general, in 1913. Here would be real irony.

Moreover, researchers found that in 1869, after the stinging "greenback" case, the House of Representatives had passed a similar bill and for similar reasons. Here, in a field where precedent meant everything, was a precedent. Cummings' solicitor general, Stanley F. Reed, was put on the trail for more research and remained a close worker on the plan thereafter. Many of the White House inner circle had put in an oar at times on the complex Supreme Court problem, but the real McCoy was authored by these two, plus another lawyer who happened to be occupying the White House.

While the ultimate plan was being researched, drafted and redrafted, the New Deal was marching along on all fronts. The elections had buoyed up the President's feeling that the country was solidly behind him and had given him as favorable a statistical picture of Congress as one could ask: only sixteen Republicans in the Senate and eighty-nine in the House.

In the Court, the very important Tennessee Valley Authority case had been decided in the government's favor, in spite of dissents by Butler, McReynolds and Sutherland.[1] But later New Deal measures were working their way up to the highest Court for almost certain rejection: the National Labor Relations Act, Social Security Act and Public Utility Holding Company Act.

On February 3, 1937, the President and Mrs. Roosevelt held their customary annual full-dress dinner for the judiciary. Two days later, the President mysteriously summoned chairmen of the congressional judiciary committees to a Cabinet meeting, placed before them hastily mimeographed copies of his explosive court plan, read the gist of it aloud and went down the hall to a waiting press conference, asking his top advisers to leave the papers where they found them. In a few minutes, and with the gusto of a child playing a sure trick, he broke the story to the press. A couple of hours later, a reading clerk was letting Congress in on the secret and a microphone in the House was spreading the news to the people. To revert to an atomic comparison, a chain reaction had been started.

The plan was simple enough. For each federal judge who failed after ten years of service to retire upon becoming seventy an additional judge would be appointed to his bench, whether district, circuit or Supreme Court. Each new judge would have to be confirmed by the Senate, as usual, and there would be no more than fifty appointed in the entire system—no more than six to the Supreme Court.

In addition, judges appointed thereafter were to be assignable by the chief justice to any court where needed, and a new job of proctor would be created to help the chief assign judges, do other housekeeping functions and generally expedite justice. It was just that simple.

To make its language even more clearly understood, the President wrote a message elaborating on it. Speaking of the crowded affairs of the judiciary, he declared that "the personnel of the Federal judiciary is insufficient to meet the business before them. . . . Delay in any court results in injustice." He pointed out that in the preceding fiscal year the Supreme Court received 867 petitions for review, but declined to hear 717 of them.

Turning to the capacity of the judges themselves, Roosevelt said: "This brings forward the question of aged or infirm judges—a subject of delicacy and yet one which requires frank discussion." He pointed out that twenty-five of the 237 judges appointed for life and serving at that time were over seventy years of age and eligible to retire on full pay, and noted that the Army and Navy retirement age is sixty-four.

That was the gist of his message to Congress on the plan which was to take its place in history as a crisis. There was not a word about nullification of New Deal legislation, the power of judicial review in general or the fact that his plan would have offset the vote of or forced into retirement all justices but Stone, Cardozo and Roberts.

It was what the President did not say that made Congress and the country rise in arms. He had not met the issue head on, had not said what he meant. Instead, he had chosen the age issue to stand on. His opponents—and his friends—had only to cite one fact to weaken the age argument: the oldest member of the Court was the President's most consistent supporter, eighty-year-old Louis Dembitz Brandeis. Also, there was the ghost of the grand old man of the law, Oliver Wendell Holmes, who at ninety-one had turned out some of the greatest of all opinions.

The smoke screen was thin. And Roosevelt had alienated, by failing to consult them even a little, the men he would have to count on to get his bill through Congress. Take Henry Fountain Ashurst, for example, the grandiloquent solon from Arizona who was then chairman of the Senate Judiciary Committee. When NRA was hardly cold in its grave, Ashurst had denounced criticisms that Roosevelt intended at some time to increase "by some legerdemain" the membership of the Supreme Court.

"A more ridiculous, absurd and unjust criticism of a President was never made," thundered the old orator. "No person whose opinion is respected has favored attempting such a reckless theory and policy."

Two years later, Democrat Ashurst was to tell the Senate: "That bill is the mildest of all bills that could have been introduced on the subject, and I marvel, in the present circumstances, at the moderation of the President."

Vice-President John Garner emerged from the Senate chamber, after hearing Roosevelt's court plan read aloud, to indicate his instinctive reaction by holding his nose. Other loyal Democrats had plans of their own in the hopper, making it difficult, especially in the absence of wooing, to tear them away. Ashurst pushed a broad amendment to the Constitution; Senate Majority Leader Joseph T. Robinson and House Speaker William Bankhead also declared for an amendment. House Judiciary Committee Chairman Hatton W. Sumners, of Texas, had already introduced a judicial retirement bill of his own, he being one of the very few who sensed that the bitter-enders

DON'T FORGET—THAT LEASE EXPIRES EVERY 4 YEARS!

The fear that later presidents might follow Roosevelt's lead in changing Court personnel was illustrated in 1937 by Talburt in the New York *World-Telegram*.

might bring down ruination on the system he fundamentally liked.

Opposition from conservative Democrats and Republicans was of little surprise to administration wheelhorses, but they soon started losing some liberals. Senators Joseph C. O'Mahoney, of Wyoming, and Edward R. Burke, of Nebraska, defected early in the game. The venerable and independent George W. Norris, a Roosevelt adviser on judicial matters, had also urged other approaches.

Outside Congress it was the order of the day for every public figure to take a stand, or weasel on the issue, for quotation. Debate simmered right down to the potbelly-stove level as well. For months editorial writers and political cartoonists had to look no further for copy.

Around the White House, President Roosevelt gathered his action men for the big assault. In the Senate he would rely on rough Joe Robinson, his faithful majority leader, and two administration men: Thomas G. Corcoran, White House handy man then in his heyday as "Tommy, the Cork," and Joseph B. Keenan, assistant attorney general, who had been handling Capitol Hill matters ably for some time. Strategy in the House was left in the hands of under secretary of the interior Charles West, former congressman from Ohio, who had also been turning in a good game.

To these, as a sort of general staff, Roosevelt added his eldest son, James; the veteran Democratic party publicity chieftain, Charles Michelson; and Assistant Attorney General Robert H. Jackson, who had helped with the plan at points and was rising as a bright star in Washington.

At once it was apparent that a five-man majority of the House Judiciary Committee, through which the bill would have to pass, was hostile to the President's plan; so it was decided to buck the Senate's line first. Noses there didn't count much more favorably, but more room was left for persuasion. Roughly one third of the senators could then be relied on, led by Sherman Minton, who later was appointed to a circuit court, Hugo Black, who was to become Roosevelt's first appointee to the Supreme Court, and Progressive Robert LaFollette, Jr.

Another third, out of the middle, included mostly conservative Democrats who were harried by the rash of sit-down strikes and New Deal philosophy in general. Fires were built under local Democratic party machines, including that of a new senator from the Pendergast country by the name of Harry S. Truman. Because the junior senator from Missouri was later to be on the appointing end of the Supreme Court issue, his remarks at that time are significant:

"I am in favor of rehabilitation of the Federal courts of the country. It is my opinion, although I doubt its 'constitutionality,' that there should be a retirement age for justices and judges. I am not in favor of packing any court to obtain any special set of decisions any more than I am in favor of jury-fixing.

"I am therefore of the opinion that the Supreme Court cannot be packed and that when a man becomes a member of it, after investigation and approval by the Senate, he becomes just what he should be—judicially independent.

"If, therefore, the condition of the docket warrants it, I see nothing against increasing the membership of that court. It should be very cautiously approached, however."

Probably unwittingly, former Senator Truman was summing up the reluctance of many of his colleagues to accept the President's plan for doing something that they would like to see done—in some way.

The third group of senators never swayed from original and violent opposition to the bill. For strategy purposes, this group was divided into two sections by party label. The Republican strategy was set a few days after February fifth in a meeting of elder members—Charles McNary, clever minority leader; William Borah, Idaho's ancient orator; and Arthur Vandenberg, Michigan's veteran. What these three agreed on was a conspiracy of silence which was to throw the Democrats into a quarrel among themselves that threatened to burst the party at its seams without having put the Republicans on record. The conspiracy spread from the Senate to national party leaders and succeeded completely for months.

Leadership of the Democratic opposition was assumed early and on a plane of religious fervor that the party regulars were never able to muster in behalf of the President's plan. When administration efforts failed to capture the dubious bronco from Montana, Senator Wheeler, the opposition quickly made him its chieftain and lost few tricks thereafter. With the aid of professional research from a small staff furnished by the American Bar Association and the GOP, the opposition capitalized on every break in the game and picked up every trump misplayed by the advocates of the plan.

During the bitter debate the administration was to take many a body blow, but it scarcely expected the hardest ones from the Supreme Court itself. Thus, when Senator Wheeler opened the opposition's half of the hearings by reading a letter from Charles Evans Hughes, the Jovian chief justice, the administration could feel the props being pulled out from under the plan. By attacking vigorously the technical arguments that the Court's docket was overcrowded, Hughes emasculated the President's ostensible reason for adding new men to the Court. Debate continued on the screened but vital issue of bringing in new blood to rejuvenate the Court's economics, but the administration's case was never strong after the Hughes letter.

It was also the Supreme Court that polished off most of the rejuvenation argument. The technique used seems simple in retrospect but it was done with considerable mental torture. It was merely to swing around to the administration's viewpoint on federal powers. The revolution in Supreme Court doctrine was conceived just before Roosevelt unleashed his packing plan and was born without benefit of a name during the public hearings.

Its life story began just as the year 1937 turned onto the calendar and lawyers came to the Supreme Court with a challenge of the Washington state minimum wage law. A chambermaid by the name of Elsie Parrish had not been paid the $14.50 per forty-eight-hour week specified in the law and she hailed her employer, the West Coast Hotel Company, into court. The hotel pleaded what many employers had pleaded before it; namely, that such legislation was unconstitutional because it denied them of the due process of law guaranteed by the 14th amendment. It was the *Adkins* case all over again and the result was foregone. One month before the President's Court plan was announced, the Court heard Elsie's plea, took its ultrasecret vote and started drafting the opinion.

While the *West Coast Hotel* case was in gestation and only a few days after Roosevelt's February fifth announcement, the Court heard a series of labor relations cases which seemed equally destined to fall on the rocks of precedent. Five appeals, headed by the *Jones & Laughlin Steel Corporation* case, were grouped together for a test of the constitutionality of the Wagner Act. Soon thereafter, the Court took on the cases that would decide the same issue for the New Deal's social security legislation. A lot of coins had been dropped in the slot; the jackpot was full.

On March twenty-ninth the jackpot was hit! Favorable decisions started streaming out of the white marble temple. Roberts turned a four-man minority into a five-man majority to uphold the Washington state wage law. The chief justice wrote an opinion which frankly admited that the *Adkins* case was no longer law and got around the similar New York case of a year earlier by distinguishing it on technical grounds. Chambermaid Elsie Parrish was entitled to the difference between the wages paid her and those set by the state law, now touched by the magic wand of constitutionality.[2] Due process of law was unsullied by the statute, except for the bitter dissents from Justices Sutherland, Van Devanter, McReynolds and Butler.

As a sort of judicial encore the Court on the same afternoon upheld unanimously the Railway Labor Act as a valid regulation of interstate commerce[3] and sustained the revised Frazier-Lemke Farm Mortgage Moratorium law.[4]

Hardly had administration lawyers finished reading these leases on life than the Court, again by a 5-to-4 division, gave a sweepingly legal status to the National Labor Relations Board and the Wagner Act under which the board had been turning out decisions. The upshot of the five opinions handed down that April twelfth was that manufacturing was brought within "interstate commerce." Moreover, the regulation of that commerce authorized by the Wagner Act was a valid regulation.[5]

By the time the social security opinions came along, on May twenty-fourth they were quite anticlimactical.[6] Franklin D. Roosevelt clearly had a majority of the Court on broad social issues and wavering congressmen could see no reason to tamper with the institution.

But across the Capitol grounds the mastodons of the Senate were still locked in bitter debate; the bill had to be disposed of in some way. As Roberts' shift gave the administration more and more favorable decisions, the word "compromise" was heard more often in the cold dingy halls of the Capitol. However, compromise was held up by more than the stubbornness of President Roosevelt—Senator Robinson had been kindled by the promise of a place on the expanded Court. Procrustes' helper was to have a bed to fit his own tired body.

Among thc public at large, the President had counted on unstinting support from farm and labor organizations. Pledges from both were not so difficult to get, but neither really went to Congress with blood in the eye. Even defeat in the AAA case did not put a burr under the farmers' saddles. The two interest groups typified the course of battle on all fronts—those who opposed did so bitterly and with religious zeal, while those who favored the President's plan did so only mildly and from behind posts. The Supreme Court had inertia on its side. As the foundation of New Deal labor legislation was approved by the Court, organized labor definitely started dragging its work shoes.

By mid-May a number of compromises had been rejected by the White House, and the Democratic party was suffering from attrition. The long hearings ended, the Senate Judiciary Committee took its vote: ten to eight against the President's bill. Roosevelt appeared to be headed for defeat, though some lukewarm supporters found comfort in pointing out that he had his favorable Court, albeit by one shifting justice. Roosevelt thought the margin too fleeting.

The same day of the vote, however, reactionary old Willis Van Devanter dispatched to the White House his resignation, giving the President a two-man majority and that much less to fight about. Still he fought on, partly because his upcoming appointment of Joe Robinson would have to be offset; for the sixty-five-year-old Arkansas conservative might stray from the liberal reservation when he ascended to the well-paying independence of the Court. Two weeks later, without appointing Robinson, Roosevelt gave the majority leader a green light on some kind of compromise, and lines started re-forming around the proposal of Senator Carl Hatch, from New Mexico. The plan of Hatch, who had been the "candlestick" on the Judiciary Committee teeter-totter, raised the age for retirement to seventy-five and allowed presidential appointment of only one offsetting justice each year for those who failed to retire at that age.

Before final debate on the compromise began in the Senate, the President summoned opposition leader Burton K. Wheeler for a last-minute effort to patch up both the Court issue and the Democratic party: The Montana bronco balked again, just as Joe Robinson, a powerful orator, opened the administration's case in Congress. He started from the floor with a terrific haymaker, but the opposition swarmed over him mercilessly. By the time Wheeler fired the first opposition oration, Robinson's health was breaking and the Democrats were doing most of their work in the cloakroom, fighting over who Robinson's successor would be when he assumedly would move up to the Court vacancy.

As more Democrats defected, newsmen predicted for the first time that the president would be defeated. Five days later, Joe Robinson was found dead in his room, holding a copy of the Congressional Record containing the opposition speeches he had been too ill to hear. There was now neither a leader nor many waverers to win over.

Joe Robinson was literally not in his grave when administration leaders tried other compromises, including one that would have retained the original plan but would not have taken effect until after the justices then sitting had been replaced by the next generation. The funeral trip to Robinson's native Arkansas was likewise used for patching up the Democratic party. Vice-President Garner, who had ducked out of the Senate fight for a rest in Uvalde, Texas, joined the large group of official mourners in Arkansas and started picking up the pieces of Democracy.

One of the first orders of business was the election of Robinson's successor, for which a cleavage had developed between friends of Pat Harrison, veteran and orthodox senator from Mississippi, and Kentucky's younger senator, Alben Barkley, whom Roosevelt had subtly boosted for his unflagging help in the court fight. No matter who won the election, the Democratic donkey was bound to be a sadder animal for the beatings taken. Barkley finally eked out a 38-to-37 victory, which gave neither side cause for rejoicing.

About this time, Garner got from the White House the go-ahead signal for a compromise of his own liking, which eventually became that of Senator Wheeler's liking. It took the form of a nice quiet motion to send the bill back to its committee, with a gentlemen's agreement to substitute a reorganization bill which would apply only to tribunals below the Supreme Court. When the result of the gentlemen's agreement was put before the same Senate sometime later, it passed in one hour.

On July twenty-second, five and one-half months after springing his plan on friend and foe alike, Roosevelt had lost one of the nation's most bitter *battles*—but the *war* was not over.

CHAPTER IV

A Study in Black

IN FACT the President suffered a bulge in his battered line just twenty-one days later, when a surprised nation learned that his choice for the first vacancy was Hugo Lafayette Black, the senior senator from Alabama. It was not so much that Black had enemies—he had those, too—but few would have thought of the crusading New Deal senator as Supreme Court material.

The first thing they looked for was experience, but Black could show only a brief period on a police court plus some private practice. Then they looked for judicial temperament, that ubiquitous soothing quality which defies precise description but might even be acquired synthetically. If Black had any, it was obscured by his fighting temperament in Congress. The whole thing looked like a political pay-off, protected by a club rule known as "senatorial courtesy." Five days later the appointment was confirmed by the Senate.

A month later, while Black was vacationing in England, the public learned through a sensational newspaper break what it should already have known: that Black had been a member of the Ku-Klux Klan. Editors dipped their pens into the slimy record of the night-riding Klan and lambasted the selection of a card holder for the nation's highest court. But that's getting ahead of the story, for no appraisal of this man is worth the paper it's written on unless it begins in Clay County, Alabama.

Hugo Black was born to Tobacco Road in 1886, with all that connotes in narrowness, ignorance and defeatism. At the age of five he got his first slight boost when his father moved to the small town of Ashland to set up a general merchandise store. Young Hugo worked for his father and picked cotton before he was old enough for a job he really liked: writing for the local paper and setting his own type. He went to school there "through algebra," as he once put it; but his main interest was the local courtroom, especially when big-name lawyers would come from outside to argue cases. He would sit there for hours, always trying to figure out how he would handle the case were he standing before the bar. Another fascination was the polls. Beginning as early as the age of nine, Black would stick around until the last vote was counted.

All this time he had been reading widely from the heavier books, and his family wanted him to be a doctor like his older brother. But after a year at Birmingham Medical College, where he crowded in two years of study, Black confessed to his brother that his real interest was the law. The family shifted plans and Black went to the University of Alabama law school, from which he was graduated with honors.

The next few formative years were hard ones, years that tested his tenacity for the legal profession and shaped his type of practice. Choosing Birmingham, Black hardly even had a place to hang a shingle. He lived in a boarding house with four men to a room and took desk space anywhere around town he could get it. When an out-of-state insurance company sent him a few dollars' worth of business it was a life saver.

Lawyer Black's first big break came in a tiny case that he fortunately handled so well that he attracted the attention of the presiding judge, A. O. Lane. Willie Morton, a Negro convict, had been kept prisoner in a mine twenty-two days after his sentence had legally ended. The lawyer in whose office Black then had a desk turned the case over to Black, who worked on it for weeks. Willie got $150 out of the victory, of which Black got $37.50.

Judge Lane later became a city commissioner and made Black the recorder (judge) of the Birmingham police court at the same time that he consolidated numerous suburban courts into one. Black took the job reluctantly and left it after only a year and a half, when he decided to file for the county solicitor's job. At the age of twenty-eight, Black was not taken seriously by the political dopesters to win over the incumbent of sixteen years' service. The young opponent went all over the county talking to people to see what was on their minds and found that they didn't like having hundreds of Negroes arrested every payday for shooting craps, thus crowding the county jails. Black promised to clear the docket of long-standing cases and concentrate on the big offenders. The voters agreed and he was elected.

The first act of County Solicitor Black was to drop charges against some five hundred men whose names cluttered the absurd docket and who had been victims of the fee system, whereby the county profited in proportion to the amount of fines collected from defendants. Then he started on the professional gamblers and, within one year, had that docket cleared as well.

The United States was by now at war with Germany and Black resigned his post to enlist in the Army. He entered officers' training, was made a captain and acted as adjutant of his regiment. He had toured three camps in the United States before the armistice released him to go back to Birmingham and the law. After a slight intermission to marry a Navy yeomanette, Josephine Foster, a minister's daughter, Black settled down to real law. In the few years, as law practices go, from the war to 1925 he had become known as a leading attorney, when the old political bug bit him. He entered the five-way campaign for the United States Senate in 1926, opposed mainly by Oscar W. Underwood, an opponent of the Klan during its peak of operation, and won the election. In the course of the campaign he covered every county of Alabama.

Black's record from 1926 through 1932 established him as a liberal before the term "New Dealer" was thought of.[1] He shared leadership with Nebraska's George Norris in the fight to make Muscle Shoals a federal power and fertilizer operation and saw it vetoed twice before the New Deal bailed it out. He opposed the type of pump-priming that dripped big money in at the top, relying on it to trickle down to the little fellows. Rather, he proposed in 1931 a $25,000,000 appropriation for direct food relief in Alabama. Black never resisted centralized government moves to combat the depression; but he fought for decentralized administration, lest the system become a weapon for Republican power over southern states.

Black took time out in 1930 to speak in opposition to his senior senator, Catholic-baiting Tom Heflin, who was defeated by the late John Bankhead. And, along with organized labor, he opposed the appointment of Judge John J. Parker to the Supreme Court.

In 1929, Black took a typically courageous stand against a bill that would have given Treasury clerks the power to exclude importation of books they felt to be immoral or insurrectionist. On the tariff question in general Black favored sharp reductions. However, being mortal and being a politician, he made an exception in the case of graphite, a Clay County commodity. Of more interest to historians than this slight meander into buttering his own bread was the fact that he proposed that there should be a consumer counsel at all tariff hearings. On the Foreign Relations Committee, Black favored Philippine independence and attacked the secrecy of the London Naval Conference.

By the time of the 1932 Democratic landslide, when he came back for a second term, Black was regarded as a skillful parliamentarian and powerful adversary. Both barbs and humor were in his arsenal. On the eve of the change in administrations, the Senate was debating whether to fire its sergeant at arms, alleged to have engaged in wrong dealing. Some, however, thought the man should have counsel to protect himself. Black noted that there were probably a great many others in the chamber who would receive the same punishment on inauguration day—and without benefit of counsel.

In his second term Black took his full place as an anomaly in the Senate—an intellectual left-winger from the deep South. In fact, by the time he was nominated for the Court, Black was probably the most radical man in the Senate. One of his main programs was the thirty-hour-week bill, designed to attack both the symptoms of depression (by spreading employment) and its cause (by increasing purchasing power). The future justice cited Court cases which he believed were decided wrongly and which had blocked the regulation of wages and hours. His radical measure passed the new Senate in its second month, but was destined to idleness in the House until after he left the Senate. Then it was the Fair Labor Standards Act, calling for no more than forty hours a week but retaining Black's name.

Black was as wary of the National Industrial Recovery Act as he was enthusiastic about some of its goals. He tried to amend it to curb the power he felt trade associations would wield within it, an opinion long since vindicated, and declared that if competition were to be openly scrapped there should be some way to limit profits.

Early in the Roosevelt administration Black turned his blowtorch on the holders of mail subsidies. An investigation conducted by him turned up the rigged bidding, collusion with a postmaster general and excessive subsidies which caused Postmaster General Farley to cancel the contracts and fly the mail by Army plane. Shortly thereafter he put the heat on steamship lines subsidized by mail contracts, finding the same thing. Then, in 1935, he got himself made chairman of a committee to investigate the opposition to one of his favorite bills, which became the Public Utility Holding Company Act, and basked in the spotlight of publicity when it was discovered that the corporations had faked telegrams to congressmen from names in the phone book. The light dimmed, however, when Black subpoenaed many telegrams. By doing so he was invading the privacy which his liberal friends held more sacred than the legislation he was trying to help. Admittedly, his action was a valuable incident in the span of legislative history, but it was a dangerous precedent—and an injudicial act.

A year later Black lost a bit more of his liberal luster by speaking against the Costigan-Wagner antilynching bill, though there was little reason to expect more from a southern senator. His reasons, whether advanced from sophistry or not, are interesting in retrospect: First, the law could be used to protect corporations from injury by three or more people (the number established as the nucleus of a lynch mob). Second, it would supersede local jury trial with federal regulation, a move which would set back labor's hard-fought gains. Third, it established a loose standard of negligence. Fourth, it would disrupt the educative process at work on the problem in the South; and, fifth, its supporters were playing politics in their own districts.

This was the man to whom President Roosevelt finally turned to fill the first vacancy on the Supreme Court. His choice was deliberate; it represented a long culling process carried on before the wounds of the Court battle had healed. If Roosevelt wanted to force a bitter pill down the throats of his opponents, as observers of the time believed, he accomplished his purpose. Liberals such as Schwellenbach, LaFollette, Minton, Norris and even Borah were pleased as punch; but the reaction of most senators was a mixture of disbelief and anger. Not only had Black gored most of them at one time or another on the floor of the Senate but he was obviously a partisan. Senatorial courtesy put the nomination through the Judiciary Committee without a hitch, but debate on the floor could not be controlled so easily.

Some of the opposition paralleled a New York *Herald Tribune* editorial lamenting Black's "meager technical equipment" and labeling the choice "as menacing as it is unfit." But there would have been even more oratorical opposition had other senators not felt as did a Washington correspondent, writing a few pages away in the same issue of the same paper. According to him, Black was "one of the most learned members of the Senate," whose convictions came to him by a reasoned, intellectual process rather than by a natural or opportunist sympathy. . . . The Senate learned to respect his industry and intelligence."

Nevertheless, there was one item in Black's past which just had to be mentioned: his Klan connection. It didn't have to be dredged up, as most people nowadays falsely think; rather, it floated on the surface like a drowned body. Senator Copeland of New York pointed to the corpse, and Senator Burke said he could bring in two witnesses to identify it beyond doubt. Others mentioned the odor; the subject was far from covered up. A small group of friendly colleagues confronted Black with the talk, asking him to say something about it. With the coveted Court prize almost in his hands (though Black had hesitated before accepting it), he gave them a characteristic, thoughtful answer: He was not then a Klan member, but those who were concerned about it should vote against confirmation. Borah told the Senate that there was not "a scintilla of evidence" that Black was a Klansman, a statement from which he later had to backtrack, though in doing so he made it plain that Black had not misled him into making it. Five days after nomination, Black was confirmed, sixty-three to sixteen. He took the oath and sailed for a vacation abroad.

It was not a very satisfactory vacation, for in the next month came proof that he had been a Klan member. Headlines across the country beat a tattoo; reporters in England heckled the new justice unceasingly for a statement. He returned and announced that he would make a comment on the radio in a few days. On October first, as Black took to the air, a pin could have been heard to drop around the radios of millions of homes. In a soft, supersincere voice, Black admitted his KKK membership, offset it with an affirmation of his current beliefs and denied that any Klan prejudices could be found in him.

Because it will long be debated how damaging the Klan eipsode was to Black's reputation, the issue should be briefly summarized before looking at his record on the Court. First, the case against Black: Aside from the fact that the Klan stood for everything base and degrading and should never have been joined, Black was excoriated for not making a clean break with it at the first opportunity. Even if the voters who sent him to the Senate were predominantly Klansmen, that allegiance would make him unfit for a judicial post, in which prejudice must be absent. And—the bitterest of all—Black should have been man enough to admit his affiliation to the President (who expressed anger at Black's failure to confess it) or to his friends in the Senate. In its strongest form, this argument runs that Black could not have been confirmed in the face of the facts, that he knew that was so and that he got his life appointment through trickery.

The case on Black's side is one of what the lawyers would call mitigation of damages rather than one of denial. Many in Alabama at that time belonged to the Klan, including stanch union men and others who should be ashamed of themselves, and Black might never have risen to a position inimical to all the Klan stands for if he had not played the political game. (Some did, however.) He definitely rose above the taint. If his affiliation were criminal, he has "served his time" and is a new man. It is pointed out, too, that a speech he made to the Klan pleaded for an end to lawlessness and religious intolerance.

Black's dramatic radio talk stilled the raging debate considerably, but it was then time to see how this controversial figure would vote on cases involving Klan issues and how Roosevelt's first appointee would get along with the eight old men left in the temple of justice.

Like the man in the old ads for correspondence courses, they laughed when Hugo Black sat down at the piano. But before he got up from the bench after his first term, Black had struck several chords that had everyone paying attention. The most far-reaching and dumfounding one was missed by lawyers and laymen because it was a solitary dissent on a very technical matter, but two months later the Court had adopted his lonely view and had overruled nearly one hundred years of cold precedent! This was not a social issue and it was not effected by Court packing. The question was whether federal courts, in ruling on the common law, should be bound by state decisions on the point or should decide what they thought it ought to be. Since *Swift* v. *Tyson,* in 1842, federal courts had been deciding their own law, making two sets; but after *Erie* v. *Tompkins* in April of 1938 all this was changed.

The revolution happened like this: After a man had died of gunshot, the executors of his estate sued his insurance company on the grounds that he had died accidentally. An argument ensued as to whether he had committed suicide; the judge's instructions to the jury on points of law came to the Supreme Court and the insurance company won.[2] Black held that the contrary rule of the state of Montana, where the contract was entered into, should prevail. He did not mention *Swift* v. *Tyson,* but was content to confine his views to the point at bar. Two months later, *Swift* v. *Tyson* was expressly overruled.

It was Brandeis who wrote the historic opinion that tossed nearly one hundred years of precedent in the wastebasket.[3] He neither ducked the issue nor hesitated to say that the Court's previous course had been an unconstitutional seizure of power over state courts. The immediate issue before the Court was a money suit—Tompkins against the Erie Railroad. Tompkins had been walking along the tracks when an open railroad car door struck him, he said. The question was whether Tompkins was trespassing on Erie property or whether Erie owed him a legal duty to keep its doors shut. The answer depended on whether the Court applied the federal rule of law or the local rule.

Brandeis started off by listing attacks on the old doctrine. Also, he pointed out that the doctrine had not worked, had not brought the uniformity that was hoped for.

A few days before word of the reversal flashed through the legal world, with general applause, a magazine article had hit the streets with a body blow at Black. Writing on "The Supreme Court Today," in the May, 1938, *Harper's,* Marquis W. Childs put into the mouths of anonymous justices an attack on their freshman colleague. Childs being a responsible Washington correspondent, the story was picked up by the daily press with gusto.

"During his brief service on the bench," wrote Childs, "Justice Black has caused his colleagues acute discomfort and embarrassment. . . . It has grown out of the lack of legal knowledge and experience, deficiencies in background and training, that have led him into blunders which have shocked his colleagues on the highest court."

The *Erie* case was too technical to be widely interpreted at the time as any rebuttal of the article. However, as Childs wrote eight years later in his column, one consequence of the incident was that Black "worked harder than perhaps any justice in the history of the court" to "vindicate himself and to justify in the law his liberal opinions." Gossip at the time pinned the criticism mainly on Stone, talks with whom had been the "basis" for the article, as Childs later admitted. Maybe neither writer nor informant had meant a personal vendetta against Black, but the attack left a deep wound in Black's reputation, if not in his feelings toward his brethren.

An even more dramatic dissent had been penned by Black two weeks before that already mentioned, but it had struck fear where this one created hope.[4] And it has picked up no other votes. The state of California had laid a tax on insurance companies in such a way that part of it fell on out-of-state business as well. A company challenged constitutionality of the tax on the grounds that it violated this phraseology in the 14th amendment: ". . . nor shall any State deprive any person of life, liberty, or property, without due process of law. . . ." It was an old argument against legislative regulation of business which had worked for more than fifty years. Black thought it was an old gag which ought to stop. His argument: The word "person" in that clause does not include "corporation," for the amendment was passed as a result of the Civil War to protect Negroes and does not mention corporations.

His lonely dissent was particularly eloquent coming from a deep southerner who was still scorching from the heat of his KKK incident, but it was bold for anyone to fly in the face of the hundred and more instances in which the clause had been used to beat off state measures in the economic and social realm.[5]

"A constitutional interpretation that is wrong," declared Black, "should not stand. I believe this Court should now overrule previous decisions which interpreted the Fourteenth Amendment to include corporations. . . . The history of the Amendment proves that the people were told that its purpose was to protect weak and helpless human beings and were not told that it was intended to remove corporations in any fashion from the control of state governments. The Fourteenth Amendment followed the freedom of a race from slavery. . . . Corporations have neither race nor color."

He worked the history over and over, pointing out that it was not until 1886 that the Court included corporations as "persons." He noted that "of the cases in this Court in which the Fourteenth Amendment was applied during the first fifty years after its adoption, less than one-half of one per cent invoked it in protection of the negro race, and more than fifty per cent asked that its benefits be extended to corporations."

The bar was singularly unimpressed by this dissent and none of Black's brethren latched onto it. But that doesn't prevent its standing as one of the greatest displays of independence and courage seen on the bench. A friend of Black's, asked if other justices would pick up the doctrine, replied with a dismissing laugh: "That one strikes the pocketbook."

Two other landmarks of Black's first term were really warm-ups for his all-out attack on the due process clause and corporations. His first dissenting vote—cast significantly with Brandeis, Stone and Cardozo—was a protest against a decision that a payment was a tax-free gift rather than a taxable compensation for services rendered.[6] Black and the others not only felt that the Board of Tax Appeals should have been allowed to determine which the payment was, without judicial review, but complained that a "large body of decisions . . . would be annulled by such a test" as the majority gave it. It was certainly no indication of disrespect for precedent. The other landmark, the first dissent to be written by Black alone,[7] was one of those cases in which the Court threw out a state's attempt to devise a rate formula. Black stated his attitude bluntly: "I believe the State of Indiana has the right to regulate the price of water in Indianapolis free from interference by federal courts. The courts did not deny this right to the states for the first hundred years after the adoption of the Constitution." Black has often been accused of departing from the Constitution, but here was an instance in which he insisted on going back to the document. There were to be many others.

Other decisions that first term were revealing of the new justice's opinions in a wide range of tangles. He dissented alone when the Court held that a state's long-term contracts with its teachers were binding against subsequent legislatures,[8] when it found no continuing liability on the part of a shipowner for an incurable disease contracted by a seaman[9] and in two patent cases—one protesting departure from precedent and one against extending the patent privilege.[10] He wrote the opinion reversing the conviction of a man who had been unattended by counsel,[11] concurred in two opinions departing from the old doctrine giving state agencies immunity from federal taxation[12] and concurred in most of a decision that Congress may exclude such products as filled milk from interstate commerce.[13]

Notable opinions in which Black went along silently that term included rulings that municipal ordinances against distribution of literature of any kind are unconstitutional (the first of the Jehovah's Witnesses cases), that efforts of a Negro organization to get an employer to hire Negroes constituted a labor dispute and thus were protected from an injunction by the Norris-LaGuardia Act and that the systematic exclusion of Negroes from a jury is unconstitutional.[14]

The upshot of Black's initial term was that liberals had cause to rejoice, while conservatives had equal cause to despair. Black had followed the formula, if there was one, for reversing the trend of the Court. But it was too early to tell how much of his voting record was formula and how much of it was Hugo Black. Was he the first of a series of rubber stamps (Reed joined the Court halfway through the term) or would his momentum carry right on through? His numerous opinions since the 1937 term will be considered under loose headings by subject matter of the cases involved.

In the area of problems caused by our federal system and our separation of the legislative and executive branches from the judiciary, Black has played a balanced game. He has seldom voted to curb centralized power, yet some of his most outspoken opinions have upheld a state's right to legislate as it wishes, even though the result is anything but uniform. Thus, by way of dissent, Black would have upheld a Florida law requiring imported citrus juices to be labeled with the state name, an Arkansas statute limiting motor vehicles to twenty gallons of gasoline in their fuel tanks at the time of entering the state without paying the Arkansas gasoline tax, and an Arizona law limiting the length of trains.[15] It is highly doubtful that Black personally liked any of the jigsaw puzzle laws, but he was fighting the judicial interference which got the Nine Old Men in trouble. However, Black dropped his dissent in these situations when the Court nullified a Virginia Jim Crow law affecting interstate busses. He still believed "that Congress can regulate commerce and that the courts cannot," but since the burden on interstate travel from the Jim Crow law was even greater than that in cases where he had been outvoted, Black "acquiesced" in the majority ruling.[16]

When the Court decided that the domicile of Edward Green was in Massachusetts when he left an estate of over $44,000,000 fought over by three other states, Black dissented with Frankfurter that the Court should not have taken original jurisdiction of the suit.[17] Though the individual states might mess up the estate—and eat it up in overlapping taxes—the dissenters felt that states should be allowed, if not forced, to work out a system. But when Pennsylvania passed an alien registration statute Black wrote the Court's 6-to-3 opinion declaring it null as having been superseded by federal laws on the subject.[18] When the Court ruled, in the famous divorce case, that North Carolina could ignore a Reno divorce as not based on jurisdiction of the divorcees, Black dissented that North Carolina was not giving "full faith and credit" to a Nevada court order, as required by the Constitution.[19] When the Court narrowly decided that the United States could tax sales of bottled water from New York's Saratoga Springs, a state-owned business, Black dissented with Douglas that the national government could not tax such an "exercise of sovereignty." They feared that the ruling would open the door for restrictive taxes on future state-owned enterprises.[20]

Black's devotion to civil rights is by now too well known to require a lengthy analysis separate from that subsequently given the Court as a whole. As a matter of fact, it would be hard to filter out Black's work from the Court's work in this area of constitutional law, for he has contributed hard-hitting leadership to the establishment of several key principles in the law of individual rights. It is in the Constitution's requirements of speedy trials by impartial juries and with counsel furnished that Black sees the real meaning of "due process of law." It is to him just what it says—a matter of *process*.

The systematic exclusion of Negroes from jury panels was reviewed extensively by Black, writing for a unanimous Court during his second term, and the conviction of a Louisiana Negro was reversed. In a similar case, from Texas, Black wrote the same result.[21] "The Fourteenth Amendment," he stated, "requires that equal protection to all must be given—not merely promised." His conclusion about the evidence: "If there has been discrimination, whether accomplished ingeniously or ingenuously, the conviction cannot stand."

A broad-gauged defense of the jury system in its entirety was written by Black as a dissent (joined by Douglas and Murphy) when the Court held a jury trial unnecessary for adjudication of a claim arising from a government war insurance policy.[22] "Today's decision," wrote Black, "marks a continuation of the gradual process of judicial erosion which in one hundred fifty years has slowly worn away a major portion of the essential guarantee of the Seventh Amendment." He dipped deeply into the founding of the Constitution to show how highly the people regarded trial by jury.

But the part of a criminal proceeding with which Black is most concerned is that which takes place before the trial. He has done as much as any justice to eliminate the third degree. In this field, his opinion for a unanimous Court in *Chambers* v. *Florida* is a real landmark.[23] A group of Negroes had been rounded up as suspects in an atrocious crime and put through a week of questioning, including an all-night session during which they "broke." Black reviewed the birth of freedom through the days of the rack, the thumbscrew and the wheel right down to modern third-degree methods. He noted that those who usually are subjected to such torment come from lowly stations in life and are of low intelligence.

"Under our Constitutional system," he wrote, "courts stand against any winds that blow as havens of refuge for those who might otherwise suffer because they are helpless, weak, outnumbered, or because they are non-conforming victims of prejudice and public excitement. Due process of law, preserved for all by our Constitution, commands that no such practice as that disclosed by this record shall send any accused to his death. No higher duty, no more solemn responsibility rests upon this Court, than that of translating into living law and maintaining this constitutional shield deliberately planned and inscribed for the benefit of every human being subject to our Constitution—of whatever race, creed or persuasion."

In a number of other cases Black wrote dissents when the Court seemed to him to depart from this line.[24]

In the matter of guarding the right to counsel, Black has been even a little more vigilant than the watchful Court. He wrote the Court's reversal of the conviction of "an ignorant layman" who, without counsel, pleaded guilty to plain burglary and who then learned that he was being charged with burglary with explosives.[25] The trial court had sentenced him to twenty years and refused to let him change his plea.

Black once wrote an opinion for the Court rejecting a plea that lawyers appointed to defend a poor defendant had not had enough time to prepare their case, but he is usually on the other side. In a later instance of this general type Black wrote a dissenting chastisement of a Maryland court that did not furnish counsel to an indigent defendant.[26] "A practice cannot be reconciled with 'common and fundamental ideas of fairness and right,' which subjects innocent men to increased dangers of conviction merely because of their poverty," he protested.

Freedom of speech, press, assembly and religion are equally dear to Black, though the press certainly does not reciprocate. He wrote the famous Bridges-Los Angeles *Times* opinion[27] in which the Court set aside an important contempt of court order on the grounds that there was no "clear and present danger" to the orderly dispensation of justice. And when the Court knocked out Jersey City's much-publicized ordinance which gave city officials the right to ban public meetings, Black was with the majority.[28] Black wrote several of the Court's opinions in behalf of the Jehovah's Witnesses, including those invalidating anti-handbill ordinances and banning door-to-door solicitation.[29] Last term, through an opinion by Black, the Court extended this protection to property within company-owned towns and federal housing projects.[30] More spectacularly, Black was one of the three justices who admitted they had been wrong in requiring Witnesses to salute the American flag and had guts enough to make the correction.[31] When that chance came, Black wrote briefly with Douglas to explain his position. His original decision, he declared, had been based on reluctance to make the Constitution a "rigid bar against state regulation of conduct thought inimical to the public welfare." After long reflection he still thought that principle was sound but was not as compelling as the freedom of religion also written into the Constitution.

"Words uttered under coercion are proof of loyalty to nothing but self-interest," he wrote. "Love of country must spring from willing hearts and free minds, inspired by a fair administration of wise laws enacted by the people's elected representatives within the bounds of express constitutional prohibitions."

Among the miscellany of civil rights cases, Black dissented vigorously for three other justices when the Court upheld the refusal by Illinois to let a conscientious objector practice law.[32] He concluded that if the state could do that it could "bar every person from every public occupation solely because he believes in non-resistance rather than in force." And he voted with four dissenters from the Court's upholding of a federal rule of procedure which requires plaintiffs in certain damage suits to submit to physical and mental examinations.[33] When three federal employees sued to get the salaries that Congress had denied them by singling them out in an appropriation measure, Black wrote the Court's divided opinion nullifying the rider as a bill of attainder, banned specifically by the Constitution. Black tread no legal tight wires in delivering the opinion.[34] If the rider weren't attainder in the conventional sense, it amounted to one—amounted to finding three men guilty without a trial.

A case in which it was surprising, offhand, to find Black dissenting was the *Classic* case,[35] named after one of the Louisiana election commissioners who had been indicted for willfully subjecting some people "to the deprivation of any rights . . . protected by the Constitution and laws of the United States." The Court upheld the indictments, an action which seemed natural enough in view of the fact that the commissioners were charged with altering ballots. But Black, Douglas and Murphy were repelled by a joker—the federal law under which the men were indicted was so vague as to be unworthy of supporting convictions. One would not have to know Black (and the other dissenters) well to know that he personally liked the purpose of the law, but he was doing the hard thing: rejecting it as too vague. Four terms later he took a similar stand, even though it meant ruling in favor of sheriffs who had beat a Negro to death while he was handcuffed and under arrest.[36]

A sort of offshoot to Black's stand on civil liberties is the pattern of his decisions in damage suits—nearly always in favor of the individual trying to collect.[37] His arguments, most often from the minority side, are usually based on setting aside legal niceties in the interest of accomplishing justice with a minimum of delay[38] or in behalf of full jury consideration of the claim.[39] Douglas and Murphy have joined in most of his dissents in favor of the individual seeking recovery.

The many economics-laden cases coming before the new Court find Black following the line of the Brandeis-Stone-Cardozo-Holmes dissents—that legislators should be allowed to experiment in that field—and turn up a liberal outcropping of the economic views Black held as a New Deal senator. Sometimes, of course, the two are indistinguishable. Naturally, the economics behind a legal dispute are never before the Court, as such; but Black makes little effort to play legal hopscotch in such a way as to pretend to ignore them.

Thus, when the Court twice took a relatively narrow view of state legislation for land debtors during the depression, Black fairly screamed (with Douglas and Murphy) that the Court was upsetting legislation of deep economic import.[40]

At the confluence of economics and law which becomes the stream of rate-making decisions, Black stands for the new doctrine of allowing public utility commissions a comparatively free rein with a formula for profits based on prudent investment, a doctrine finally evolved out of many dissents. In the *Natural Gas Pipeline* case, which he gladly labeled as starting a new chapter in the regulation of utility rates, Black was with Douglas and Murphy in agreeing with the Court's result but insisting on a bolder opinion.[41] They noted that the Court "had returned in part at least to the constitutional principles which prevailed for the first hundred years of our history." Then they added: "But in so far as the Court assumes that . . . the due process clause of the Fifth Amendment grants it power to invalidate an order as unconstitutional because it finds the charges to be unreasonable, we are unable to join in the opinion just announced." Of the conventional doctrine of due process as a curb on rate-fixing in public utilities they said: "And in no field has it had more paralyzing effects."

When the Court handed down another regulatory opinion he didn't like, Black spoke bluntly on economics:[42] "The issue in this case is whether the farmers and shippers of the middle west can be compelled by the Interstate Commerce Commission and the railroads to use high-priced rail instead of low-priced barge transportation for the shipment of grain to the east. I agree that . . . 'this record is replete with complexities and technicalities' which have almost, but I think not quite, successfully obscured that simple issue."

In antitrust litigation Black is always to be found on the government's side, partly because he has the broad congressional charter of the Sherman and other acts to work from and partly because his career has made him sensitive to the economic facts of life. There appears to be no record, however, that he is a disciple of the Brandeis school of thought which would make little firms out of big ones as a solution in itself to the problems of corporate concentration.

Among the opinions in which he has done more than cast his vote silently with the Court, Black wrote the majority opinion in the ground-breaking cases extending the antitrust laws to insurance, sustaining action against the Associated Press and breaking up a cozy arrangement in the garment industry used ostensibly for stopping "style piracy."[43] Also, he wrote the opinions upholding laws of two states against ASCAP, the society for protection of copyrighted music.[44] "The constitutional right of States to pass laws against monopolies should now be beyond possibility of controversy," he asserted.

Among Black's dissents in the antitrust and trade regulation fields is one insisting that the United States government, like any other purchaser of goods, is entitled to sue for treble damages under the Sherman Antitrust Act.[45] Also, he joined the dissent when the Court held that the Federal Trade Commission, in the course of prohibiting an unfair method in the sales of candy in interstate commerce, could not order the same practice stopped within the state, even though such a result left the interstate dealers at a competitive disadvantage.[46]

Nowhere has Black recorded more bluntly or humorously his refusal to go along with the Court on many patent cases than he did in a dissent (joined by Douglas and Murphy) from a flashlight battery decision:[47]

"Those who strive to produce and distribute goods in a system of free competitive enterprise should not be handicapped by patents based on a 'shadow of a shade of an idea.' The microscopic structural or mechanical improvements inevitably must reduce the United States Patent Office to a mass production factory for unearned special privileges which serve no purpose except unfairly to harass the honest pursuit of business. If the patentee here has 'discovered' anything, it is that the creamy substance in a dry cell will not leak through a steel jacket which covers and is securely fastened to the ends of the cell. For that alleged discovery this patent is today upheld. I do not deny that someone, somewhere, sometime, made the discovery that liquids would not leak through leak-proof solids. My trouble is that, despite findings to the contrary, I cannot agree that this patentee is that discoverer. My disagreement is not based solely on the narrow ground that the record shows previous patents have been issued to others who put jackets of metal and other substances around dry cells. Antiquarians tell us that the use of solid containers to hold liquids predated the dawn of written history. That the problem of the quality and strength of the walls of such containers was one to which ancient people turned their attention appears from the widespread currency at an early age of the maxim that 'new wine should not be put in old bottles.' It is impossible for me to believe that Congress intended to grant monopoly privileges to persons who do no more than apply knowledge which has for centuries been the universal possession of all the earth's people—even those of the most primitive civilizations."

Black has often dissented along this line, that the new device is not patentable,[48] as well as for holding the economic advantage of a valid patent down to a bare minimum so that its use will be more widespread.[49] The attitude prevails also in copyright cases,[50] such as those involving "When Irish Eyes Are Smiling" and Drew Pearson.

It surprised no one to see Hugo Black join with the Court in expanding labor law in favor of the workingman, but he has gone even beyond most justices in a number of significant cases. In the course of scrapping for the National Labor Relations Board's power to interpret the Wagner Act relatively freely, Black has stuck his neck far out. In the *Fansteel* and *Columbian Enameling* cases, where the board ordered reinstatement of strikers, Black and Reed stood in the minority and for the board.[51] Likewise, when the Court sent a case back for more evidence about the dynamiting of company property by employees, Black dissented (with Douglas and Murphy) because the punishment for dynamiting should not be allowed to interfere with the choice of collective bargaining agents.[52]

A labor issue that has constantly plagued the Court—the use of injunctions and antitrust suits against unions—has involved Black deeply. An early case, in which he wrote the unanimous opinion, was easy. An injunction against the Milk Wagon Drivers' Union was dismissed where the union picketed nonunion stores selling cut-rate milk. It was clearly the kind of picketing allowed to be free from injunction by the Norris-LaGuardia Act. Three months later, however, the same union carried a case to the Court which involved the thorny problem of violence mingled with regular picketing.[53] Frankfurter, for six justices, upheld the injunction this time because the past violence had a coercive effect which carried through to the admittedly peaceful picketing. Black exploded. He conceded that the state could enjoin violence, but he protested vigorously the sweeping terms of the injunction, even banning discussion of the cause of the strike—different methods of distributing milk.

"Freedom to speak and write about public questions is as important to the life of our government as is the heart to the human body," said the ex-medical student. "In fact, this privilege is the heart of our government. If that heart be weakened, the result is debilitation; if it be stilled, the result is death."

When the Court, again through Frankfurter, upheld an injunction against a union picketing the restaurant of a man whose contractor was using nonunion labor on a building a mile and a half away, Black exploded again.[54] To him (and to Douglas and Murphy) the Court was upholding a restraint on admittedly peaceful picketing (by one picket at a time) and thus on a right protected by the Constitution.

The mixture of violence with peaceful picketing gives the Court no more trouble than does the mixture of restraints of trade by employers and unions in the same industry. Black wrote a far-reaching opinion for the Court in the *Allen Bradley* case holding guilty under the Sherman Act a union that worked with its employers to boycott electrical goods bought outside the locality and threatened to strike against employers who did not play the local game. However, the same day he wrote a 5-to-4 opinion for the Court in a similar case that didn't show the necessary degree of collaboration with employers. Thus he agrees with the Court's principle but calls the facts in each case more closely on the side of labor.[55]

When a 5-to-3 Court held that tips are a part of the wages of redcaps at railroad stations, for the purposes of the wage-hour law, Black dissented (with Douglas and Murphy, again) that the statute imposes the duty of paying a minimum wage on the employer—not on someone else.[56] "The tip paying public," he protested, "is entitled to know whom it tips, the redcap or the railroad."

Black escaped the heavy moral-legal problems of wartime litigation without expressing very strong opinions, though he came closer to vigorous spokesmanship when upholding the government's wartime powers than when finding an excessive use of them. In the former category he dissented when the Court released George Sylvester Viereck, charged with violating the enemy-agent registration law and when the Court, in its first case of treason, interpreted that crime so strictly as to reverse the conviction.[57] He wrote the Court's opinion which expedited draft procedure by denying judicial review until after induction and the decision sustaining the "relocation" of United States citizens of Japanese ancestry from the West Coast.[58]

On the other hand, Black spoke for the Court in allowing a Japanese alien to sue in American courts even after the declaration of war, concurred in the dismissal of the case against Bund leaders for counseling to evade the draft law and concurred vigorously when the Court set aside denaturalization proceedings against a former German for lack of evidence.[59] His name is on the opinion that released two men convicted by military courts in Hawaii under the system of martial law which the Court found was maintained there longer than necessary.[60] In general, Black's votes were not embarrassing to the government in its exercise of war powers.

Among Black's miscellaneous opinions, perhaps none is more typical than a lone dissent in a puny case involving a state's condemnation of one fish net.[61] The point was that the case was not really puny. The formal issue was whether a state is precluded by the Constitution and laws of the United States from entertaining a suit in rem (against a thing) or whether there is only federal jurisdiction of such suits. The California law allowed seizure of the fish net because it was being operated in forbidden waters.

"If this case involved only a fish net," wrote Black, "I should be inclined to acquiesce in the holding of the Court. . . . But the principle laid down here involves far more than a fish net, for under it state courts are authorized through in rem proceedings to seize and condemn, for violation of local law, any equipment or vessel employed in maritime activity. Today's in rem action is against a fish net used in patently illegal fashion; tomorrow's may be an action against a tramp-steamer or ocean liner which violates a harbor regulation or otherwise offends against the police regulations of a state or municipality."

Also, he dissented when the Court dismissed a suit to force Illinois officials to reapportion election districts.[62] He disagreed that the case was "political" rather than judicial. And he wrote the opinion of the Court in three Indian cases in which he was on the other side of the fence from Justice Murphy, the Court's main defender of obligations to Indians.[63]

Finally, Black wrote a dissent in the 5-to-4 decision that a judge could not deduct from his income tax expenses incurred in his campaign for re-election.[64] Black's view was realistic: The lawyer had accepted appointment to a vacancy on the bench with assurance that he would be backed for return to the job at the next election, providing he would make a campaign contribution. To Black it was a legitimate part of doing a judge's business.

The opinion illustrates why the suspicion refuses to die that Black is a politician wrongly on the Court. He is a hapless man. The public reads into each of his votes an ulterior purpose. Just as Black's critics accuse him of following his personal predilections in casting his vote, they also work back from the end result to see if it checks with an opinion held by Black in the Senate. Like the gossipy women who learn that a newlywed is to have a baby, the critics start counting back on their fingers in search of premarital scandal.

But the outstanding thing about Black is that he can take it. They don't come much more relaxed and good-natured, and criticism seems to lash him into harder work. In good weather he has, like as not, put in an hour or so on the tennis court before reaching the Supreme Court for the grind of reading cases and picking out citations with mental tweezers. His frame does not bespeak the vigor of his mind, for it stoops a bit and he walks in an uncertain stride. Enough of what hair he has left is white that he now looks the oldest on the Court (Reed

QUALIFYING TEST FOR SUPREME COURT JOBS

The most common feeling against the Court plan—that it would make rubber stamps of the justices—was shown at the time by cartoonist Brown of the New York *Herald-Tribune*.

is a bit older). Nevertheless, his age and position don't keep him from quipping good naturedly about some of the art work with which the Court building is blessed.

Black's personality accounts almost as much as his legal theories for his leadership of the Court's liberal bloc. By virtue of having been there to welcome each of these justices, plus his skeptical look at legal formalities, Black has almost naturally come to the fore on the left side of the Court. Moreover, his forthrightness has made believers of some doubters.

This is by no means to say, however, that all Roosevelt appointees wandered into his fold. The fact that all were appointed by the same man may have started some that way—Frankfurter voted with Black frequently at first—but the new men were by no means rubber stamps, as hardly needs stating at this date. Douglas, Murphy and Rutledge found Black to their liking as well as to their way of thinking.

When Jackson arrived on the Court, from a brilliant career in the law, he found four years of Black's influence ahead of him. For some reason he chose to take a different path. The fact seems to be, however, that it was he who moved over—not Black. When the differences developed into a personal "feud" between the two justices and were thrown into the headlines by Jackson, from Nuremberg, it was again Jackson who did the moving—not Black. The story of that histrionic phase of the new Court is properly considered fully in the chapter on Jackson, but it should be noted in passing that Black showed no signs of emotional reaction. He attended a large press party a few days later, as scheduled, and enjoyed himself as unconcernedly as if nothing had happened. At the Court, he was whistling a nondescript tune as he puttered around the chamber getting ready for the summer vacation by cleaning his desk of the papers he accumulated as acting chief justice for several weeks after Stone's death.

Nearly everyone stepped into the fracas with a statement, editorial or private opinion, the consensus of which was that even though Jackson's specific charges might be flimsy and were definitely in bad taste, both men should resign. The reasons for demanding Black's resignation, however, were nebulous, ranging from the assertion that he should do it for the good of the Court on down to the charge that he doesn't have a judicial temperament. The latter was an omnibus charge, admittedly not directly connected to the Jackson feud incident; but it cannot be brushed off lightly.

Analyzing why Black supposedly has no judicial temperament gets into all kinds of rhetoric and metaphysics. Is it because he votes wrong, or because he doesn't take time to consider both sides of a case? Is it because he was once a Klansman—or a senator? Did his pleading of union cases ruin him as a judge? All these are really oblique approaches to the more general and appropriate question: What makes a Supreme Court justice a good one?

No total answer to that poser will be attempted, but several features of Black's career should be noted as sign posts along the way to the ultimate appraisal of him as a judge. At the outset, he is an affirmative justice rather than one who holds up a forbidding hand to the operating branches of the national and state governments. If the quality of being affirmative seems to conflict with the concept of judiciousness, it should be noted that the great judges of the past did not get that way by being neutral in their impacts. By definition, the good judge in a dynamic society must move ahead.

It is a distinct possibility that much of whatever fame Black may acquire will come not through his expertness in the law but through his ignorance of the law. That sounds both harsh and strange but is based on the belief that Black was able to cut through to the crux of legal situations largely because he was unencumbered by years of legal rigmarole which would have bogged down men higher in the profession. A man with a slingshot has been known to best a warrior with heavy armor and no plan of battle other than the one that had never failed him.

But the most popular fear about Black is that he will go too far "forward"—so far as to upset the vital role of the judiciary as the stabilizer of government. A major curb to this possibility lies in the fact that his loosest interpretations are on acts of legislatures, which can easily be amended if the interpretation doesn't suit those who passed the law.

In the field of civil liberties, where Black has been most outspoken and where the Constitution leaves most of the say-so to the Supreme Court, Black has already received a nod from history. In *The Republic*, Charles A. Beard wrote of Black's opinions in *Chambers* v. *Florida* that it "will ring with power as long as liberty and justice are cherished in our country."

Then, as if addressing those concerned with the stability of Black's opinions, Beard added this advice about the *Chambers* opinion: "The whole document ought to be read by all citizens who care for the perpetuity of the Republic."

CHAPTER V

The Judgment Seat

THE Court has often stated as a cardinal principle that it will function only on the basis of specific cases before it. For example, by its self-imposed limitation it could not have said what it did in the *Chambers* case in any way other than by deciding the particular issue brought before it. The Court could not have announced that principle in a press release nor in a letter to the governor of Florida nor in an edict posted on its big front door.

Therefore, the work of the Supreme Court progresses case by case. Similarly, an analysis of the Court must be concerned to a large extent with the march of cases. It would be much easier if one could say, for example, that Mr. Justice Doe believes that a suspect must be formally charged with a crime within five hours after his apprehension. But, no, the attitude of Mr. Justice Doe can be brought out only by looking at his position in a sequence of cases. He may vote in one case (continuing with the hypothetical situation) that two hours is quickly enough and, later, that eighteen hours is too long. A zone of speculation is left between the two positions.

The following seven cases, selected almost at random from those in which the Court has split recently, will illustrate what crosscurrents each justice meets at voting time and will give the reader a chance to put himself briefly in the judge's seat.

1. A forty-three-year-old man, named Smith Betts, was indicted for robbery in Maryland.[1] He asked for counsel, which he could not afford to hire, was denied it and was sentenced to prison. The trial judge described Betts as having "ordinary intelligence," but turned down the request for a state-paid lawyer on the grounds that one is not warranted for anything less than murder or rape in Maryland. Betts appealed that he had been deprived of due process.

Roberts wrote the majority opinion, confirming Betts' conviction, for Stone, Reed, Frankfurter, Byrnes and Jackson. The 6th amendment's right to counsel applies only in federal trials, the Court said; and the due process clause of the 14th, which applies to states, does not formulate a hard-and-fast rule. Each case must be looked at to see if the defendant suffered from lack of counsel. This one did not. A reading of common law and state statutes on the subject shows that many states allow counsel but only a few compel it to be furnished. The Court refused to require counsel in all cases or in this one.

Black dissented vigorously, also for Douglas and Murphy. They felt that Betts, whom they described in more sympathetic terms, did not have a fair trial and that passage of the 14th amendment made the 6th amendment's right to counsel applicable to the states. It was not the first time Black had urged this view on the Court, only to have it rejected. The right to counsel is "fundamental," wrote Black, citing a precedent decided before his appointment. Then he quoted historic attacks on trials without free counsel and asserted that study of state provisions on the subject shows that thirty-five states have some provision for granting counsel on request.

2. Several officers, directors and large stockholders of a typical holding company were involved in a Securities and Exchange Commission proceeding.[2] The SEC rejected a plan for reorganization of the company on the grounds that these managers of the firm had brought stock in it while the shuffle was in progress and stood to gain financially by their deal. The stock was bought openly; SEC made no charge of fraud but felt that such a transaction violated the managers' duty to their stockholders. SEC based its ruling on the principles of equity as laid down by the Court through the years.

The opinion, by Frankfurter, was joined in by Stone, Roberts and Jackson. The Court agreed that the managers held positions of trust, which must be upheld, but asked to whom they owed the trust. The majority found nothing in the SEC decision to indicate that other stockholders had been affected adversely by the managers' shrewd but open stock purchase. Since the commission's decision was based on principles of equity, Frankfurter reasoned, the Court had full authority to see if the SEC followed the correct principles. It had not. Whether the commission might have reached the same result by basing its opinion on administrative determinations, rather than a rule of equity taken from the courts, did not matter, Frankfurter decided; but the case was sent back to the commission for further proceedings.

Again, Black dissented—this time also for Reed and Murphy. Douglas had disqualified himself in the case.) "The grounds upon which the Commission made its findings seem clear enough to me," wrote Black. Of the managers he wrote that "they bought preferred stock and then offered a reorganization plan which would give this stock a book value of four times the price they had paid for it." That the SEC saw fit to "draw support for its own administrative conclusion from decisions of the courts should not detract from the validity of its findings," he protested. And, finally, Black felt that the principle of equity followed by the SEC was correct, anyway.

3. The setting of the *McNabb* case might have come out of a storybook.[3] The scene was the McNabb Settlement, twelve miles from Chattanooga and long-time home of a clan of Tennessee mountaineers. One summer night in 1940 federal revenuers swooped down on five of the McNabbs and upset a moonshine deal in the family cemetery. The McNabbs fled, but the officers stayed to dump the illicit liquor. However, when a large rock dropped among the officers, one of them went off to investigate. He was shot and died without knowing who had fired the gun.

Five of the clan were rounded up for grilling. Freeman and Raymond, twenty-five-year-old twins who had never gotten beyond the fourth grade or the near-by town of Jasper, were questioned fourteen hours in a bare room without benefit of friends or counsel. Their twenty-year-old cousin, Benjamin, whose formal education was no greater and whose travel had been even less, came in after this first session; but all three spent long hours before officers for two more days. Finally, they had confessed enough to give the government a case and all were arraigned before a court official and charged with murder. Eventually they were sentenced to forty-five years in prison; their appeal was based on the irregularities during the period before their trial.

The question facing Frankfurter, for a 7-to-1 Court, was whether the main evidence against the McNabb boys had been unfairly extracted from them or whether the federal officers had used legitimate zeal in bringing to book the moonshining slayers of their fellow law enforcer. Frankfurter decided that, by various laws, Congress had ordered its agents to take suspects to the bar of justice before holding them for questioning.

"A democratic society, in which respect for the dignity of all men is central, naturally guards against the misuse of the law enforcement process," Frankfurter wrote. The officers in this case showed "a plain disregard" of the duty imposed upon them by Congress; the confessions were not admissible and the McNabb boys were freed.

Reed, by himself, protested that confessions were adequately protected by the requirement that they be voluntary, that the time element didn't matter. "I am opposed," he said, "to broadening the possibilities of defendants escaping punishment by these more rigorous technical requirements in the administration of justice." Finally, he observed that no point was made at the trial of the failure to take the McNabbs to a magistrate for commitment.

4. The *Elgin, Joliet & Eastern Railway* case[4] came up as a complicated administrative law problem, labor division. Under a well-established system in the railway industry, the union that has been duly chosen as collective bargaining agent handles grievance cases before the National Railroad Adjustment Board. This beautiful bureaucratic machinery was challenged in this case, however, by a demand for court review of a grievance settlement arrived at in the customary manner.

In 1945 the Court threw the world of railway unions into a dither by holding, five to four, that courts can upset adjustments of the board unless there is legal evidence that the aggrieved employee made the union his bargaining agent on the specific problem at issue. The four dissenters—Stone, Roberts, Frankfurter and Jackson—soon had lots of company, for the railroad brotherhoods, the AF of L, the CIO and the government flocked in to ask the Court to reconsider what havoc it had wrought in the industry. The impressive list of objectors raised the specter of thousands of adjustments being gone through all over again by the courts after elaborate administrative proceedings.

The Court agreed to a reargument and handed down a second decision in 1946. But it adhered to the former one. The Court pointed out that the burden of upsetting an administrative decision rests on him who would do so, but the dissenters got little satisfaction out of the second try. Jackson was absent and Roberts had resigned, but Burton took the latter's place in the minority.

Frankfurter, for the dissenters, noted that the Court had erected enough hurdles in the way of an employee, that few would be able to get courts to reverse administrative decisions adverse to them. "But since litigation is authorized and hope springs eternal in a litigant's breast," he said, "the far reaching mischief of unsettling nonlitigious modes of adjustment under the machinery of the Railway Labor Act largely remains." Twenty-five years of successful method was being undercut, he feared. And finally, Congress created the railway system for the very purpose of "replacing the ordinary judicial processes in resolving railway labor controversies," except where specifically retained. "We ought not to read the new law through the spectacles of the old remedies," he thought.

5. The case of William Schneiderman was one of those which gets tried as much in the newspapers as in the courts.[5] The appearance of Wendell Willkie as counsel for Schneiderman, an avowed Communist, not long after Willkie had been presidential candidate of the Republi-

can party, added considerably to the drama of the case. The government, for the first time, was seeking to nullify a citizen's naturalization papers on the grounds that they were obtained years before "unlawfully," even though by court order.

Schneiderman came to the United States from Russia when he was three. At the age of sixteen he became active in Communist party operations, rising through such important posts as candidate for governor of Minnesota, member of the party's national committee and secretary of the party in California. The question was not whether he was a Communist but whether that "attachment to principles" conflicted with the requirements under which he got his citizenship papers. Briefly, the law requires that he "has behaved as a man of good moral character, attached to the principles of the Constitution of the United States, and is well disposed to the good order and happiness of the same." The government argued that when Schneiderman applied for citizenship he was affiliated with a party which "advised, advocated and taught the overthrow of the Government, Constitution and laws of the United States by force and violence."

Murphy wrote the Court's opinion, also for Black, Douglas, Reed, and Rutledge. His emphasis was on Schneiderman's behavior rather than on general questions of political thoughts. An analysis of evidence in the case, including testimony of professors that Marxian theory did not include overthrow of the government by force and violence, failed to convince the majority that Schneiderman fell within the legal language. The Court conceded, as had the government, that no one has been able to settle the Communist party's exact attitude about overthrow and concluded that evidence against Schneiderman was not adequate to support denaturalization. In passing, the Court spoke eloquently of the gravity of removing one's citizenship after the all-important right had been granted.

Douglas concurred briefly to emphasize the standards of evidence that were not present in this case and to declare that he would not upset the original finding of the court that naturalized Schneiderman. Rutledge, also concurring, emphasized the civil-liberty angle. If Schneiderman's citizenship could be canceled after twelve years, he argued, it could be canceled after thirty or fifty years; "if it can be done for Schneiderman, it can be done for thousands or tens of thousands of others." Moreover, said Rutledge, "no citizen with such a threat hanging over his head could be free."

Chief Justice Stone, with Roberts and Frankfurter, wrote a long dissent that the findings of the two lower courts—against Schneiderman—"are abundantly supported by the evidence" and hence should not be set aside. Freedom of thought is not involved, Stone wrote; the question is only that "the declared will of Congress shall prevail—that no man shall retain his citizenship who does not show attachment to the principles of the Constitution."

Stone was irked by Douglas' proposal that the Court should not go behind the original naturalization proceedings, This, he felt, "emasculated the statute," allowing cancellation of naturalization papers obtained unlawfully. Then, for page after page, Stone reviewed excerpts from Communist doctrine which were enough to convince him that its adherents would overthrow the government by force and violence.

6. The appeal of murder sentences against Morris Malinski and Sidney Rudish, New Yorkers, gave the Court great trouble.[6] Most of it came from Malinski, who was arrested on his way to work one morning and taken to a Brooklyn hotel room instead of to a court for arraignment. He was stripped and kept naked for about three hours, then allowed to put on his shoes, underwear and a blanket and kept there until six o'clock that evening. Though he was charged with murder (of a police officer), Malinski was kept in the room three days and allowed to see only one friend. It was after a private session with him that Malinski confessed and was allowed to dress. Then he was taken to the scene of the crime to explain how it happened. Five days after his arrest, Malinski made out a confession at a police station, after which he was jailed and arraigned.

Of the many technicalities presented at the trial as to whether the jury should consider this and other evidence, it is essential to note a few. The first confession was not offered in evidence, though the subsequent one was and the jury decided that it was voluntary. In the presentation of the written confession by Malinski, the identity of Rudish was hidden from the jury by using symbols for other defendants' names, but both men claimed before the Supreme Court that they had been denied due process of law. Besides the circumstances surrounding the confessions they cited remarks such as these which were made by the prosecutor in closing his case before the jury: Malinski "was not hard to break. He did not care what he did. He knew the cops were going to break him down. Why this talk about being undressed? Of course they had a right to undress him to look for bullet scars, and keep the clothes off him. That was quite proper police procedure. That is some more psychology—let him sit around with a blanket on him, humiliate him there for a while; let him sit in the corner; let him think he is going to get a shellacking."

Douglas spoke for a five-man majority which couldn't agree fully within itself. The Court held that Malinski's confession had not been made voluntarily but that Rudish had been protected at the trial from the taint of that defect and must pay the penalty for murder. Douglas noted that Malinski had had no lawyer during his questioning and that the prosecutor made no effort to conceal the "applied psychology." A majority also felt that even if the later confession were voluntary the trial would have to fall because the coerced admissions were referred to repeatedly before the jury. "Constitutional rights," Douglas wrote, "may suffer as much from subtle intrusions as from direct disregard."

Black and Frankfurter agreed with this judgment by Douglas; but Murphy and Rutledge thought Rudish's sentence should also be reversed, while Stone, Roberts, Reed and Jackson thought that both should be upheld. Frankfurter, concurring separately, laid out a professorial treatise on the due process clause of the 14th amendment, distinguishing it from similar phraseology in the 5th amendment. In the 14th, which applies to state action, he found only generalities, but generalities that have deep roots of procedure which have given years of freedom. But though due process is general, Frankfurter had no doubt that the Malinski trial fell short of its standards, especially where a death sentence was involved.

Rutledge and Murphy insisted that all Malinski's confessions were nullified by the coercion of the first one, and that the device used for separating Rudish from them was no good. They branded Malinski's first five days of arrest as third-degree methods for which the Constitution has no room. The due process clause which protects one from a confession wrung out of him by coercion "should not allow him to be convicted upon a confession wrung from another by coercion," they said of Rudish.

Murphy added a few remarks of his own, characterizing Malinski's first four days as a "reign of mental fear and terror" and pointed to statements by the prosecutor that "were indicative of a desire to appeal to racial and religious bigotry." The prosecutor had referred to Malinski (a Jew) as a "jerk from the East Side" (center of Jewish population).

The Stone-Roberts-Reed-Jackson dissent that both men should die noted first the conflicting testimony. Its main point, however, was that the Supreme Court had no business upsetting the jury's verdict that the confessions were not coerced. "It is not the function of this Court . . . to sit as a super-jury," they complained. The requirements of due process were met in submitting the case to the jury, at which point the Supreme Court's concern had hitherto ended. As for the prosecutor's remarks, said the dissenters, "at most, his remarks were an ill advised attempt at justification of the coercion which the defense had alleged." Besides, he had not testified before the jury as a matter of evidence.

7. One of the most beautiful examples of differing attitudes within the Court, though not a typical line-up of voting blocs, occurred in a case

as obscure as is most people's knowledge of the law affecting Indians.[7] The Court's 5-to-4 opinion was written by Reed in behalf also of Stone and Rutledge. He said, in effect: "There is nothing this Court can do for the Shoshone Indians, suing under the Box Elder Treaty of 1863." He didn't even say, "Sorry." Jackson and Black voted with this trio, but wrote a joint concurrence to express regrets.

Reed's opinion was as drab as they come. He traced negotiation of the treaty and explained that under well-settled law (which was not contested by any justice) the Shoshones could sustain their suit for $15,000,000 for the taking of an equal number of western acres only if the treaty recognized that the Indians held title to the land. The crux of the case became an interpretation of the treaty, which might as well have been recorded in Indian sign language as far as the layman is concerned. After reviewing its circumstances and the terms embodied in it, Reed concluded that it did not recognize title. What it amounted to was an agreement by the Indians not to molest travelers, stagecoaches, telegraph lines or projected railroads. The United States agreed to protect the Indians, to increase their annuity $5,000 and to give them $2,000 "to relieve their immediate necessities." This, plus much more history, did not recognize title in the Indians, the Court decided. The Shoshones had no suit.

The concurrence by Jackson, joined by Black, was unique. It contained barbs directed at both sides of the Court, as well as at the United States' policy toward Indians. First, they pointed out that even if the Indians won the case they would get no wampum, for an act of Congress requires that funds recovered in such suits go into the Treasury—after deduction of "reasonable" lawyers' fees. They rebelled against resort to the courts to settle this kind of a question, saying that "to apply the litigation process to such a problem as we have here seems farfetched." And: "The Indian problem is essentially a sociological problem, not a legal one."

"We would not be second to any other," they wrote, "in recognizing that—judgment or no judgment—a moral obligation of a high order rests upon this country to provide for decent shelter, clothing, education, and industrial advancement of the Indian. Nothing is gained by dwelling upon the unhappy conflicts that have prevailed between the Shoshones and the whites—conflicts which sometimes leave one in doubt which side could make the better claim to be civilized."

The generation of Indians who suffered from the westward white march, they observed, has gone to the Happy Hunting Ground, leaving their descendants to get whatever debt is paid. However, "it is most unfortunate" to measure that in legal damages. "Here we are asked," they protested, "to go back over three quarters of a century to spell out the meaning of a most ambiguous writing made in 1863. One of the parties did not keep, or know how to keep, written records of negotiations. . . . The whites brought forth their armies and reduced the Indians to submission. Then the whites 'negotiated' a treaty. . . . The most elemental condition of a bargain was not present, for there was nothing like equality of bargaining power."

The Indians, they wrote further, didn't have a word for property concepts and their representatives in making the treaty "appear to have been softened for the job by gifts of blankets and trinkets." Thus they agreed with Reed that the treaty gave no legal rights and they agreed with the dissenters as to the Indians' moral deserts.

Douglas and Murphy each wrote dissents, in both of which they were joined by each other and by Frankfurter. Roberts merely noted a dissent. Douglas was poetic but he mainly disagreed with the Court's interpretation of the legal treaty. He felt it clearly recognized the Indians' title in the land and created a right to sue for the taking of that land.

"He who comes to my abode," wrote Douglas, "and bargains for free transit of a right of way across the land on which I live and which I proclaim to be my own certainly recognizes that I have a claim to it. That and more was done here. . . . The United States . . . could have invaded this Indian country and extinguished Indian title by the sword or by appropriation. But it did not choose that course. It chose to negotiate a treaty."

Douglas also noted the unfairness of the negotiation ("But we should remember that no counsel sat at the elbow of Pokatello when the treaty was drafted."). Then he urged a liberal interpretation of the treaty. He protested that "what these Indians did not lose to the railroads and to the land companies they lose in the fine web of legal niceties." Finally, he cited a book about one of his favorite characters, Chief Joseph, in support of his feeling that the "downtrodden people" were not getting a break in the case.

Considering Murphy's usually sentimental approach to an Indian case, the dissenter restrained himself considerably this time. For his own opinion, he dealt mostly with a detailed analysis of the negotiation, paralleling but disputing the majority's version of the same deal. He pointed out that the secretary of the interior, as late as 1934, admitted that the 1863 treaty recognized the title of the land to be in the Shoshones. Of the argument that any money recovered would go into the Treasury, anyway, Murphy pleaded that this should not keep the Court from deciding the principle of the case.

These seven samples do more than illustrate the complexities facing a justice as he votes one way or the other on a given issue. They go far in disabusing one's mind of any idea that there is a right and a wrong answer to each case. These are differences of opinion which may be honestly held. Only time can chalk up one side or the other as correct. Even then, more time can erase the first scoring and reverse it. One side may be more popular than the other; but, happily, men even before the founders of the Constitution rejected popularity as a test of judiciousness.

Here we have nine grown, thoughtful and hard-working men subsidized for life to look over the conflicting arguments. Yet they come up with different interpretations of the same pieces of paper. To many this is disconcerting. Soundness, according to some, is closely correlated with unanimity. Where correctness exists, they argue, there must also be error. But such reasoning ignores the basic process of judging cases. A judge has before him two or more piles of precedents, heaped up by opposing counsel, who are—in theory, at least—agents of the Court. He then must make up his mind which pile represents the better law and select from it for his written opinion. Neither pile is wrong. One may be more desirable to contemporaries, but the other may prevail even before the dissenter who advocates it is gone. If nine men agreed perfectly day after day in making their choices it would more likely be a sign that something was wrong than that they had found some oracular source for enduring correctness.

The differences of opinion in the *Betts* case were both of principle and of interpreting agreed-upon facts. Black, Douglas and Murphy sought to make the 14th amendment include the specific rights of the 5th, which would have tightened up state criminal procedure. A majority, including Frankfurter, thought that there should be no hard-and-fast rule under the 14th amendment's due process clause and that the denial of counsel to Betts in that particular case was not covered by it. Yet when the fate of Rudish was at stake, Frankfurter thought that the same clause protected him from a third degree before arraignment.

Then there was Chief Justice Stone, often a courageous defender of civil liberties, finding himself unable to help either Betts or Malinski, the latter because the jury had found no coercion around his confession. Yet Black, generally a stanch defender of letting juries have their say (once they have been properly chosen), voted to upset the jury's findings and substitute the Court's. In the *Schneiderman* case is found the ridiculous situation of three justices saying that the findings of the two lower courts were "abundantly supported by the evidence," while five of their colleagues were saying there wasn't enough evidence. Even "abundance" is not a well-settled term.

And so it goes. Each case is a wheel within other wheels. The Court accepts for decision mostly those cases that are not clear cut; it seldom gets a crack at a simple one. One principle seldom disposes of a case; others cut across it sharply, touch it at angles or impinge on it with a broad sweep. No justice is free from this pulling and hauling necessary to a decision in each case, but none illustrates the fact better than the Court's center man, Justice Reed.

CHAPTER VI

Center of Gravity

WHEN President Roosevelt put Stanley Forman Reed on the Supreme Court in January of 1938, the packing job was statistically complete. Though Reed was only the second Roosevelt appointee, he made the fifth sure liberal vote. (Brandeis, Stone, Cardozo and Black were the other four.) Reed was the very man who had stood before the Nine Old Men to argue the New Deal's legal case. Now, after teaching all the new wrinkles to the Court, he was stepping around the bench to vote. Presumably, his votes would follow the pattern of his painstaking, pioneering legal briefs to the Court. At the age of fifty-three, Reed seemed the most predictable appointment Roosevelt could make, yet seven years later, Reed was definitely the "swing" man, the man hardest to place in either the conservative bloc or the liberal bloc.

Reed's three years as solicitor general, lawyer for the world's biggest client, were the most hectic three years that office ever experienced. When he took over, in March of 1935, the gold cases had shaken the land, but there were many other tremors to come. One of the greatest chapters in Supreme Court history was just being started, and while someone else caused it, Reed was right in the middle of it, putting it in legal form like a harassed editor.

Nearly all of the cases argued for the government by Solicitor General Reed are landmark cases. Opinions in them will be studied for many years in the law schools and will be cited equally long by other administrations claiming legal power to extend control over new phases of national economic life.

It was Stanley Reed who successfully argued the constitutionality of the Tennessee Valley Authority, the Railway Labor Act (first real application of collective bargaining as a government policy) and the Wagner Act. In winning this list of class A cases, Reed had to whip the highest-priced legal talent money could buy, both as foe in each case and as general adversary through such well-heeled organizations as the American Liberty League, dedicated to the proposition that the Nine Old Men—or, rather, a majority of them—were infallible.

Good as his batting average was, Reed didn't win all his cases. In fact, it was two of his losses, as much as any other New Deal defeats, that goaded Roosevelt into his Court plan of early 1937. In 1935, Reed lost the NRA case by a unanimous decision; next year he lost the AAA case by a 6-to-3 count, stunning him deeply. In the next two years, however, Reed taught the Supreme Court more than it taught him about the law of a republic taking drastic steps to fight a drastic depression and extend the benefits of government to a new strata of the population.

The name of Stanley F. Reed apparently was first spoken in Washington by two top officials of the old Federal Farm Board. It was November of 1929, days which few need prodding to recall. Even before the depression struck with full fury, burdensome surpluses in farm commodities had forced the lethargic Herbert Hoover to set up a bureau for buying commodities for resale on world markets at different prices. The chairman and vice chairman of the Farm Board were discussing the problem of finding a counsel for their agency.

"I won't be satisfied until we find a man who has all the qualifications," declared the chairman.

"I know a man who has all the qualifications, all right," replied his assistant, "but—he happens to be a Democrat."

"That makes no difference," countered the Hoover administrator. "If he's the right man, get hold of him and put him to work. What's his name, and where is he from?"

"His name is Stanley Reed and he's from Maysville, Kentucky," was the reply.

He might as well have suggested Joe Doaks, of Plainfield, for all the country knew about the Democratic lawyer from the town of 6,500 in upstate Mason County, where Reed still has a medium-sized tobacco farm. However, the people of Kentucky were beginning to know the name. Reed had been born on the right side of the tracks, into a doctor's family, and had enjoyed more than his share of higher education. After Kentucky Wesleyan, Reed went to Yale for a bachelor's degree, majoring in economics and history. For law he chose the University of Virginia but shifted to Columbia, from which he was graduated. About that time, Reed married Winifred Elgin, a hometown girl whose later accomplishments include being registrar general of the Daughters of the American Revolution and mother of two lawyer sons. As a combination honeymoon and postgraduate course, the Reeds went to Paris for a year of study, mostly in the code of civil law and in international law, at the Sorbonne.

In 1910 lawyer Reed took his high polish back to Maysville to try it on the hometown. Two of his main clients from then on were the Chesapeake and Ohio Railroad and the Burley Tobacco Growers' Cooperative Association, a combination which made him seem right for the Farm Board job. In fact, the man who chose him for that position worked with Reed as head of the tobacco co-op.

Meanwhile, the young lawyer was getting into politics. He had been home only two years when the good people of his district sent their budding legal light off to the state legislature for four years, a period in which Reed made local history by introducing Kentucky's child labor and workmen's compensation laws, a radical step. In the Wilson campaign Reed was active as president of the Kentucky Young Democrats.

This was the man who was called to Republican Washington to help the government bail the farmers, including his tobacco friends, out of an economic hole. In doing so, as counsel to the Farm Board, Reed was only getting a good warm-up for the myriad problems dumped on him later. Less than a month after the landslide election of Roosevelt, he was transferred to the more important post of counsel to the Reconstruction Finance Corporation, with which economic stagnation was to be broken up by loans to start the ball rolling again.

It was at the RFC that Reed learned the finer points of using legal power for the administration's concept of economic justice—and expanding traditional concepts of legal power when that was necessary. Reed hadn't been at RFC long before the Roosevelt program for buying newly mined foreign and domestic gold came under attack. The administration hoped to lower the value of the dollar on foreign exchanges by this expedient, raising domestic commodity prices; but it was immediately argued that there was no basis in law for such a measure. The Treasury declared itself flatly on the negative side, but Reed, whose agency would have to do the buying, issued an opinion that legal authority existed. The program was carried on.

At RFC, Reed's assistant counsel was the dashing, brainy, politicking Tommy Corcoran. The junior member of this long-standing partnership used his office for many activities other than RFC legal work, contrasting sharply with his boss, who kept close to the work at hand. Because of the association some people were inclined to view Reed as a finagler, pulling strings all over town, but it is a significant trait in Reed's character that he was not.

As a sort of transition from RFC to the rich, paneled offices of the solicitor general, Reed was used as a special assistant to the attorney general to lead the fight for the government tinkering with the gold value of the dollar. His plea to the Supreme Court, on the private contracts case, was that probably $100 billion was at stake unless the Court upheld the right of the government to manage its currency. The Court believed him, and Reed moved to the second highest post in the Department of Justice, where the United States government consulted him all hours of day and night.

His new boss, Attorney General Homer Cummings, called Reed in and told him that his first case before the Supreme Court as solicitor general should be a sure thing. The list was looked over and Reed selected the case in which President Roosevelt was seeking the ouster of Federal Trade Commissioner Humphries. The official was a presidential appointee and presumably could be removed by the President; victory was certain. But Reed chuckles as he recalls how the Nine Old Men upset his applecart by holding in Humphries' favor.

Big as the solicitor's job was, there was one big legal project in which Reed was not consulted as much as his title might indicate. That was the President's packing plan. Reed wrote at least one memorandum on a minor phase of judicial reorganization, but for the most part he happily worked away at his heavy job of pleading personally with the Court to change its ways. Through diligence, long hours, letter-perfection and alert arguments, Reed did that job well. Incidentally, Reed is one of the few justices who had practiced before the Court before moving to Washington. His reputation as a good lawyer, broad as that term can be, was well established. Equally apparent was his loyalty to the administratian, a characteristic that had marked him for a federal judgeship just as soon as the tory Sutherland retired. Roosevelt immediately appointed Reed to the vacancy, his second to fill, and thirteen days later Reed was confirmed overwhelmingly by a Senate which he had not brushed against in the Court fight. Mother nature was accomplishing the Court change which Congress had felt should not be done artificially.

•

Those who thought that the vote of Stanley Reed was sewed up for the New Deal side (and there were few who didn't) were gradually proved wrong. Unlike Hugo Black, Reed played the game of being a good freshman justice and made little noise. In a year or two, however—by the time the young men were beginning to show their independence—Reed's vote was getting harder and harder to classify.

In the 1943 term he dissented with Roberts nine times, his most frequent combination when in the minority, and was almost never protesting with the Black-Douglas-Murphy group. However, most of the cases in which the Court was split were technical or procedural matters rather than issues fundamental to the Constitution. The 1944 pattern was the same: Reed dissented with Roberts and Stone much more than with the liberal bloc, which had by that time been joined by Rutledge. Thus, when Reed dissented he was on the conservative side; however, an analysis of his affirmative opinions in recent years shows that Reed was more nearly in the center of the Court than was any other justice.

An analysis of 5-to-4 splits shows that the two most predictable blocs, right and left, exclude Reed. Thus, Reed is in the position of hardest man to get when lawyers address the Court, much the same as Roberts was when Reed was standing before the Court as chief pleader for the government.

Governor Ellis Arnall, of Georgia, demonstrated this fact when he argued that the Court should take original jurisdiction of a suit against northern railroads for allegedly discriminating against the South in freight rates. At one point in his oral presentation, Arnall pointed his finger mildly but directly at Reed and said, "Now, Mr. Justice Reed, I want you to get this point." He did. The 5-to-4 majority included Reed.

However, there are some principles of law for which the center man has been outspoken and for which he is particularly tagged. They are not the dramatic principles engendered by criminal cases, for example, but then that's not the kind of lawyer Reed is. One of his strong points is administrative law, a subject in which he would be expected to follow the pressure of Washington's myriad bureaus, ever seeking more freedom for themselves and less judicial review of their actions.

Much of the organized bar's enmity for the New Deal came from the flood of administrative orders, decrees, regulations, findings, determinations, certifications and promulgations. Most of these were born of emergency and given only bastard status by lovers of old-fashioned, cut-and-dried law. Agencies such as the National Labor Relations Board were bound hand and foot in their early days by injunctions filed in lower courts to keep them from issuing any orders at all. Then, when the Supreme Court came to their rescue to hold that complainants must fight their cases through the agencies before running to the courts, the orders themselves were attacked from all angles. Courts were asked to upset administrative findings of fact as not supported by evidence, as being arbitrary, wrong or based on improper hearings. Before the Nine Old Men had exited, the Court established the principle that administrative findings of fact, based on expert handling, would not be set aside and rejudged as to merit by the courts. Meanwhile, the Supreme Court built up a body of decisions telling administrative agencies what constituted fair proceedings—adequate notice, opportunity to be heard, etc. The division of work between agencies and courts was a convenient one, for the courts would bog down overnight if they assumed the many functions of administrative agencies; but the division continued to rankle the bar. Most of the discontent came from clients who were being regulated (adversely) by the many administrative decisions, but lawyers also took exception professionally to the procedure of agencies acting as their own prosecutors, judges and juries. This prospect was not pleasing to some justices, but their alternative was far worse; namely, trying all issues from the beginning to see if they agreed with the administrative agency.

As personnel on the Court shifted and as the huge new crop of agencies settled down to a routine, the legal arguments on this important issue milled around in the Court chamber. Stanley Reed, as much as anyone, helped nail it down. In 1941 he wrote for a 5-to-3 Court one of the most extreme opinions ever written on administrative power.[1] The bituminous coal division of the Department of Interior had concluded that a railway was not entitled to exemption from the Bituminous Coal Code. The railroad insisted that it consumed its own coal and hence came within a specific exemption of the act; it asked the Court to review the administrative decision on the grounds that it was a finding on the scope of the act, not a mere finding of fact.

Reed, for the Court, would have nothing to do with the argument that the bureaucrats were deciding statutory interpretations. "Where as here a determination has been left to an administrative body," Reed wrote, "this delegation will be respected and the administrative conclusion left untouched." Roberts, Stone and Byrnes felt that the bureau had exceeded the limits to which administrative officers may go in interpreting a statute so as to accomplish aims which Congress might not have wanted.

However, Reed balked when the Court voted to refuse to review a National Mediation Board decision designating one group of employees as appropriate for selecting their own bargaining representatives, freezing out another group.[2] The majority felt that this was an example of a decision that Congress wanted administrators to settle, but Reed (for Roberts and Jackson, too) protested that "the special competence of the National Mediation Board lies in the field of labor relations rather than in that of statutory construction."

Reed lost the point in that case, but regained considerable ground a few months later when he wrote a 7-to-2 opinion giving milk producers the right to sue the Department of Agriculture to stop certain deductions from the settlement price of milk under the Marketing Agreement Act of 1937.[3] The aggrieved milkers insisted that the administrators were making the deductions from their complicated payment formula without authority in the law. The government pleaded that Congress wanted the department to decide such matters, that the Court should not intervene.

Reed decided that the milkmen had very real complaints and that the courts should hear them. Though Congress did not specifically grant judicial review in this particular law, he conceded, the principle exists in the scheme of things. Besides, no forum other than the courts was provided in this law. Reed's opinion was doubly convincing, for he helped organize many such marketing co-operatives when he was with the Federal Farm Board and wrote the 5-to-4 opinion upholding constitutionality of the very act under which this dispute arose.[4]

Two years later he collected his philosophy of administrative law in an opinion for the Court that "back pay" awarded an employee by the National Labor Relations Board for being wrongfully fired must be counted as "wages" for the purposes of the Social Security Act.[5] In keeping its accounts, the Social Security Board had defined "wages" more narrowly, depriving thousands of employees of having their checks for back pay counted toward old age benefits. The issue was important; in five years recalcitrant employers had paid $7,700,000 in back pay.

The Supreme Court's holding on the true definition of "wages" was not as important, however, as its ruling that it need not follow the administrative agency's interpretation of the statute under which the agency operated. The Court conceded that those interpretations deserved "great weight," but declared that "an agency may not finally decide the limits of its statutory power." That is a judicial function, and in this case the agency had exceeded its limits.

These opinions by Reed are not easily classifiable, but they are more so than are many of his other opinions. They stand for the ultimate balance between the legislative, executive and judicial branches of the republic, each strong—but only so long as each stays within its proper confines. But the judiciary will set the confines. Administrative agencies can decide factual questions, such as whether an employee was fired for union activity or for being incompetent, whether XYZ or ABC union won an election for collective bargaining rights, etc. However, when an administrator issues an interpretation of the statute under which Congress has set him up in business, the Supreme Court will step into the argument, hear it all over again and make the final determination.

Looking at it another way, Congress may now delegate broad authority to administrative agencies—and of course has—but when a doubt arises as to how much authority has been delegated, the umpires will wear black robes. It is a convenient division of authority, for it keeps the multitude of lesser decisions away from the slow-moving judicial process and allows the people's elected representatives to set the general course of policy. At the same time, it keeps the Supreme Court close enough at hand to detect deviations from the Constitution, from the master copy of the rules of the game of government. The presence on the Court of former senators and former administrators has helped an intelligent drawing of the boundaries.

In another area in which lines often have to be drawn, Reed is bolder with his strokes. That is the area between states' rights to tax business operations and the federal right to conduct its own business unhampered. A typical situation involving this old argument was before the Court in 1943.[6] In the interest of protecting its farmers from buying adulterated fertilizer, the sovereign state of Florida started an inspection system under which each sack of fertilizer sold in the state had to bear a tag showing that it had been inspected and a fee paid for the service. The United States government bought fertilizer outside of Florida and shipped it in to farmers of that state who were participating in the national soil conservation program. Uncle Sam refused to pay the inspection fee and got an injunction against Florida officials from enforcing the local law.

Reed, for a unanimous Court, made quick work of this interference with a national program and declared the federal supremacy in terms so broad that Florida and the other states whose officials poked their noses into the case understood their defeat. ". . . the activities of the Federal Government are free from regulation by any state," Reed wrote. "No other adjustment of competing enactments or legal principles is possible." Such fees are allowable, he said, where the United States is not the owner, but "these fees are like a tax upon the right to carry on the business of the post office or upon the privilege of selling United States bonds through federal officials."

It is in the field of civil rights that Reed's friends have been most disappointed, though the justice's career offered little from which to predict which way he would vote in personal liberty cases. Reed is kindly, rather than oppressive, by nature; yet his experience has been in allocating power among government branches and in arguing technicalities of the law rather than in umpiring the hard knocks of life—or even sharing in them. He assumes the role of a jurist, as opposed to a plain lawyer, yet he shows little of the philosophy that marks a jurist in deciding civil rights cases.

In the few opinions Reed has recorded on this subject, his language is singularly uninspired, though in perfectly good form. His arguments are firm but don't rise to the heights of the Bill of Rights under which they are pleaded. His opinion upholding conviction of Earl Browder for use of a passport obtained by false statements is historic because the leader of the Communist party was sent to jail by it, but Reed's brief statement for the Court is purely legalistic.[7]

The subject on which Reed hit his literary high is treatment of Jehovah's Witnesses, an issue on which he generally upholds local ordinances against the religious sect. He wrote the majority opinion in the three cases that were later reversed by the Court.[8] Reed made an eloquent plea that the rights guaranteed by the first ten amendments are not absolute but are subject to restraint whenever they collide with other rights in a community. The core of Reed's attitude in these cases is that one who sells Bibles must pay the same tax that is assessed against sellers of other books. To the argument that such taxes restrict religious freedom, Reed answered that the religious practitioners here were vending their religious books and tracts as a source of funds, properly subjecting themselves to a reasonable fee. "It would hardly be contended," he wrote, "that the publication of newspapers is not subject to the usual govermental fiscal exactions," yet freedom of the press is also guaranteed by the Constitution.

A minority, led by Stone, attacked the fees as restrictive on their faces and as liable to abuse. When the decision was reversed Reed clung tenaciously to his original attitude in a dissent which some regard as one of his best opinions. When the same minority helped overthrow the *Gobitis* flag salute case, a month later, Reed dissented laconically that he was standing by the famous decision to make young Witnesses salute the flag or be expelled from school.

More recently, Reed exasperated some of his liberal friends by an opinion that the state of Illinois may deny an otherwise qualified lawyer the right to practice law because his creed as conscientious objector made it impossible for him to take an oath to support the state constitution, which requires willingness to perform military service.[9]

Again, when the rest of the Court joined to set forth boldly the meaning of a "speedy" trial, as guaranteed by the Constitution, Reed dissented that rights of suspects in criminal proceedings were adequately safeguarded so long as confessions were not wrung from them by third degrees.[10]

Reed's only real landmark clearly on the side of civil liberties came in 1944 when he wrote the Court's opinion which overthrew the legal fiction that primaries are not elections within the meaning of the Constitution and laws.[11] The opinion ended the southern ruse for keeping Negroes from voting by banning them from the primaries, which really are the elections in that one-party area. Southerner Reed braved the criticism that attends any disregard of precedent to hold that the primary, though operated in Texas by each political party, was in reality being operated by the state. "Constitutional rights would be of little value if they could be thus indirectly denied," he wrote.

Reed's civil rights votes in the 1945 term indicate his vacillation, using four important ones as bench marks. He dissented when the Court reversed three cases to hold that an alien conscientious objector, applying for citizenship, may choose noncombatant duty instead of promising to bear arms and when the Court branded as a bill of attainder the appropriations rider which barred salaries to three federal employees who were disliked by Congress.[12]

These were balanced by his authorship of two majority opinions, one against a Florida court which felt that the Miami *Herald* had been contemptuous of it and the other striking down Virginia's racial segregation law, as applied to interstate busses.[13] But the latter decision was based legally on the interstate commerce clause rather than on any consideration of racial equality.

As the pattern of the new Court's right, left and center emerged, Stanley Reed became more of a question mark to those who follow the Court. Some became interested professionally because their arguments were channeled largely at Reed; others became interested because this justice, unlike most, seemed to have no philosophy of the law.

Some see Reed as a man who was a liberal only among conservatives. As a young Turk sponsor of Kentucky's child labor and minimum wage laws, Reed looked good to the liberals. However, the analysis runs, his liberalism was only comparative. When he got in a crowd of liberals he was just another guy.

Others see him as a man who is so wrapped up in the law as an institution that he seldom lashes out boldly in criticism of its dogma. This is an ironical analysis to hang on the man who guided New Deal laws through the roughest kind of going in the Supreme Court and really amounts to saying that Reed has relaxed and fallen behind times. It is true that he is wrapped up in the law and conscious of its every attribute. The old, old saying that "the law is a jealous mistress" applies well here. Until his Court routine, which is not easy by any means, he worked day and night without vacation. He is steeped in the law; some would say a slave to it.

Certainly, the pile of precedents cited on each side of a legal case gives Reed as much trouble as it does any man on the Court. He is an inner struggler, wanting above all else to be fair, honest and just in each decision. The quality of adroitness which makes it possible for a good lawyer to take either side of a case without making his argument of it the less forceful seems to seize Reed as it does few others on the Court.

This is not to say, however, that he wavers easily from influence or will do what others tell him. It would be cute to say that he's like a reed in the wind, but that is not accurate because it implies that he's swayed from external influences. On the contrary, he is swayed from within, oversensitive about doing the right thing each time.

One of his former colleagues explains that Reed cannot be labeled on the Court because he goes after each decision there just as he did as general counsel to the RFC. There, in the midst of an economic slump, Reed would fix up a small loan for a fishery on the Florida coast, a group of apple growers in Wenatchee, a shrimp business in New Orleans and a firm about to fail on its pay roll in New Hampshire. Each problem had to be solved then and there, had to be wrapped up in a bundle without much fuss over what the books had to say about it. According to this same observation, Reed has no vain sense that history is snapping up each line of his decision; nor does he display pride of authorship in his plain opinions.

His brethren on the bench and his former associates around town have a genuine affection for Stanley Reed. On the Court, he looks—with his large bald pate, massive jowls, pince-nez and stern composure—like a cold, unfriendly judge. However, his nature is one of the most pleasant, his informal manner humorous. His eyes sparkle and his voice is friendly. It is, therefore, with reluctance that the popular lawyer is criticized by his acquaintances. Thus, one of the associate justices meant no malice when he said of Reed that he is a very good lawyer and a fair judge but would never be missed from the Court. If the statement is true, and there are few off the bench either liberal or conservative who would debate the point vigorously, it is an interesting commentary on modern jurisprudence. In public opinion, Reed is probably damned by the paradox that people admire neutrality as an abstract virtue but remember longer and admire more the man who takes a stand—right or wrong—and keeps working at it. Ask a dozen lawyers who are familiar with Reed's record how to appraise him and one will get about the same reaction from each—a thoughtful pause, then a slowly drawn conclusion: "A good, middle-of-the-road lawyer."

CHAPTER VII

Open for Business

IN 1943 the country's broadcasting networks stood figuratively before the Supreme Court, resisting an order the Federal Communications Commission had issued for shaking them up. The case presented a model in governmental procedure for regulating an industry—hearings extending for six months had resulted in 8,000 pages of testimony, mostly from the networks themselves, and the FCC had worked out its conclusions carefully. But the conclusions called for drastic pruning, and the legal authority for such an operation had not been spelled out in the Federal Communications Act of 1934.

The FCC had found that public interest demanded a change in the contract relationships between local radio stations and the networks through which more than 97 per cent of the total nighttime wattage of the country passed. Exclusive clauses in network contracts were eliminated, stations were given freer right to reject unwanted programs and other steps were taken to loosen cozy arrangements. Only the Mutual network, a comparative newcomer, approved the surgery.

For a 5-to-2 Court, Frankfurter reviewed the sweep of radio legislation and found that Congress had authorized such regulations.[1] "The facilities of radio are not large enough to accommodate all who wish to use them," he wrote. "Methods must be devised for choosing from among the many who apply. And since Congress itself could not do this, it committed the task to the Commission." The justice went on to deny that the FCC had been "arbitrary and capricious" in drafting the orders.

Murphy (with Roberts) dissented, on mainly a civil liberties basis. He strained to uphold the administrative agency's interpretation of its power but found no basis in legislation for the regulations. However, the root of Murphy's objection was in this sentence: "In the dissemination of information and opinion, radio has assumed a position of commanding importance, rivaling the press and the pulpit." Thus, the dissenters wanted Congress to spell the authority out rather than let bureaucrats infer it.

The case was argued by big-name lawyers. John T. Cahill spoke for NBC; Charles E. Hughes, Jr., appeared for CBS; Louis G. Caldwell pleaded against them for Mutual; and Solicitor General Charles Fahy defended the government's position. Homer Cummings and Morris Ernst filed a brief for the American Civil Liberties Union which, interestingly, ran contrary to the dissent of Murphy. Nearly the entire radio industry was in the hands of the justices, arguing the FCC's interpretation of the words "public interest, convenience, or necessity."

Whether or not the justices liked it—or admitted it—the Court was tangled up in the public responsibility and the economics of a business. The new era of regulatory bodies would have plunged the justices into the whirl, anyway; but pushing isn't necessary to get these justices interested in the nation's economics. Before the incumbents came to the Court they helped create and run the agencies. They were part of the era of governmental consciousness of economics.

One of the points at which law is most mixed with economics is in the application of the antitrust laws, all of which were passed before the New Deal. It is natural, then, that the economics-conscious justices would be interested in the antitrust laws and that they would vote to uphold prosecutions of those exceeding corporate privilege and abusing economic power. But the new Court has done more than merely stamp OK on each charge of restraint of trade that came along. It has gone far beyond the pre-1937 concept of what business practices could be construed as being banned by the old legislation.

Under the onslaught of the Roosevelt administration, with an antitrust staff much larger than that ever dreamed of by such former attorney generals as McReynolds and Stone, the Court was asked to go well beyond the usual case of price-fixing or monopolizing. Particularly under the buzz-saw drive of trust-buster Thurman Arnold, the Court recognized modern business techniques for violating laws passed to snare clumsier trusts. It has often done so unanimously.

The chief legal barrier that Arnold helped the new Court hurdle with its muscular young legs was the "rule of reason," a doctrine found nowhere in the Sherman Antitrust law but applied by the Nine Old Men to throw out antitrust suits if the admitted restraints were "reasonable." This meant frequently that a group of companies could fix prices so long as they did not dominate the market.

The case that Arnold won, in 1940, to brush away much of that vague standard is one of the biggest and most complicated antitrust cases, but it illustrates well the mixture of economics and law—with a dash of politics thrown in. It all started in 1936 with an indictment in Madison, Wisconsin, against a number of major oil companies, headed by Socony-Vacuum.

Thirty-four lawyers, led by William J. Donovan, once a Republican trust buster and later head of the Office of Strategic Services, filed briefs for the companies; the Court used 102 pages in deciding the tangled case in favor of the government.[2]

The charge was that companies selling about half the gasoline in the midwestern area conspired to maintain prices artificially high by getting together in two big purchasing programs. The companies relied heavily on the fact that they had combined to end the ruinous price warfare and the flood of cheap gasoline which had culminated in legislation and an NRA code aimed at ending it. The NRA had allowed many industries to run their own production and prices with immunity from the Sherman Act, but the government contended that nothing like the practices complained of had been approved by the late NRA or its petroleum administrator, Harold Ickes. More than 1,000 exhibits were scattered through 3,900 pages of the trial court record.

It fell to Douglas, then hardly more than the Court's freshman, to dig into this mountain of evidence. First, he turned aside the argument that combinations rising from beneficial motives had anything to do wth the case, citing forty years of precedent that price-fixing agreements are unlawful on their faces under the Sherman Act. The Court "has not permitted the age-old cry of ruinous competition and competitive evils to be a defense to price-fixing conspiracies," Douglas wrote. "It has no more allowed genuine or fancied competitive abuses as a legal justification for such schemes than it has the good intentions of the members of the combination. If such a shift is to be made, it must be done by the Congress."

As to the defense that Uncle Sam had helped establish the programs through NRA codes, the Court said that only Congress could give immunity from the Sherman Act, even though employees of the government "may have known of these programs and winked at them or tacitly approved them."

That was in 1940. Five years later the Court had handed down many equally far-reaching decisions, the most recent of which upheld a broad prosecution of the big three of tobacco.[3] Though a new principle was established by its decision, the Court was without dissent—in fact, Republican Burton wrote the opinion. The three companies were indicted for conspiring to restrain and monopolize trade. The big question was whether it was necessary to show actual exclusion of competitors in order to prove an illegal monopoly. The Court decided it was not, citing with endorsement the opinion of the second circuit court of appeals in upholding the similar antitrust suit against the Aluminum

Company of America. (The circuit court had disposed of this case under a special act of Congress because the Supreme Court was unable to muster a quorum of justices who would participate in its decision.)

In the five years between the oil and tobacco opinions the Court grappled with a number of vital cases, seldom modifying the government's position in the briefs before it. Several of these demonstrated the Court's eagerness to bring business within the orbit of the antitrust laws.

One of these created a stir mostly because it declared that the ancient and honored profession of medicine might also be a plain, everyday "trade." But the merits of the government's suit against the well-organized profession also attracted attention.[4] The AMA and affiliates had ganged up on Group Health Association, a co-operative medical clinic and prepaid insurance system among federal employees in Washington, D.C. The profession, claiming such a scheme violated its code of ethics, denied membership to doctors who joined Group Health's staff, restrained hospitals from caring for patients of Group Health physicians and ordered other doctors not to consult with staff doctors. Suffice it to say that the Court, without dissent, swept aside legal technicalities and medical ethics, self-asserted, to prescribe a strong dose of restraint from further interference with Group Health.

An equal furor was raised a year later when the Court brought the insurance business within the Sherman Act, admittedly "for the first time in the history of the Court."[5] Even while the Court had insurance on its operating table, diagnosing it, a number of congressmen were working frantically to exempt insurance from the antitrust laws for sure. The Court's hoary concept of interstate commerce being confined to a stream of goods, a traffic, had kept insurance companies free from any federal control since 1869. Assuming themselves to be beyond the arm of federal law, the insurance companies snuggled up to state regulatory bodies so cozily, as proved by a Temporary National Economic Committee investigation, that they violently feared any federal control. Their protests that Congress had not intended to include them in the antitrust laws were shouted so loudly that the issue of their guilt or innocence was lost in the roar.

The din or arguments over the merits theoretically, at least, did not penetrate the marble walls of the Court building, but the Court left no doubt as to where it stood on the technical question involved. It held that insurance companies fall within "commerce" and that the Sherman Act was intended to prohibit fire insurance companies from restraining or monopolizing trade. "No commercial enterprise of any kind which conducts its activities across state lines has been held to be wholly beyond the regulatory power of Congress under the Commerce Clause," declared the Court. "We cannot make an exception of the business of insurance."

As the medical and insurance decisions made the Court unpopular with doctors and insurance men throughout the country, the *Associated Press* case[6] alienated most of the country's newspaper publishers. The Department of Justice had hauled the AP into court because of its bylaws, under which it was next to impossible for a newspaper to join the AP—technically a co-operative enterprise for gathering news—if its competitor already belonged. This neat little system had been accomplished by giving each member of AP the "right of protest" to a competitor's application, an obstacle which could be overcome only by a four-fifths vote of the AP membership. In 1942, with the Department of Justice breathing hot on its neck, the AP modified its bylaws so as to admit a competitor after he had paid 10 per cent of the established, competing member's assessments since 1900 and received a majority vote of the membership.

Spice was added to the dispute by the fact that the best-known applicant who had been blackballed by the AP was the Chicago *Sun* a pro-administration paper locked in mortal combat with the Chicago *Tribune*, the administration-hating paper of Colonel Robert McCormick, a pillar of the AP's board of directors. What didn't get so well reported was the fact that another blackballed applicant was the Washington *Times-Herald*, paper of the Colonel's like-thinking cousin, Eleanor Patterson.

The Court admitted that some competing newspapers had gotten along without AP service, but pointed out that morning papers controlling 96 per cent of the nation's total circulation have AP news. Moreover, to meet the rigid requirements of the bylaws it would have cost $1,432,142.73 to enter the AP morning field in New York or $416,631.90 in Chicago. By pooling their economic and news control power, the Court found, the AP agreements were "plainly designed in the interest of preventing competition."

Arguments that AP deserved special treatment to conform to its idea of freedom of the press were brushed aside with the statement that "freedom to publish is guaranteed . . . but freedom to combine to keep others from publishing is not." Besides, the Court reasoned that members of the AP "are engaged in business for profit exactly as are other business men who sell food, steel, aluminum or anything else people need or want."

The dissents and concurrences were many and long. Roberts and Stone drew a distinction between denying *news* to competitors and denying *AP* news to them and pointed out that there is no dearth of competition in news gathering. They also felt that the majority in effect rendered AP a public utility, "subject to the duty to serve all on equal terms." This, they protested, "is Government by injunction with a vengeance." They then warned that the decision threatens to be but a first step in the "shackling of the press."

Frankfurter, in a concurrence, dealt mainly with an opposite view of the AP's status. The case, he wrote, "calls into play considerations very different from comparable restraints in a cooperative enterprise having merely a commercial aspect. . . . Truth and understanding are not wares like peanuts or potatoes." Douglas, also concurring separately, called this a "public utility theory," and declared that it had no place in the argument because the AP was not charged with being a monopoly.

Murphy would have gone along with the majority had there been a clear finding of restraint, he wrote, but he found "a complete lack of any relevant proof justifying the conclusion that the Associated Press membership policy has prevented or hindered the birth of a competing newspaper . . . or caused one to be discontinued."

One of the main ways by which the new Court has dug deep into business practices is by pruning away control over patents and copyrights. Arnold and his successors, Tom Clark and Wendell Berge, hit the justices over their dignified heads with case after case of abuse of patents. The Court rewarded their diligence with a procession of opinions outlawing a variety of patent uses by which the spirit, at least, of the Sherman Act had been gotten around for years.

In the *Ethyl* case a major policy was laid down.[7] The Ethyl Corporation, which makes the nation's supply of the special fluid for increasing efficiency of gasoline engines, allowed sale of it to jobbers and retailers under very rigid requirements. Of the 12,000 jobbers in the United States, 11,000 were licensed by the corporation, ostensibly to maintain standards of the product and premium prices above ordinary gasoline. All dealers were subjected to a company investigation before getting a license. It was largely in this investigation that the government—and the Court—found a violation of the antitrust laws. For the corporation refused licenses to firms not conforming to "business ethics," the term admittedly denoting compliance with "marketing policies and prevailing prices of the petroleum industry" and prices posted by its leaders. The latter included the Standard Oil Company of New Jersey, which happens to own one half of the Ethyl Corporation. Therefore, the Court found, Ethyl had used its patents "as a means of controlling jobbers' prices and suppressing competition among them," going well beyond its patent monopoly.

In the *Univis Lens* case,[8] a little later, the Court ruled unanimously that the owner of a patent on the manufacture of spectacle lenses could not use his patent monopoly to force price-fixing on the product all down the line to the consumer.

Then came the whopping big *Hartford-Empire* case[9] against the glass container industry for restraining trade by controlling about 840 patents among seven companies. "It is clear," the Court ruled, "that, by cooperative arrangements and binding agreements, the appellant corporations, over a period of years, regulated and suppressed competition in the use of glass making machinery and employed their joint patent position to allocate fields of manufacture and to maintain prices of unpatented glassware."

The use of copyrights to effect restraints of trade was similarly kicked in the teeth, in 1939, when the Court upheld the prosecution of motion picture film distributors for agreeing among themselves to require exhibitors to charge a higher admission price than they had been charging and to keep their films out of double features.[10]

Another way in which the Court helped the government get a new impact into the antitrust laws was by sweeping aside the argument of numerous defendants that other legislation made their activities legal. In the *Borden* case[11] the Court held that neither the Capper-Volstead Act, allowing farmers to distribute their commodities co-operatively, nor the Agricultural Marketing Agreement Act, giving the secretary of agriculture power to regulate farm marketing, repealed the antitrust laws. Later the Court decided that the Webb-Pomerene Act, allowing combinations for the purpose of exporting commodities, was no excuse for certain restraints of trade practiced by an export association.[12]

A thornier problem has been what some thought was a conflict betwen the antitrust laws and the Miller-Tydings Act, under which makers of a trade-marked article can control the resale of the article in states which provide for it. The act was passed largely to prevent cut-rate stores from slashing prices on big-name brands; it was a deliberate modification of the antitrust laws. However, the government started cracking down on companies using the act for additional restraints.

The Court went along. Without dissent, it upheld a conviction breaking up the system by which the sole distributor of Soft-Lite (pink-tinted) lenses controlled wholesale and retail prices and boycotted dealers who wouldn't go along with its scheme.[13] In another case, involving liquor in Colorado, the Miller-Tydings Act was found no defense to an agreement for setting prices up and down the line and refusing to deal with noncomformists.[14]

Similar resale price control, but not involving the Miller-Tydings Act, was rejected by the Court in the *Masonite* case,[15] in which the manufacturer of hardboard, a construction material, signed individual "agency" agreements with others in the industry who then embraced a standard price. The system was struck down, even though the firms insisted that they had not acted together, that they had signed their agreements with the Masonite Corporation only. The Court found that each participant knew the purpose of the deal and that trade was restrained thereby. Thus the Court helped unmask a complex price-rigging system.

In the *Crescent Amusement* case the Court got tough with motion picture operators and distributors who "crushed competition" by threats of retaliation in areas where those holding the whip hand had monopolies over showing of films.[16] The Court went so far as to order the exhibitors to divest themselves of stock in other firms engaged in the same business, on the ground that "the proclivity in the past to use that affiliation for an unlawful end warrants effective assurance that no such opportunity will be available in the future." It was harsh but realistic treatment.

In another film case, this time a private suit, the Court upheld damages of $360,000 to a community theater for being frozen out of first-run pictures until downtown Chicago theaters were through with them.[17]

Among the miscellaneous practices found to be violations of the antitrust laws was a combination to stop "style piracy."[18] The Fashion Originators' Guild, a regimented trade association of garment makers and fabric designers, set up a blacklist for boycotting dealers who handled goods of style pirates, those who copied designs and sold them at a lower price as soon as they hit the market. The guild argued that neither patents nor copyrights were available to them under law, that something had to be done for protection; but the Federal Trade Commission found the system to be clearly illegal and was backed by the Court.

Another miscellaneous though far-reaching practice cut down by the Court is that of using a single "basing point," by which the delivered price of a product is calculated on a fictional, rather than actual, place of shipment.[19] For example, the sales price of all caraway seed might be computed by adding freight costs from Pittsburgh to the point of delivery, even though the seed were shipped from Kalamazoo or Seattle. An accompanying practice in the same case was the "booking" practice, whereby favored customers were allowed to buy at the lower price after a general price increase had become effective. It, too, was knocked in the head.

Late in the 1944 term, the Court shocked railroad lawyers by allowing the state of Georgia to bring an original suit in the Supreme Court against northern railroads which the state alleged to have conspired to discriminate against the South in setting freight rates.[20] The discrimination charges were old; what was new was the Court's acceptance of jurisdiction over the case rather than sending Georgia to the Interstate Commerce Commission for relief. It was a close decision (five to four, by Douglas) but demonstrated the new Court's eagerness to tackle economics.

One of the oldest economic stumbling blocks of the law which New Dealers set out to overthrow was illustrated in *Smyth* v. *Ames,* decided in 1876. Volumes have been written about this old landmark and the cases decided under it, but a layman's version of the issues can be boiled down to a couple of paragraphs.

In the early days of railroad and utility regulation, after the legal power to do *any* regulating was pretty well settled, the lawyers found themselves confronted with a new and highly technical problem: What standard was a rate-making commission to use in order to comply with two provisions of the Constitution; namely, that no property shall be taken without "just compensation" and that no property shall be taken without "due process of law"?

In *Smyth* v. *Ames* a lawyer by the name of William Jennings Bryan pleaded successfully that the proper procedure is to base a utility rate of return on a valuation of the property as it would cost at the time of the decision. That is to say, the utility's property should be assessed at its very latest value—as if it were being constructed at the time of the rate-making. This, of course, gets into pure theory, for no one could actually rebuild the property to check the cost figures; but it kept the concept current. Bryan's opponent argued that the commission should use the original cost of the plant as the basis for valuation. A practical reason for the fight was that property values had gone down after the plant was built, meaning considerable difference in the dollar-and-cent return which the company would be allowed—and consumers would pay.

However, the *Smyth* v. *Ames* rule fell into disrepute because of two factors. First, property values started rising sharply thereafter, putting the shoe on the other foot, as between regulators and those being regulated. Second, it became more obvious that "reproduction costs" were too theoretical to guide the mushrooming commissions. In 1923, Brandeis and Holmes started hacking away at the doctrine, and the former started preaching in its stead the original cost idea.[21] As Brandeis pointed out, immediate reproduction of a plant would be impossible without Aladdin's lamp.

Legal writers took to the chase, and soon the original cost concept became known as the "prudent investment" theory, meaning really that a company should be allowed to make a fair return on its investment, excluding bookkeeping items which commissions found had no legitimate place in the financial structure. ("Fair return" has come to be an average of 6 to 6½ per cent.)

The Court, as a majority, floundered around in this quagmire of accountancy, law and legislation with the net effect of leaving commissions with no idea of what they *could* do, though they were often told what they could *not* do. In 1939, after Roosevelt had appointed three new justices, a case came along for the New Dealers to try their skill on.[22] One appointee, Reed, wrote a majority opinion which pretty well continued the floundering process; but the other two, Frankfurter and Black, stepped out boldly with separate concurrences.

Their complaint was that "the Court's opinion appears to give new vitality needlessly to the mischievous formula for fixing utility rates in Smyth v. Ames." They pointed out that Congress has tried to get away from it and that various states, too, have "sought to escape the fog into which speculations based on Smyth v. Ames have enveloped the practical task of administering systems of utility regulation."

In 1942, with seven Roosevelt appointees on the bench, the issue arose again when Stone, for a unanimous Court, upheld a natural gas rate fixed by the Federal Power Commission.[23] The long opinion reached a result that might have been reached by straight application of the "prudent investment" theory, but its reasoning was not doctrinaire. In fact, the conclusion was that a commission is bound to no single formula.

Black, Douglas and Murphy liked the result but protested two main points. First, they objected to Stone's use of the 5th amendment's due process clause for asserting the Court's power of review of the commission's rate order. Second, the three young men issued a call to battle on an old point: ". . . we think this is an appropriate occasion to lay the ghost of Smyth v. Ames, which has haunted utility regulation since 1898." Quoting heavily from dissents of Brandeis, they added that "the havoc raised by insistence of reproduction costs is now a matter of historical record." Their concurrence wound up with a demand for wider discretion in the regulating commissions.

But Brother Frankfurter could go only halfway with these radicals who would restore the Court to its first hundred years of decisions on the Court's function in rate-making. According to him, the doctrine of "confiscation," as a limitation to be enforced by the courts upon the legislatures, was authored by Chief Justice Waite and concurred in through the years by such advocates of utility regulation as Justices Miller, Bradley and Harlan. Next, the former professor took his colleagues to task for first holding that the commission should be unhampered (by the due process clause), then telling the commission what rules to use.

Two years later it fell to Douglas to write an opinion for a 5-to-3 majority in a similar case that was to climax the new version of evaluation for rate-making purposes.[24] The Hope Natural Gas Company argued for a base calculated on the cost of reproduction new; the Federal Power Commission rejected the theory as unworkable and based its computation on "actual legitimate costs."

Douglas first affirmed the rule of the preceding case, that no single formula need be used, then observed that the commission was justified in rejecting the reproduction theory on the grounds that use of it from 1937 through 1940 would have netted the company 3.27 per cent, whereas it actually averaged about 9 per cent. The conclusion that the company's rate base was inflated seemed inescapable. The commission was upheld.

Thus, with three cases the new Court cleared away most of the fog in which regulatory commissions had been operating for years. Whether right or wrong, they gave commissions some affirmative guideposts instead of constantly telling them each new attempt must be discarded. And, of more importance in the long run, a majority of the new Court agreed to let the commissions do the expert calculating instead of substituting the Court's opinion for that of the administrators. It was one of the dullest, least-publicized and most important of Roosevelt's victories over the old Court.

On April Fool's Day of 1946 the Court handed down another decision in the public utility field which got little attention. The Court upheld the constitutionality of one of the New Deal's most drastic laws—the Public Utility Holding Company Act, commonly known as the "death sentence." At 12:16 P.M., when Murphy quietly intoned the death warrant, specifically against sprawling subsidiaries of the North American Company, an era of Supreme Court history ended, for the act was the last of the major New Deal legislation to be tested judicially.[25]

Under the "death sentence," Congress empowered the Securities and Exchange Commission to lop off those tentacles of utility corporations which it feels do not fit into a well-integrated corporate structure, geographically and economically. The North American system did business in seventeen states and the District of Columbia, providing electric service alone to more than 3,000,000 customers. The SEC pruners ordered the corporation to divest itself of property worth about $190,000,000. The company, which the Court called "the pinnacle of a great pyramid of corporations," protested that the act conflicted with constitutional provisions as to commerce and due process of law.

There were no curves in Murphy's opinion. Neither objection had merit and there were plenty of precedents by this time to prove it. But the significant thing about the decision was that there was no dissent—not even from Republican and ex-utility lawyer Burton. Death came quietly to the era of fighting against New Deal legislation in the courts.

CHAPTER VIII

Associate Professor of Justice

"I'M SCARED," Felix Frankfurter is said to have told a friend who came to see him while the professor packed to leave his comfortable Cambridge home to move to Washington and the Supreme Court. Theoretically, no man should have been less afraid of the prospects, for a Court appointment meant in several senses a comedown rather than a promotion. A long period of freedom for writing, speaking and politicking about the Court and the Constitution from the vantage point of a leading university had been ideal in many ways. The life of a justice, with its relative gags and austerity, left much to be desired by comparison.

An uglier view of the change in Frankfurter's life would explain it on the basis that no sideline critic does so well when put in the position of power which was the object of his criticism. As an abstract principle, this view applies to Frankfurter as well as the next man. It is lent credence—still according to the uglier view—by a conundrum aimed at Frankfurter by a key New Dealer after Frankfurter had been on the Court a couple of terms.

"What is the difference between Justice Frankfurter and Justice Sutherland?" the quip goes. "Sutherland's whiskers were on the outside," goes the cutting answer.

Historians of another century may have less trouble appraising the contribution of Felix Frankfurter to the Supreme Court and to constitutional life, but contemporaries are plagued by question marks and character complexities. The problem is not, however, that the justice with the funny name has been a sphynx or a recluse. On the contrary, no justice has reduced his thoughts to writing so often or has a wider circle of acquaintances.

What one can say about Frankfurter without fear of contradiction is very limited. He is short of stature (a little over five feet), usually is seen wearing pince-nez, is a booklover, has a high-pitched voice, is troubled by a sacroiliac condition, has a razor-sharp mind, enjoys the company of people and came to the Court as one of the very most learned authorities on the subject. Add to these facts the usual biographical items from *Who's Who* and from then on controversy attends the pursuit of the Frankfurter nature and works. Beyond these cut-and-dried notes one is strictly on his own.

The extreme view of Frankfurter on the poisonous side was published in *Harper's* (October, 1941) by Fred Rodell, needling, subjective professor of law at Yale, never an institution to show love for a son of Harvard. Under the title of "Felix Frankfurter, Conservative," Rodell goggle-eyed readers who still thought of the new justice as a radical or liberal pillar of the New Deal. The author chortled over the fact that a poll of lawyers, a barometer of conservative attitude, put Frankfurter first on the list of candidates for the Court vacancy which he later got. Rodell painted Frankfurter as a man whose reputation as defender of civil liberties was highly synthetic and who enjoyed flitting around the bright lights of government rather than furnishing any real candlepower for them. Many Frankfurter friends subscribed softly to the title of Rodell's piece but thought it got off the track and was a smear.

The sweetness and light extreme was furnished in *Life*, February 12, 1940, by Frankfurter's very close friend, Archibald MacLeish, poet, editor, librarian of Congress and Roosevelt handy man. The genteel MacLeish brush-painted a drawing-room picture of a great man of legal letters exuding the philosophy of a good life—great companionship, fine books, good food, interest in uplifting souls, and full-time teaching of youth to follow the high road of public service. Beautiful prose made the subject equally beautiful (with technicolor pictures, too) but left by conspicuous omissions a hole big enough to put the Court building in.

A well-balanced, objective story of Frankfurter up to his appointment to the Court was done in three parts by Matthew Josephson in the *New Yorker*. Here, in 1939, was a competent biographer taking plenty of time to poke into the crosscurrents of a full life, disinterested in what he found; yet more than forty errors are said to have found their way into the profile.

To gather a truly fair account of Felix Frankfurter is a humbling undertaking, if nothing else. Perhaps the most maddening thing encountered in talking to the usual sources of information about Frankfurter—students, lawyers, associates around the Court, social acquaintances and others—is the opening sentence of most: "Felix is really quite simple to analyze." At the end of the "simple" explanation one has been led through a dizzy course; however, the early part of most analyses adds up to understandability. Paraphrased as a summary it runs like this:

After years and years of fighting for changes in the interpretation of the Constitution, Frankfurter came to the Court after the basic changes had been made. Moreover, he hadn't been there long before a liberal bloc consisting of Black, Douglas and Murphy appeared at one side of the Court—and without benefit of a blessing from the great expert on constitutional law, Felix Frankfurter. This bloc, with votes occasionally from others, began to jell into a group which would seldom let red tape stand in its way of arriving at an end it felt to be desirable. In trying to stave off departure from procedural barriers, which Felix thinks make freedom rather than destroy freedom, he was driven into fancy dialectics and picayunish distinctions. He withdrew into a strict construction of his favorite document and laws passed by legislatures. Hence his many separate concurrences and dissents.

Now add to this difference in principle the matter of personalities. In the first place, Felix is not a man to play second fiddle to anybody. He has always lived by his brains and he has always had a high regard for his brains. Also, he has the Rooseveltian feel that history is looking over his shoulder. In the second place, most other members of the Court didn't take kindly to Felix's lectures to them or to his heckling of counsel. They had traveled roads far different from Felix's and refused to tumble for his high dialectics. Add it all up and you have a split which will get wider before it narrows.

That's the consensus, the area in which there is rough agreement. Before exploring the other areas, it would be best to spread out the map of Frankfurter's life. It begins in Vienna, Austria, where he was born in 1882 to parents not wealthy but well enough fixed to keep young Felix from the Horatio Alger category. Before he was in his teens, Frankfurter's family had moved to New York City, where Felix was schooled. Eight years after an immigrant's landing, Frankfurter had been graduated with high grades from the College of the City of New York and was well on his way to the mastery of his new language for which he is now known. Thereafter, he worked a year for the city, for $1,200, and hied off to Harvard for law school. His high scholastic standing there landed him in a big Wall Street law firm in 1906, but he stayed just two months. Thereafter, he never engaged in private practice; he turned to public service.

The offer that lured Frankfurter to public service was in the United States attorney's office for Manhattan, then in charge of Henry L. Stimson. The well-known Republican had been appointed by Teddy

Roosevelt to bust trusts, a job which Frankfurter ably helped him with for five years, much of which was spent in courtrooms. Then, when Stimson was appointed President Taft's secretary of war, Frankfurter went to Washington as law officer for Stimson's Bureau of Insular Affairs.

It was during these few years in the nation's capital that Frankfurter's propensity for gathering influential, intellectual and interesting friends about him fully blossomed. In his comfortable bachelor quarters, which he shared with three others, Frankfurter gathered socially a nucleus of young, sharp-minded government men such as was not seen again until the New Deal enticed diploma holders ahead of stump speakers. Justice Holmes, one of Frankfurter's patron saints, spoke of the residence humorously, but not derisively, as the "House of Truth."

In 1914, Frankfurter returned to Harvard to teach law, but the war pulled him back to Washington and into several administrative jobs dealing with labor. By 1918 he was chairman of President Wilson's War Labor Policies Board, on which the Navy was represented by its assistant secretary, Franklin D. Roosevelt, a New Yorker Frankfurter had met before. The friendship grew into what their mutual friends call a truly great one and what their mutual enemies saw as a sinister relationship to thwart the will of the electorate. A favorite epithet reduced Frankfurter to being Roosevelt's Rasputin.

In 1919, Frankfurter returned to his love, teaching law at Harvard. For twenty years he built his distinctive name into a place of prominence by straight study and research and by subjective explorations of constitutional law and public affairs. In the former category, he had already edited *Cases under the Interstate Commerce Act* and was to collaborate on texts in labor injunctions, federal jurisdiction and administrative law.

Frankfurter was no old-line teacher. His lectures were by no means cut and dried; rather, he took his classes along the byways of legal evolution, into the reasoning behind legal points and into the philosophy of the law. In fact, many of his Socratic lectures rambled so thoroughly that he was accused of teaching more about Felix Frankfurter than about the curriculum. Be that as it may, Frankfurter succeeded in stimulating students in a subject best known for reverence of the past.

Much of his own stimulation came from the lives of Holmes and Brandeis, two unorthodox operators in the law whose personal likings differed but whose outlook on the Constitution was to allow it flexibility for social change enacted by legislatures. No student of Frankfurter's left Harvard without paying attention to the dissents of both heroes.

Other Frankfurter needles may have been fashioned around Harvard Yard, but they were used extracurricularly. The most famous of these activities was his defense of Sacco and Vanzetti, the two Italian anarchists who were found guilty in 1921 of murder. Only a handful of known names joined the militant radicals who cried "Foul," at the trial of these insignificant men, but Frankfurter was one of them. In stepping into the fight he was risking his standing at Harvard, for the president of that dignified institution was notably on the other side of the fence, with most of the "right" people. Sacco and Vanzetti were executed, though popular opinion has since vindicated them; and Frankfurter's unusual name was circulated widely, if not favorably at the moment, around the country. Even before this celebrated cause, Frankfurter had defended the imprisoned Tom Mooney, but that he had done in the form of a technical report for President Wilson.

Moreover, Frankfurter helped found the American Civil Liberties Union, an organization to defend the legal rights of persons who find themselves at the short end of the popular stick. And he was a founder of the *New Republic,* weekly journal of liberal opinion. Black-bound volumes from the first issue to the present fill one tall set of shelves in his outer office today, for they contain many unsigned editorials on the Court which he wrote for years. His authorship of many of them was revealed in *Law and Politics,* a volume of his writings edited by MacLeish and Edward F. Prichard, Jr., formerly his clerk.

One impact of Frankfurter's pedagogy and social reward at his home for the brighter students was to send hundreds of embryo lawyers into the world with psychological strings attached. He kept in touch with many of them, steered many of them into jobs and almost ran a one-man fraternity. The fact that many of his placements were with the New Deal was largely because he tried to shove students toward public careers and the New Deal was then expanding public service so vastly. The corny but adhesive term "happy hot dogs" was applied with glee to these fledglings, whether they arrived after Roosevelt or before, as was the case with Tommy Corcoran, the most famous. While the professor stayed at Harvard, pepping up his friends with hundreds of laconic notes and occasional visits, this big team worked smoothly, sparked the New Deal greatly. But as one of the happy hot dogs now puts it, shortly after Frankfurter moved to Washington the team fell apart. Mutual friends began wondering, as they disagreed with more and more Frankfurter decisions, whose idea it was to bring him down. Questions grew into blame and quarrels; the New Deal spirit weakened and gave up. Some say flatly that Frankfurter's arrival killed the New Deal he had blessed with such great energy.

At various times in the 1930's, Frankfurter was called many names. He was seen as a Svengali, the administration's Iago (by the Hearst press), a Jimminy Cricket to Pinocchio Roosevelt and the "most single influential individual in the United States" (by Hugh Johnson).

But his legal acumen in a dynamic society was as famous among the majority as it was snorted at by a minority. A man from Mars wouldn't have needed five minutes on earth to conclude that Felix Frankfurter just had to be appointed to the Supreme Court. Teddy Roosevelt had been unable to tempt him away from the academy with a federal judgeship offer. In June of 1932 he declined appointment to the Massachusetts Supreme Court, replying that he preferred to continue teaching. (To the delight of those who think of Frankfurter as utterly vain, he blandly includes the refusal in his biographical summaries.) In 1933, Roosevelt quite naturally asked Frankfurter to be his solicitor general but was turned down. "Felix is a stubborn pig," Roosevelt is said to have remarked.

Nearly everyone has taken for granted that Frankfurter yearned feverishly to be on the Supreme Court. However, in view of some new evidence it appears that an injustice may have been done the man by this speculation. The new and illuminating fact is that when Frankfurter rejected the solicitor generalship, in 1933, Roosevelt told his friend that he wanted him to be on the Court eventually. The President explained that he could elevate Frankfurter to the Court from the solicitor general's post but said that he could not do so from Harvard Law School. In the face of this alternative, Frankfurter repeated his negative answer, thus having reason to believe that he had turned his back on the Supreme Court forever.

Only after six years did fate, in the form of old age on the Court, make it possible for Roosevelt to change his mind and appoint his friend to the nation's highest court—from Harvard Law School.

The hearings held by a Senate judiciary subcommittee on Frankfurter's nomination were out of this world.[1] A collection of professional and largely self-appointed patriots exercised their privileges of opposing Professor Frankfurter, mainly on the grounds of his foreign birth, alleged love for Communism, supposed authorship of the NRA, long affiliation with the American Civil Liberties Union and ubiquitous "un-Americanism." Such strange groups as the Constitutional Crusaders of America, the League for Constitutional Government and the American Federation against Communism crawled out of the wood for the occasion.

The most dramatic moment of the four-day sessions came when Senator William Borah, who spent many years in penitence for having fought confirmation of Brandeis, jumped up, shook his mane and his finger and shouted at a witness: "I do not propose to listen to an argument against a man because of his religion."

The drollest moment, as Frankfurter labeled it, occurred when the professor pointed out that the ACLU once defended the right of one witness, Elizabeth Dilling, to speak on the air. Other droll moments came when senators sought elementary facts about the organizations some witnesses claimed to represent. Even free love was dragged across the path of the professor.

For his own part, Frankfurter appeared reluctantly, read the solons a paragraph from history observing that only one other nominee for the high bench had appeared before the Judiciary Committee, then begged off. However, he spent an hour or two in a rehash of old facts and a listless discussion with Senator McCarran of the books of his British friend, Harold J. Laski. The good senator was slightly handicapped by not having read the books he was worried about, but Frankfurter chose unnecessary snippiness to cut him down. However, if he hadn't made friends he had apparently influenced people, for he was easily confirmed.

But because Frankfurter has remained a mystery to so many and because he really is complex, it is necessary to examine his legal opinions at greater length than is required for those of his colleagues.

A large pile of cases was disposed of on January 30, 1939, the day Felix Frankfurter took his specially padded chair behind the big mahogany bench which nearly hid him from the public. Seated below the new justice were Harold Ickes, Ben Cohen and Tommy Corcoran. Two of the cases were highly significant. The Court decided a copyright case in favor of Drew Pearson and Robert S. Allen, spicy authors of *The Nine Old Men,* the book which had lampooned the old Court mercilessly. Then Roberts read an opinion brushing aside the plea of nineteen public utilities that sale of electric power by the Tennessee Valley Authority would be unconstitutional. Frankfurter faced Roberts, as the latter in his loud, clear voice, disposed of one of the last of the issues which had started all the hubbub.

Frankfurter's first term was probably as fruitful as any first term in history. It should have been, for the professor required no boning up to begin his duties there. Frankfurter stepped in boldly, both as majority spokesman and as concurrer.

The most noteworthy contribution of the 1938 term came in the Court's abandonment of the double doctrine that states may not levy taxes on the incomes of federal employees[2] and that not even the federal government may impose income taxes on federal judges.[3] The latter doctrine was based on the constitutional mandate that judicial pay not be reduced while judges hold office. Frankfurter did not write the opinion wiping out federal immunity from state taxation of official salaries, but he added a significant concurrence. It first expressed his sentiment that justices should each write opinions "when an important shift in constitutional doctrine is announced after a reconstruction in the membership of the Court," then pointed out that the 120-year immunity had no basis in the Constitution. Also, he went far in laying to rest what he called the "seductive cliché" that "the power to tax involves the power to destroy." That utterance, he said, was an "unfortunate remark," made "partly as a flourish of rhetoric."

One of the most striking features of his first term was the frequency with which he voted with Black, an association not long in breaking up. Another feature was that not one old Frankfurter fan raised an eyebrow at his opinions up to this point.

Early in the next term, 1939, Frankfurter wrote civil rights opinions for the Court which were as liberal as his last opinion of the term, in the flag salute case, was later regarded as conservative. For example, after a defendant in a narcotics trial had refused to take the witness stand, the judge had told the jury that "it is the privilege of a defendant to testify as a witness if, and only when, he so elects. . . ." The judge refused to add a paragraph to the effect that "failure of any defendant to take the witness stand and testify in his own behalf, does not create any presumption against him. . . ." The Supreme Court, in an opinion by Frankfurter, reversed the conviction on the ground that the trial judge should have given both charges to the jury.[4]

Because the second case has been used by so many for beating Frankfurter over the head, it deserves extra attention. In weighing the right of parents to teach their children not to salute the American flag and the right of a State to force such a ceremony "in the promotion of national cohesion," Frankfurter first laid out the reasons for protecting religious freedom.[5]

"Certainly the affirmative pursuit of one's convictions about the ultimate mystery of the universe and man's relation to it is placed beyond the reach of law," he wrote. But then he brought it within the law. "National unity is the basis of national security" and "we live by symbols," he stated for the Court. "What the school authorities are really asserting," he added, "is the right to awaken in the child's mind considerations as to the significance of the flag contrary to those implanted by the parent. . . . The preciousness of the family relation, the authority and independence which give dignity to parenthood, indeed the enjoyment of all freedom, presuppose the kind of ordered society which is summarized by our flag."

In other cases that term Frankfurter spoke for the Court in upholding Puerto Rico's law placing an upper limit of 500 acres on land ownership[6] and upholding a Virginia law against sales of insurance not handled by resident sales agents.[7]

In the next term Frankfurter wrote a 6-to-2 opinion for the Court putting outside of the antitrust laws a time-worn jurisdictional dispute between two AF of L unions over which would install machinery in a brewery. Congress specifically excepted such labor activities by passing the Clayton Act, he wrote.[8] Known as the *Hutcheson* case, it soon became bitterly debated in Washington and elsewhere. Thurman Arnold, for instance, was furious with having the door slammed in his face against other union prosecutions. Organized labor, however, hailed it as a great victory against union smashing.

Frankfurter was still holding fast, in general, to a devotion to civil liberties. When the majority held that Congress had power to authorize federal courts to require physical examination of persons suing for personal injury, Frankfurter wrote a scintillating dissent.[9] To him, "a drastic change in public policy in a matter deeply touching the sensibilities of people or even their prejudices as to privacy, ought not to be inferred from a general authorization to formulate rules for the more uniform and effective dispatch of business on the civil side of the federal courts."

Halfway through this 1940 term—four years, to the week, after Roosevelt had announced the plan which his enemies said would pack the Court—a split opened. For the Court, Frankfurter upheld an injunction against a Chicago union of milk wagon drivers.[10] It was a double-barreled injunction—against both peaceful picketing and a considerable amount of violence directed at employees of an unorthodox dairy. The rule of the case was clear; namely, that *peaceful* picketing could be enjoined if "blended with violence." Black, Douglas and Reed dissented sharply. Things were never again as cozy on the Court.

The very next Monday these three dissented from Frankfurter's opinion in a case reversing the Federal Trade Commission.[11] The FTC had ordered an Illinois candy manufacturer to stop a sales practice which it felt created unfair competition in the Illinois market for manufacturers who shipped in interstate commerce and who had already been barred from the practice by the FTC. However, FTC nominally has no authority over firms operating within one state. That was about enough for Frankfurter—the point would not be strained. The dissenters felt that the practice complained of was "in commerce" and therefore within jurisdiction of the commission. A few weeks later, Black, Douglas and Murphy dissented from Frankfurter's opinion in a complex case arising from a National Relations Board order.[12] The pattern was to become familiar.

In the term beginning in 1941, Frankfurter voted with the conservatives in four out of six important civil rights cases. When, on the day after Pearl Harbor, a majority of five justices freed Harry Bridges and the Los Angeles *Times* from contempt of court charges for commenting on pending cases in California, Frankfurter wrote the four-man dissent.[13] "Our whole history," he began his dissent, "repels the view that it is an exercise of one of the civil liberties secured by the Bill of Rights for a leader of a large following or for a powerful metropolitan newspaper to attempt to overawe a judge in a matter immediately pending before him." Then he charged the majority opinion with containing "careful ambiguities and silences." The majority had found no "clear and present danger" to the administration of justice, but Frankfurter would tolerate no interference with the judicial process. In fact, he accused the majority (Black wrote the opinion) of turning its back on history and indulging "in an idle play on words unworthy of constitutional adjudication." The state of California, under our federal system, had a right to forbid publications having "a reasonable tendency to interfere with the orderly administration of justice in pending actions," he insisted.

Then when the Court set aside the conviction of a man who had been forced to share counsel with a co-defendant whose interests were different from his, Frankfurter dissented.[14] The whole appeal was to Frankfurter "obviously a lawyer's after thought," for the defendant in the case was a former assistant United States attorney. The record, he felt, showed that the defendant went along with the arrangement and got a fair trial.

In two other cases of this kind Frankfurter wrote the Court's opinion, while the Black-Douglas-Murphy team dissented. One was a complex appeal of a death sentence which involved close examination to see whether a long trial had been fair and without coercion of witnesses. The Court thought everything was in order.[15] In the second, Frankfurter wrote that a state has power to ban picketing of the place of business of a man who has contracted with an employer of union labor for the construction elsewhere of a building not connected with that business. The argument that such a ban violated free speech in the form of picketing, advanced by an array of labor and civil liberty lawyers, was weighed but found wanting.[16] The dissenters noted, however, that the carrying of banners on the sidewalk was peaceful and declared that the union had a right to carry its case to the public by means of picketing.

But after voting with the conservatives on these four issues, Frankfurter upset the dope bucket by voting with Stone and Murphy against wire tapping, while Black and Douglas shifted to the conservative side. Two cases were involved; in both, the law banning use of intercepted telephone messages was at issue. In one, it was complained that the verdict of guilty had been obtained by confronting co-conspirators with evidence from tapped wires, causing them to turn state's evidence.[17] The Court turned aside the objection, but Frankfurter joined in Murphy's vigorous protest. In the other, the Court upheld use of a "detectaphone," a new sleuthing gadget that enables one to overhear a telephone conversation in the next room.[18] Frankfurter would have had the Court overthrow its famous *Olmstead* decision, which held that wire-tapped messages may be used against persons not a party to them.

Another case that found Frankfurter on the unexpected side of the decision concerned the long-fought suit against the Bethlehem Shipbuilding Corporation for allegedly unconscionable profits (22 per cent) from World War I contracts.[19] A majority of the Court, led by Black, felt that only Congress could handle the question by legislation; but Frankfurter felt that the judiciary should step into the dispute—and settle it in favor of the government.

In the field of interstate commerce, Frankfurter dissented from a 5-to-4 opinion holding that federal legislation on renovated butter excluded a state from acting against a violator of a state law on the same subject.[20] Frankfurter loosed a blast at his colleagues for misreading the congressional intent in the issue: "If ever there was an intrusion by this Court into a field that belongs to Congress and which it has seen fit not to enter, this is it." He was referring to the fact that the drafters of federal butter legislation had never sought to curb state action in addition to their own.

The term beginning in 1942 found the Court badly split on civil liberties cases, particularly those involving Jehovah's Witnesses. In fact, Frankfurter suffered the minor indignity of having the Court reverse one of the majority opinions written by him—the *Gobitis* opinion.[21] The occasion called for a strong dissent from the man who was being left behind.

"One who belongs to the most vilified and persecuted minority in history," Frankfurter wrote of himself, "is not likely to be insensible to the freedoms guaranteed by our Constitution. Were my purely personal attitude relevant I should wholeheartedly associate myself with the general libertarian views in the Court's opinion, representing as they do the thought and action of a lifetime. But as judges we are neither Jew nor Gentile, neither Catholic nor agnostic. We owe equal attachment to the Constitution and are equally bound by our judicial obligations. . . ."

Frankfurter then lectured his colleagues on self-restraint from expressing their personal views from the bench and in such a way as to prevent states from exercising their legitimate power. His lengthy analysis ably marshaled from history all the possible reasons for letting states require a flag salute in schools; it will probably become a classic of the law, though not accepted. Near the end of his treatise Frankfurter inserted several rebukes—assertions that the Court had passed on the issue five times previously with only one dissent (Stone), that the thirteen Justices who passed on the issue included men like Brandeis and Cardozo and that no other reversal in history took the direction of restricting the "powers of democratic government."

Similarly, when the Court reversed several previous decisions upholding local license taxes on the Witnesses, Frankfurter stood his ground.[22] With Reed, he believed that religious freedom was not the issue, that no harm had been wrought on the Witnesses' activities and that they were opposing trifling taxes. However, he went along with the Court (after attacking the opinion for lack of clarity) when it struck down a municipal law keeping literature distributors from ringing doorbells or otherwise summoning housekeepers to the door.[23]

Frankfurter was across the line from Black, Douglas and Murphy (and some others) in two other civil rights cases that term. He wrote the opinion holding that a defendant may waive trial by jury, even though having no counsel, and may even waive counsel, as long as the trial court supervises his choice.[24] Also, he voted with the dissenters from the ruling that William Schneiderman, Communist, could not have his citizenship papers canceled.[25]

But in two major civil rights cases Frankfurter spoke boldly for an almost unanimous Court. The well-known *McNabb* opinion[26] established the far-reaching principle that a defendant in criminal proceedings must be taken promptly before a judicial officer for formal charges (arraignment). "The history of liberty," he said, repeating one of his favorite expressions, "has largely been the history of observance of procedural safeguards."

The same day he wrote a politically courageous opinion releasing, for similar reasons, eight unionists who had been convicted of conspiring to dynamite two TVA power lines in connection with a strike against the Tennessee Copper Company.[27] The men were quizzed nearly a week before being allowed to see anyone; the treatment was so raw that the government couldn't even defend legality of the arrests.

In an important case on federal authority over property Frankfurter was on the government's side. He wrote the precedent-making opinion upholding the power of the Federal Communications Commission to restrict practices of the radio networks.[28]

Frankfurter wrote a concurrence in the famous *Williams* divorce case[29] in which a quick Nevada divorce was upheld even though one of the spouses was not there to contest it. Under our federal system tangled marital situations inevitably arise, he wrote, adding that "these complications cannot be removed by any decisions this Court can make—neither the crudest nor the subtlest juggling of legal concepts could enable us to bring forth a uniform national law of marriage and divorce."

In the next term—1943—the split in votes between Frankfurter and the Black-Douglas-Murphy contingent was inflated into something just short of open warfare. What had been simple differences of opinion became polemic traps and thinly veiled digs at colleagues. Three cases, on widely varying subjects, produced the bitterness—all within the month of January, 1944.

The first was the *Hope Natural Gas* case,[30] in which the Court moved further away from the corpse of *Smyth* v. *Ames* and associated itself with the "prudent investment" theory of utility regulation. Jackson and Frankfurter started an argument over the relative powers of Congress and the Court in ultimately regulating utilities. According to Frankfurter, "it was decided more than fifty years ago that the final say under the Constitution lies with the judiciary and not the legislature." Moreover, he asserted, Congress had acquiesced in that position. Black and Murphy jumped on the latter sentence, branding it "patently a wholly gratuitous assertion as to constitutional law." Then they flung in Frankfurter's face his own words: "That issue is not here in controversy." They disagreed that Congress had acquiesced in the doctrine, then wrote: "The salutary practice whereby courts do not discuss issues in the abstract applies with peculiar force to constitutional questions."

In the very next case, Frankfurter used a dissent to hurl practically the same charges back at Black, Murphy and probably others. It was a complicated patent case;[31] Frankfurter dissented on technical grounds, but added a few remarks about the majority's position. The charge was that "litigants and lower courts ought not to be embarrassed by gratuitous innuendoes against a principle of the law which . . . is accredited by legal history as well as ethics. . . . The experience of centuries is behind the wisdom of not deciding, whether explicitly or by atmospheric pressure, matters that do not come to the Court with the impact of necessity."

Black and Murphy rose to the bait, "in order that silence may not be understood as acquiescence in the views expressed in the dissenting opinion of Mr. Justice Frankfurter." It seemed to Black that "the judicial error of discussing abstract questions is slight compared with the error of interpreting legislative enactments on the basis of a court's preconceived views on 'morals' and 'ethics.'"

The third case was far more remote in subject matter but much more histrionic. A merchant seaman fell from a staging because of defective rope which the mate had used in rigging it. The seaman sued the ship owner on the grounds that he had not kept the ship "seaworthy," as he is bound by law to do. Chief Justice Stone, writing for the Court, upheld the seaman's theory of the case, frankly discarding one part of a precedent.[32] Roberts dissented, finding no reason to "liberalize" maritime law in favor of the seaman.

Had he stopped at that point the case would have been unnoticed, but what he said in addition put it on the front pages.

"The evil resulting from overruling earlier considered decisions must be evident," said Roberts. For nearly a page he went on to outline the evils. An example: "The tendency to disregard precedents in the decision of cases like the present has become so strong in this court of late as, in my view, to shake confidence in the consistency of decision. . . ." Even this blast would have evaporated with the departure not long afterwards of Roberts, if it had not been for seven words at the end of the opinion which gave it historical continuity and contemporary harshness: "Mr. Justice Frankfurter joins in this opinion."

Besides these institutional arguments, the unending problems of the federal system plagued the Court in the 1943 term. The most thorny of these arose when Minnesota levied a property tax on the entire fleet of planes of the Northwest Airlines, whose center of business is in that state. Frankfurter wrote the majority holding that Minnesota acted within her power, regardless of the consequences to Northwest Airlines in other states.[33]

When the Court narrowly (four to three) upset seventy-five years of negative thinking to bring fire insurance within the meaning of interstate commerce for the purpose of an antitrust suit, Frankfurter dissented.[34] He had no doubt that Congress could regulate insurance, but since it had never chosen to do so he was unwilling to bring about the "far-reaching dislocations" indicated by the majority holding.

Frankfurter's votes in civil liberty issues were mostly opposed to the individual, with two important war cases involved. In the *Ashcraft* case,[35] in which the Court released an accused murderer largely because he had been quizzed incessantly for thirty-six hours under bright lights before "confessing," Frankfurter believed that diligent police methods had not overridden the constitutional guarantee of due process. Ashcraft, the dissenters pointed out, "was a white man of good reputation, good position, and substantial property" and was allowed to be at large for a week before the questioning under discussion. In the *Feldman* case [36] Frankfurter wrote a bitterly contested opinion for the Court upholding the conviction of one whose testimony against himself in the federal criminal trial had been taken from a previous state trial in which he had been guaranteed by state law that it would not be used against him in any criminal proceedings. Frankfurter's opinion ruled that the 5th amendment's ban against self-incrimination was a ban only on the federal government, whereas it was the *state* which had the evidence. The evidence was allowed.

The *Baumgartner* denaturalization case[37] and the *Hartzel* espionage case[38] were decided the same day and involved a question of sufficiency of evidence to carry out the government's attempt to put both men away as detrimental to the war effort. In the first, Frankfurter wrote for the Court that the evidence was not enough. All justices agreed with the conclusion, though the four men to Frankfurter's left were compelled to write a separate concurrence to state their convictions a little more strongly. In the second, the majority felt the same way about the evidence, but Frankfurter was on the dissenting side with Reed, Jackson and Douglas.

Similar problems were presented during the 1944 term in two cases arising from the Selective Service Act. In both, Frankfurter was on the side of strict construction of terms under which men were facing prison sentences. The *Singer* case[39] turned on whether the words "or conspire to do so," appearing at the end of a list, applied only to the last item on the list or to all above it. Five justices gave it sweeping application; but Frankfurter climbed in bed with Murphy, Rutledge and Roberts to write a dissent. As a master of the English language, Frankfurter felt that his reading was the natural one; he also declared that when Congress wants to make conspiracy unlawful it carefully spells out that fact.

A few months later, in the *Bund* case,[40] Black joined these dissenters to form a majority of five which reversed indictments against twenty-five Bundists charged with counseling evasion of the draft. Much of the argument was semantic, but it also involved sufficiency of evidence.

In the Japanese relocation cases Frankfurter went along with the government and with the Court. In the ruling that the Army's evacuation of American citizens of Japanese descent from the West Coast was lawful,[41] Frankfurter filed a brief concurrence pointing out that war powers are as much a part of the Constitution as are peacetime powers and that most of the "hardheaded" framers had participated in war.

Regular civil rights cases that term were not highly exciting so far as Frankfurter's written opinions were concerned, and his vote was about half and half. He wrote dissents twice when the Court held that persons had unlawfully been deprived of the right of counsel, placing his reliance on the wisdom of lower courts.[42] When the Court unanimously brushed aside the amazing argument that New York's law against race, creed or color discrimination violated the Constitution when applied to a union of mail clerks, Frankfurter stuck in one of his unnecessary concurrences that leaves lawyers just a bit cold.[43]

Two other cases that term blended labor and civil rights law. One that got headlines across the country was the test of a recent Texas law requiring a permit for soliciting membership in a labor union. The majority released the challenger, R. J. Thomas, then head of the auto workers, on the grounds that his freedom of speech had been violated; but a minority of four declared that the state had power to regulate union organizers in the same way that it could regulate other business practitioners. Frankfurter joined in this dissent.[44] Similarly, when a majority struck down Florida's licensing system for union business agents, Frankfurter wrote the dissent.[45] The majority ruled that Florida's restrictive law clashed with the National Labor Relations Act, which underwrites free collective bargaining with agents of employees' own choice. Frankfurter once again protested on the grounds of state rights: "The Court is striking down a State law not because such a statute in and of itself is beyond the power of a State to enact. The Florida statute is nullified because . . . Congress has barred Florida from lawmaking, although Congress has neither expressly nor by fair inference forbidden Florida to deal with the matter with which Florida has dealt and Congress has not."

Another labor case really involved an argument over what is interstate commerce. Frankfurter, for a 5-to-4 Court, ruled that maintenance employees, such as elevator operators, in a forty-eight-story building devoted to offices leased to more than one hundred tenants of widely varying businesses were part of local, rather than interstate, commerce.[46] The same day, however, he joined with a different majority to put in interstate commerce the maintenance employees of a building owned by the Borden Company, a firm clearly engaged in interstate commerce.

Other Frankfurter opinions that term included a separate concurrence against the Associated Press in the antitrust case[47] and the dissenting opinion when the Court (five to four) allowed individual members of railway unions to challenge in the courts settlements arrived at by collective bargaining and administrative processes.[48] Also, Frankfurter took a major part in deciding whether campaign expenses could be deducted for income tax purposes by a judge who had not been re-elected.[49] For the majority, Frankfurter wrote that even though being a judge constituted "carrying on any trade or business," campaign expenses were laid out for trying to be a judge, not for being one.

The 1945 term was a big one for Felix Frankfurter. With Jackson off the bench he became more of a spokesman for one wing of the Court. He frequently dissented with the chief justice, always a pleasure, and he found a new friend to take the place of the retired Roberts: Harold Burton. In a term marked by a record number of cases which had to be postponed for reargument when Jackson would be back to break the tie, Frankfurter was a busy bee. He wrote only a handful of opinions for the work-laden Court, but he emerged as the most vocal dissenter.

His two most noteworthy majority opinions dealt with our system of government. He announced the Court's judgment upholding a federal tax on the water bottled by New York from its Saratoga Springs against the argument that to do so would destroy the historic immunity from taxation between federal and state units.[50] Citing an earlier case in which the Court upheld a tax on South Carolina's liquor business Frankfurter said: "We certainly see no reason for putting soft drinks in a different constitutional category from hard drinks." However, four of the justices who voted with him wrote a separate opinion to disclaim his sweeping remarks against the general theory of intergovernmental immunity, a theory that Frankfurter has held consistently and effectively. In another majority opinion he turned aside the pleas of three voters that Illinois districts were not apportioned correctly under law.[51] Frankfurter concluded: "To sustain this action would cut very deep into the very being of Congress. Courts ought not to enter this political thicket."

On the subject of labor Frankfurter dissented when the Court held that the federal Kickback Act was not intended to apply to an agent for a closed shop union who collected money from employees to be applied on their initiation fees.[52] According to him the loose language of the act clearly covered the union situation. "The statute is for the protection of the laboring man and the taxpayer," he summarized. Again, when the Court set aside a settlement between an employer and his employees for back pay due under wage-hour regulations, after a Supreme Court decision clarified the company's liability, Frankfurter blew his top.[53] He felt that the deal (by which the workers agreed to less than the letter of the law allowed them) was arrived at by arm's length bargaining, but his anger came because Congress had said nothing on which the Court could have based its holding. The dissent was joined by Burton and Stone.

"For purposes of judicial enforcement," wrote Frankfurter, "the 'policy' of a statute should be drawn out of its terms, as nourished by their proper environment, and not, like nitrogen, out of the air."

Frankfurter always delivers his opinions in an assertive, almost strident manner, leaning on the bar as if it were a barrier he wanted to push aside so that he could get right down in the front row. In at least two civil liberties cases that term he fairly left his seat with indignation. In both of them he was on the individual's side, with Black and Douglas across from him. Probably his major opinion of the term falls into that category.[54] The Court, four to three, sustained the conviction of a gasoline station operator from whom OPA inspectors had taken A coupons as evidence. The officials had no search warrant, though they had plenty of time to prepare for the arrest. They didn't physically force the operator to give up his tickets, but the record showed that he finally unlocked the door rather than have them break it down.

Frankfurter (joined by Rutledge and Murphy) first noted that one reason the OPA men had no search warrant was that they could not legally have obtained one; hence, he argued, the Court sustained a search and seizure without a warrant when it couldn't have sustained one even with a warrant. But it was the broader aspects of the case that infuriated Frankfurter, the "travesty" he saw on the 4th amendment—against unreasonable search and seizure. We are in danger, he said, "of forgetting that the Bill of Rights reflects experience with police excesses. It is not only under Nazi rule that police excesses are inimical to freedom." He scoffed at the idea, held by the Court, that the operator had yielded the evidence "voluntarily."

Then he reviewed the long history of the 4th amendment and cases under it. "The Court's opinion has only its own reasoning to support it," he asserted. "Nothing that this Court has ever decided or sanctioned gives it strength." Farther on he inserted two more barbs: "The Court in this case gives a new label to an old practice and to an old claim by police officials" and ". . . enforcement presupposes a moral atmosphere and a reliance upon intelligence. . . ."

The same day he dissented with the same justices against the Court's affirmance of the conviction of a Negro for the gruesome murder of the Washington Cathedral librarian.[55]

The trio protested that the murderer had not been shown to have premeditated the bludgeoning and strangling. For example, he had been provoked by the librarian's calling him a "black nigger," had choked her because of fear when she screamed and didn't seem to know that he had murdered her. "A shocking crime puts law to its severest test," said Frankfurter, adding that "it is not enough that a trial goes through the forms of the law."

In other civil rights cases that term Frankfurter was usually on the government's side. He went along with protection of Jehovah's Witnesses both in company-owned towns and in government-owned housing projects,[56] but in all other notable cases he went conservative. He concurred in Burton's dissent favoring the Army in the case concerning military law in Hawaii and he joined in Stone's last dissent—protesting the overruling of three old decisions on conscientious objection and the naturalization laws.[57] He felt that Congress had acquiesced in the earlier interpretations of the law, thus binding the Court to exclude those who would not take the customary oaths in seeking citizenship.

Moreover, he wrote a dissent from the Court's reversal of a conviction on the grounds that daily wage earners had been excluded from the jury.[58] He would not have stood for the exclusion of all workers, but he felt that the lower court had acted within its discretion in not picking those workers who would probably be excused anyway on the grounds of financial hardship. And he filed a concurrence in the decision that struck down as a bill of attainder the congressional rider banning funds for three federal employees suspected of radical activities.[59] He (and Reed) condemned the rider, but from his reading of history he denied that it was a bill of attainder (singling out by a legislature of persons for punishment without a trial).

Significantly, the session closed with a near record number of cases for one day, but one of the opinions carried the terse notation that Frankfurter dissented and would file his opinion sometime later. He had dissented so much that he hadn't been able to finish with his brethren. The notation was as ominous as it was unique.

The pattern of Frankfurter's votes, in relation to those of his brethren, is fairly clear. In dissent, he was most likely to agree with Roberts, until recently, then Stone, Jackson, Reed and Burton. However, this behavior pattern does not make Frankfurter's vote predictable, not even against the background of volumes of his writing about the Court and the Constitution. Theoretically it should; but the best test—reactions of lawyers who have to follow the divisions closely—shows the professor to be unpredictable.

Another feature of his record is the high number of concurrences, often by himself. Those who have no love for Frankfurter are inclined to write this habit off as an outgrowth of his vanity, but that is an oversimplification. He possesses such a fund of knowledge on the innuendoes of past opinions that none of his brethren can quite get the exact shading Frankfurter sees. Those of the bar who are annoyed at his added remarks are impatient with history writing, for there are frequently nuggets tucked away in his lonely opinions.

Some experts have also overreached in tabulating Frankfurter's votes mathematically as to his being pro or con labor, administrative agencies, criminal defendants, the taxpayer and other subjects. Frankfurter seldom throws a straight ball that will fit into any of those grooves. The main factor which cuts across Frankfurter's approach to many cases in his outright worship of the federal system. He believes it is a bulwark of freedom and has written lovingly of it as an answer to the problems raised by maintaining democracy in a large geographical area.[60] Thus, when one of the many disputes within the federal system reaches the Court, Frankfurter will keep it a long time under the microscope of his long study of the system.

Another favorite Frankfurter doctrine is that the Court should interfere with legislation only as a very last resort. Of course this is the doctrine of all justices now sitting, but Frankfurter makes more noise about it. His heroes, the dissenters on the old Court, firmly established it as a principle of interpretation. However, in the absence of a lie detector or a bench of nine immortals it is hard to say whether Frankfurter interferes with legislation less than do his colleagues who accuse him of the same error. The nearest that one can come to a factual statement on the issue is to note that it makes a convenient epithet to hurl by any justice dissenting from an interpretation which he doesn't like.

These crosscurrents, though legitimate differences of opinion, do not make for harmony on the Court—for whatever that is worth. There are two things that make Frankfurter grate on many people, lawyer and layman alike. The first is his incessant and often snippy quizzing of lawyers who stand before the bar pleading their cases. Many are the men who have remarked that Frankfurter thinks he's still conducting a seminar at Harvard. And not all of his interruptions are for questions: some are for assertions of his own, delivered in a dogmatic, high-pitched tone. One of these once prompted McReynolds, who always showed enmity for Frankfurter, to tell the lawyer before the bar: "I want to hear *your* argument."

A more pointed incident arose when Frankfurter was shooting questions endlessly at lawyers in a medical hearing. The medicos, so the story goes, had craftily brought into the chamber two lip readers to pick up clues as to how the argument was going. After the first part of their oral presentation the barristers huddled with their lip readers for a report which they hoped would enable them to switch emphasis for the second part if all was not going well. The lip artists had a one-sentence conversation to report from one justice leaning toward another: "I wish Frankfurter would shut his goddam mouth."

The incessant interrupting is definitely annoying. During the oral argument of the fate of the Nazi saboteurs Frankfurter injected questions or statements exactly eighty-nine times. The main object of his heckling, Colonel Royall, told reporters afterwards: "It was just like old times, with the professor crowding me to the wall, and me holding out to the last." Royall had been a student of Frankfurter's.

On top of this, Frankfurter's long words and involved structures let him in for some caustic remarks. If it is a crime to use the English language expertly, the justice would probably plead guilty, but some observers are convinced that he is merely putting on airs. Rare words in Frankfurter opinions include: aliquot, trivialize, indefeasible, finicking, gossamer, feckless, bifurcate, meretricious (a favorite), adumbrate, truncated, animadversion, nexus, rubric and lacunae. Another of his favorite words is "mischief," used in various forms to describe a legal situation displeasing to him. However, each word is used precisely; Frankfurter's writings will undoubtedly stand up as good literature rather than mere verbiage.

His literary perfection is sometimes achieved at the expense of litigants and his brethren on the Court—litigants because he tries to keep cases away from the Court so that more time can be spent on each opinion, his brethren because his labors over one opinion force others to write more in order to keep the docket current. Last term he wrote only eleven opinions for the Court, even though there were only eight, sometimes only seven, justices to do all the work. His own passion for detail is reflected in a *Harvard Law Review* article he once did on Brandeis' technique, including a reproduction of one page which Brandeis drafted twenty-six times before it was released. In support of giving the justices more time for deliberation of only crucial cases Frankfurter once wrote a lengthy dissent, quoting Taft, Holmes and others in support of his contention.[61] Moreover, Frankfurter has proposed that each justice deliver a separate opinion in each case, as the British do. Incidentally, he cites innumerable British and other foreign citations in his opinions, often to the boredom of the bar.

Another criticism which hangs over Frankfurter is one of substance rather than form: his real and imagined influence at the White House on Franklin Roosevelt. It was real enough from 1933 and for about ten years thereafter, including about two years while Frankfurter was on the Supreme Court. It will be many more years before the record of that influence is gathered, if it ever is, but no one doubts that Roosevelt's old friend was in on much of the New Deal by telephone, letter, personal friends and trips to Washington. He was in on appointments, and he was in on policy, until he retired behind a program of relative judicial austerity.

However, there was one big program he was not in on, try as

the public would to hang it around his neck. That was the 1937 Court plan. Everyone waited eagerly for even a public expression on that issue from Frankfurter both because of his closeness to Roosevelt and because of his position as an historian of the Court. After his prolific writings on the subject, surely the professor would have a few words on an outright crisis. The answer was one of those silences so loud that it could be heard all over the country. A clue to his attitude, obviously not wholly favorable, appeared in England, where the *Round Table* magazine printed a letter from him protesting its statement that his friends Corcoran and Cohen helped write the plan.

There was much wonderment current in those years, and later, about Frankfurter's motives. Was he studying the law first, then the wisdom of governmental programs—or was it the other way around? The two need not always conflict, theoretically, but the question was asked and remains substantially unanswered.

From his genuflections toward the shrine of the much-loved philosopher of the law, Justice Holmes, one would judge that Frankfurter is a Holmes man through and through. Yet, subjectively, this is discarded by several Frankfurter intimates who say that he wraps Holmes about him as a flag for phony protection. Objectively, few reasonably prudent men could read Frankfurter's opinions during the war and find anything about them that resembled Holmes' famous wartime opinions which Frankfurter praised so highly in his book, *Mr. Justice Holmes and the Supreme Court*, published in 1939.

As successor to "the scholar's seat" on the Court—warmed for him by such luminaries as Gray, Holmes and Cardozo—Frankfurter came to the Court with the biggest tradition to uphold, so far as the never-sleeping eye of history is concerned. History has already recorded the vast erudition he brought to the job, but in the application of erudition to specific cases there is room for much mischief.

CHAPTER IX

Any Stick to Beat a Dog

THE story is told that the Supreme Court, during John Marshall's term as chief justice, found itself tippling in conference so much that it disciplined itself by ruling that there would be no drinking at those times—except on rainy days. Soon thereafter, when the justices were assembled in conference, Marshall opened the business by asking if there were any signs of rain. One of the associates obliged by peering outside, but he was forced to return with a negative report. The chief was disappointed in his colleague. "Are you not aware," he asked, "that the jurisdiction of this Court is nation-wide and that somewhere in this vast country it must be raining? Let's have a drink."

Apocryphal or not, the incident is one of the few times when jurisdiction has been more than a boring subject. Unfortunately, it is far from enough to say that the Court's jurisdiction is nation wide. To do so ignores the mass of problems arising from relationships among the states and the national government. The corner grocer at Wahoo, Nebraska, for example, is subject to both national and state executives, legislatures and judiciaries. When there is a conflict, the only way he can tell which authority to heed is to carry his problem to the U. S. Supreme Court. There his case will be thrown in with thousands of others, past and present, in an effort to iron out the myriad wrinkles of our "federal system," our federation of states.

In the course of riding herd on these jurisdictions, plus the District of Columbia and the territories, the Court has had rough going. The niceties of umpiring disputes from so many governments is enough in itself to tax the legal ingenuity of great men—every state line is a tight wire for the justices—but there has also been a willful lack of help from litigants. Cases arising under the federal system have frequently been brought to confuse the issue rather than simplify it. Especially has this area of litigation been made fruitful in negating state power by arguments that the power complained of can be exercised only by the national government—or vice versa, depending on which side of the bread the butter is on. The result of these pressures on an unimaginative, reactionary Court, was the no man's land for social legislation into which President Roosevelt rushed his troops in 1937.

One of the objectives in the battle was to upset the Court's negative attitude toward legislation on behalf of young workers. In 1916, Congress passed a law banning interstate shipment of goods manufactured in plants employing children under fourteen years of age more than eight hours in a day or more than six days in a week or between seven in the evening and six in the morning. The Court, five to four, nullified the statute on the grounds that Congress had exceeded its power over commerce.

This famous case of *Hammer* v. *Dagenhart*[1] became a martyr. However, the intense twenty-year debate which followed it centered not on the wisdom of outlawing child labor but on the narrower issue of whether such a law was really a proper exercise of power over interstate commerce. Thus, when President Roosevelt laid his Court plan before Congress and the people, *Hammer* v. *Dagenhart* was one of the main exhibits of judicial horrors. Lawyers kept up their argument that regulation of child labor was a valid control of interstate commerce.

Technically speaking, it was of course a regulation of interstate commerce. If one pound of goods made by one kiddie was kept out of a freight car crossing a state line, interstate commerce was obviously affected. But putting the regulation of child labor on such grounds had a very phony ring, a sound still echoing where constitutional issues are debated, for the battle was never put on the simple but honest grounds of whether Congress has the power to control child labor.

Nor did the Court itself use other than commerce grounds when it finally got around to reversing the decision, twenty-two years later. The precedent actually started slipping when Roberts gave the Court a majority to uphold the Wagner Act. When Black replaced Van Devanter its ultimate fate was certain, but it was a Coolidge appointee, Stone, who wrote finish to the case. The occasion was the *Darby* case, upholding the Fair Labor Standards Act, on February 3, 1941. The Court made no bones about reversing the *Dagenhart* case and in adopting what it referred to as the "classic" dissent of Holmes therein.[2] By coincidence, the winning lawyer that day was a former Holmes law clerk, Francis Biddle, then solicitor general. There was no dissent. Two days before, McReynolds had announced his retirement; the last of the old conservatives was gone. Five days later, Van Devanter died in retirement. A major milestone had been passed.

Lawyers have special categories for litigation within the federal system, but for purposes of a digestible explanation of what the change

IF HE DEFEATS COURT REFORM, LET'S CROWN HIM AND BE DONE WITH GOVERNMENT BY THE PEOPLE

C. D. Batchelor, in the New York *Daily News*, depicted the charge that the lawyers, in 1937, were setting themselves above the will of Congress.

in Court personnel has done to national-state relations few of the legal niceties can be observed. Among these special angles none has been more subject to pulling and hauling or become more fouled up than the plain old commerce clause of the Constitution: "The Congress shall have power . . . to regulate commerce with foreign nations, and among the several States, and with the Indian tribes."

It all started in 1824 with the case of *Gibbons* v. *Ogden*[3] in which the Court held through its strong Federalist, Marshall, that "commerce" includes "navigation" and is subject to regulation by the United States government, superseding any state government.

At first the fuel for the flames of dispute over interstate commerce was supplied from the broader dispute over state rights, spearheaded by the differing philosophies of Alexander Hamilton (favoring strong central control) and Thomas Jefferson (championing strong state powers within the federation). But it was not long before the issue spread far past navigable water into the growing industrialization of America. State lines meant less and less as, first, states subordinated their selfishness into the federal system and, second, crossing state lines meant nothing in daily trade and commerce.

But the latter transition threw before the Court increasingly important cases in which the question was: What is interstate commerce? Is it anything that crosses a boundary, or is it to be strictly interpreted as traffic and physical movement? The Court vacillated with great dignity. It held, for example, in the *E. C. Knight* case[4] that though the companies controlling 94 per cent of the nation's sugar production had fixed prices the action was local. It refused to extend the meaning of interstate commerce to trade, but confined it to manufacture. Even before that the Court had ruled that the insurance business was not interstate commerce.[5]

As recently as 1932, an expert on the commerce clause, commenting specifically on that ruling, stated: "The expression 'Insurance is not commerce' has became almost a classic. There is nothing more to be said for it."[6] Yet fifty-one years after the insurance decision the Supreme Court held that a correspondence school is engaged in interstate commerce and hence out of reach of a state regulation.[7] A number of other "intangible" businesses have been just as clearly classified as interstate, including a dealer in futures, the business of credit reporting and a vaudeville booking agency. Seventy-five years after the old insurance case, the Court finally accepted the government's contention that insurance should not be exempted from the commerce clause and could be regulated for at least the purposes of the antitrust laws.[8]

The device of stretching the commerce clause was not invented by New Deal lawyers; it was originated by their predecessors, who found it a convenient legal vehicle to latch sundry legislation onto. In 1940, Stone was able to put in a footnote an imposing list of federal laws passed after 1890 "imposing penalties for obstructing or misusing interstate transportation."[9] It included statutes regulating lottery tickets, obscene books, illegally killed game, white slavery, prize fight films, stolen cars, kidnapped persons, threatening letters, and strikebreakers.

Following this successful legal lead—any stick to beat a dog—the New Dealers set out to club social evils to death with the interstate commerce clause. Regulation of coal, oil, agriculture, railroad employees' pensions, and the National Recovery Act were sought mainly on interstate commerce grounds—and denied on the same grounds. Yet Roosevelt never proposed an amendment to the troublesome clause; he placed all his eggs in the basket of trusting younger minds to interpret the old clause liberally enough to achieve social change.

That they have done. It was the old Court which held in April of 1937 that the Wagner Act constitutionally regulated interstate commerce by prohibiting employers from interfering with collective bargaining. From then on, the interstate commerce clause grew and waxed exceedingly strong. Following up on the Wagner Act and wage-hour basic victories, the government, with organized labor, kept the Court hopper full of cases seeking broad interpretations of coverage. Interstate commerce was stretched to the limit, if not beyond, in efforts to corral every possible worker within its haven for collective bargaining, higher wages or shorter hours.

Only a few of the NLRB cases are needed to illustrate the Court's attitude in the many cases brought to extend coverage of the Wagner Act. In the *Consolidated Edison* case,[10] decided in 1938, the NLRB had found the electric power company guilty of unfair labor practices and ordered six discharged men reinstated with back pay. The utility's defense was that it did not engage in interstate commerce and it cited the significant fact that none of its power crossed a state line.

This was all very interesting, but the Court was more concerned about the dire consequences of a stoppage at Consolidated Edison: "Instantly, the terminals and trains of three great interstate railroads would cease to operate," wrote Hughes; "interstate communication by telegraph, telephone, and radio would stop; lights maintained as aids to navigation would go out; and the business of interstate ferries and of foreign steamships whose docks and lines are operated by electric energy would be clearly impeded."

The Court decided that Congress had power, through the Wagner Act, to avoid such tragedy, Justices Butler and McReynolds still to the contrary and still feeling that the "sick chicken" case was better law.

The Court's approval of the Fair Labor Standards Act, better known as the wage-hour law, had followed the Wagner Act pattern, except that there was no dissent. It upheld provisions for minimum wages and maximum hours for employees engaged in "the production of goods for commerce." But the circles that spread from this splash in the judicial pool became extremely wide. The Court later extended coverage of the act, for example, to elevator operators, watchmen and carpenters in a loft building where businesses produced goods for commerce and to similar employees of the headquarters building of a company largely engaged in interstate commerce but not producing any goods in that building.[11] Most recently the Court included in the act a daily newspaper of about 10,000 circulation, only forty-five of which were sent out of the State.[12]

A similar revolution occurred in the old supposition that nothing could be more local than agriculture. In the *Currin* case[13] the Court okayed a system for uniform grading and inspection of tobacco which the administration had said in the Tobacco Act of 1935 was necessary to remove conditions burdensome to interstate commerce. Nearly all of the tobacco sold in the auction centers involved moved across state lines and the Court affirmed a rule that where goods are purchased in one state for transportation to another the purchase is a part of interstate commerce. The tobacco which was used locally, never crossing boundaries, was held to be validly regulated along with that which went up in smoke in other states.

The old AAA case was reversed, for most purposes, when the Court upheld the Agricultural Adjustment Act of 1938.[14] Roberts, for the Court, found, first, that the marketing quotas of the new act got around the Court's former objections to the AAA by not controlling production. The act placed no limit upon the acreage that could be planted, merely restricting the amount of tobacco that could be marketed in any one year at auction warehouses, which are "the throat where tobacco enters the stream of commerce." To frame it within a well-known cigarette ad, the Court established a sort of interstate "T" zone—the throat of commerce in the tobacco industry.

Also, the Agricultural Marketing Agreement Act of 1937 was upheld as a valid power over commerce.[15] The Court decided that, though the act of selling milk may be a local deal, the commodity becomes an article of interstate commerce, thus drawing the entire system into the broad commerce power. Five years before, the Nine Old Men had reluctantly found authority for a state to fix the price of milk,[16] so the 1939 Court had little trouble in finding power for federal control of interstate milk, Justices Butler and McReynolds to the contrary notwithstanding.

Another agriculture case, *Wickard* v. *Filburn*,[17] is cited by lawyers as the high point of extending the commerce power. An Ohio farmer, standing against the legal talent of the government, tried to stop the

Department of Agriculture from collecting from him the penalty payments for harvesting more wheat than was established as his quota under the Agricultural Adjustment Act of 1938. After a referendum among farmers had approved the general plan, officials had set for this farmer a quota of 11.1 acres. He harvested, however, twenty-three acres. The government dunned him forty-nine cents for each of the 239 bushels reaped from the excess acreage. His legal argument was that his wheat was not to be sold in commerce but to be used right on his farm.

The government argued that under the scheme of the 1938 act, which was to control the total amount of wheat in commerce so as to prevent a surplus, every little bit had its impact on the whole. A unanimous Court decided against the farmer, thus putting the home-used wheat under as much control as if it had crossed state lines.

If the sublime is hard to find in interstate commerce law, the ridiculous is not so elusive. It frequently manifests itself in the many cases arising from state barriers against sister states. These restrictive laws were not originated by the New Deal—in fact, one of the best reasons the founders had for creating this government was to minimize Balkanization of that type. Before the Constitution, retaliation between states was rampant, but there was some hope that the new government of the United States might remedy the situation. The Supreme Court, no less than travelers and businessmen, has trouble with the barriers—good and bad ones alike.

For example, an Indiana law required the carcasses of dead animals to be disposed of under sanitary rules within the Hoosier State. The law was challenged as an unlawful burden on interstate commerce, but the Court found no such burden and the dead horse had to be decently buried or turned into glue in Indiana.[18]

An exceptional case? No, the Court keeps getting into these weighty matters. A trucking company operator was licensed for interstate business but not for trucking within Missouri. When that state cracked down on his carryings on in that area, he pointed out that he hauled freight from St. Louis, in Missouri, to Kansas City, Kansas, where he had a place of business, then across the river into the Kansas City which lies in Missouri, making him part of interstate traffic. The state—and the Supreme Court—held, however, that he was resorting to a subterfuge by unnecessarily hauling his freight out of the state and then back in again.[19]

One of the best known of the extremely restrictive laws was the 1937 "inspection fee" imposed by Florida on all cement sold and used there. Florida felt that foreign cement, like bathing beauties and citrus fruit, was of inferior quality and added the assertion that it therefore menaced public safety and "amounts to unfair competition being forced on this great industry in Florida."

The facts, stripped of advertising flavor, showed that 30 per cent of the cement used in Florida was imported. The "inspection fee" imposed on this quantity was fifteen cents per hundred pounds, sixty times the cost of inspection. The Court, not being in the Florida cement business, declared that "it would not be easy to imagine a statute more clearly designed to circumvent what the commerce clause forbids."[20]

The Court was probably right, but there were plenty of other trade walls built around states to give the Court some hard times. Acting under what is generally known as the "police power," states have Balkanized the nation with a multitude of laws both legitimate and phony. The Court often had to tell which was which, then apply the Constitution while giving state legislatures the benefit of all doubts as to the real intent of their statutes. In its mellower mood the Court approved a California license fee of $15 each six months on caravans of cars for sale, finding it a reasonable classification of traffic requiring more control and maintenance on roads, and upheld a Pennsylvania ban on transporting autos over the cab of the carrying vehicle.[21] Nor could it find an unconstitutional burden on interstate commerce in the rule of a state commission requiring a terminal railroad company handling interstate trains to provide caboose cars for protection of the employees.[22]

Yet the Court felt compelled to strike down a number of seemingly similar state actions. It ruled against the Arkansas prohibition on trucks entering the state with more than twenty gallons of gasoline for their own fuel, declaring it to be an undue burden on commerce.[23] Also, it was against an Arizona law limiting the length of trains to fourteen passenger or seventy freight cars, as applied to an interstate train.[24] And the state of Virginia had no better luck with its law requiring segregation of Negroes when it was tested by an interstate passenger.[25]

Then there are arguments over taxation of goods bought from out of state. On a single day, for example, the Court took on three of these problems, splitting badly on the following results.[26] It held that a state may not impose a sales tax on goods bought by mail from another state, but it permitted levy of a tax on the use of such goods after their purchase. This distinction was too fine for the dissenters in the first case, as it must be for most laymen. Third, the Court allowed a state to impose a gross income tax on the receipts of the out-of-state company from such interstate sales.

Nor could the dissenters see any reason for distinguishing the nullification of the sales tax from an earlier New York case in which a sales tax was upheld on a delivery of coal from outside the state but contracted for within the state.[27] The New York case also touched off an attack on a long line of "drummer" cases, in which the Court had knocked out license fees against itinerant solicitors of orders from out-of-state firms. However, the Court stood firm, finding that a Richmond, Virginia, license on solicitors was an unconstitutional burden on commerce, largely because it was discriminatory in effect.[28]

If these cases are dull, though necessary, other subjects of dispute among the family of states are more dramatic. For example which state has the power to tax a company owning a fleet of airplanes that fly into many states? If one state holds the authority, can it tax the entire fleet? The Court ran into these and many shadings of them when Minnesota assessed the Northwest Airlines for a property tax on all its planes.[29] A 5-to-4 Court upheld the tax, even though other states had taxed part of the fleet. The corporation was organized under Minnesota laws and had its home port there. It would have been hard to avoid, but the decision left hundreds of airplanes flying all over the country without any way for their owners to tell how much tax they would have to pay or where.

That doubt is pale, however, compared with one left by the fantastic case of *Williams* v. *North Carolina*.[30] It was one of those divorce situations in which a man and a woman went to Nevada to shed their respective wife and husband and then to marry each other. They returned to North Carolina as man and wife, but were greeted inhospitably by a prosecution for bigamous cohabitation, as the lawyers put it. Their Nevada marriage license being unconvincing to North Carolina courts, they appealed to the Supreme Court, where they were upheld by a ruling that the latter state must give "full faith and credit" to the action of its sister state.

The proceedings then took a change—North Carolina attacked the famous six-weeks jurisdiction which Nevada has so long declared to be bona fide for a divorce. This was something else, and the Supreme Court found the newlyweds again before it, still charged with bigamy. This time the Court ruled against the couple, throwing the fear of bigamy into thousands of other Nevada divorcees scattered through the country. If Nevada did not have proper jurisdiction, the Court ruled, North Carolina need not follow its decision. Parties who were not litigants in the Nevada proceedings—that is, the man and woman left behind—could attack Nevada's jurisdiction, or the other state could. And a jury could find from the facts that Nevada residence—an auto court for six weeks in this case—was not truly acquired. The conviction for bigamy was affirmed. It was one of those cases in which the Supreme Court could not win, in terms of satisfying everyone, no matter which way it turned. Its rule was harsh on Williams and his second wife, but it established a pattern which could be followed from then on, and it left to each state control of divorce—something the Court tries to do in other subjects as well.

Disputes between the federal government and a state, usually in the form of who can tax whom and how much, have undergone a great change by the new Court. The most publicized of this transition has been in the degree of immunity between the two, established as a gulf many years ago when the Court was more fearful that states would use the tax weapon to cripple the national government. Part of this fear was engendered by the half-truth that "the power to tax is the power to destroy," uttered by Chief Justice Marshall in keeping Maryland from taxing the United States Bank back in 1819. As Frankfurter wrote many years later, Holmes gave this remark its intellectual *coup de grâce* with one pithy stroke when he said: "The power to tax is not the power to destroy while this Court sits."

While the Court was sitting in 1939 it overruled, in effect, four decisions to hold that New York could levy a nondiscriminatory income tax on an employee of a federal agency, the Home Owners' Loan Corporation.[31]

A question of similar import has arisen over federal taxation of state operations. Last term the Court upheld an excise tax on the water bottled at New York State's Saratoga Springs, following a precedent in taxation of state liquor monopolies, though with considerable misgiving among the justices.[32] Earlier, when only Black and Reed of the new justices were sitting, the Court had taken a big bite out of the old immunity of state employees from federal taxation when it allowed income levies on employees of the Port of New York Authority.[33]

A different angle of the argument arises from local taxation of property owned by the United States government, but the Court has been liberal in allowing the taxes. For example, it held that Pennsylvania could tax a company's property which included machinery placed there by the government for war production.[34] The majority saw no threat to the federal system so long as the tax was not at a discriminatory rate.

Among the other, more sundry cases handed down in an effort to keep the federal system from being hopelessly tangled are two which took power away from states. In one, Ohio was prevented from taxing hemp from the Philippines, the Court reasoning that the Constitution quite clearly reserved import taxes to the national government.[35] In the other, Pennsylvania's law requiring aliens to register was invalidated as being superseded by the national law on the subject.[36]

Among the more confusing are two dealing with the federal regulation of *intrastate* commerce as an incident to control of interstate business. In contrast to the *Consolidated Edison* case and the wheat penalty situation, already referred to, the Court once held that the Federal Trade Commission had no power to ban "break and take" candy sales made within the borders of one state.[37] The FTC had already banned the practice—which makes the amount of candy received by the purchaser depend on chance—from interstate sales. Thus the interstate dealers were put at an unfair advantage by those merchants who used the unfair trade method within the safety of a state boundary. The majority of six felt that to uphold the FTC would "give a federal agency pervasive control over myriad local businesses in matters traditionally left to local custom or local law." The dissenters countered that "unfair competition involves not only an offender but also a victim. Here some of the victims . . . are engaged in interstate commerce. The fact that the acts of the offender are intrastate is immaterial."

One year later the Court allowed the Department of Agriculture to regulate milk sold within a state's borders on the grounds that it "directly affected" regulation of milk in interstate commerce.[38] The effect was the opposite of that in the candy case, yet there was no dissent.

That there are wheels within wheels in the federal system is abundantly illustrated by the Court's interpretation of "navigable" water, control over which belongs to Congress as against states by virtue of the Constitution. Late in 1940 the Court opened a new vista in the law of navigability by the *New River* decision.[39] The federal government was trying to stop construction of a dam on the New, tributary of a clearly navigable stream, the Kanawha. The company proposed to build a hydroelectric dam, asserted that it could not be denied that authority because the New was not navigable and rallied to its support the attorneys general of nearly every state in the union.

Nothing indicated the Court's problem more clearly than the fact that official reports on the river had alternately called it navigable and not navigable for many years back. Both lower courts, relying on a very early Supreme Court ruling that a river is navigable in law if navigable in fact, held against the government.

The Court first reviewed the mass of facts about the New, including testimony by a Confederate veteran that during the Civil War keelbottom boats had navigated part of the New with supplies, then settled the case on a novel principle: that navigability must be determined in the light of the effect of reasonable improvements which could be made. "Navigability . . . is but a part of this whole" of flood protection, watershed development, recovery of the cost of improvements through use of power generated, etc. In short, if the river could be made navigable at "reasonable" cost it was navigable in the eyes of the law. Two dissenters declared that the Court had completely ignored the many rapids and other obstructions in the New and attacked the majority for its vague reference to "reasonable" cost. They observed also that under this doctrine any creek in the United States could, by enormous expense and all kinds of blasting, be made navigable enough to carry a boat drawing two feet of water and come under the federal power.

A few months later the Court added another principle to the definition of navigability.[40] This time the state of Oklahoma was trying to stop federal construction of a dam on the Red River, between that state and Texas. Oklahoma wanted no part of the flooding which would cover 100,000 acres of her territory if the Denison Dam were built. She declared that the project was not connected to the navigable part of the Red River and hence was beyond federal power to build. But a unanimous Court declared that the dam would bring into control part of the general Mississippi watershed by controlling drainage from an area half again as large as New England. "Floods," said the Court, "pay no respect to state lines" and they paralyze commerce. Of the *New River* decision the Court said: "And now we add that the power of flood control extends to the tributaries of navigable streams." The two cases left little doubt that the new Court would resolve disputes over navigability in favor of federal control of the waterway.

A fitting case on which to conclude an analysis of decisions applying to the federal system is that in which the Court opened California borders to free access by the migrant Okies who had found the Sunshine State's famous hospitality conditioned on financial independence.[41] Fred F. Edwards was prosecuted under a California law against bringing into the state "any indigent person who is not a resident of the state, knowing him to be an indigent person." Edwards, a Californian, had gone to Texas to bring his brother-in-law, a WPA beneficiary, back with him. By the time they hit California the relative's $20 capital was exhausted; he was indeed indigent.

Though the Court's vote was unanimously in favor of Edwards, the grounds of the decision were not. Byrnes, for the majority, found the California law to be a plain and intended burden on interstate commerce; Jackson thought it was the privileges and immunities clause of the Constitution which was violated. Douglas, Black and Murphy objected to placing people in the category of cattle, fruit, steel and coal in their movements across state lines and believed the right to go from state to state is a privilege of national citizenship. The differences of opinion were indicative of the Court's desire to avoid Balkanization of the country and its reasonable doubt as to which of the several constitutional clauses should be applied in each new, troublesome situation.

Frankfurter once summed up the toughness of these decisions when he was settling the jurisdiction of the Wage and Hour Administration over many loft buildings. "To search for a dependable touchstone," he wrote, "by which to determine whether employees are 'engaged in commerce or in the production of goods for commerce' is as rewarding as an attempt to square the circle."

Stone, in dissenting from the Court's inclusion of the janitors in a company's headquarters office building, put his judicial finger on some of the troubles to which Frankfurter alluded. "No doubt there are philosophers who would argue," he said, "what is implicit in the decision now rendered, that in a complex modern society there is such interdependence of its members that the activities of most of them are necessary to the activities of most others. But I think that Congress did not make that philosophy the basis of the coverage of the Fair Labor Standards Act. It did not, by a 'house-that-Jack-built' chain of causation bring within the sweep of the statute the ultimate causa causarum which result in the production of goods for commerce."

The most recent and sharpest example of the straining undergone by the commerce clause was the Virginia Jim Crow bus law, already cited, which the Court nullified as a burden to that ubiquitous movement across the jigsaw puzzle of state boundaries. The resulting grist from the Court's mill is confusing; but one thing stands out: the phrase "interstate commerce" is getting worn pretty thin.

The conversation of two intelligent but puzzled observers of the legal scene, overheard just after the Court had found elevator operators to be enmeshed in interstate commerce, is pertinent. The men were discussing the case as they entered the men's room in a Manhattan office building similar to that which had just been touched by the magic wand of interstate commerce. As they spotted an acquaintance who had arrived ahead of them and was exercising an easement of necessity, one called to him:

"Say, Joe, do you realize that you are engaging in interstate commerce?"

CHAPTER X

Life Begins at Forty

"THAT guy can take a look at a corporate statement and tell you in a minute if there's been any fornicating going on in the back room," said one of the justices when William Orville Douglas moved to the Supreme Court from the chairmanship of the Securities and Exchange Commission. Even Justice McReynolds, a hater of anyone connected with the New Deal, once said that Bill Douglas would probably develop into one of the best men the Court ever had. The bitter-ender was impressed with his legal brilliance and with the way Douglas held his fire until the right time.

A third justice chose for comment a better known trait: "Bill Douglas is the most uninhibited member ever to serve on the Court." If the assertion needed proof it was borne out when Douglas showed up in his soft western fedora at the White House reception honoring the Court's 150th anniversary. His colleagues appeared in the traditional black silk toppers.

The incident illustrates superficially how Douglas epitomizes the "new blood" demanded by President Roosevelt for the bogged-down Court. At the age of forty, Douglas took his seat as the youngest man to be so honored since Joseph Story's appointment 128 years before at the age of thirty-two. But more than youth, Douglas brought with him a maverick quality, a Horatio Alger success story and a liberalism geared to the techniques and language of modern fast-stepping business and finance. Everywhere Douglas had been—from Columbia Law School to Washington bureaucracy—he had come like a breath of fresh air. His recognized brilliance in such heavy subjects as bankruptcy and corporate finance made him a natural to tilt with the lawyers of the "economic royalists" whom Roosevelt was attacking.

A favorite Douglas story illustrates the quality of homespun skepticism into which he wove his technical proficiency in this field. It concerns an Indian who wanted to borrow from a western bank but who was rejected until he forked over twenty ponies as collateral for the loan.

Later, the Indian struck it rich, returned to the bank, peeled off enough from his huge bank roll to discharge the debt and claimed his ponies. The banker, eyeing the fat bank roll, suggested that the Indian deposit the money in his bank.

"How many ponies *you* got?" asked the Indian.

In addition to his skill and skepticism, Douglas' open approach to problems made him adept at the job of sweeping cobwebs from the judiciary. How did Douglas get this way?

At a time when he could look forward to thirty years on the Supreme Court before the ordinary retirement age, Douglas could also look back on forty years as packed with color and interest as most men see in their entire careers. By the time he was old enough to start remembering it (five), his circuit-riding father, a Presbyterian preacher from Nova Scotia, had died and the Douglas family had moved to Yakima, Washington, to start an even tighter battle on its economic front. For those days and parts there was nothing unusual about the odd jobs with which Bill started supplementing the family income: selling the arch-Republican Yakima *Republic* (which attacked him in later years), running errands for a jewelry store at ten cents an hour and peddling junk. As a schoolboy he was nicknamed "Peanuts" because of his puny size, but as a scholar he carried off the valedictorian honors and a scholarship to Whitman College, in Walla Walla.

Douglas' energy in getting through college, and with a Phi Beta Kappa key, almost makes one weary just to read about. He set the pace by pedaling the 131 miles from Yakima to Walla Walla on a bicycle, then hooked onto campus jobs, such as washing windows and "hashing." By pitching a tent in a near-by grove and staying there throughout college he was actually able to send a little money home and afford one luxury —membership in Beta Theta Pi fraternity. Between terms he learned about the pre-Steinbeck indigents of the West Coast farming country by picking fruit alongside them and sharing their paltry subsistence.

Years later, just after Douglas joined the Court, he helped nullify a California law to keep the Okies out. But it took a separate concurrence to express his indignation at a law that "would prevent a citizen because he was poor from ever seeking new horizons in other states."

After leaving college, in 1920, Douglas spent a couple of years finding himself. For a while he taught at his old high school in Yakima, then he took a flier in business of his own with the $500 he had saved. The insurance venture which he favored with the sum promptly folded, seeming to take with it his hopes for an eastern law education. However, it merely set his determination, and in September of 1922 he boarded a freight train as caretaker for a carload of sheep headed for Chicago.

A rail strike ahead of his woolly charges forced him to leave them short of Chicago and reduced his traveling status even further—down to bumming his way on a caboose. The only casualty of the trip was a one-dollar shakedown from a brakeman along the way, but he came within inches of being snuffed out by an iron signal standard when he jumped the freight at Chicago to avoid entanglements with the railroad police. A wire to his brother brought coach fare to New York, where he arrived with a face full of whiskers and a pocket full of six cents—not enough to claim his baggage.

Badly in need of fraternity, Douglas went to the Beta quarters in Manhattan; but he had not reckoned with how little like a Greek brother he then looked. He was saved from a bouncing only when a Whitman classmate spotted him behind the two-weeks beard and advanced $75 for rehabilitation. From then on everything moved fast, though not more comfortably for some time.

On the verge of leaving Columbia Law School because everything was running up hill, student Douglas heard of a correspondence school operator who needed a course written. In six weeks the freshman student had whipped off the job and pocketed $600, then he tutored enough undergraduates so that he was able to go back to Yakima the first summer to marry Mildred Riddle, the pretty schoolteacher who now is a quietly popular Washington wife and mother of his two children.

In two more rough years, Douglas had finished Columbia Law School with second high honors and had attracted the attention of the dean, Harlan Fiske Stone. By graduation, in 1925, he had the eastern law practice bug. Later, he was to reject a partnership chance with a classmate, one Thomas E. Dewey; but, at the time, he signed up with a large firm and taught a couple of courses at Columbia on the side. At the end of two years he was ready to return to the West.

Douglas had hardly hired himself out as a Yakima law clerk, however, when Columbia wired a $5,000-a-year offer to rejoin the law faculty, which he did. From that day on, the Douglas legal career boomed in spite of the fact that not long after he arrived at Columbia he resigned in protest against President Nicholas Murray Butler's appointment of a new law dean without consulting the faculty. He soon happened to meet Yale Law School's young dean, Robert Maynard Hutchins (now president of the University of Chicago), and was immediately offered a better job at Yale. Within two years he was Sterling professor of law.

By this time Douglas had become a specialist in those parts of the law often regarded as the dullest: corporate reorganization and bankruptcy. But he made the law books sing by using actual corporate cases in his classes and showing the connection between the law and the corporation as an institution in the national economy. He started rebelling at the system of law which allowed voting trusts and other corporate devices to freeze out ordinary stockholders and creditors in the race for the remaining assets of defunct businesses.

Strange as it may seem now, it was the Hoover administration which first recognized the governmental talents of Bill Douglas. His expertness attracted Republican officials, searching for the cause of bankruptcies, just as it did New Dealers a few years later. In 1934, the first chairman of the new-fangled Securities and Exchange Commission, Joseph E. Kennedy, spotted an article by Douglas and summoned the untamed educator to Washington. Congress had ordered a study of such things as corporate reorganization and Kennedy hired Douglas to run it.

After shuttling between Yale and Washington until he had finished it, Douglas submitted a blistering report on the finer arts of thievery in the name of reorganization, and eventually Congress converted his recommendations into law. In January of 1936, Douglas was appointed an SEC commissioner and moved to Washington to supervise, in particular, the activities of securities exchanges. The next Douglas target was reform of the New York Stock Exchange. By 1937, at the age of thirty-nine, he was moved into the chairmanship of the commission as a sort of clean-up batter to clinch the progress of predecessors.

The clean-up batter slugged out a home run. Douglas read the riot act to the New York Stock Exchange in an effort to get the exclusive club to take on a public responsibility. That Douglas eventually would have won the pitched battle no one doubts, but he was aided greatly by the scandal that broke around the head of Exchange President Richard Whitney and sent the financier to prison for grand larceny. The Exchange installed its first full-time, paid president and launched a program of self-regulation.

By this time the praises of Bill Douglas were being sung all over town. His unorthodox behavior as a top bureaucrat, such as his fondness for a quick hot dog and coffee at the lunch counter next door to the SEC, made reams of feature copy for Washington reporters and he was tagged as a man bound somewhere higher. Yet few quite knew what made the man tick. In an administration full of professional intellectuals Douglas could match brains with ease, yet he operated differently.

One answer to what made him tick was given by the man, himself, at his first press conference after being named SEC chairman. "What kind of a bird am I? To tell you the truth, I think that I am really a pretty conservative fellow from the old school, perhaps a school too old to be remembered. I am the kind of conservative who can't get away from the idea that simple honesty ought to prevail in the financial world. I am the kind of a fellow who can't see why stockholders shouldn't get the same kind of fair treatment they would get if they were big partners instead of little partners in an industry."

This belief in simple honesty has been ascribed by at least one biographer, Jack Alexander, in a *Saturday Evening Post* article, to the early Douglas family routine of church attendance four times on Sunday, plus prayer meeting during the week. The observation may well be true, though Douglas is not known as a churchman now, but there is much more to the "old school" with which the SEC chairman identified himself. In its economic aspects, the Douglas outlook is taken from another jurist, the late Louis D. Brandeis.

As a disciple of the venerated dissenter, Douglas has an abiding faith in little business and an inherent mistrust in the other kind. "Bigness taxes the ability to manage intelligently," Douglas once told an audience of Chicago businessmen. "Bigness concentrates tremendous economic and financial power in the hands of a few. The growth of bigness has resulted in ruthless sacrifices of human values. The disappearance of free enterprise has submerged the individual in the impersonal corporation. When a nation of shopkeepers is transformed into a nation of clerks enormous spiritual sacrifices are made. Service to human beings become subordinated to profits to manipulators."

In many ways, then, it was natural when, in March of 1939, President Roosevelt appointed Douglas to wear the mantle put aside by Brandeis. It was also natural that the retiring justice wrote the forty-year-old heir to his chambers that he had wanted him to have that place. The central exhibit in Douglas' outer office is an etching of the white-haired Brandeis, and an autographed portrait of his predecessor hangs in his inner office next to one of Roosevelt.

But Brandeis' successor, in 1939, didn't have the Senate confirmation trouble Brandeis had suffered in 1916. Senator Frazier was worried about the thirty years, at least, which Douglas had ahead of him on the Court; but the tributes of men like Senator Borah rolled up a quick 62-to-4 vote. Significantly, it was discovered that Douglas had never been admitted to practice before the Supreme Court.

The comparative youngster chafed at first under Court work and Court routine. As a near chain smoker, Douglas found it hard to keep his nicotine pocketed during each two-hour session on the bench, and—until McReynolds left the Court—the Saturday conferences were also unsullied by tobacco smoke. He squirmed in his high leather swivel chair, brought to the bench his habit of cocking a pencil behind one ear, left his sandy hair tousled and grated for six months under piddling decisions.

Almost from the first, Douglas teamed up with Hugo Black to stick pins in old majority opinions or strike out in new directions with the new majority. The close relationship continued for about seven years with as few interruptions as any other combination on the Court and could almost be predicted in any case. Then, in 1945, he started veering away from his friend in a manner difficult to analyze. His style of expression in writing is almost as plain as his soft western hat, his literary flourishes as infrequent as his appearances in high society.

Many of the opinions assigned to Douglas to be written for the Court are given him in his role as chief preventer of corporate dishonesty. Few who are not lawyers, and some who are, can see what attracts Bill Douglas, the "regular fellow," to such horribly dull and painstaking cases, but he eats them up. Few readers do likewise, but someone has to write bankruptcy cases and they do help place the young westerner as something much more than a maverick.

One of the earliest Douglas financial opinions for the majority was a long one which removed any doubt that the new Court was still in love with the rule that bondholding creditors of a defunt company must be satisfied in full before stockholding and directing vultures descend on the carcass.[1]

In the next term Douglas injected high fiduciary standards into municipal reorganizations, tossing out a plan in which a city had been represented in the deal by one who gained considerably and anonymously by the shuffle of finances.[2]

Later in the same term the sharp-nosed justice wrote the unanimous Court's opinion in an extremely complicated bankruptcy reorganization of a holding company and two of its subsidiaries.[3] It was a good example of craftsmanship in ferreting out devices by which creditors might be left holding the bag in a reorganization. The odd feature of the three cases is that by ruling that bondholders must be paid off completely before stockholders can take anything home, Douglas was being as conservative in his financial thinking as any member of the Union League Club.

Probably the most complicated opinion Douglas ever wrote was that which sent back to the lower court a mazelike reorganization for the Chicago, Milwaukee, St. Paul and Pacific Railroad.[4] Lawyers swarmed over the fat case like ants on a fallen lollypop; it takes twenty-five pages to capsulize the arguments, compared with the usual three or four. It took Douglas fifty pages to return the case for more work below—fifty pages of high finance which have come to stand, briefly, for giving the Interstate Commerce Commission power to project the earnings of a reorganized railroad and otherwise cut away excess capitalization. It was major surgery, but was calculated to put the road back in shape.

In a 1942 case, after the Court had unanimously upheld a Federal

Power Commission's rate for a natural gas company,[5] Douglas joined with Murphy and Black in a bold move to start a new chapter in the tedious, basic subject of evaluating utility property for the purpose of setting rates. Writing bluntly, the three urged their colleagues to "lay the ghost of Smyth v. Ames, which has haunted utility regulation since 1898." The ramifications of this pronouncement are explained elsewhere; the significant thing about it in a chapter on William Douglas is that he was picking up where his patron saint, Louis Brandeis, had left the attack on the precedent which had fouled up regulators for nearly fifty years.

Two years later Douglas wrote the majority opinion in a case[6] which, in cautious language, swung the pendulum to the old position of Brandeis, Holmes and law review authors. The upshot was to leave commissions free to work out "reasonable" rates without being straitjacketed by any single formula.

Another heavy case[7] arose when the Tennessee Valley Authority condemned land for a dam site and offered up to $165,000 in payment. The owner, however, demanded $7,500,000 on the grounds that he could use the land, together with more he could acquire, to build an elaborate four-dam hydroelectric project. For a six-man majority, Douglas held that the owner was entitled only to the market value fairly determined, exclusive of the projected addition of other land which he could get by use of the power of eminent domain, given him by the state. Three years later Douglas got a more direct taste of condemnation and eviction: he was ousted from his lovely colonial home outside Washington in favor of an enlarged business zone.

The business expert also had a share of patent and antitrust opinions to write. In 1941 he upset the patent bar by an opinion involving a dashboard cigar lighter.[8] After reviewing the genesis of the lowly gadget, Douglas held for the Court that it was not the result of invention but a "mere exercise of the skill of the calling," an advance "plainly indicated by the prior art."

"Strict application of that test," he wrote, "is necessary lest in the constant demand for new appliances the heavy hand of tribute be laid on each slight technological advance in an art."

As a tool for springing loose technological skills for broadening economic horizons, the justice can be counted on to uphold a conviction under the antitrust laws. In fact, he wrote the Court's opinion in several important cases: the agency agreement device of the *Masonite* case;[9] the *Crescent Amusement* case,[10] in which dissolution of stock ownership was actually ordered; and the controversial railroad case,[11] in which the state of Georgia was allowed to sue the alleged combination of railroads discriminating against the South.

A substantial part of the new Supreme Court's outright reversal of precedent has been recorded for history in opinions written by Douglas as spokesman for the majority; in other cases he tried mightily for frank reversal but was in a minority. It was Douglas who spoke for the unanimous Court in overthrowing *Ribnik* v. *McBride*, a 1928 precedent in the way of regulating businesses such as employment agencies. In the course of his opinion,[12] Douglas also made sure that a doctrine rejected before 1937 was cold in its grave: the doctrine that only businesses "affected with a public interest" could be regulated as to prices and rates by legislatures and Congress. In doing so, he picked up the strong thread of a well-known Holmes dissent.

And in a minor part of the opinion, Douglas declared the new Court's independence from the technique which got the old Court into trouble: the substitution of justices' opinions of a statute's wisdom for the opinion of the legislature that passed it. "We are not concerned," he stated, "with the wisdom, need, or appropriateness of the legislation"—again citing the steady erosion of Holmes on the old Court's idea that it was a super-legislature. Douglas dissented in this vein when the Court found an Arizona train limit law and a Richmond, Virginia, tax on traveling salesmen to be burdens on interstate commerce,[13] but he remained silent when the Court struck down Virginia's Jim Crow law as applied to interstate busses.[14]

The justice could dissent in that vein over and over without impressing his many critics who think that he, like Black and others, decides cases by emotion, then looks for support in legal citations. Stated that baldly the charge is unfair, though Douglas is a part of the school of thought that holds it is naïve to think that judges can put their own feelings high on a shelf while deciding cases. Because this school is somewhat dominated by Yale professors, Yale-man Douglas cannot escape the label. And, in fact, he helped create it. Moreover, some Washington circles see Bill Douglas as a past and present schemer for bigger political things. This angle of his character is more easily gossiped than documented, but there is enough about his purposeful approach to cases to leave much room for his enemies to drive wedges between him and Frankfurter, representing the more aloof Harvard school. As will be seen later, much of this supposed judicial restraint, contrasted to judicial interference in legislation, is a shibboleth that can be hurled by anyone who wants to embarrass the other side. But it does get hurled.

In the next term Douglas was spokesman for the Court in overruling, seven to two, a 1932 precedent against dual taxation of intangible property. Under the new line[15] the state of Utah was allowed to impose a transfer tax on stock in a Utah corporation when its owner died, even though the stock was in New York and was also taxed there.

The following term Douglas wrote an attack on another landmark of the law, *Eisner* v. *Macomber*, for the team of Douglas, Black and Murphy.[16] The Court had taken jurisdiction on the possibility of overthrowing the precedent, but had decided not to go so far. That case had stood since 1920 for the proposition that an ordinary stock dividend is not income for the purpose of taxation because the dividend remains part of one's capital, is not separated from the investment. The Court rejected a contention that Congress had tried to get away from the old decision, then refused to do so itself.

"Eisner v. Macomber dies a slow death," Douglas dissented. He thought that Congress had tried in 1936 to make stock dividends taxable as income and that the old decision should not be tacked onto it as a phantom rider. "Our task ends," he wrote," if we erase Eisner v. Macomber and give Congress a clean slate on which to write. Then and only then can Congress design a tax system treating stock dividends consistently." He then quoted Brandeis' dissent in the old case and declared that the wealth of stockholders normally increases as a result of stock dividends.

As long as Douglas is fighting to change precedents he thinks are wrong and as long as he is urging restraint in setting aside the acts of legislatures and as long as he is supporting the little fellow against the big one, the Brandeis mantle looks good on the young disciple. But the luster of Brandeis in another and vital field of law has tarnished in his care. That is the field of civil liberties, especially in wartime.

It is not that Douglas, the democrat, the plain guy, is an enemy of civil liberties. In fact, he has frequently voted with the minority in courageous defenses of liberty. For example, he joined Black and Murphy in frankly declaring that their former votes in the *Gobitis* flag salute case were wrong.

Also, Douglas has written several heavyweight opinions for the Court in behalf of safeguarding individual rights. He was the spokesman in knocking out Oklahoma's loosely worded law for sterilizing habitual criminals;[17] for reversing the conviction of Charles Williams, who was sentenced to the Missouri penitentiary without benefit of counsel;[18] and in reversing Morris Malinski's conviction for murder, after he had been coerced into making the first of several confessions.[19] Two of Douglas' best-known civil rights opinions for the Court prevented deportation of Harry Bridges[20] because of insufficient evidence and pulled the rug from under the Post Office Department for banning *Esquire* magazine from second-class mail.[21] Also through dissents Douglas has occasionally shown a protective attitude. For example, in the *Adams* case[22] Douglas dissented from upholding a conviction in which the defendant, without advice of counsel, passed up his right to a jury trial.

It is in the wartime cases that the Douglas record looks little like that of his mentor. Whereas Brandeis had dissented so strongly against wartime excesses against personal liberty, Douglas seldom climbed off the government bandwagon, a bandwagon on which martial music was nearly always played. In the language of the GI, when it came to prosecuting the war Douglas was an "eager beaver."

He dissented sharply when the Court freed Cramer[23] from charges of treason and he voted against George Sylvester Viereck, charged with failing to disclose fully his German propaganda activities in a registration statement. Douglas rode with the Court when it upheld Japanese relocation and when it upheld the trials of Yamashita and Homma. True, he was also with the Court when it released those Japanese-American citizens whose loyalty had been established. However, one might expect a different record from a disciple of Brandeis.

Last year Douglas showed one flash of Brandeis, then lost his gain. He spoke forcefully for the Court in reversing three cases and following the dissents of Brandeis and others on the question of requiring alien conscientious objectors to agree to bear arms as a condition of citizenship.[24] He thought that Congress had finally upset an old fallacy by recognizing that noncombatants also render national service. Six weeks later, however, he wrote an opinion that set back many years the traditional protection of citizens from unreasonable search and seizure, a safeguard which Brandeis had brilliantly nurtured. For the Court, Douglas upheld a conviction based on OPA gasoline coupons which had been obtained from their unwilling owner only after long badgering by officers and a threat to break the door in if the owner would not unlock it.[25] The facts in the case were borderline, perhaps; but Douglas wrote into the law, by his opinion, two dilutions of the constitutional guarantee against unreasonable search and seizure; namely, that places of business are not as sacred as homes and that public papers, such as OPA coupons, are not protected as are private papers. The decision helped OPA in its enforcement of wartime laws, but it weakened civil rights for as long as the Court uses the Douglas opinion as a precedent.

In plumbing the depths of Douglas' mind—and it is deep—it is hard to escape the conclusion that the justice was swayed in wartime decisions by his intense support of the war itself. To inject personal opinions into decisions on law is a great temptation and one to which humans have usually yielded. Douglas, being one of the most human justices on the bench, does a fair share of the yielding. His speeches during the war clearly reflected his known personal concern for mobilization for total war in the cause of right.

Ten weeks before Pearl Harbor, in a speech entitled "Citizenship," delivered at Atlanta, Georgia, Douglas stated that "the world has taken sides: the sons of freedom are aligned against the hosts of tyranny."

Then he declared proudly that "those who would immobilize us were not successful," that we were not "confused by that much abused word 'peace.'" Then, continuing: "Through a vast preparedness program we have sought to purchase insurance against the day of aggression." As an all-outer, Douglas lectured the Oregon Newspaper Publishers Association, in June of 1942, for presenting too much news of victory and not enough on the gloomy side.

However, the firm-minded justice should not be classified as one who always works hard at the immediate goal without looking ahead to see how the task at hand will fit into the whole. The man has a vision far beyond the capacity of better-than-average political figures. On legal subjects his radarlike mind has contributed greatly to the ironing out of legal inconsistencies or wrong decisions in the corporate field and others. In the political realm it has sent impulses considerably beyond the United Nations organization and the loose league concept. Grasping the twin problems of world organization and control of atomic energy, Douglas boldly allied himself with a small group dedicated to world government backed by law, not world meetings backed by nothing more than speeches and moral suasion. Douglas would amend the United States Constitution to yield enough sovereignty to a world body to control firmly the atomic bomb, a step not envisioned by his contemporaries in Congress or the administration.

Because of his interest in these and other current events Douglas has always been suspected of having ants in his robe, only grinding out legal maxims and citations until the right thing comes along to return him to the outside world. Bill Douglas likes that outside world—whether he's fishing in its Wallowa Mountains, where he has a summer cabin, or whether he's thinking about its vast water resources which could be harnessed for more public benefit.

However, Douglas repeatedly insists that he's happy on the Court, where he enjoys "making democracy work all the time." His Court work confirms that attitude, though it is sometimes hard to believe when he musses his hair, puts his feet on his highly polished desk or spits quickly at a receptacle behind his desk. Politicans have speculated many hours on whether this man who never ran for an office might be persuaded to try. His name was kicked around for months when, early in the war, Roosevelt needed a production czar—not because Douglas knew anything about machine tools or airplanes, but because he was a tough, action-minded administrator who could also see beyond his nose.

The bullish feeling about Douglas' vote-getting ability was reduced to a definite plan during the 1944 Democratic National Convention in Chicago when Franklin Roosevelt sent word that if he couldn't have Henry Wallace as his running mate he would accept Douglas or Senator

Harry Truman. The senator's name was seized eagerly by his fellow Missourian Robert Hannegan, Democratic party chairman, who pushed it through to victory. Douglas' political appeal was not tested and therefore was not dimmed. The man who might have been President, upon Roosevelt's death, went on reading petitions for certiorari as if nothing had happened.

But the man who did get the job had not forgotten Douglas. Early in 1946, when Harold Ickes left the Department of Interior in a huff, Truman called the associate justice to the White House for an hour's chat and an offer of the Cabinet post. Why Douglas chose to stay on the bench is not known—the Interior job seemed a natural for his western interest—but it is known that one of the subjects discussed in the President's office was the need for getting the message of democracy to millions of Chinese.

There was a time when Douglas fans, intent on getting him into politics, argued that he could easily be replaced on the Court. The reasoning, which was intended as no slur on his Court work, was true in a general sort of way so long as it was a matter of having Roosevelt appoint a successor to the bench. However, when Truman started doing the appointing, it became obvious that the conservative side of the bench was being built up to a point where Douglas would have to stay put or the liberals would be reduced to the status of chronic dissenters.

Thus, it probably will be all or nothing at all for Bill Douglas—if he jumps it will presumably be for big stakes. For a man still in his forties that leaves boundless room for speculation. American politics being what they are, the sky is the limit for a young man who was born in Otter Tail County, bummed his way into the big time, purged Wall Street, was written up flatteringly in the *Saturday Evening Post*, doesn't wear a silk topper to White House receptions for the Court and lights matches by scratching them on the seat of his pants.

CHAPTER XI

Justice with a Union Label

IT IS almost impossible to separate the rise of organized labor from the victorious attack on the old Court, with its high-buttoned thinking and outmoded economics. The same forces caused both reactions. Theoretically, the Supreme Court remains aloof from economics, labor and other facts of life. In 1936, however, it was about as aloof from those subjects as a cow browsing on the tracks is aloof from a train speeding down on her.

The analogy is not casual. A railroad engineer does not stop his train for every cow. He often plows through her, or eventually his company sees to it that cows are fenced off the right of way. Social legislation, whether good or bad, could not be held up by the Supreme Court indefinitely. The new administration splattered a few cows, then—in 1937—tried to fence in the remaining ones. Chief Justice Hughes tried to get his herd off the tracks with the art of persuasion, and Roberts finally decided to browse elsewhere.

Douglas was typical of the new blood on the Court. His background was not that of organized labor; he was the product of a generation busily getting on with its affairs. How the Court discarded years of negative law to uphold the constitutionality of the National Labor Relations (Wagner) Act, the Fair Labor Standards (wage-hour) Act and a state minimum-wage law has already been explained.[1] The first two basic laws were approved by the old Court; the third was put into place effortlessly by the new justices. Refinements of these basic decisions, which came in the form of defining terms such as "commerce" and "necessary to production," were nearly always extensions of government authority and hence of labor's gain. Most are of interest only to specialists, but a few—including two major setbacks—are worth brief attention.

Two of labor's greatest victories came in mining cases, in which unions claimed that the wage-hour law required their employers to pay them for time spent in traveling from "portal to portal." That is, they argued that they should not have to spend their own time getting from the company gate to the location of their day's job, often miles away, and back. In the first case, involving the Tennessee Coal, Iron and Railroad Company, the Court ruled that the "work week" should include this type of travel time and the workers had to be paid for it.[2] Two justices noted that they went along with this conclusion only because there was no contrary custom shown in the case. A year later, when a similar case arose from the Jewell Ridge Coal Corporation, a majority of the Court stuck to its previous conclusion, but the two who had spoken separately joined the two previous dissenters because they felt that established custom in the new set of facts clearly showed "work week" to exclude travel time. The majority of five still reasoned that no custom could be used to defeat what it regarded as the terms of the Fair Labor Standards Act.[3] It was an important victory for organized labor, but it split the Court deeply and served as Jackson's chief document in declaring an open feud with Black.

In the 1945 term, when a group of pottery workers from Mt. Clemens, Michigan, sought to come under the generosity of these cases, the Court affirmed the principle of portal-to-portal pay; however, it sent the suit back to the district court for an exact determination of how much time was spent in walking from the time clock to the place of work and preparing for the work. In doing so, the Court noted that the rule of *de minimis* (that the courts do not concern themselves with trifles) could be used to eliminate some claims. Within a few months, unions throughout the land had filed suits on the same grounds for more than $5,000,000,000 in back portal-to-portal pay. The huge sum was an exaggerated idea of what the Supreme Court had indicated might be collected, but it was enough to bring editorial denunciation of the Court in nearly every paper.

Perhaps the biggest defeat for labor in the wage-hour field came in a controversy over the system of counting the tips of redcaps at railroad stations.[4] The company required these employees to report each day's take of tips, which was then substracted from the minimum wage required by law and the difference paid as wages. The redcaps argued that tips were given for personal services and the gratuities were their property —not part of their legal wages. The Court decided against the redcaps, holding that tips were part of wages. Black, Douglas and Murphy protested briefly that the statute requires employers, not someone else, to pay the minimum wage and that the majority's decision diverted tips to employers, for whom tippers do not intend them.

A similar setback came when a 5-to-4 Court refused to interpret the Fair Labor Standards Act broadly enough to include a ban on employment of children under sixteen in the Western Union Telegraph Company.[5] The Court was unable to define several key words so as to include the type of work done by messengers, and it was impressed by the fact that Congress had repeatedly refused to pass a child labor law, as such. The minority thought this interpretation to be "far-fetched."

Another defeat for organized labor, not connected with wages or hours, was handed it by a unanimous Court in holding that a union official cannot hide behind the Constitution to keep from producing the union's books for a grand jury.[6] Self-incrimination, the Court decided, is not involved, because no member can be held liable for acts of his organization unless it is proved that he personally authorized or participated in them.

Of the three broad sections of labor law—wage-hour regulation, collective bargaining and picketing—the right to picket is in many ways the most fundamental. It has been found to be deeply rooted in the Constitution (though the word is not mentioned in that document) and does not depend on legislation for its vigor. It is further beyond the reach of shifting tides of legislative opinion than are wage-hour and collective bargaining rights, which the Court merely approved as being within the power of legislatures.

The groundwork for the new Court's expansion of the right of picketing was laid just before any of the present justices joined the Court. In the *Senn* case[7] the old Court split five to four to uphold a Wisconsin law prohibiting injunctions against peaceful picketing and publicizing labor disputes.

Three years later, when only McReynolds was left to dissent, the Court met the issue more directly and answered it more sweepingly. In *Thornhill* v. *Alabama*[8] the Court declared invalid on its face a state law forbidding persons from going near, loitering about or picketing the premises of any other person with the intent of influencing others not to trade with or work for the person complained of. In striking this broad law down, the Court quoted with approval language from the *Senn* case that publicity on the facts of a labor dispute might be guaranteed by the freedom of speech of the Constitution. Typical of the Court's strong feeling on the subject was this sentence:

"Free discussion concerning the conditions in industry and the causes of labor disputes appears to us indispenable to the effective and intelligent use of the processes of popular government to shape the destiny of modern industrial society."

A year later, however, the Court wrote into the law of picketing an important modification: picketing mixed with violence is lifted out of the free speech category sufficiently that states may curb it.[9] In addition to peaceful picketing of three outlets for an unorthodox system of milk sales in Chicago there was evidence of more than fifty instances of window smashing, bombings, wrecked trucks and beatings. A minority of three felt that the peaceful activities could easily be separated from the violent ones for injunction purposes, but a majority felt that a general injunction was warranted.

A year after this *Meadowmoor* decision the Court allowed Texas a curb of another kind.[10] Ritter's Café was picketed, not because of a labor dispute there, but because the owner refused to use union labor on his construction job a mile and a half away. No violence was involved. The Court held that Texas could try to localize disputes by enjoining such picketing without trampling on the right of free speech. A minority of three thought the *Thornhill* case clearly governed the situation, as did the *Swing* case, decided a year before.[11] In the latter the Court nullified the common law policy of Illinois, under which a union was enjoined from picketing a beauty parlor where it had no members but was trying to get some.

In 1943 the Court moved toward a firm position near the *Swing* doctrine, that there need not be an employer-employee relationship in order to invoke the guarantee of free speech.[12] A cafeteria was picketed, even though it had no employees. (The proprietors ran it by themselves.) Ugly words like "unfair" and "Fascist" were hurled, but the Court found that they did not approach violence and voted unanimously for the union, setting aside an injunction.

These cases, one might say, merely enable unions to get up to the line of scrimmage. Another group of decisions lays down the rules of collective bargaining. Once a majority has been established the Court has protected it from attempts by employers to erode away its power or authority.[13] In the *J. I. Case* decision[14] the Court found that an employer cannot defeat collective bargaining by signing identical contracts with its individual workers. In the *Medo* case[15] the Court struck down an employer's tactic which the NLRB found to be an unfair practice because it went behind the backs of the chosen representatives. The board was sustained in this case, even though the negotiation which got the boss in trouble was initiated by a group of employees who repudiated their union representatives. The newcomers had told the employer they were dissatisfied with the union and would abandon it if their wages were increased. The employer got along with them nicely, then refused to recognize the union which it had once acknowledged as representing the majority.

The May Department Stores got into similar trouble with the NLRB and the Court by applying to the National War Labor Board for permission to raise wages of all employees except those represented by union bargaining representatives.[16] The employer advertised this distinction and tried to justify it on the grounds that the representatives were improperly chosen and were being contested in the courts. The Court upheld the board's finding that the employer presented his petition for higher wages in such a way as to coerce employees, instead of continuing to bargain with them and consult the union on the wage request.

The Court has also protected workers' freedom to bargain through representatives of their own choosing from state attempts to curb it. Florida was rebuffed by the Court for a law requiring that all union business agents pay $1.00, show good moral character and prove United States citizenship for more than ten years. This clash with the Wagner Act was resolved in favor of the federal law.[17]

But the majority by no means has unlimited power in the conduct of its negotiations. The Court has imposed a number of curbs on it in the name of protecting the minority and has put a plague on unions participating in certain types of misconduct in the course of their bargaining. When the Brotherhood of Locomotive Firemen and Enginemen, after becoming the exclusive bargaining agent under Railway Labor Act machinery, agreed with a railroad company to get around the seniority of several Negro employees who were not union members, the Court upheld an injunction filed by a Negro.[18] Under union rules Negroes were not eligible for membership, but the Court held that a union chosen as the bargaining agent must consider requests of non-union members of the craft and give them a chance to be heard.

Also, the New York Civil Rights Law, prohibiting any labor organization from discriminating because of race, color or creed in the admission or treatment of members, was upheld by the Court from attack by the Railway Mail Association.[19] This group argued that it was not a labor organization and that, even if it were, the law was unconstitutional. The Court rejected both ideas, opening up the association's ban on members other than whites or Indians.

These two cases were simple for the Court, but it had a hard time with a third, arising from an NLRB decision.[20] The Court agreed with the board that it is an unfair labor practice for an employer to sign a closed shop agreement with a union when he knows that the union intends to deny membership to a minority of his employees. Had the agreement been allowed to stand, the minority employees would have been thrown out of their jobs by the closed shop, but the Court found a clear obligation on the majority to represent the interests of all employees "fairly and impartially." Four justices dissented, mainly as to the interpretation of facts but also to insist that Congress had given the board no power to supervise union membership.

The most important instance in which the Court looked at violence as an abrogation of rights under the Wagner Act came in 1939, when seven of the old justices remained.[21] Significantly, the first two newcomers—Black and Reed—dissented. In the *Fansteel* case the employer had discharged all men participating in a bitter sit-down strike (two battles with police) and refused to recognize the union after regaining possession of the factory. The Court reversed the NLRB order for reinstatement of the strikers, even though the strike had been brought on by unfair labor practices and some of the strikers had been re-employed after the violence.

Two years later the new majority was in the saddle but the Court ruled that the NLRB had no power to order reinstatement of seamen who had been discharged for peacefully striking while under shipping articles, action which technically made them guilty of mutiny, even though their ship was tied up to a dock.[22] A minority of four justices felt that the misconduct in this case did not put it in the *Fansteel* category.

Other controversial labor cases are those trying to trap unions in the antitrust laws. Some of these suits were brought by outraged employers, but some were prosecuted by the Department of Justice, particularly under Thurman Arnold, who cared more about the existence of restraint of trade than about who caused it. Of the four noteworthy decisions in this category, that in the Apex case[23] will set the legal stage, as well as illustrate how the Court is certain to be cuffed politically no matter which way it turns.

In May of 1937, when only eight employees of the Apex Hosiery Company were union members, a demand for a closed shop was served on the firm by the president of the union and numerous brethren from near-by struck hosiery factories. Refusal of the demand was met by a sit-down strike, along with considerable violence and damage. For six weeks strikers refused to let the company ship the 130,000 dozen pairs of hose on hand; a jury awarded the employer damages, which amounted to $711,932.55 when trebled by the Sherman Act provisons.

At the Supreme Court, where most of organized labor filed briefs in behalf of the hosiery workers, the issue centered on interpretation of the Sherman and Clayton acts. The former states that "every contract, combination in the form of trust or otherwise, or conspiracy, in restraint of trade or commerce among the several States or with foreign nations is hereby declared to be illegal." It sounded simple enough—80 per cent of the hosiery would have been shipped in interstate commerce.

But the union argued that Congress intended to exclude labor from the Sherman Act by later passing the Clayton Act. The Court, through Stone, answered that for thirty-two years it has held that the Sherman Act embraces labor unions "to some extent and in some circumstances."

Precedents were then cited to show that labor was brought under the act by the Court whenever it restrained commercial competition in the marketing of goods, but not when a local strike merely resulted in the stoppage of goods in interstate commerce. The Sherman terms meant, Stone wrote, what they had meant in the common law, where striking was not regarded as a conspiracy to restrain trade. In fact, the subsequent Clayton Act states that "the labor of a human being is not a commodity or article of commerce." Finally, the Court ruled that "restraints not within the Act, when achieved by peaceful means, are not brought within its sweep merely because, without other differences, they are attended by violence."

However, Chief Justice Hughes, with McReynolds and Roberts, read the same precedents and came up with an opposite conclusion. "There was plainly a conspiracy here," wrote the chief, citing particularly the Court's decisions upholding the Wagner Act for preventing interruptions of interstate commerce.

Thus, organized labor clearly reaped a gain from the new personnel on the Court. Had the Nine Old Men still been sitting, a majority would have upheld the $700,000 fine against one union for stopping the flow of goods by striking—and the Wagner Act decisions might well have been the deciding factor against the labor organizations who hailed the act as labor's Magna Carta.

A year later the Court was presented with a somewhat similar legal mess but a factual variation—this time it was a jurisdictional feud between the carpenters and the machinists of the American Federation of Labor.[24] The scene was a brewery; the action involved a bitter fight over which union would install some machinery. The carpenters were beaten but called a strike, picketed and called on all good union carpenters to stop buying Anheuser-Busch beer. The Department of Justice brought a criminal case under the Sherman Act. The Court decided that this type of prosecution had been specifically lifted from the Sherman Act by the Clayton Act, read in conjunction with the Norris-LaGuardia Act's extension of immunity from injunctions in labor disputes "regardless of whether or not the disputants stand in the proximate relation of employer and employee."

Government attempts to crack these situations were sometimes repulsed by mere citation of this *Hutcheson case*,[25] but finally a big change came in the *Allen Bradley* case.[26] This time the Court caught a union in the Sherman Act because it combined with businessmen to violate the act. The union had signed agreements with electrical contractors and manufacturers in the New York City area by which it agreed not to work on electrical goods shipped in from outside the city, while the employer groups agreed to buy and sell only from local firms in that business. It was an outright attempt to create more business and more jobs—at higher prices and wages. The scheme worked very well until an outside manufacturer took his objections to the Supreme Court. The justices could find nothing in the books to indicate that Congress intended to exempt unions from the antitrust laws when they combined with businessmen to violate those laws.

Yet the same day the Court was on labor's side in a modification of the old routine. A group of AF of L trucking unions, culminating an old grudge against a trucking company, refused to let its employees join the union, then got the company's business cut off by putting pressure on its best customers. The unions were strong and operated under closed shops; the trucking firm was practically driven out of business.[27] A five-man majority, led by Black, ruled that the Sherman Act did not apply because there is nothing illegal about a union's refusing to work for an employer. The angry minority felt that this was not a mere withholding of work (the trouble came when the union blamed the company for the death of a member) and failed to see the difference between this case and the *Allen Bradley* situation for using businessmen in their restraint of trade.

A similar kind of reasoning, applied to a different law a few years before, left the Court with all kinds of brickbats in its chambers. Under the federal Antiracketeering Act of 1934, the government had prosecuted teamsters in New York City for requiring outside truckers to hire a union member upon entering the city or pay up to $10 for a "standby" teamster. The object was ostensibly to better working conditions in that area, but it looked like a racket to Uncle Sam, especially in those instances when the truck owners paid the fee but refused the proffered services.

But the Antiracketeering Act was not that simple. The Court reviewed its history and found that Congress did not intend to include ordinary labor union activities.[28] In fact, Congress exempted "the payment of wages by a bona-fide employer to a bona-fide employee." Hinting at the reprehensibility of the union practice, the Court felt bound to throw out the suit because the union was engaging in legitimate activities. Also, the Court rejected the argument that truck drivers entering New York paid the money for protection rather than for work. The teamsters, it noted, were ready to work if wanted.

The Court had similar trouble with the federal Kickback Act of 1934, making it unlawful to induce any person employed on a project financed by the United States to give up any part of the compensation to which he is entitled. The Court unanimously sustained the conviction of a project foreman who forced men under him to kick back part of their pay or lose their jobs, even though the foreman argued that the act applied only against employers.[29] However, the Court refused to extend coverage of the act to four officials of the Hod Carriers Union who were indicted for pocketing installments on initiation fees.[30] The case arose from a big wartime construction job on which the Hod Carriers had a closed shop agreement. The officers collected $5.00 a week from new employees as part payments on their initiation fees. Failure to pay resulted in being discharged. The officers got in trouble because they did not report the many payments made by men who left the project before completing membership requirements. The Court reviewed the history of the act and concluded that it was aimed at extortion by contractors. "There is nothing in the legislative history to support the thesis that the statute was intended to affect legitimate union activities," said the Court. Embezzlement and failure to obey union rules are something else, it added. Frankfurter, Stone and Burton, however, felt that the word "whoever" clearly snared union leaders.

The decision typifies the new Court's approach to labor cases—it may not have been right, but it was not wrong. The majority cited ample logic to support its feeling that Congress intended no such use of the Kickback Act, yet it could as easily have said that the single word "whoever" included the crooked bosses of the closed shop union. Instead, it chose to find that Congress did not intend to cover "legitimate" union activity.

One might conclude from a number of such cases that the present Court is weighted with former lawyers for unions, but there is only one justice (Black) who would remotely fit into that category. Rather, most of the present justices have arrived at their guardianship of organized labor by ideological processes. The Court is in no sense a partisan body on which are members of interested pressure groups. There is no farmer, worker, businessman or banker—as such. (That Presidents have consciously placed there one Jew and one Catholic is beside the present point.)

The man who wrote the opinion that protected the four hod carriers from the Kickback Act was Frank Murphy, never a union member, though often a public official in places where labor counted heavily, quantitatively and qualitatively. His most famous experience with organized labor—settling the Michigan sit-down strikes of 1937—gave him a big headache and came close to ruining his career, but he is one of the majority of the modern Court which gives organized labor the corners of home plate.

CHAPTER XII

Justice Tempered with Murphy

IF ONE were out to do a smear job on a Supreme Court justice, Frank Murphy would be the best target. In his fifty-six varied and colorful years, all but three of them in the public service since adulthood, Murphy made himself as vulnerable as any politician does. But on top of that he opened himself to the type of gossipy anecdote that always seems to surround bachelors more than married men. When, in January of 1940, he took his famous bushy red eyebrows up to the mahogany bench, Murphy became the butt of many stories, both idle and productive.

The case against Frank Murphy might start appropriately with the remark passed by a Court attaché after hearing the freshman justice read his first opinion rather clumsily: "Mr. Justice Huddleson has just handed down his first opinion." Few wanted to think that he had written the document himself; Huddleson was his law clerk. Also, the story got around that the new justice at first wanted a law dictionary beside him on the bench so he could look up the technical terms.

From this line of thinking it was logical that rumor should mention Murphy for any number of jobs off the Court. No one wanted to believe that he belonged there and his restless nature kept the story factory grinding out new jobs for the Michigan New Dealer. One day he would be special envoy to India, then he'd be running the War Department, then he'd be about to return to the attorney generalship, after which he'd be reported in the military machine headed for the fallen Philippines, or returning to run for governor of Michigan.

For a year or two the stories were plausible; Murphy really grated under the annoying, petty decisions always tossed the freshman. Then seniority came to his aid in the form of a couple of controversial issues with real meat in them for the Irishman's fervor. The causes of safeguarding jury procedure, striking down the third degree and defending religious liberty seized him almost all at once. From that time on,

Murphy turned his attention to making his saucy critics eat crow—and a very large portion of crow he has fed them since.

But the case against Murphy took a more personal form. Pictures of him riding horseback with a girl much his junior, soon after his Washington arrival in January of 1939 touched off an examination of his private affairs that has really never ceased, though it has let up considerably.

Another source of suspicion has been the justice's life-long abstinence from alcohol and nicotine. The Washington press corps long ago turned cynical on politicians who claim no vices, and when Murphy started buttonholing some of them to note that he used neither of these two stimulants his virtue took on a phony aura. The Murphy ban on tobacco and liquor are genuine articles, however, though the bachelor does *hold* a cocktail glass occasionally to avoid offending some of the many hostesses who put him on their social lists.

A case of vanity has clouded many persons' interpretation of the man Murphy, not only by creating suspicion but by building up such a contrast with his ultrahumble legal opinions in behalf of the underdog. His conversation is a nervously fervid repetition of the theme of Frank Murphy. Friends say he sees himself as a man of destiny, and he has been known to ask if a man by the name of Murphy could ever be President.

His inability to settle down to a trot has made it hard for contemporary historians, such as newspapermen, to write a normal story about the man, all of which is compounded by the semblance of truth in the lofty sentiment of a gilt-framed motto which was on the mantel of his attorney general's office. It was entitled THE PENALTY OF LEADERSHIP, and starts as follows: "In every field of human endeavor he that is first must perpetually live in the white light of publicity." The white light has been strong for his eyes.

Since Frank Murphy's birth, at Harbor Beach, Michigan, on April 13, 1890, his career has followed the traditional pattern of American politics. But if his advancement in jobs was conventional, the way in which he conducted the duties of office was not. His party label was always Democrat, but often it might as well have been Republican, for he pursued his course quite independently of any machine concept—either good or bad.

Murphy's undergraduate and legal education was completed at the University of Michigan just in time for three years' practice before World War I, in which he was a captain of infantry with the American Expeditionary Forces. Twenty-three years later, just after Pearl Harbor, Murphy renewed his military career in a most unique manner. Like some of his brethren on the Court, Murphy had found it hard to read hoary precedents after the world was set on fire, and he even wanted to resign. Had he done so, there would have been little criticism. Instead, however, he went back to the Army as a trainee in the armored forces, drawing down his $20,000 Supreme Court pay while holding the rank of lieutenant colonel, and all for no perceivably good reason.

When the Court was hastily summoned from its collective vacation to hear the final appeal of the eight Nazis who landed one night in a rubber boat to sabotage American production, Lieutenant Colonel-Associate Justice Murphy came bounding back from camp, but sat only long enough to disqualify himself in the case. The act annoyed officialdom considerably—Attorney General Francis Biddle had to issue a press release denying that his department had rendered an opinion on the legality of Murphy's dual role—but it pleased society circles. Igor Cassini, then gossip columnist for the Washington *Times-Herald*, drooled:

"Going without sleep for three days, using a tank as a table for meals, drilling, driving tanks at night without lights, enduring heat and rain—none of this bothered Frank Murphy. When exhausted, he went to his cot in the field. He felt as comfortable there, he said, as in his hotel room here. By the time he comes back Justice Murphy will be a perfectly trained officer in mechanized warfare. Whenever he wishes, he will be able to discard the robe of an associate justice for the grim outfit of a warrior. Yes, we think that Frank Murphy is a fine justice, a fine soldier. And, more than anything else, a fine American."

Though some were concerned with Murphy's voluntary destruction of the independence of the judiciary, the Army didn't go so far with its training of soldier Murphy that it got him to vote the GI line in cases before the Court later. On the contrary, he later blasted the military position with verbal blockbusters.

So much for the military digression. The day Murphy was released from World War I he was sworn in as assistant district attorney in Detroit, from which post he prosecuted and won many cases, including a whopping war fraud. Then, from 1920 to 1923, he resumed private practice with the prominent firm of Monaghan and Monaghan until election to recorders court, where he served six years, including a re-election.

The foundation of Frank Murphy's good government record was laid in this court. When he took office, Detroit jail cells bulged with 617 prisoners awaiting trial; when Murphy left office he was proud to say that only twenty-one were waiting. He set up a bond bureau to shake the unsavory influence out of the jail bond business; he took jail-house psychiatry out of politics and put in on a scientific basis; and he installed a merit system for probation officers, men who got lots of work during his term of office.

Probably Murphy's most sweeping change was to create a sentencing board. Instead of handing down a sentence that he personally might think reasonable, he called in a sociologist and a psychologist to go over each convicted man's record, after which Judge Murphy, a mere lawyer, passed sentence.

From 1930 to 1933, Murphy served the automobile city as its mayor, and its good mayor, during a period of extreme depression in autos and everything else. In 1933 he called a meeting of mayors throughout the country, an idea for which he was rewarded by being elected first head of the United States Conference of Mayors.

About this time the name of Frank Murphy was high on Franklin D. Roosevelt's list. Of course it had never hurt Murphy's relationship with the White House to have found a dignified job (city comptroller) for Mrs. Roosevelt's hapless brother, Hall Roosevelt. There is good evidence that Mrs. R. was convinced, as well, that Murphy was a twenty-four-carat liberal. Be that as it may, Congress heard one day that Mayor Murphy had been nominated governor general of the Philippine Islands.

The Philippines left a deep imprint on Murphy. Ever since his three years there as top United States authority, Murphy has taken on a glow in discussing the accomplishment of rough democracy for that stepchild of Uncle Sam's. He loved the climate, the people and the life; he was in on the first Philippine election, then was appointed first United States high commissioner to the Islands.

It was now 1936, making Murphy forty-six years old. He had established his vote-getting ability and had pleased the administration in many ways. It was decided to call him home to run for the governorship of Michigan, which he won just in time to put him in one of the hottest seats a governor ever sat in—the new governor had to figure out what to do in the great sit-down strikes of 1937.

Because Murphy refused to dispatch his state troopers to rout the workers out of the company plants, he was roundly damned as an enemy of private property, an ancient legal concept; but he cemented his friendship with organized labor. And when the dust had settled he received letters of gratitude from Alfred P. Sloan, Jr., of General Motors, and Harry Bennett, of Ford, as well as laudatory editorials from the Detroit papers. About three years later, after he had been confirmed by the Senate without a hearing for the Supreme Court, Murphy requested a public hearing at which he defended his handling of the sit-down strikes.

But before his elevation to the Court, Murphy's record in Michigan had pleased President Roosevelt enough to win him an appointment as attorney general of the United States. The voters of Michigan had not been so pleased; they had defeated Murphy for re-election, though the issues were too complex to be hung entirely around Murphy's neck.

Murphy went right to work in the Department of Justice. He gathered a young, energetic and high-caliber staff of top assistants and started putting out front-page stories so fast that his press conferences rated up with Roosevelt's and Secretary Ickes' in popularity.

On the administrative side, he brought closer co-operation between his department and the far-flung federal district attorneys, appointed a committee to study bankruptcy laws, speeded the appointment of judges and asked Congress to put all 992 United States deputy marshals under civil service. However, his rank-and-file employees were glad to see him leave because of several old maidish rules he started around the building, such as a ban on private phone calls.

He not only retained the services of chief G-man J. Edgar Hoover but started whipping around the country with the supersleuth and being seen with him in Manhattan night spots. The association was more than social—Murphy started prosecuting the erstwhile sacred cows of the Democratic party who were vulgarly known as "political bosses." Murphy moved in on the remnants of the Huey Long machine and started the Kansas City boss, Tom Pendergast, on his road to prison—all to the horror of the party regulars who started thinking of him as an ingrate. Certainly the Pendergast convictions alienated a Missouri politician by the name of Truman. With less controversy, Murphy successfully prosecuted Moses Annenberg and Judge Martin Manton.

It probably can't be proved, but all indications are that Murphy was ready to probe Democratic Ed Kelly, in Chicago, and Frank Hague, in Jersey City, when his pipeline to the White House started running poison. Whether he was "kicked upstairs" to the Supreme Court because he couldn't be controlled, or whether—as some say—he had "loused up" the Department of Justice will be debated for some time. However, Murphy has never been in doubt. Nor is there much doubt that his old pals of the White House inner circle shed few tears over his departure from the prosecutor's role.

It should not be inferred, however, that Murphy used his aluminum-trimmed office for a big witch hunt. On the contrary, one of his proudest accomplishments was the creation in his department of a civil rights unit. Though the unique office operated on a starvation budget—and still does—it gathered information on violations of personal liberties and actually obtained a few convictions on peonage and other unlawful oppressions.

Stripped of eccentricities and gossip, Murphy's term as attorney general pretty well bore out the motto, albeit a corny one, which governed Murphy's thirteen months there: "Speak softly and hit hard." If he gained no great reputation as a lawyer, it is partly because the attorney generalship is only partly a legal job. An attorney general who kept his eye on nothing but the law would not do justice to his job, one might say, for the work also involves great discretion in delicate matters affecting many lives. The Frank Murphy who was to move on up to the Court was an emotional man who also was a lawyer. As he said in closing his last press conference before joining the Court: "Yes, I've plenty of feelings—How's an Irishman going to get on without feelings?"

Among Mr. Justice Murphy's feelings the most interesting come under the heading of religion—Catholic denomination. It has long been an unwritten law that the Supreme Court membership include a Catholic and a Jew, a fact that helped elevate Murphy when Pierce Butler died. The fact alone that Murphy fills the "Catholic seat" on the bench makes a look at his religion legitimate, but the amazingly blunt manner in which Catholic Justice Murphy has defended the right of other groups to try to destroy his own church makes it imperative.

A former high official of the Department of Justice put Murphy in character with this remark to a friend: "If the President appoints Murphy to the Supreme Court he will have achieved his Supreme Court Plan, because when Murphy goes on the Court so do the Father and the Son and the Holy Ghost." At a press conference three days after his nomination to the Court, Murphy himself spoke of the high tribunal as the "Great Pulpit." When he was sworn in at the White House he brought along a Bible given him by his mother and which he keeps at his bedside wrapped in a towel to preserve it from dog-earing. Murphy took the oath with the Bible opened to the book of Wisdom: "Love justice, you that are the judges of the earth. Think of the Lord in goodness, and seek him in simplicity of heart."

It was after he completed the ceremony by kissing the Bible that a relative was quoted as saying: "Frank looks more like Christ every day." As a matter of fact the justice does have a Christlike appearance in his pensive moments. A reporter once put it a little more crudely in describing the justices after their return from the 1941 vacation, when he said that Murphy looked like a fighting angel of the Lord with a terrific sunburn.

An archbishop of his own faith refers to communicant Murphy as "a lay bishop," and a fellow Catholic who was one of Murphy's best friends in politics has called him "the modern counterpart of the fighting priests of the middle ages." Describing Murphy's boldness in prosecuting political bigwigs, another reporter remarked that he takes long chances but talks to God first.

The fact that many Catholics see him as a renegade giving aid to sects who would tear down the Catholic church only makes Murphy more zealous in his fight for freedom of all religions, which ultimately, he feels, does his own faith more good than opening the door for legal bigots and political persecutors of minorities. The extent to which he is establishing his point in the Court could hardly be illustrated more soundly than by the wholly sympathetic remark of another justice: "If Frank Murphy is ever sainted it will be by the Jehovah's Witnesses." If that is to be his reward in heaven, it will be enough; but evidence is already abundant that the opinions of Frank Murphy will be required reading at the pearly gates for centuries after individual denominations have had their say on earth.

The Jehovah's Witnesses litigation started back in 1938 when the sect's belligerent methods of soliciting converts from door to door were repulsive to many not only because they were largely based on anti-Catholicism but because they collided with the sovereignty of a nation buckling on its shield for war. A series of colorful cases was touched off when the Minersville (Pennsylvania) school ejected children of the Gobitis family for refusing to salute the American flag, an act which their parents had taught conflicted with their religion. The case appeared in the Supreme Court in 1940,[1] where it was paid little attention except by Harlan Fiske Stone, who dissented vigorously and alone.

The majority opinion was whipped up by Felix Frankfurter in a mood of indignation and wrapped in the flag which the Gobitis kids had not been allowed to salute. The whole matter might have been dropped with the 8-to-1 decision, but Frankfurter's eagle screaming immediately started pricking the consciences of Murphy, Black and Douglas. Murphy, at least, was frankly ashamed of himself and vowed to amend the Court's overzealousness at the first opportunity. When that chance came,[2] Murphy concurred separately. "The right of freedom of thought and of religion as guaranteed by the Constitution against State action includes both the right to speak freely and the right to refrain from speaking at all . . . ," said the devout Catholic.

There were other means used by local authorities for hemming in the doorbell-ringing evangelists, particularly by the use of ordinances against distributing literature without a license. The Court struck these down, but Murphy occasionally felt compelled to write a concurrence. In one such opinion[3] he said that the right to worship freely "extends to the aggressive and disputatious as well as to the meek and acquiescent. The lesson of experience is that—with the passage of time and the interchange of ideas—organizations, once turbulent, perfervid and intolerant in their origin, mellow into tolerance and acceptance by the community, or else sink into oblivion."

Shortly after the licensing cases, the Court decided that not even freedom of religion was enough to make the Witnesses immune from a Massachusetts child labor law under which a Witness was prosecuted for allowing a nine-year-old in her custody to distribute religious literature on the streets.[4] Murphy couldn't go along with the Court. After stating several more technical reasons, he philosophized that "the sidewalk, no less than the cathedral or the evangelist's tent, is a proper place, under the Constitution, for the orderly worship of God."

In the same dissent, Murphy summed up his feelings about the law and the Witnesses as follows: "From ancient times to the present day, the ingenuity of man has known no limits in its ability to forge the weapons of oppression for use against those who dare to express or practice unorthodox religious beliefs. And the Jehovah's Witnesses are living proof of the fact that even in this nation, conceived as it was in the ideals of freedom, the right to practice religion in unconventional ways is still far from secure. Theirs is a militant and unpopular faith, pursued with fanatical zeal. . . . To them, along with other present-day religious minorities, befalls the burden of testing our devotion to the ideals and constitutional guarantees of religious freedoms."

In another case that term[5] Murphy issued what his friends regard as his most noteworthy dissent of the year. A member of the Witnesses, claiming that he was a minister entitled to exemption from active service under the draft laws, was ordered by his board into a conscientious objectors' camp. Because he felt the action of his local board was illegal and arbitrary, the Witness refused to report and was prosecuted criminally. The Court rejected these arguments, but Murphy blew a dignified fuse.

"That an individual should languish in prison for five years," he said, "without being accorded the opportunity of proving that the prosecution was based on arbitrary and illegal administrative action is not in keeping with the high standards of our judicial system. . . . The law knows no finer hour than when it cuts through formal concepts and transitory emotions to protect unpopular citizens against discrimination and persecution. I can perceive no other course for the law to take in this case."

The first six Murphy years on the Court saw the Irishman rise from an extra-long period of hazing to a continuing period of great fertility. He wound up the 1944 term having written eighteen majority opinions, six concurring ones and thirteen dissents—a total of thirty-seven documents and somewhat of a record. He developed a cross-fertilization of genuine literature with cold legal procedent that puts some of his opinions on that high pedestal with Holmes, Brandeis and Cardozo. It is too early finally to rank the contemporaries with such bench marks as Holmes in total legal thinking, but Murphy's style of opinion lends itself to the quotation of phrases, much as Holmes' did, and his decisions are similarly based on human rights.

Murphy's written opinions cover, besides religion, many subjects, though he is by far most eloquent when confined to guaranteeing fair trials, protecting minority groups from technicalities, defending freedom of the press and interpreting labor legislation broadly. Excerpts from some of these furnish a pattern from which Murphy can be placed in relation to his colleagues and from which the Murphy vote on a given case can be fairly well predicted.

In the department of assuring fair trials, the Court as a whole has been definitely liberal to defendants, but Murphy often goes even further. In protesting the use of a confession obtained from an Oklahoma Negro twelve hours after the third degree had been applied, Murphy based his opinion[6] on opening his eyes to "the realities of human nature."

"An individual," he wrote, "does not that easily forget the type of torture that accompanied (his) previous refusal to confess, nor does a person . . . so quickly recover from the gruesome effects of having had a pan of human bones placed on his knees in order to force incriminating testimony from him."

Murphy's dissent in another criminal case[7] took note of remarks by the prosecutor which hinted at an appeal to racial and religious bigotry; then he laid upon judges a duty beyond that of being a mere arbiter: "Instead of an attitude of indifference and carelessness in such matters, Judges and officers of the court should take the initiative to create an atmosphere free from undue passion and emotionalism."

Murphy again dissented when a majority of his colleagues freed on technicalities three local police officers who had beaten a Negro to death while in their custody.[8] The justice felt that the policemen's own consciences, if not the Criminal Code and the Constitution, told them they had no right to take a life.

"The significant question, rather," according to the former recorders court judge, "is whether law enforcement officers and those entrusted with authority shall be allowed to violate with impunity the clear constitutional rights of the inarticulate and the friendless."

In another Negro case,[9] Murphy dissented from the majority conclusion that Texas had not gone too far in hand picking the jury that convicted a Negro to die. One Negro had been deliberately put on the jury panel to get around earlier Court decisions against their outright exclusion from juries. However, Murphy wanted to carry the mandate one step further—from exclusion to limitation. There would be absolutely no consideration of color in a Murphy jury panel.

The labor relations opinions of the justice who was governor of Michigan during the sit-down strikes began with the widely cited case of *Thornhill* v. *Alabama*[10] in 1939, his first term. Speaking for the Court, Murphy knocked out an Alabama antipicketing law which was so broad as to include a ban on nearly everything. Murphy nullified the law on the grounds of its abrogation of free speech; and as he was often to do later, refused to confine his examination of the case to its immediate, narrow issue. Rather, he looked ahead for the continuing impact of the statute in question.

"The existence of such a statute," he warned, "which readily lends itself to harsh and discriminatory enforcement by local prosecuting officials, against particular groups deemed to merit their displeasure, results in a continuous and pervasive restraint on all freedom of discussion that might reasonably be regarded as within its purview."

Three other major labor decisions in which Murphy spoke for the Court involved "portal-to-portal" pay. The question was whether certain kinds of workers are entitled, by wage-hour legislation, to wages for time spent getting to and from the actual location of their work. The affirmative answers in all cases[11] are not here so important as is the way in which Murphy approached them. The issue, he said at the outset, "can be resolved only by discarding formalities and adopting a realistic attitude, recognizing that we are dealing with human beings and with a statute that is intended to secure to them the fruits of their toil and exertion. . . . We are not here dealing with mere chattels or articles of trade but with the rights of those who toil. . . . (The) statute must not be interpreted or applied in a narrow and grudging manner."

However, Murphy does not always vote on the union side. For a unanimous Court he held that union officials must open their official books in spite of the constitutional privilege against self-incrimination,[12] and he went beyond the Court in ordering a railway union to exercise its powers on behalf of all members, including Negroes.[13] In a separate concurrence, Murphy fairly screamed:

"The utter disregard for the dignity and the well-being of colored citizens shown by this record is so pronounced as to demand the invocation of constitutional condemnation. To decide the case and to analyze the statute solely upon the basis of legal niceties, while remaining mute and placid as to the obvious and oppressive deprivation of constitutional guarantees, is to make the judicial function something less than it should be."

Some of Murphy's most strongly worded opinions have been generated by his concern for the rights of the foreign born, citizen and alien alike. When, for example, the Court set aside the denaturalization proceedings against German-born Carl Wilhelm Baumgartner,[14] Murphy wrote a separate concurrence for three other justices in which he said, in part:

"American citizenship is not a right granted on a condition subsequent that the naturalized citizen refrain in the future from uttering any remark or adopting an attitude favorable to his orginal homeland or those there in power, no matter how distasteful such conduct may be to most of us. He is not required to imprison himself in an intellectual or spiritual strait-jacket. . . ."

In the deportation case against Australian-born Harry Bridges, CIO leader, Murphy wrote another concurrence which went beyond the Court's setting aside of the deportation.[15] The entire opinion is a masterful attack on, first, the broad statute relied upon by the government in trying to deport Bridges and, second, on the persecution of a single man. The opening remarks must suffice to show how Catholic Murphy felt about deporting the alleged Communist affiliate:

"The record in this case will stand forever as a monument to man's intolerance of man. Seldom if ever in the history of this nation has there been such a concentrated and relentless crusade to deport an individual because he dared to exercise the freedom that belongs to him as an individual and that is guaranteed to him by the Constitution."

Again, in the denaturalization case against an avowed Communist, William Schneiderman, Murphy upheld the new citizen as having rights demanding delicate consideration.[16] This time speaking for the Court (six to three), Murphy put the case of the defendant in perspective, as follows:

"We are directly concerned only with the rights of this petitioner . . . , but we should not overlook the fact that we are a heterogeneous people. In some of our larger cities a majority of the school children are the offspring of parents only one generation, if that far, removed from the steerage of the immigrant ship, children of those who sought refuge in the new world from the cruelty and oppression of the old. . . . Here they have hoped to achieve a political status as citizens in a free world in which men are privileged to think and act and speak according to their convictions. . . ."

But it was in wartime Japanese relocation cases that Murphy really hit the forty-four-foot ceiling of the chamber. In the *Korematsu* case,[17] after the majority had sustained the 1942 exclusion of all persons of Japanese ancestry, from the West Coast, citizen and noncitizen alike, Murphy protested that the "exclusion goes over 'the very brink of constitutional power' and falls into the ugly abyss of racism." After granting that military authorities might act on the basis of necessity, Lieutenant Colonel Murphy reviewed the military evidence and decided it was snafu.

"Justification for the exclusion," he found, "is sought mainly upon questionable racial and sociological grounds not ordinarily within the realm of expert military judgment, supplemented by certain semi-military conclusions drawn from an unwarranted use of circumstantial evidence. . . . I dissent, therefore, from this legalization of racism."

In the companion case,[18] in which the Court ordered the release from a relocation center of a Japanese-American whose loyalty had been established, Murphy concurred briefly. The detention, he said, was "not only unauthorized by Congress or the Executive but is another example of the unconstitutional resort to racism inherent in the entire evacuation program."

Murphy's high blood pressure had hardly subsided from these cases when, early in 1946, he wrote long blasts in the *Yamashita*, *Homma* and Hawaiian military law cases. While the Court refused to set aside the death sentence of Japanese General Yamashita, imposed hastily by an Army commission, Murphy dissented at white heat that there had been no fair trial.[19]

"The immutable rights of the individual," Murphy wrote, ". . . belong not alone to the members of those nations that excel on the battlefield or that subscribe to the democratic ideology. . . . No court or legislature or executive, not even the mightiest army in the world, can ever destroy them. . . . To conclude otherwise is to admit that the enemy has lost the battle but has destroyed our ideals."

The next week when the Court refused even to review the similar sentence of General Homma, leader of the Bataan death march, Murphy dissented:[20]

"This nation's very honor, as well as its hopes for the future, is at stake. Either we conduct such a trial as this in the noble spirit and atmosphere of our Constitution or we abandon all pretense to justice, let the ages slip away and descend to the level of revengeful blood purges. A procession of judicial lynchings without due process of law may now follow."

Murphy voted with the Court in declaring that civilian courts, rather than military tribunals, should have been allowed to dispense justice in Hawaii before the end of the war; but he filed a nine-page opinion of his own in behalf of applying the Bill of Rights to the legal issue.[21] Excerpts illustrate his anger:

"Abhorrence of military rule is ingrained in our form of government. Those who founded this nation knew full well that the arbitrary power of conviction and punishment for pretended offenses is the hallmark of despotism. . . . From time immemorial despots have used real or imagined threats to the public welfare as an excuse for needlessly abrogating human rights. . . . Civil liberties and military expediency are often irreconcilable. It does take time to secure a grand jury indictment, to allow the accused to procure and confer with counsel, to permit the preparation of a defense, to form a petit jury, to respect the elementary rules of procedure and evidence and to judge guilt or innocence according to accepted rules of law. But experience has demonstrated that such time is well spent."

Another Murphy obsession is freedom of the press. He enjoys all such cases, but he took particular delight in voting with the five-man majority which upheld the Los Angeles *Times* against a contempt citation.[22] The newspaper, trying to discount the antilabor editorial which California courts decided would influence the dispensation of justice, argued that it was the paper's consistent editorial policy. One of its exhibits in this novel argument was an editorial bitterly attacking Frank Murphy for his conduct in the sit-down strikes.

In two other cases involving the commercial distribution of ideas, Murphy crossed swords with both the majority and the administration. In the government's antitrust suit against the Associated Press,[23] which the Court upheld on the basis of a look at the AP's bylaws, Murphy dissented on two grounds.

First, he felt, that the bylaws merely secured a fair competitive advantage to the business and should not be struck down without more evidence. Second, he felt the precedent to be dangerous to freedom of the press in general.

"The tragic history of recent years," according to Murphy, "demonstrates far too well how despotic governments may interfere with the press and other means of communication in their efforts to corrupt public opinion and to destroy individual freedom."

Similarly, when the Federal Communication Commission's regulations cracking down on chain network broadcasting reached the Court, Murphy dissented from the Court's approval of the far-reaching regulations.[24] He felt that his brethren of the majority had gratuitously bestowed upon the FCC power which Congress had not granted. In arriving at that belief, Murphy pointed out the importance of radio as a rival of the press and the pulpit in disseminating information and asked, therefore, that the case be approached "with more than ordinary restraint and caution."

Actually, both the AP and radio dissents were motivated more by Murphy's fear of censorship and his dislike for bureaucratic excesses than by any expert reading of the laws involved. That is not to reflect on his integrity as a judge, for there was plenty of room for argument on both sides of both cases; it is only a comment on what makes Murphy tick.

This same suspicion of bureaucratic meddling has led Murphy to strike down laws solely because they were vague, failing to set standards for officials acting under them. Also, it accounted for his dissent, with Roberts, in a little-noticed case[25] involving the secretary of labor's administration of the Walsh-Healey Act, which requires persons supplying goods to the government to meet certain labor conditions. Secretary Perkins issued a subpoena to force the examination of the Endicott Johnson Corporation books. The company fought the subpoena to the Supreme Court, where it lost, but not until Murphy had said the following about administrative agencies:

"Yet, if they are freed of all restraint upon inquisitorial activities and are allowed uncontrolled discretion . . . to invade private affairs through the use of the subpoena . . . under the direction of well-meaning but over-zealous officials, they may at times become instruments of intolerable oppression and injustice."

To round out Murphy's special interests, it must be noted that he has become quite a writer of opinions in Indian cases, almost invariably upholding the red men against their paleface exploiters, and that Murphy feels strongly in patent law cases that patents are imbued with a great public interest which allows strict regulation.

His up-and-coming specialty, however, is a field in which one might not expect to find the Court's religion expert: the Mann Act for abolishing interstate white-slave traffic. Murphy got into this incongruous situation because he felt the government was not confining its prosecutions to white slavery and was using the statute as a catch-all.

For example, Murphy protested loudly when the Court upheld the Mann Act conviction of one who paid the four-block taxi ride of a voluntary prostitute in the District of Columbia.[26] "The act is applied here," Murphy protested, "not because white slavery is present. . . . Such distortion of the legislative purpose . . . can only serve to subject residents of the District of Columbia to the evils of blackmail and persecution and to punish unjustly those whose immoral acts do not constitute white slavery. No principle of stare decisis and no rule of statute or reason can justify such a result."

Similarly, one of the most novel cases ever to come before the Supreme or any other court found "the fighting angel of the Lord" protecting the proprietors of a Nebraska bawdy house.[27] These characters had been apprehended while crossing a state line on their way with a few of their girls for an annual vacation. Said Justice Murphy, for a straight-faced but not strait-laced majority of the Court: The girls were not transported for "the purpose of prostitution or debauchery" within the meaning of the Mann Act, even though they resumed their trade upon return from the innocent holiday trip.

Two dissents which one would scarcely expect to come from a former attorney general were written by Murphy in the 1939 wire-tapping cases.[28] When evidence gathered by wire tapping was used to turn several defendants into witnesses against others, Murphy protested (for

Stone and Frankfurter, too) that Congress had banned all "use" of such evidence. In the second case, where a detectaphone was held against a wall to record conversations, Murphy was repulsed by the thought that officers should be allowed to go around listening to people.

Murphy believed that the framers of the Bill of Rights would have excluded the modern gadget had they known about it, and said that "science has brought forth far more effective devices for the invasion of a person's privacy than the direct and obvious methods of oppression which were detested by our forebears."

If any justice uses the "gastronomical" approach to decisions—that is, votes by the nausea or pleasure he gets from hearing the case—it is Murphy. His vote can be more nearly predicted than can that of any other justice, which is another way of saying that one can predict which cases will offend Murphy's sensitivities. Some will immediately charge that no one of that description should be on the Supreme Court, but more are inclined to read a particularly lonesome Murphy opinion and comment along this line: "The Court could hardly have voted that way, but it's a good thing to have that opinion on the record."

Sometimes such an observation is a lame apology for the law not being able to face up to the moral considerations of a case—the *Yamashita* case, for example. Murphy can take that kind of criticism; in fact, he thrives on it. His opinions are delivered almost inaudibly and nearly always stop at the name, number and judgment in the case. To sit in the chamber when opinions are being handed down, one would think that Murphy never does anything, but he prefers to concentrate on a written record—written with indelible ink.

CHAPTER XIII

The Right to be Wrong

THOUGH there is not a man on the Supreme Court who was there during World War I, the present justices learned much from that previous experience—much about what *not* to do in wartime. Only part of the ugly cases of war prosecutions in the earlier war reached the highest court, but they were a sorry sample of a democracy at war.

Thanks mainly to the two famous dissenters, Holmes and Brandeis, the former a twice-wounded veteran of the Civil War, the way was pointed for a more enlightened treatment in World War II of those with whom the majority of people and the government disagreed. Supreme Court justices, having emotions, blushed between wars, along with millions of laymen, at the disgraceful chapter in jurisprudence. To put in focus the decisions these latter-day judges handed down during the second war, it is necessary to glance at the precedents which the Nine Young Men could have followed had they ascended the high bench wearing blinders.

In the *Abrams* case[1] five Russian sympathizers distributed 9,000 leaflets proposing strikes in protest against the government's dispatch of troops to Russia in mid-1918, after President Wilson had repeatedly declared that the United States would not interfere in Russia's political development. The authors, isolated New York youth, conceived their pamphlets in a garret and produced their work in a basement; their products seem ridiculous now, but a frenzied government sent them to prison and seven strict constructionists on the Court sustained their convictions.

It remained for Holmes, with Brandeis, to say in defense of the obscure characters: "I think that we should be eternally vigilant against attempts to check the expression of opinions that we loathe and believe to be fraught with death, unless they so imminently threaten immediate interference with the lawful and pressing purposes of the law that an immediate check is required to save the country."

There was not a scrap of evidence of any stoppage of war production, but an even better commentary on the case came later from Secretary of War Newton D. Baker, who said that "the expedition (to North Russia) was nonsense from the beginning," and General William S. Graves, who said: "I was in command of the United States troops sent to Siberia and, I must admit, I do not know what the United States was trying to accomplish by military intervention." The five prisoners were released in November, 1921, on the condition that they return to Russia at their own expense.

In 1920 the Supreme Court got a similar case[2] based on a speech by a Non-Partisan League leader named Gilbert, as unreconciled to the war as were many of his northwestern fellow citizens. Excerpts from his speech give the tone: "We are going over to Europe to make the world safe for democracy, but I tell you we had better make America safe for democracy first. . . . Have you had anything to say as to whether we would go into this war? . . . We were stampeded into this war by newspaper rot to pull England's chestnuts out of the fire for her. . . ."

A majority of seven justices upheld the Minnesota antisedition law, under which Gilbert was convicted, in an opinion which included the following: ". . . every word that he uttered in denunciation of the war was false, was deliberate misrepresentation of the motives which impelled it, and the objects for which it was prosecuted."

Another famous case arose when Victor Berger's *Milwaukee Leader* was banned from the mails under the Espionage Act.[3] Articles in the Socialist paper denounced the draft law as unconstitutional, arbitrary and oppressive, with the implied counsel that it should not be respected or obeyed.

Soldiers in France were represented as becoming insane and being conveyed from the front in long trains of closed cars; the Food Control law was denounced as "Kaisering America." The first fact was later substantiated; the Supreme Court itself had knocked out the Food Control law one week before the Socialist paper denounced it. But only Holmes and Brandeis spoke out against the postmaster general's power to kill publications he did not like.

Perhaps the most ludicrous case[4] was decided in 1925. It involved a left-wing Socialist named Benjamin Gitlow, apprehended for publishing a manifesto so dull as to be nearly unreadable. Tucked into thirty-four pages of boredom was this passage: "Strikes are developing which verge on revolutionary action, and in which the suggestion of proletarian dictatorship is apparent. . . . The mass struggle of the proletariat is coming into being." Then there were scattered calls to the shackled worker for mass strikes.

This was too much for congressional under-the-bed lookers, and an obscure 1902 law against criminal anarchy was clamped on Gitlow. The splinter Socialist put in almost three years at hard labor, Holmes and Brandeis notwithstanding, before Governor Alfred E. Smith pardoned him.

A majority of the human beings on the World War I Court exhibited such frailties that it seemed as if no Court could approach World War II without being determined to protect civil rights from the flame throwers of temporary public opinion. How well did the new Court have its lesson learned?

Three general types of war cases plagued the Court this time: prosecutions of civilians for disloyalty to the United States, conduct of military justice and scrutiny of the emergency powers granted administrative agencies to expedite the war effort. First, the disloyalty of civilians.

One of the first and most impassioned of these tangles involved an admitted German agent by the name of George Sylvester Viereck,[5] writer for the German Library of Information, reporter for German newspapers and author of a bitterly anti-British book. Registration of these connections was duly made by Viereck before Pearl Harbor, under the 1938 law requiring disclosure by all enemy agents of their bosses. In addition, however, Viereck distributed propaganda through, and helped form, the Make Europe Pay War Debts Committee and the Islands for War Debts Committee and propagandized through congressional mailing franks. The Department of Justice, eager to be rid of Viereck, even though there was no law against entertaining his opinions, prosecuted him for failure to disclose more about himself than "author and journalist."

The jury was told by the judge that Viereck could be found guilty even if the propagandizing was on his own behalf, as he claimed. Chief Justice Stone, speaking for the Court in the middle of the war, sided with the venomous Viereck. The law required Viereck to register only his business done for Germany.

The freeing of Viereck was a bitter blow to lawyers for the administration, but a stronger blow came later in Stone's opinion. The chief warmed up on a brief lecture on the Court's place in wartime: ". . . men are not subjected to criminal punishment because their conduct offends our patriotic emotions. . . ." Then his haymaker landed. Well down in Viereck's defense was a complaint that the Department of Justice attorney, in his closing remarks to the jury, sought to arouse passion and prejudice. The attorney, William Powers Maloney, was regarded as an ace prosecutor by the department, and what the chief justice of the United States said about him in the last paragraph shouldn't have happened to a dog.

"He may prosecute with earnestness and vigor—indeed, he should do so," said Stone of Maloney. "But, while he may strike hard blows, he is not at liberty to strike foul ones."

Black and Douglas dissented, first as to the chief's construction of the statute, and, second, as to Maloney. "A prosecutor must draw a careful line," wrote Black. "On the one hand, he should be fair; he should not seek to arouse passion or engender prejudice. On the other hand, earnestness or even a stirring eloquence cannot convict him of hitting foul blows."

The case made hot news copy and editorial writers had great sport sainting or damning Stone or Maloney. Shortly after Stone's punch, Attorney General Biddle shifted Maloney to other work.

In the next session the Court took on its first sedition case of the war,[6] against Elmer Hartzel, an American financial analyst who had lived a normal enough life, including Army duty in World War I, until he wrote a number of prewar scurrilous attacks on the English, the Jews and President Roosevelt. In 1942, Hartzel mailed anonymously about six hundred copies of three articles to widely divergent recipients, ranging from America Firsters to men of the American Legion. Government attorneys particularly jumped on the fact that copies were received by the commanding general of the United States Army Air Forces, a colonel on the General Staff and numerous persons registered under the draft act, such as one twenty-year-old clerk who opened incoming mail at the Lions International office. In addition, envelopes addressed to at least eighteen high-ranking Army officers were found secreted under Hartzel's bathtub.

Behind bars, Hartzel declared that his purpose in writing the articles lay in "the hope that they might tend to create sentiment against war amongst the white races and in diverting the war from them, to unite the white races against . . . the more dangerous enemies, the yellow races."

Concerning himself narrowly with the language of the Espionage Act of 1917, under which Hartzel was arrested, Murphy wrote the Court's opinion reversing Hartzel's conviction. In the first place, Murphy found, there was no evidence from which a jury could find "beyond a reasonable doubt" that Hartzel had *willfully* caused or attempted to cause "insubordination, disloyalty, mutiny, or refusal of duty, in the military or naval forces of the United States" or willfully obstructed the recruitment of armed forces. In the second place, the government did not prove existence of "a clear and present danger" that the activities of Hartzel would bring about the mutiny, etc., that Congress has a right to prevent. Roberts, in a nine-line concurrence, said "there was not sufficient evidence in the case to warrant submission to the jury."

Four justices, however—Reed, Frankfurter, Douglas and Jackson—

believed that the evidence was sufficient. "Papers or speeches may contain incitements," Reed wrote, "for the military to be insubordinate or to mutiny without a specific call upon the armed forces so to act." It is interesting to speculate on what the reasoning of the majority opinion would have been if the majority had been against Hartzel. Could they have said, with four distinguished colleagues to the contrary, that there was no "reasonable doubt" as to Hartzel's guilt? The question illustrates the spot the Court is on when it has to weigh evidence—it is as subject to doubt, reasonable or otherwise, as are juries of laymen.

A similar shortcoming in the evidence was found by the Court in the *Cramer* case, one term later.[7] This time the charge was treason, the only crime defined by the Constitution itself. Treason against the United States, according to the good document "shall consist only in levying war against them, or in adhering to their enemies, giving them aid and comfort." Also, "no person shall be convicted of treason unless on the testimony of two witnesses to the same overt act, or on confession in open court."

Anthony Cramer had been snatched for meeting, drinking and conferring with German saboteurs in a restaurant and keeping $3,600 for them. The Court first held that two witnesses must swear to both overt acts, not merely to one or the other; then it weighed the evidence and found it wanting. There was no two-witness proof of what the saboteurs said, or that Cramer gave them any information, had any to give them, or gave them encouragement or shelter. There wasn't even proof that he paid for their drinks!

Not even a little imagination was allowed to be substituted for the stricture of the Constitution drafted by men who had known so well the charge of treason as a tool against political enemies in the Old World.

Another method used by the administration for getting persons out of the way whose loyalty was heavily doubted was removing the citizenship of those who had obtained naturalization papers. It would have been easy for the Court to uphold this stripping process by reasoning that naturalized citizens have something less than the rights of native-born citizens, but the new Court did it the hard way. The case of Carl Wilhelm Baumgartner, formerly a German, illustrates.[8]

Eight months after this country declared war on Germany and ten years after his naturalization, the government raised the claim that Baumgartner had not truly renounced his allegiance to Germany and never intended to be loyal to his new country. He had been an officer in the German Army in World War I, then became an electrical engineer. Shortly thereafter he was employed by a Kansas City utility company, but employees complained so much about his praise of the

Hitler movement to overthrow the German government that Baumgartner had to be transferred to another section of the plant. Later, he spoke of democracy as a farce, compared Roosevelt unfavorably with Hitler and even aroused complaints from the Sunday school class he taught that he was preaching Nazism. His diary showed that Baumgartner attended one meeting of the German Vocational League, at which the extended arm salute was given, and that he was violently anti-semitic.

Frankfurter, for his brethren, reviewed this evidence and found it fell short of the narrow legal question at issue: regardless of what Baumgartner thought politically after his naturalization, was he disloyal at the time of his oath? Did he get the papers fraudulently? Then Frankfurter, himself a naturalized citizen, repeated earlier Court opinion of the rights of newcomers: "Under our Constitution, a naturalized citizen stands on an equal footing with the native citizen in all respects, save that of eligibility to the Presidency."

One of these prerogatives, he added, is the right to criticize public men and measures— "and that means not only informed and responsible criticism but the freedom to speak foolishly and without moderation." He also pointed out that the country to which Baumgartner gave up allegiance was the Weimar Republic, that Hitler came to power later on.

But Murphy, Black, Douglas and Rutlege weren't quite satisfied, even with this forceful opinion. Murphy, writing for them, thought the issue was simply that the government had failed to meet the standard of proof laid down in the earlier *Schneiderman* case: "clear, unequivocal, and convincing" evidence of obtaining citizenship papers illegally. "With one unimportant exception," the four justices felt, "the Government proved only that [Schneiderman] displayed certain Nazi sympathies and was critical of the United States" several years after his naturalization. The final score: nine to nothing against the government prosecutors.

A more technical though still important group of war cases came to the Court from the legal scramble to give the President and his bureaus the maximum amount of power to act quickly in administering selective service, price control and other wartime laws. In general, the government fared better in its court tests of emergency actions than it did in the loyalty cases.

The keystone of the administration's power to control inflation was set in place by Chief Justice Stone in the *Yakus* case,[9] decided two years after the Emergency Price Control Act was written by Congress. The law was attacked on numerous grounds by a wholesaler of beef who felt that it delegated too much authority to the executive branch of the government and set up such a strict method for appeal that it violated the constitutional provisions for due process of law.

The Court found that the price law, unlike the invalidated NRA, laid down plenty of standards within which its administrators had to stay. The procedural short cuts were legitimately designed to avoid having the country's eighty-five district courts delaying inflation control by handing down eighty-five different interpretations of the law.

Justice Roberts dissented on the grounds that Congress had not placed enough limits on the executive branch, thus unlawfully delegating power; but a more interesting dissent—for studying the new Court—was filed by Rutledge, joined by Murphy. Rutledge, who had then been on the Court only a year, took his brethren of the majority to task because Yakus was denied a chance to attack the wholesale beef ceilings in answer to a criminal prosecution for violating them.

"The procedural pattern is one which may be adapted to the trial of almost any crime," he warned. "Once approved, it is bound to spawn progeny."

Other inflation cases were laid into place around the *Yakus* decision, in which the Court wrote seventy-five pages. Constitutionality of the rent control program was decided the same day by an 8-to-1 vote against Mrs. Kate C. Willingham, of Macon, Georgia.[10]

"We need not determine what constitutional limits there are to price-fixing legislation," the Court decided. "Congress was dealing here with conditions created by activities resulting from a great war effort. A nation which can demand the lives of its men and women in the waging of that war is under no constitutional necessity of providing a system of price control on the domestic front which will assure each landlord a 'fair return' on his property."

Roberts again dissented that no standards had been set by Congress. "Without further elaboration," he wrote, "it is plain that this Act creates personal government by a petty tyrant instead of government by law. . . . I do insist that, war or no war, there exists no necessity, and no constitutional power, for Congress' abdication of its legislative power. . . ."

Two lesser decisions on stabilization were important only for significant dissents filed by Black, Douglas and Murphy in behalf of the government. In the first,[11] a warehouse company tried to avoid price control on the grounds of an exemption in the Price Control Act for "rates charged by any common carrier or other public utility." The state in which it was located, California, had declared warehouses to be public utilities; the majority of the Court agreed that warehouses were therefore exempt. "The war against inflation is a grim affair," three dissenters complained, and "every exception read into the Act creates another point of leakage."

The second case [12] involved an intervention by OPA in a rate hearing before the Public Utilities Commission of the District of Columbia in an effort to keep down the rates of the capital's gas and electric services. The law provided for the intervention and required all such commissions to give OPA a chance to show the relation of proposed changes to inflation. This time, however, OPA tried to broaden the scope of the hearing in order to go behind a sliding-scale system of rate increases the commission had previously set up. Roberts, for the majority, held against OPA; but the trio of dissenters felt the decision allowed commissions "so to shape the issues as to exclude the data most relevant to a determination of whether any rate increase should be allowed," making OPA's right to intervene "an empty right indeed."

A more troublesome area of war powers was served up to the Court in the form of selective service cases. The justices were over draft age, but they were by no means exempt from draft woes. Consider, for example, the legal snafu presented by conscientious objector Whitney Bowles, whose draft board denied him the classification of CO, after which he was charged with violating the draft law for failing to report for induction. Bowles claimed that his denial had been based on a misinterpretation of the law. The prosecutor refused to let him see his selective service file, though required by law to do so. The majority of the Court[13] felt that the undisclosed parts of the file didn't help his case and therefore upheld his conviction, but Jackson and Reed wanted to help him.

"The citizen of necessity has few rights when he faces the war machine," Jackson wrote; but "one of them is the right to know what happened to him and why, as shown by his Selective Service file, even if he is not able to do anything about it." Denying the records to Bowles, Jackson said, "seems to let the prosecution eat its cake and have it too."

In the case of Nick Falbo,[14] who claimed to be a minister of the Jehovah's Witnesses faith, the Court had to deal with one who was classified as a CO, but refused to report for work of national importance. He insisted that his ministerial status exempted him from any kind of service and was sentenced to five years in prison. For the Court, Black held briefly that Falbo should have complied with all orders before going to the courts for relief, that Congress granted no judicial review in advance of service.

Only Murphy dissented, but in more words than the majority used. He noted prejudice against Witnesses by one board member, then pointed out that the war effort doesn't gain by denying examination of the validity of such an order before service. If Falbo won, Murphy reasoned, he shouldn't be in the service anyway; if he lost he would go to prison rather than the Army. Finally, he didn't like the picture of a man languishing in prison for five years without a chance to prove that the prosecution was based on illegal action.

Three months later the Court had to draw the line more clearly in a case almost metaphysical.[15] Arthur Billings, a teacher at the University of Texas, claimed to be a conscientious objector but could not convince his draft board. He resolved not to serve in the Army; but, unlike Falbo, he was determined to exhaust selective service remedies before going to court. Eventually he was called up for induction, reported to an Army camp and was accepted. He then notified officers that he wished to turn himself over to the civilian authorities but an officer read the oath of induction to him and said: "You are in the Army now." He did not take the oath and refused to be fingerprinted, for which he was charged with disobeying a military order. Finally, Billings got a lawyer to file a writ of habeas corpus to get him back under civilian jurisdiction.

The Court reviewed the entire draft process, then decided that the Army couldn't get a man by merely reading the oath of induction to him. The exact moment, the Court ruled, at which a civilian becomes a soldier is when he accepts the induction oath.

Another curb on broad government power over manpower during the war was put in place by a case reversing the conviction of a merchant seaman for knowingly failing to notify his local draft board of a change of address.[16] According to the somewhat confused evidence, Homer Bartchy, of Houston, Texas, decided to make one trip with the merchant marine before he was inducted. His board was duly notified, but after the first trip he decided to take another. He left a forwarding address with the board and his union headquarters, but was mistakenly reported as being at sea when he was actually still in port. The Court merely ruled that there was insufficient evidence to convict him, that he had tried to keep his address straight. What the ruling amounted to was a rule of reasonableness for draft registrants in leaving a chain of forwarding addresses, thus preventing local boards from snatching men on technicalities.

Two cases involving the Selective Service Act gave the Court as much trouble as any others; both were decided five to four. In the Singer case[17] the problem was an old one applied to a new law: how narrowly to interpret "conspiracy" where its use in a statute is ambiguous. Section 11 of the act listed a number of actions made unlawful, adding at the end of the last one, "or conspire to do so." Did this phrase apply to each of the outlawed actions or only to the last one, which was to "interfere in any way by force or violence with the administration of this Act . . ."? Douglas, Black, Stone, Jackson and Reed thought the conspiracy phrase applied to the entire section; but Frankfurter wrote a dissent—joined by Murphy, Roberts and Rutledge—in which he pleaded for a strict construction of the phrase, making it apply to an overt act of force or violence. One of his main arguments was that Congress customarily spells out instances in which it wants conspiracy to be made unlawful.

The German-American Bund case,[18] decided a few months later, involved a similar argument over the words "counsel" and "evade," as used in the same act. This time, Black was on the side of the strict constructionists, tipping the 5-to-4 scales from their position in the *Singer* case and releasing a group of twenty-four Bundsmen.

The government's prosecution of the Bund leaders had gone back seven years into the obnoxious *Fuehrer* system which the organization had set up in the United States in imitation of German Nazism. The prosecution's main exhibit, however, was Bund Command No. 37, which it said counseled evasion, resistance and refusal in regard to selective service obligations. The Bundsmen obviously didn't want to fight against Germany, but their specific objection to the draft law came from this proviso in the act: "It is the expressed policy of the Congress that whenever a vacancy is caused in the employment rolls of any business or industry by reason of induction into the service of the United States of an employee . . . such vacancy shall not be filled by any person who is a member of the Communist Party or the German-American Bund."

After passage of the act the Bund tried to decide what to do, especially in view of what it felt was an unconstitutional discrimination against its members. Part of its answer was this sentence from Command No. 37: "Every man, if he can, will refuse to do military duty until this law and all other laws of the country or the states which confine the citizenship rights of Bund members are revoked! We will fight to establish a precedent in this servile matter!" As Roberts said, in the Court's opinion, "the Government's case is really pitched on this command, which it construes as a counsel to evade military service."

Roberts first rapped the trial court for allowing so much evidence to be taken concerning the years before the act was passed. Then he declared that the Bund command did not counsel evasion, that evidence was insufficient to establish a case against the Bund. In essence, the majority thought, the case made by the government amounts to this: "That these men were partisans of Germany, were against our going to war with Germany, and might be disposed, therefore, to counsel evasion of military service, and were all familiar with Bund Command No. 37."

"One with innocent motives," Roberts wrote, "who honestly believes a law is unconstitutional . . . may well counsel that the law shall not be obeyed, that its command shall be resisted until a court shall have held it valid, but this is not knowingly counselling, stealthily and by guile, to evade its command."

Black, who really swung the case, concurred briefly on the point of the discriminatory language in the act. For Congress to say that Bund members could not, even after an honorable discharge from the Army, come back and get employment was a legitimate reason for the Bund to challenge the act, Black thought. In fact, he felt that the Bund's language about the discrimination was "little, if any, more condemnatory . . . than language used previously by this Court with reference to legislation of a similar pattern." Rutledge, in a briefer concurrence, thought that Command No. 37 was no more than "sheer political discussion."

The dissenters, led by the chief justice, quarreled with the majority's definition of "evade," giving it a much broader meaning. In fact, the minority said the conclusion was "inescapable" and "plain" that the Bund leaders had counseled evasion. Also they felt that a bona fide effort to create a constitutional test before complying with the act was no defense.

Two cases during the term beginning in October of 1945 were typical of cases in this category. In the first, the *Girouard* case, the Court reversed a decade of law on the obligations of a conscientious objector seeking United States naturalization.[19] This applicant stated that he would not "take up arms in defense of this country" because he was a noncombatant and a Seventh-Day Adventist. The lower court, relying on three earlier Supreme Court decisions, denied Girouard his papers.

Douglas, for the five-man majority, made no bones about overruling three precedents—*Schwimmer, Macintosh* and *Bland*—and in relying on the dissents of Holmes and Hughes for doing so. Then he added a few licks of his own, such as the fact that Girouard's religious scruples would not disqualify him from becoming a member of Congress or holding other high offices and that modern warfare dramatizes as never before the contribution of those behind the lines. Interestingly enough, one of the winning lawyers in the case was a man who had a major part in the fight to rejuvenate the Court, Homer Cummings.

The other case involved Paul Knauer, the big man in the German-American Citizens Alliance, a front for the Bund.[20] German-born Knauer was naturalized in 1939; six years later the government charged that his papers had been obtained by the fraud of not really meaning what he had sworn in the oath. Though two justices clung to their belief that no naturalized citizen should be denaturalized, the Court found an abundance of solid evidence of Knauer's fraud. The rigid standards of the *Baumgartner* and *Schneiderman* cases had at last been met.

The decision illustrated clearly how the case-by-case approach of the Court ultimately sets in place a formula which prosecutors and defendants can latch onto. It also shows how the first few cases in that process may look unrealistic at the moment and may even rescue some repulsive characters but nevertheless serve the purpose of guiding the law down the ultimately correct channel.

CHAPTER XIV

Prelude and Feud

AMONG the belongings of Mr. Justice Jackson is a framed picture from a very old magazine showing a lonely student working at a dingy desk. The caption is from Kipling: "He travels fastest who travels alone."

The picture and its moral are significant for many reasons. The biggest headlines ever created for history by Jackson were made from Nuremberg, thousands of miles from the Supreme Court, when, alone, he loosed the strongest blast ever delivered by a member of the Court at another member. Yet even then, as American prosecutor at the quadripartite trials of Nazi war criminals, Jackson was making history in international and military law. He was making it literally; he had only scraps of law on which to build a bold and frank precedent for any future war lords. He was traveling alone. The consensus was that he was traveling fast.

Also, Jackson is his own kind of student. He had less formal education than any of his colleagues, but he has spent many hours outside of big jobs studying legal and political history. He has no contempt for the more formal kind of scholarship, yet he looks with more approval on the man who has wrestled in the pit with opposing legal gladiators, a jury occupying the choice seats.

Jackson once put the contrast fliply to a young job seeker who had emphasized his study under Frankfurter, at Harvard. "If you have learned your legal theory under Felix Frankfurter thoroughly and are willing to unlearn most of it under me," replied Jackson, "I think there is hope for you."

That Jackson was being flip is indicated by the fact that he urged Frankfurter's appointment and a few years later he was voting quite consistently with Frankfurter on the Supreme Court. That he was still traveling alone is shown by the fact that his chief enemy on the Court was Hugo Black, the man who worked hard in the Senate toward the same Court reorganization which Jackson slaved for.

In that shift lies the story of this Court, indeed of any Court; for majorities have long tended to split like an amoeba and become two groups from one. This phenomenon is believed by some to be more basic than the resulting labels of the new groups. That is, the amoeba principle works on liberal and conservative majorities alike. Jackson, himself, is an authority for a big chunk of this observation. By way of a preface to his hard-hitting book, *The Struggle for Judicial Supremacy*, Jackson wrote in September of 1940 the following:

"But our history shows repeated disappointment of liberal Presidents in their efforts to effect a permanent or even long-enduring change of attitude or philosphy of the Court by additions to its personnel. Why is it that the Court influences appointees more consistently than appointees influence the Court? I point out certain sustained institutional and procedural pressures toward conservatism which only the most alert Justices will sense and only the most hardy will overcome. Because of these constant pressures I would underwrite no futures even now."

A few months later the author of these words was nominated by a liberal President to the Supreme Court. Five years after that he fired his guided missile from Nuremberg to Washington, aimed at Hugo Black, in many ways leader of the liberal bloc.

Jackson's reputation as a tough and eloquent prosecutor of Nazi war criminals paled beside the white-hot indictment he leveled at his fellow justice. When the angry words hit press tickers in Washington, late in the afternoon of Monday, June 10, 1946, the justices' black robes were still warm, hung in their lockers for the last time that term. The seven left to carry on the Court's work by Stone's death and Jackson's absence were tucking papers into drawers and otherwise preparing for the annual vacation. Most of the dozen reporters who gather on opinion Mondays had gone to their offices to write their stories. Thirteen cases had been decided that last day, with bad splits in ten of them, but the top news in the morning papers was Jackson's cable.

His long "statement" was addressed to the House and Senate judiciary committees, the latter of which was then considering the confirmation of Vinson as chief justice; but just what he expected the congressmen to do about it was not clear, for he specifically praised Vinson's appointment. Jackson said he was bringing what he bluntly called the "feud" out into the open so that Vinson could "take up his task without the cloud hanging over the court." When Vinson was confirmed, a few days later, the cloud was gone but a storm had taken its place.

Jackson's blast was prompted mainly by a column written by Doris Fleeson in the Washington *Star* nearly a month before. It purported to disclose Black's anger at Jackson's behavior when the Court refused to hear a reargument of the *Jewell Ridge* case, urged because Black's former partner won it by a 5-to-4 vote. More of the case later. It was on the record, but columnist Fleeson connected the differences of opinion in that case with what she called the "inside story" of what happened thereafter when it was laid before the President: "The harassed President, a Southerner himself, was quick to perceive the affront which Mr. Black feels he suffered. He had confided to a Senator: Black says he will resign if I make Jackson Chief Justice and tell the reasons why. Jackson says the same about Black."

Other columnists had said similar things before and after the Fleeson piece; Washington read them all with interest but little more. Reporters were unable to confirm the gossip. But even if it were only gossip, Jackson felt he had to go after it. Besides, he was convinced that they were "inside jobs." He decided to turn the Court inside out to answer them—"not by inferred innuendos, but over my signature."

According to Jackson's cable, Black insisted in the no-longer-secret conference that the petition for a rehearing be denied by a one-word order of the Court, as is customary. "This," said Jackson, "would not draw attention to his participation or to other circumstances. If his action were later questioned, the denial would be construed as vindication by the court on the facts." But none of the justices who had dissented wanted to lend their names to "blind and unqualified approval."

Jackson then disclosed that Stone, then chief justice and one of the dissenters, "attempted to compromise the matter." Stone drafted a short opinion, which Jackson printed posthumously in the cable: "The court is without authority and does not undertake to pass upon the propriety of the participation of members in the decision of cases brought here for review. The petition for a rehearing is denied."

Jackson admitted that he was willing to accept Stone's compromise. Roberts (another dissenter) was out of town and did not get involved in the final argument. However, Jackson told his brethren that "the petition should be denied on the grounds that each member is reponsible for his own decision on whether to sit or decline to sit on any particular case. I did not say it was wrong of Mr. Justice Black to sit. But I did say it was questionable for him to decide and the responsibility for approving a decision should not by inference be put on the court. . . ."

Still according to Jackson, "Mr. Black became very angry and said any opinion which discussed the subject at all would mean 'a declaration of war.' I told Justice Black in language that was sharp but no different than I would use again that I would not stand any more of his bullying and whatever I would otherwise do I would now have to write my opinion to keep my self-respect in the face of his threats."

The chief justice withdrew to the sideline; Jackson wrote his opinion (discussed later, with the controversial case) and Frankfurter added his name to it.

Of Black's position, Jackson said: "I must join in covering up facts or have war. . . . I refused to buy my peace at that price." He then denied that he had threatened to resign if Black were named chief justice, and continued his feud: "If war is declared on me I propose to wage it with the weapons of the open warrior, not those of the stealthy assassin." Then, as a sort of postlude, Jackson added: "Further, I do not want it inferred that I charge that Justice Black's sitting in the Jewell Ridge case involved lack of 'honor.' It is rather a question of judgment as to sound judicial policy."

Finally, he made it clear that his feuding iron was still cocked, by saying of Black's practice that "if it is ever repeated while I am on the bench I will make my Jewell Ridge opinion look like a letter of recommendation by comparison."

The telephone in Black's chambers and at his home was rung incessantly that night by reporters looking for a statement, but there was none. They turned their journalistic attentions to trying to learn from other quarters what would happen. Congressmen had no idea what could or would be done with Jackson's long cable to them; White House aides were dumfounded, incredulous. Nothing was ever done—except damage to the Court.

Little else *could* be done. There was no point in looking to the President for intervention, though Truman later told a press conference that Jackson had disclosed his plan via telephone the night before its publication and that he had discouraged the justice from issuing it. Congress had nothing but Vinson's nomination before it. Even if it wanted to launch a witch hunt on the Court it would be dependent on getting other justices to testify, and that would be a cold day in hell.

Reporters who went to the books for clues as to what might be done ran, ironically, only into the fact that justices "shall hold their offices during good behavior." It would take outright impeachment to force either justice to resign. But what had Black done that *he* should resign? The "plague on both your houses" which ran through the majority of editorials that week was as vague in its reasoning as was Jackson's original reasoning, now that it has cooled and can be handled more slowly. Two things stand out in Jacksons' indictment: first, Black did not disqualify himself from a case in which his ex-partner participated; second, Black allegedly hurled some ugly words at Jackson.

The issue of disqualification, alone, could be kicked around for years without solution. Black had always disqualified himself from Federal Communications Commission cases because his brother-in-law, Clifford J. Durr, is a commissioner. Other justices had withdrawn as they saw fit, practically never stating their reasons. After the feud broke into the open, researchers came up with a number of instances in which several justices could be criticized for not disqualifying themselves. One of the offenders, if it is an offense, was Roberts, whose former partner, Robert McCracken, argued a number of big cases before the Court. Roberts was not criticized—in fact, some think it is a disadvantage to have an old friend pass on one's argument. The system had worked well enough. Jackson, as former solicitor general and attorney general, undoubtedly has as many former associates appear before him as does anyone on the Court. In his cable he mentioned that 40 per cent of the Court's business involves the United States government as a litigant.

It seems reasonable to believe that Jackson had a chip on his shoulder about Black's slip into possible censure. Two years before, quite unnoticed, he had stuck a needle into Murphy in the *Schneiderman* case by noting at the end that he, Jackson, had disqualified himself from the case because, as attorney general, he had inherited the prosecution of it. The unwritten point was that the attorney general who handled the case on to him was Murphy, who wrote the Court's opinion —*against* the government.

What didn't often get mentioned about Black's participation in the *Jewell Ridge* case, though Doris Fleeson pointed it out, was that Black's absence would not have changed the outcome. (A tie vote sustains the lower court, which in this case sustained the union's position.)

The ugly words, if one can take Jackson's version of them, were certainly not becoming the dispassion of a judge. However, there is one sin which is even more unpardonable than feuding in the chamber. That is revealing what occurred in a conference. Jackson not only did that, but he quoted a deceased member of the Court. This, by any standard, was stooping lower than his adversary. As public reaction to his charges simmered down, it became fairly evident that no one likes a tattle-tale, even if he is right and even if he wears black robes.

Jackson's friends in Washington were at a loss to find any rational basis for the Nuremberg cable. They declared the action completely out of character and muttered observations about the work being hard at Nuremberg and the focus of affairs back home being hazy. Supreme Court lawyers were equally at a loss to understand the motives. Both groups could understand the feud within the confines of the conference, where, incidentally the two men sat opposite each

One version of the feeling of disgust with the Court that was caused by Jackson's feud with Black was drawn by Jim Berryman in the Washington *Evening Star*.

other at the time; but where was the judiciousness in Jackson that he implied was gone from Black?

As Jackson admitted, he was willing to accept Stone's compromise. A reading of that undelivered compromise statement makes it difficult to see any difference except personal overtones and undertones between Jackson's attitude and Stone's. For these reasons, and the political dynamite involved in boring any deeper into the affair, other Washington quarters let it drop. Jackson returned two months later for an interlude from Nuremberg, refusing to add to his cable.

The feud will be recalled as long as there is a Supreme Court. It could very easily be fanned within the Court, for while Jackson was gone he had his furniture moved into the more desirable chamber vacated by Roberts—less than twenty paces from Black's door.

Pieces of the puzzle will be slow in falling into place—some probably never will—but one key piece is that Jackson never did like Black, never could get along with him, though he kept his dislike on the plane of honest differences of opinion over close cases. The huddle over the petition for reargument was the beginning of a feud, in the true sense of the word. Though Jackson disclaimed, in his statement, any reflection on Black's honor, readers could not be so delicate in choosing what to believe. One of the nation's greatest lawyers had based his greatest case on the wrong grounds.

The key to what is left of the mystery lies in the life of a great and disappointed man. But before retracing the biographical clues, it is best to review his career in the daily routine of the Court, highlighted by his own opinions.

Jackson's first important opinion for the Court was delivered under inauspicious circumstances. The Court was split five to four, and it was almost the very hour in which Congress declared war on the Axis.[1] At the time it looked as if another symbol were present, for Jackson joined with Black, Douglas and Murphy, a combination that might have been expected in terms of liberal and conservative. However, the combination was seldom together after the first session.

As a freshman, Jackson did not often dissent or concur separately, but when he did speak out it was with feeling. By way of lone concurrence he took the Court to task three times. First, he felt that his brethren decided a liquor case on the wrong grounds, slighting the constitutional clauses on the subject.[2] By ruling that Arkansas, under its police power, could stop a shipment of liquor passing through it, Jackson felt that the Court "adds another to the already too numerous and burdensome state restraints of national commerce and pursues a trend with which I would have no part."

Jackson said he differed basically "as to whether the inertia of government shall be on the side of restraint of commerce or on the side of freedom of commerce. The sluggishness of government . . . and the relative ease with which men are persuaded to postpone troublesome decisions, all make inertia one of the most decisive powers in determining the course of our affairs and frequently gives to the established order of things a longevity and vitality much beyond its merits. Because that is so, I am reluctant to see any new local systems for restraining our national commerce. . . ."

Jackson conceded that he wanted a minimum of judicial interference with legislative action but warned: "We must be cautious lest we merely rush to other extremes."

Second, Jackson differed with the grounds for striking down California's Okie law.[3] He felt that the commerce clause was not the proper one to use; the privileges and immunities clause seemed more proper to him.

"This court," said Jackson, "should . . . hold squarely that it is a privilege of citizenship of the United States . . . to enter any state of the Union. . . ." If the Court is not willing to do that, he added, "then our heritage of constitutional privilege and immunities is only a promise to the ear to be broken to the hope, a teasing illusion like a munificent bequest in a pauper's will."

Third, he differed with some of his colleagues on the clause to use in nullifying Oklahoma's sterilization law, but he expressed his agreement with the unanimous result as follows:[4] "There are limits to the extent to which a legislatively represented majority may conduct biological experiments at the expense of the dignity and personality and natural powers of a minority—even those who have been guilty of what the majority define as crimes."

Jackson's first-term dissents were few and in technical cases. When the Court reversed a precedent to hold that intangible property can be taxed in more than one state, Jackson said that he could "see nothing in the Court's decision more useful than the proverbial leap from the frying pan into the fire."[5]

The second term, beginning in 1942, involved deeper water. Right off the bat, Jackson wrote four majority opinions from which Black, Douglas and Murphy dissented as a trio. One sent back to the National Labor Relations Board for more testimony a case in which several employees dynamited company property.[6] Another ruled that evidence was insufficient for a jury to find negligence on the part of a shipping company for loss of a seaman's eye.[7] In the third, Jackson wrote the majority's refusal to reverse an often-attacked principle that stock dividends cannot be taxed as income.[8] The fourth case upheld an ICC rate which was discriminatory against water transportation.[9]

Two other Jackson opinions for the Court were highly important.[10] He wrote the unanimous opinion in the "wheat penalty" case, probably the greatest extension on record of the interstate commerce power of Congress. Also, he wrote the dramatic opinion by which the Court reversed itself quickly on the flag salute. Excerpts from this highly literary opinion reveal Jackson's ability as an advocate and his craftsmanship with a pen.

He pointed out that early Christians were persecuted for refusal to participate before symbols of imperial authority, recalled how William Tell was forced to shoot an apple off his son's head for refusal to salute a bailiff's hat and noted that the Quakers suffered punishment rather than uncover their heads in deference to civil authority.

"Compulsory unification of opinion achieves only the unanimity of the graveyard." he warned. "It seems trite but necessary to say that the First Amendment to our Constitution was designed to avoid these ends by avoiding these beginnings."

Finally, Jackson wrote that "if there is any fixed star in our constitutional constellation, it is that no official, high or petty, can prescribe what shall be orthodox in politics, nationalism, religion, or other matters of opinion or force citizens to confess by word or act their faith therein."

Jackson's other major opinions that term were dissents. He refused to go along when the Court reversed a group of Jehovah's Witnesses' municipal license taxes.[11] In a long dissent he raised many of the practical questions which laymen might raise, such as exactly what power *does* a community have to reckon with nuisances, albeit religious ones. Instead of searching for an answer to that, he complained, "the Court has, in one way or another, tied the hands of all local authority and made the aggressive methods of this group the law of the land."

Then his warning: "This Court is forever adding new stories to the temples of constitutional law, and the temples have a way of collapsing when one story too many is added. . . . Civil liberties had their origin and must find their ultimate guaranty in the faith of the people. If that faith should be lost, five or nine men in Washington could not long supply its want."

In another civil rights case, Jackson was bitter over the Court's refusal to help an inductee who claimed to be a conscientious objector but who was denied a look at the draft board records.[12]

He also complained against the Court's forcing North Carolina to accept Nevada divorces, asserting that the former state should be empowered to protect her people.[13] To the argument that a conclusion other than the Court's would result in "bastardizing" children of the divorces, Jackson quipped: "I had supposed that our judicial responsibility is for the regularity of the law, not for the regularity of pedigrees."

When the Court upheld an "informer's suit," based on information taken from a criminal indictment obtained by the government, Jackson dissented alone.[14] His colleagues had very narrowly construed the words of the 1863 statute to permit such an action, though the informer had done nothing, as Jackson complained, but run down to the courthouse and copy an indictment in order to cash in on the archaic law allowing him one half of the amount defrauded from the government. Jackson agreed that laws should be interpreted strictly, yet he felt the interpretation should make sense when the Court was through with it.

"If ever there was a case where the letter killeth but the spirit giveth life, it is this," he wrote, explaining that he was sure Congress never intended to "enrich a mere busybody" for such easy work.

By the 1943 term Jackson was writing many attention-attracting opinions. Some were noticed mainly because liberals were becoming convinced of year-old suspicions that Jackson was "going conservative." Others were noticed because he writes the kind of opinion that can't help being spotted for phraseology and force. As former general counsel of the Bureau of Internal Revenue, he was being assigned a man-sized share of the Court's tax work. But Jackson, the political scientist, was overshadowing Jackson, the tax expert.

In the economics cases of importance he was never in the Black, Douglas and Murphy corner. When the Court upheld a rate order of the Federal Power Commission, based on the modern theory of "actual legitimate costs," rather than the abandoned "reproduction costs" idea, Jackson urged a different treatment for natural gas cases than for other utilities.[15] He agreed with the discard of the latter formula but felt that use of any single formula suggested "legalistic rituals" instead of "economic functions." He would have distinguished natural gas from other utilities on the grounds that its production is characterized by being exhaustible and irreplaceable.

In a complicated patent suit[16] he seemed to enjoy his dissent. Of the theory involved in patents he said: "Thus we have an abstract right in an abstruse relationship between things in which individually there is no right—a legal concept which either is very profound or almost unintelligible, I cannot be quite sure which." Later in the case, speaking of ethics, Jackson said that the parties seem to be "as much on a parity as the pot and the kettle." Another quip was that "the less legal rights depend on someone's state of mind, the better."

In the controversial case by which the Court suddenly put insurance in interstate commerce, Jackson agreed that insurance was, in fact, commerce; but he disagreed with the "drastic" and "reckless" legal maneuver of the Court in upsetting decades of state regulation without congressional declaration.[17]

Organized labor could not complain much that term about Jackson's two written opinions on that subject. He spoke for the Court in upholding a National Labor Relations Board ruling that an employer may not refuse to bargain with representatives of employees because he has already signed individual contracts with each of them.[18] Also, he concurred in the Court's prounion decision that travel time in certain mines had to be paid for as working time under the wage-hour law.[19] His reasoning was simple.

"This case in my view probably does not present any question of law or, if so," he wrote, "it is one with a very obvious answer." That was that no custom existed in the mines involved, so the Supreme Court was bound by the findings of the two lower courts. The concurrence was to become important in the next term.

Jackson's civil rights opinions ran half and half. He spoke for the Court in nullifying a Florida law which the Court felt amounted to peonage and involuntary servitude,[20] and he dissented from three freedom decisions.

The first decision helped the "I Am" movement by holding that, in the prosecution of its leaders for using the mails to defraud, considerations of the truth or falsity of the religious doctrines of the accused must be excluded.[21] The defendants had claimed, via mail, great divine powers, to put it mildly. Jackson had fun telling why he would dismiss the proceedings "and have done with this business of judicially examining other people's faiths." (He is an inactive member of the Episcopal church.)

"Religious symbolism," he said, "is even used by some with the same mental reservations one has in teaching of Santa Claus or Uncle Sam or Easter bunnies or dispassionate judges."

As he saw it, the wrong done by those like the "I Am" defendants "is not in the money the victims part with half so much as in the mental and spiritual poison they get." He was quick to add, however, that this is "precisely the thing the Constitution put beyond the reach of the prosecutor." The price we pay for this freedom, he added, "is that we must put up with, and even pay for, a good deal of rubbish."

Also, Jackson dissented for himself, Roberts and Frankfurter when the Court brushed aside a Tennessee court's findings of fact to conclude on its own that a "confession" was coerced and therefore no good.[22]

"The claim of a suspect to immunity from questioning," wrote Jackson, "creates one of the most vexing problems in criminal law—that branch of the law which does the courts and the legal profession least credit." But his legal argument against voiding the "confession" was that findings of state courts should be given a stronger presumption of validity.

With the same justices he dissented when the Court put a state's right to control child labor ahead of the claim of a Jehovah's Witness that children are protected by freedom of religion in selling religious pamphlets on the street.[23] Jackson's dissent was not so much for or against the religious right claimed as it was a protest that the Court was not being consistent. He used the occasion to sum up his views in all the Witnesses cases, as follows:

"I think the limits begin to operate whenever activities begin to affect or collide with liberties of others or of the public. Religious activities which concern only members of the faith are and ought to be free—as nearly absolutely free as anything can be. But beyond these, many religious denominations or sects engage in collateral and secular activities intended to obtain means from unbelievers to sustain the worshippers and their leaders. . . . All such money-raising activities on a public scale are, I think, Caesar's affairs and may be regulated by the state so long as it does not discriminate against one because he is doing them for a religious purpose. . . ."

Federal system cases that term were as troublesome, if not more so. Jackson tipped the 5-to-4 scales in a case under the "full faith and credit" clause so that the Court ruled that a man who received a workman's compensation award for an injury in one state was barred from recovering in another state, the state of his employment.[24] In other words, each state has to abide by the award of the first state—give it full faith and credit. Jackson wrote a concurrence to explain that he saw no difference between this situation and the North Carolina divorce ruling, where the majority reached a similar conclusion about Nevada decrees. He objected to the divorce result, but so long as it was on the books he felt bound to follow its dictates. A few of his words in behalf of discarding the divorce decision were particularly interesting:

"Overruling a precedent always introduces some confusion and the necessity for it may be unfortunate. But it is as nothing to keeping on our books utterances to which we ourselves will give full faith and credit only if the outcome pleases us."

When the Court held that Minnesota, the home state of an airline company, could tax all of the airline's planes, Jackson went along with the result but served notice that he was doing so only because that state included the "home port" and not because each state through which the planes traveled should thereafter be allowed to duplicate Minnesota's tax.[25] Also, he frankly confessed his inability, without a federal statute to work from, to devise any result that would be sound and would let air travel progress without local obstruction.

Similarly, he dissented when the Court upheld Iowa's right to collect a "use" tax on a nonresident seller of goods to citizens of Iowa.[26] "I can think of nothing in or out of the Constitution," he protested, "which warrants this effort to reach beyond the State's own border to make out-of-state merchants tax collectors because they engage in interstate commerce with the State's citizens."

By the next term, beginning in 1944, war cases were plaguing the justices. Jackson stepped into them boldly, coming up with at least two decisions that might not have been expected of the man who was to leave the Court, at the end of the term, to prosecute war criminals. For example, he spoke strongly for the five-man majority which freed Anthony Cramer of treason charges for giving aid and comfort to two of the Nazi saboteurs.[27] Jackson's forty-five page opinion in the Court's first such case reviewed at length the history of treason, then held that the evidence against Cramer did not come up to the very rigid standards written into the Constitution. Douglas, Stone, Reed and Black bitterly dissented, calling Jackson's work "hypothetical" and charging that it "makes justice truly blind."

In the Japanese relocation case, considered at length in the next chapter, Jackson's pen was sharpened on the bone of dissent, in favor of those relocated. Other civil rights cases in which Jackson's position was of interest included his vote against the conscientious objector whom the Illinois bar would not admit to practice and against dismissing the prosecution of the Bund leaders.

But the most significant opinions of Jackson that term came in five labor cases, all of which were decided by a 5-to-4 vote. In four of them, he sided with Stone, Roberts and Frankfurter. In the first of these Jackson dissented from a decision supporting the NLRB, in an unusual situation.[28] The Wallace Corporation, maker of clothespins, etc., signed an agreement with a CIO and an independent union for an election to choose the bargaining representative. The NLRB approved the agreement and the independent won. Thereupon the corporation signed a closed shop contract and the victorious independent union barred CIO members from joining it, thus requiring the employer to fire them. The NLRB found the company guilty of unfair labor practices; a majority of the Court agreed, largely on the grounds that the independent and the company had worked closely together to get rid of the CIO.

Jackson felt the company was being punished for not interfering with its union's policy, something the Wagner Act doesn't want it to do anyway, and that the Court was likewise setting union policy. He declared that the decision "is utterly at war with the hands-off requirements which the law lays upon the employers, and . . . at war with one of the basic purposes of labor in its struggle to obtain this Act and of Congress in enacting it."

In the second case Jackson spoke for a majority in favor of Western Union, fighting attempts of the government to bring its messengers less than sixteen years of age within the child labor ban of the Fair Labor Standards Act.[29] The important case boiled down to an argument over one word, "shipment." A majority decided that the telegrams handled by the youngsters are not "shipped" in commerce. Of this word Jackson said: "Its imprecision to linguists and scholars may be conceded. But if it is common in the courts, the marketplaces, or the schools of the country to speak of shipping a telegram or receiving a shipment of telegrams, we do not know of it. . . ." To define the term to cover electrical impulses, he felt, would make it embrace propositions rejected by Congress, including one written by a senator named Black. The ex-senator and three other justices did not agree.

A test of the controversial Texas law requiring permits of union organizers brought on the third labor case.[30] This time Jackson left the "conservatives," but he was forced to write a concurring opinion. He wanted to make it plain that he felt a state might regulate union organizers, as an occupation, but he agreed that it could never bar them from holding public meetings to solicit members—just as licensed doctors could always call a meeting. What worried him most about the majority opinion was that he felt it granted to organizers the freedom of expression which the Court had denied to employers under NLRB decisions. Douglas wrote a separate paragraph, also for Black and Murphy, to dispute this contention.

The fourth labor case involved the union truckers who refused to work for a company they hated, thus knocking it out of business.[31] Jackson's quarrel, by way of dissent, was with the extent to which labor was being exempted from the antitrust laws.

"Those statutes which restricted the application of the Sherman Act against unions," he said, "were intended only to shield the legitimate objectives of such organizations, not to give them a sword to use with unlimited immunity. . . . The Court now sustains the claim of a union to the right to deny participation in the economic world to an employer simply because the union dislikes him. This Court permits to employees the same arbitrary dominance over the economic sphere which they control that labor so long, so bitterly and so rightly asserted should belong to no man."

These were all important cases in Jackson's life, as well as in the life of the Court, but the fifth one has already topped them all in history. Known as the *Jewell Ridge* case, it was later disclosed by Jackson to be the basis for his feud with Black.[32] The feud may not have been on in the other cases, but it is easy to note the prelude which had been playing.

The importance of this portal-to-portal decision in the field of labor has already been noted, but several innuendoes of the affair are essential to any kind of understanding of its later importance to the justices. Jackson had gone along with the majority in the previous portal-to-portal decision because there had been no custom contrary to the standards of the wage-hour law. This time, however, there was a definite custom against counting the travel time as work time for the purposes of making up pay checks. The majority felt that the wage-hour law of Congress should override any private agreement; the minority argued that Congress had not intended to upset collective bargaining agreements.

Jackson's dissent again cited Senator Black, as floor manager of the wage-hour law in its early stages. Particularly he cited the senator's negative answer to a question whether the bill would affect collective bargaining agreements. The majority protested that "a full and fair reading of the entire debate" made it clear that Congress understood the possibility of setting aside agreements that did not come up to the statutory standards. It italicized parts of Senator Black's debate supporting this contention.

By way of conclusion of the minority view, Jackson wrote: "We doubt if one can find in the long line of criticized cases one in which the Court has made a more extreme exertion of power or one so little supported or explained by either the statute or the record in the case. Power should answer to reason none the less because its fiat is beyond appeal."

It was a bitter case legally and economically. Immediately after it was decided it became bitter in personalities—the company asked the Court for a reargument on the grounds that the victorious union lawyer, Crampton Harris, was formerly Black's law partner. Five weeks after the decision, the request for reargument was denied, as such requests nearly always are. But a one-page statement by Jackson, with Frankfurter concurring, was tacked on, much to the surprise of procedure artists.

"This petition," he wrote, "is addressed to all of the Court and must either be granted or denied in the name of the Court and on the responsibility of all of the justices. In my opinion the complaint is one which cannot properly be addressed to the Court as a whole and for that reason I concur in denying it."

He pointed out that there is no uniform practice, either by law or by decision, on disqualification of a justice from hearing a case. It is the responsibility of each justice. "There is no authority known to me," he added, "under which a majority of this Court has power under any circumstances to exclude one of its duly commissioned justices from sitting or voting in any case."

The inference was that Jackson and Frankfurter would have voted to keep Black off the case had they had the power to do so. On the other hand, there was room for thinking that a couple of individualistic justices were merely expressing a legitimate—and accurate—thought about the situation. No one dreamed at the time, June 18, 1945, that the single page was the end product of the greatest fight in the nation's highest and most secret judicial conference room.

Robert Houghwout Jackson was born in February of 1892 on the farm of his pioneer family, at Spring Creek, Pennsylvania. The first big city he saw was Pittsburgh, to which he rode at the age of fourteen in a boxcar with a horse his father had sold. He was a small-town boy on the right side of the tracks with more than a share of the prodigy about him.

After high school, Jackson went straight into a law office to prepare for the career he knew he wanted in the way that practically no one is allowed to prepare any more. It was the old apprenticeship system—"reading" the law in an established office. After a year of this, Jackson went to Albany Law School for his only formal higher education. There he compressed a two-year course into one year, but the fact that he was not twenty-one made him ineligible for a degree. Returning to Jamestown, New York, where he had received his lower schooling, Jackson "read" another year and fulfilled the New York requirement for practicing on his own.

His roots were already in Jamestown (population 42,600 in 1940), but he sunk them deeper. His first clients were strikers arrested in the violence of a streetcar strike. He won their acquittal and immediate attention. The young lawyer's practice became both lucrative and varied. At the age of forty-two, when Jackson left Jamestown for Washington, he had argued tiny cases and big cases—one by lantern light before a backwoods justice of the peace and one in which he won a whopping judgment for $1,700,000.

He appeared in court both for and against railroads, insurance companies and other corporations. He moved to Albany to handle damage cases for a railroad, but even this was too much specialization for his taste and he moved back to Jamestown. He was a well-known lawyer, citizen about town and gentleman farmer just outside of town. With his fine trotting horses he might well have settled down to the life of a western New York squire, but something was always eating on him.

Oversimplified, it was oppression by big people of little people. This was not a crusade; Jackson bit into the situation only as it came along. He defended a Communist who was arrested for selling the *Daily Worker* and *New Masses* on the public square. In bar associations he was as unorthodox as he was active. For example, on the subject of the bar's responsibility for straightening out the snarls in tax law Jackson declared that the bar had too much "intellectual inertia" to get the job done.

Jackson's most lucrative clients could be called the big interests in town, but that would tell only part of the story. They may have been big, but he represented them against bigger ones. He defended the local railroad from the big New York Central and he defended the local independent telephone system from the New York Telephone Company. A close friend of Jackson's swears that the justice still displays the independence symbolized by Jamestown's unique independent telephone system. Jackson saw these corporate trends as the economic facts of life—and didn't like them.

The political facts of life had come to Jackson in the Democratic version, handed down from his Democratic father and grandfather without interruption even by the Civil War. In a center of Republicanism, Jackson could expect to be elected to nothing, though he was corporation counsel of Jamestown a while. Bob Jackson's political hero was Andy Jackson, who was no kin but whom Bob regarded as the only President really put into office by the people.

During the Democratic inning headed by Woodrow Wilson, Jackson met Franklin D. Roosevelt, who later put him on the New York Commission to Investigate the Administration of Justice. He also knew Henry Morgenthau, Jr., and James A. Farley. Thus, it was to be expected that when Roosevelt was elected President, Jackson would be asked to take a federal job. Farley asked him to become counsel to the Works Projects Administration, but he declined. Then, in 1934, he accepted Morgenthau's offer of the same position in the Bureau of Internal Revenue. He expected to be in Washington six months or a year.

Six years later, Jackson was first on the dopesters' list of men to be groomed to succeed Roosevelt, should he not run for his third term in 1940. Moreover, most of them wanted him to be first on the list. Marquis Childs, who knew the field well, explained Jackson's standing in a March, 1940, *Forum* article on Jackson, sub-titled "The man who has always been a New Dealer." Said Childs: "If there is any single individual who represents all the qualities that commonly inhere in the term (New Dealer), it is the man who has just been made Attorney General of the United States." How Jackson got to that position and beyond is the story of one of the most interesting climbs in officialdom.

Being counsel of the Bureau of Internal Revenue is ordinarily a steppingstone into a fat law practice but no help in political advancement. But the times were made to order for a man with Jackson's legal acumen and dislike of big corporations. He stepped right into an inconceivably complicated tax suit against Andrew Mellon for three of the financier's many millions. Jackson's diligence in preparing his case, plus the news value of any investigation of the fabulous Mellon empire, attracted great attention to the new legal light and shook $750,000 from Mellon's jeans.

The winning lawyer was then assigned to prepare a defense for the Securities and Exchange Commission in its coming test of the constitutionality of the Public Utility Holding Company Act of 1935. With him on the case were Ben Cohen and Tommy Corcoran, White House expediters and legal brains. Said Jackson, not untruly: "This is easy. Ben will furnish the learning, Tom the energy and I'll furnish the horse sense to win this case." By some such division of talents, the three prepared a successful brief.

Jackson then moved to the Department of Justice, where his reputation will long endure. As counsel for the Bureau of Internal Revenue he had been in charge of nearly three hundred lawyers, so his work at the department would not be different, at first, although it would get more into the political realm. After a period as assistant attorney general in charge of the tax division, Jackson wound up on the springboard at the head of the antitrust division, an almost moribund part of the government which he proceeded to jazz up at once.

At the outset, Jackson dropped the policy of acting only on complaints from aggrieved businessmen; he stuck the public's oar in wherever he felt it should be. The prosecutions for which he will longest be remembered, though he moved on before they were finished, were those against the Aluminum Company of America (Mellon, again), the automobile finance companies and midwestern oil firms. All three were successful. Before Jackson went "upstairs" to the solicitor general's office, bringing in Thurman Arnold to keep waving the "big stick," he attained a reputation as a radical of the New Deal. Radical, that is, from the businessman's point of view, sheltered for many years from a vigorous antitrust policy. Jackson hit hard at filling in details in the Rooseveltian phrase, "economic royalists."

In March of 1938, he moved into the number two job at the Justice Department, made vacant by Reed's elevation to the Court. Reed had established a good record as a straight lawyer trying to blast away at what the administration regarded as the Court's blind spots. Jackson had a friendlier Court passing on his arguments, but he put into his job as lawyer for the world's largest client more polish, vigor and personal advocacy. Jackson had deliberately chosen, back in the Jamestown days, not to specialize. His philosophy was that a good advocate should be able to prepare a case on any subject and come as close to winning it as a specialist of narrower talents. Being a good advocate, Jackson could afford to feel that way, and there was little doubt that he *was* a top-flight advocate. Occasionally, Court observers detected spots of poor preparation in Jackson's oral arguments, but they were seldom fatal. In the 1938 term, Jackson personally argued twenty-four cases, a prodigous effort, and lost only one, something of a big record. True, the Court was swinging with him, but Solicitor General Jackson was the epitome of a great lawyer standing before the highest court of his land. He enjoyed that job more than any other because it offered real legal work for a man in love with his calling. The premise may be emotional, but it was borne out in results.

During the Court fight of 1937, in which Jackson's important role has already been outlined, his main target was the mental outlook of the justices. He was one of those who felt that the President's approach for overhauling the Court was basic enough. To the suggestion that an amendment to the Constitution, specifying the change that should be made, would be a better course, Jackson told the Senate Judiciary Committee: "You cannot amend a state of mind."

Within the strategy, therefore, of eroding away the state of mind, instead of changing it by some legal fiat, Jackson was supreme. Both the battle and Jackson's experience as solicitor general in cementing the changes, case by case, were put in writing by Jackson, himself, in *The Struggle for Judicial Supremacy*. As a job of reporting, admittedly from one side of the issue, it was enough to make any journalist take notice. As a job of dishing up to the American people a large portion of the history of their leading institutions it was brilliant. And as a job of advocating his own ideas the book was superb. As in a courtroom, one might differ completely with Jackson's ideas but it would be hard to do anything but bow to his artful role as an advocate of them. If one were allowed by some magic to select anyone he chose to represent him in a major struggle he could do no better than pick Bob Jackson. He has the clarity of a man addressing a jury of average IQ John Does, the sophistication of one impressing an enlightened judge and the smartness of one who knows that news reporters are present.

Even as solicitor general, Jackson was regarded around Washington as a man on the way to bigger things politically. In January of 1939, however, when he was passed over in favor of Frank Murphy for the attorney general post, the Jackson star dimmed. Also, the two men did not get along so well as first and second in command of the Department of Justice. When Murphy was elevated to the Court, one year later, Jackson moved around the corner to the top spot, but much bad blood existed between the two men. Jackson's friends in the department, of whom he had many loyal ones, spoke of Murphy's Court appointment as a "kick upstairs," and lesser employees heaved a sigh as the man they liked immensely took over the reins.

Jackson protested mildly that he didn't like the attorney generalship because it involved too many administrative problems. Certainly few people envied some of the policy decisions he had to make at that time. The war had broken in Europe so completely that many thought it could not help catching the United States up in its fury. Jackson was in the position of having to dispense legal advice to a President who was moving in a direction vastly different from that charted in the main legal document affecting his course: the Neutrality Act. Almost no one, back in 1940, believed that this bit of pious legislation would work, but there were many insisting on giving it a full chance. Attorney General Jackson all but threw the hollow shell of the Neutrality Act in the trash can when he advised the President, on August 27, 1940, that it would be legal for him to give Great Britain fifty over-age destroyers and a flock of "mosquito" boats in return for a ninety-nine year lease on a handful of bases. Commentators cried outrage at the legal shenanigan. Jackson skillfully steered the President around three legal obstacles by ruling that the deal need not be ratified by the Senate (as a treaty), that the President had authority to transfer title of the vessels away from the United States and that Britain's status as a belligerent need not bother anyone. It was one of the fanciest bits of legal advice ever received by a President. Small wonder that Roosevelt found no need to seek amending or repealing legislation. Legal expediency, based on the idea that Hitler was not disposed to wait until Congress got through debating, accomplished more than new legislation.

Jackson was attacked for prostituting his profession by finding means to justify the ends sought by Roosevelt. Without going into how that might differ from what a lawyer ordinarily does, it should be said to Jackson's credit that all he did was tell the President that he could do something. The President did it and got away with it.

There were a number of other vexing problems facing Jackson on the operating side. His incumbency included that weird period when the Communists were on the same side of the war as the Nazis, giving the government fits in trying to protect its defense plants, real or imagined. Also, he set up the system of registration for aliens and took over the Bureau of Immigration and Naturalization, both big headaches to their administrators. Labor will remember the time he announced, to everyone's surprise and without documentation, that the North American Aviation strike was Communist led.

It is necessary at this point to digress to Jackson's Nuremberg assignment, originated by Roosevelt and seconded by Truman in the spring of 1945. The choice of Jackson could have been made either because he was no old-line international lawyer or because he would undoubtedly make a good showing. Both were needed if the trial were to accomplish what its planners had in mind. As early as March of 1941, Jackson had told the first meeting of the Inter-American Bar Association that international law, as then known, was as dead as Hitler's good promises. "No longer can it be argued," he said, "that the civilized world must behave with rigid impartiality toward both an aggressor in violation of the treaty and the victims of unprovoked attack." Nearly five years later he was telling judges from the four major powers that military aggression is an international crime.

The Nuremberg trial is a book in itself, but the interlude it furnished in Jackson's life compels immediate mention. By frankly making some of the law as he went along, Jackson earned both bouquets and brickbats. Some synthesis of the law was necessary if the Nazi leaders were to be punished with any semblance of formal law and order, by any system other than the Nazi's own. Yet it could easily be pointed out that the procedure used and the indictment read to the miserable defendants violated several key principles of the American Constitution. The judges were obviously biased and there were only vague laws on the international books which the defendants could have read and known they were violating by waging their war. The trial that resulted was a mongrel variety, but it worked to most people's satisfaction.

Jackson labored hard at his job, which was supposed to end in time for the opening of the 1945 term of the Supreme Court. Some said he fell down on his cross-examinations, but his extremely long opening address at the trial is already historic literature. His summary, in July of 1946, was brilliant. Many newspapers ran feature stories on the adjectives used by the American prosecutor in describing defendants. Of Walter Funk, for example, Jackson said he "banked gold teeth fillings of concentration camp victims—probably the most ghoulish collateral in banking history."

But some who remembered Jackson from World War I, or even those who read his dissent in the Japanese relocation case, might well wonder how Jackson got into this particular legal job. He was accused bitterly of being pro-German in World War I for opposing the use of American troops overseas. Later, he vigorously attacked the Versailles Treaty as starting the next war. He was a 100 per cent isolationist.

Jackson's undisguised change in foreign policy came partly from the fact that he saw Hitler's government as a very different type of animal from the old Kaiser's government. He also decided that isolationism would never work as a system, however tempting it might be as a principle. He was not a pacifist, only a peace lover. The heavy reparations which he fought in World War I may be repeated this time, but Jackson does not think of the punishment of war criminals as being in the same class. His distinction is that reparations merely saddle the next and guiltless generation with the burden, whereas punishment of the war leaders strikes at the guilty generation, leaving nothing more dangerous than an object lesson for their successors.

While Jackson was in Nuremberg, stories emanated from the Court that the chief justice was angry with him for taking the leave of absence, dumping more work on remaining justices and reflecting on the nonpartisan character of the judiciary. Other justices were said to be equally unhappy about their brother. Whether they were bitter or not, circumstances of a closely divided Court that 1945 term resulted in their setting aside a score of tie cases until Jackson should return to provide a majority vote. It was a departure from custom and somewhat of a low blow to Jackson.

It will be supposed as long as nothing to the contrary is unearthed that Jackson would have been the chief justice if he hadn't been away on the Nuremberg mission. Much of this supposition is based on the undisputed but also undocumented fact that Roosevelt toyed with the idea of making Jackson the chief when Hughes retired on June 2, 1941. Jackson was known to have felt for some time that he would rather not go on the Court unless he went on as chief, which job would carry something more than mere dignity. The President chose to name Stone, but Jackson apparently overcame his reluctance to be a mere associate justice, for he was appointed on the day Stone was elevated. It was common gossip, if nothing more, in Washington at the time that Stone would serve only a year or so before retiring and Jackson would become chief justice.

When Stone died, still serving as chief, Jackson was in Germany; but dopesters believed that Truman admired Jackson, whom he had not had a chance to know intimately, about as much as Roosevelt had. Then the stories about resignations from the Court if Jackson were named began to clog the dope lines. Vinson was appointed and Jackson blasted the feud into the open.

Against this background, Jackson's charges against Black take on a heavy flavor of sour grapes. Certainly there have been a number of disappointments in Jackson's eventful life. Once a move was started to run him for governor of New York, largely to give him the elective stature believed necessary to make him acceptable as a presidential nominee soon thereafter. Jim Farley is credited with having sawed the limb off so early that it reflected on Jackson as somewhat of a political flop before he had a fair chance to try. Whether he took the incident as seriously as political observers did or not, Jackson surely had many reasons other than vanity to think that he might look toward the White House as a residence. If he brooded over these things at all, they could easily have driven him to throw caution to the winds and tell all when his last chance disappeared and the going was tough at Nuremberg. Regardless of his intentions in opening the feud, that act was to many a showing of his hand, a disclosure of his ambition.

To project Jackson's post-feud career on the Court it is necessary to combine this complexity with another—his voting position on the Court. By the time he arrived there, in October of 1944, Murphy had left Frankfurter's wing and cast his lot with Black and Douglas. Friends of Jackson's insist that he would never have joined a group containing Murphy. Some add that it was unlikely from the beginning that Jackson would have sided closely with Douglas because both men were talked of so frequently as presidential possibilities. Anyway, Frankfurter and Jackson started hitting it off smoothly, a not unnatural thing because Jackson had pushed Frankfurter for the Court. More fundamental, the big issues of the New Deal had been resolved before Jackson's arrival; cases then were mostly close interpretations, almost philosophies of law. Not being a joiner by nature, Jackson proceeded to assert the individualism which he always possessed, in spite of opposition epithets of "rubber stamp" which were hurled at him.

Impose the feud on top of this situation and one has a two-sided Court, each faction of which will be fighting to vindicate itself in history. For that struggle Jackson is well equipped, being an able advocate occupying a judge's seat. That the Court will become that kind of a center or that he should be on the relatively conservative side of the Court should be of little surprise to Jackson. Both facts are provided for in the prophetic last chapter of his book.

"The ultimate function of the Supreme Court," he wrote, before he was appointed to it, "is nothing less than the arbitration between fundamental and ever-present rival forces or trends in our organized society. . . . Conflicts which have divided the Justices always mirror a conflict which pervades society. In fact, it may be said that the Supreme Court conference chamber is the forum where each fundamental cause has had its most determined and understanding championship. . . . The Constitution, in making the balance between different parts of our government a legal rather than a political question, casts the Court as the most philosophical of our political departments."

Jackson then discussed to what extent justices should be conscious of this power of theirs and concluded that it is safer that they be aware of the implications of their decisions on all of society. But he assured his readers that this realistic approach to decisions would not lead the country astray, because the "contribution of legal philosophy to the balance of social forces will always be on the conservative side."

CHAPTER XV

Black Silk and Khaki

IT WAS an eager and record crowd that cluttered the immaculate Court building on July 29 and 30, 1942. The United States had been at war with Germany nearly eight months. Four trained German saboteurs had been landed under cover of night from a German submarine off Long Island; four buddies had put ashore at Florida. All eight had been quickly caught and hauled before a military commission appointed by President Roosevelt especially for the puropse of a speedy, noncivil trial of the country's first real, live prisoners. As everyone had expected, the secret military tribunal found all guilty of attempting sabotage and it ordered death for six of them forthwith. (Two got only prison sentences because of their help to the government.)

But the two colonels ordered to defend the Nazis, in accordance with military law, raced to the nearest federal district court, in the District of Columbia, to demand a writ of habeas corpus, that piece of paper which lawyers have been seeking for centuries in order to release their clients. The district court refused the earnest colonels, so they filed an appeal a block away in the circuit court. But it appeared that before the wheels of circuit court justice could grind the military sentence would be executed. Defense counsel fled to the Supreme Court and succeeded in having the nine vacationing justices summoned by wire from all parts of the country—on the double.

Some of the crowd that gathered hoped to see the Nazis who had crossed the Atlantic to blow up war plants; others were there to taste war vicariously. As the Court convened, confusion reigned. It had been only eight o'clock the night before that the district court had rejected the saboteurs' pleas. Colonel Kenneth C. Royall, chief of the defense, had not had time to read the government's opposing brief and had to get his colleague admitted to practice before the Court as the first order of business.

The Court wanted to know why counsel hadn't gone through the circuit court before coming to it. "I don't know whether the Court will like to have me say this," Colonel Royall answered, "but as a practical matter this is all we could do." When Royall and Attorney General Francis Biddle paused briefly to whisper together in front of the bench the crowd's laugh had to be quieted with the gavel.

The issues, subordinated to the excitement, were highly technical. Royall wasn't asking the Supreme Court to pass on the merits of the case but only to order a civil trial to supersede the military. The civil courts were functioning in spite of the war, he argued, and Germans were no less "persons" than everyone else guaranteed a trial by jury.

Next day the Court briefly announced that the military had legal jurisdiction; a few days later six of the saboteurs were electrocuted not far from the Court; and three months later the chief justice's long, technical opinion was filed for the unanimous Court.[1] War had come to the Supreme Court with little more effect than interrupting its collective vacation, but a footnote to judicial fairness was furnished by the career of defense counsel Royall. During the trial, he had parried one military question by saying: "I'll have to ask my colleague that one; you see, I've been in the Army only two months." About three years later he had worked up to the position of undersecretary of war.

But if the Court had little trouble in disposing of military questions from the European war, it had to squirm plenty in handling the issues raised later by the war with Japan and the military orders affecting Japanese-Americans on our West Coast. First, the case which will probably be argued longest in the hot-stove league and the law journals: *Korematsu* v. *United States*.[2]

Though Fred Koramatsu's parents were born in Japan, his own birth (in Oakland, California) made him an American citizen. By the time he had finished California public schools he had to use a brother as interpreter when he talked with his Japanese parents. In 1940, at the age of twenty-one, Korematsu was called up by the draft, but he was rejected by the Army because of stomach ulcers. With his $150 savings he learned to be a welder, but it did him little good—after Pearl Harbor he lost his job because of his ancestry.

On March 27, 1942, Korematsu and all other Japanese-Americans were prohibited by the Army from entering or leaving a military area along the West Coast, the idea being that persons of that ancestry might aid their enemy relatives in Japan by acts of sabotage. After a number of other brushes with the law, Korematsu wound up in one of the bleak War Relocation Authority's camps, for more than 112,000 persons of Japanese ancestry. The whole program moved like clockwork. The families were hastily routed out and transported to the interior.

The only catch was that about 70,000 of the people tossed around in this manner were American citizens, presumably protected by a Constitution replete with safeguards against manhandling. Korematsu exercised the only right of citizenship that remained for him—a law suit.

In good time, the Supreme Court granted his request to proceed as a sort of pauper, meaning that the United States would bear the cost of sending the voluminous record up to the high bench; then the Court heard oral arguments.

"The only parallel I have been able to find," said Korematsu's lawyer, "is that of Adolph Hitler, who persecuted citizens because of Jewish ancestry." Then he recited facts in rebuttal of those which the government felt compelled such drastic action. For example: On December 7, 1941, there were 5,000 Japanese Americans in the United States Army and there were no acts of sabotage during or after the attack on Pearl Harbor. His authority: the famous report made for the President by one of the justices he was then standing before, Owen J. Roberts.

Arguing for the government, Solicitor General Charles Fahy insisted, first, that the military order was valid under war powers given by Congress and, second, that the class distinction was a reasonable one to carry out the powers. When a lawyer suggested in behalf of Korematsu that the government had borrowed the device of "protective custody" from the Nazis, Fahy replied: "These people are not prisoners and are not in concentration camps." No one belabored the niceties of the incarceration, but Jackson wanted to know what would terminate it. Fahy explained the system of putting the evacuees through tests to determine their loyalty before releasing them. "The government has felt," he added, "that it must restore their full liberties as soon as it can under the national circumstances. It is one of the most difficult problems the government ever had to handle."

It was not exactly easy for the Court. Black, for a majority of six, first gave a nod to the principle that "all legal restrictions which curtail the civil rights of a single racial group are immediately suspect"; then he found the suspicion of these unwarranted. "We cannot say," he wrote, "that the war-making branches of the Government did not have ground for believing that in a critical hour such persons could not readily be isolated and separately dealt with. . . ."

Black strained mightily at the distinction between merely excluding Japanese-Americans from the area and detaining them. He reasoned that since Korematsu had been convicted of failing to report to or to remain in an assembly or relocation center, the Court didn't have to pass, in this case, on what might have happened to him after reporting there. "Our task would be simple, our duty clear," he stated, "were this a case involving the imprisonment of a loyal citizen in a concentration camp because of racial prejudice."

But the three dissenters, all bitter men that day, found the distinctions too finely drawn for them. The order to leave the area was all part of the detention system to them. Moreover, in the opinion of Roberts these citizens were being put in "concentration camps." An assembly center, he said, was "a euphemism for a prison."

It is, protested Roberts, a case of "convicting a citizen as a punishment for not submitting to imprisonment in a concentration camp, based on his ancestry, and solely because of his ancestry, without evidence or inquiry concerning his loyalty and good disposition towards the United States." Constitutional rights, which the majority opinion lightly skirted, were definitely violated in Roberts' book.

Concerning the majority's distinction between going to an assembly center and going to a relocation center, Roberts asked: "Why should we set up a figmentary and artificial situation instead of addressing ourselves to the actualities of the case?"

Murphy's dissent was concerned, among other things, that the government had shown no good reason for not giving the citizens individual investigations for loyalty. To the answer that "time was of the essence," Murphy retorted that "nearly four months went by until the last order was issued, and the last of these 'subversive' persons was not actually removed until almost eleven months had elapsed." And he found no answer to the fact that no Japanese-American had been accused of sabotage or espionage while all were free.

Jackson was equally hot under the collar but more surprisingly so: "Now, if any fundamental assumption underlies our system, it is that guilt is personal and not inheritable." Of the military necessity argument, Jackson wrote: "But if we cannot confine military expedients by the Constitution, neither would I distort the Constitution to approve all that the military may deem expedient."

It should be noted that a strong support for the Court's position in the evacuation case was its decision without dissent a year and a half before that the West Coast military curfew order against Japanese-Americans was constitutional.[3] Douglas, Murphy and Rutledge each filed concurrences to make it plain that only great and immediate military necessity got around the other constitutional barriers against such discrimination by race.

The case of Mitsuyo Endo,[4] argued and decided with the *Korematsu* case, presented an even more embarrassing situation to the government. She, too, was a citizen—formerly a California state civil service employee with a brother in the United States Army. Shortly after her evacuation to the interior by the government she applied for release. Six months later she got it, meaning that she had been adjudged "loyal"; but she still could not return to California. She refused to leave until she could go anywhere she wanted to. Her legal case was that, even if the original evacuation program were constitutional, further detention of her was not.

When the solicitor general pointed out that Miss Endo was free to leave the camp, so long as she agreed not to return to California, the chief justice asked: "Can a person be loyal in New Jersey and not loyal in California?" The answer was indirect—it wasn't wise to release persons who might go where there would be incidents.

However, the time element made it easy for the Court to dispose of Miss Endo without a dissent. Whereas it would have been in a political hot seat if it had declared the entire evacuation program illegal from the first, it could declare that the investigated and admittedly loyal Japanese-Americans should be released. That is what it did on the same day it rendered the Korematsu decision—December 18, 1944, with the war tide safely turned against the Japanese.

Sixteen months after Miss Endo had been granted general clearance, the Court declared that she should have her liberty. However, the Court did not rest its decision on the constitutional issue of military power; in fact, Douglas said for the Court that the detention here was by a civilian agency. What the Court did was examine the legislation underlying the evacuation program and find no reference to "detention." The original program being legal only as a sabotage and espionage measure, it could not survive against those who had been adjudged loyal, he said. Thus, the program had run its legal course for Miss Endo, and an "unconditional release" was ordered for her.

Murphy added a few words repetitious of his Korematsu dissent, and Roberts still insisted that the Court had skipped the vital constitutional issue: whether the detention violated the guarantees of the Bill of Rights. "There can be but one answer to that question," he declared.

Editorial writers, on the whole, agreed. One of the most extreme views was summed up in the title of a *Harper's* magazine article "America's Greatest Wartime Mistake." The argument was interrupted before long by decisions against actual Japanese war criminals.

When the Supreme Court stayed the execution of Japanese General Tomoyuki Yamashita, "The Tiger of Malaya" and "The Butcher of Luzon," it took on one of the strangest cases in jurisprudence.[5] In the spotless marble temple, 9,000 miles from the foxholes in which American troops fought to regain the Philippines from Yamashita's fanatical army, eight justices undertook to appraise the military trial of their enemy's commanding general. To make matters more confusing Yamashita was defended by three United States Army officers while he waited in a Manila jail to see if the highest court of the conqueror's land would keep its army from carrying out the death sentence.

On the surface it was ridiculous in the extreme, this legal folderol over this man whose bloodthirsty troops had pillaged the Philippines, taking the lives of maybe 60,000 innocent people. As if to flout the absurdity of it all, the chief defense counsel, Colonel Harry E. Clarke, wore a campaign ribbon earned in Buna and Leyte, as well as a Purple Heart from World War I. But the issue was far deeper than quick revenge for Pearl Harbor.

"The gravity of this case lies not in the sentence," Clarke told the Court, "for soldiers always stand close to death. Anglo-Saxon nations take pride in their justice and in their guarantees of civil rights. It may seem to some that these guarantees were never intended for a vanquished enemy general. But does not a defeated enemy general represent that very example of a besieged and helpless human being caught in the net of state power whom it was the impulse of the Bill of Rights to protect?"

No one doubted that the Japanese general would eventually be hanged, but most wondered whether our highly touted system of justice was being fouled up by a couple of "guard-house lawyers" in khaki taking advantage of our expensive technicalities. The defense briefs ran eighty-six pages and the opposition briefs, prepared by the Department of Justice, totaled another forty-eight; but the case can be boiled down to a few paragraphs.

At his trial by a special military commission, created by order of General Douglas MacArthur, Yamashita was charged with responsibility for 123 separate instances of atrocities by Japanese troops. Yamashita's borrowed lawyers contended, first, that their client had done none of the atrocities himself, nor ordered them done by his troops, and could not be charged with the guilt of someone else. Second, the defense argued that the Tiger was entitled at least to regular prisoner-of-war status and that any trial conducted after the war in the Philippines should be conducted by a civil court. Third, the fairness of Yamashita's trial was bitterly attacked, chiefly because he was convicted with the aid of written depositions instead of face-to-face witnesses, as required by law.

The government's rebuttal of these points was, first, that if Yamashita hadn't ordered the atrocities he should have known about and stopped the butchery. If present law doesn't hold a commander liable for his troops, the prosecution argued, then the time has come to write such responsibility into the common law by pioneering with Yamashita's neck. Second, the enemy general was lawfully being tried by the military force which defeated him and was following the administration's pre-VJ-Day policy of trying war criminals. Also, Yamashita could not cover himself with our constitutional guarantees by invading United States territory. Third, as to the fairness of his trial, depositions were used to support only a few of the 123 atrocity charges, leaving more than enough to hang the general.

The shadow of other war trials, chiefly those then being held at Nuremberg, was cast across the mahogany bar. In fact, Justice Jackson was then prosecuting the Nuremberg cases. The justices, in their own uniforms, listened carefully as the five and one-half hours of legal battle progressed.

"His was not a trial as Americans know the term," Clarke told the Court wearily, "and it should not be allowed to stand. The petitioner is charged not with having done something or failed to do something. He is charged with having *been* something—the commanding officer of a Japanese force."

The majority decision, written by the chief justice, was no surprise and afforded little more news copy than it took to support a headline. The ultralegalistic opinion upheld the government's case completely. The military commission was duly authorized, the responsibility for troops under one's command is part of recognized international law, the prohibition against depositions and hearsay evidence does not apply to enemy combatants, and Yamashita was not entitled to the same trial given our own Army personnel. Finally, since the military tribunal was legal, the Court had no business weighing the evidence upon which Yamashita was convicted.

The plain, lengthy majority opinion was attacked bitterly by Murphy and Rutledge, each of whom stole the headlines with dissents. All the fierce eloquence to which a dissent inherently lends itself, while a majority must be duller because it represents more opinions, was mustered by the two. The literary overtones of each belong in their personal chapters, but their imposing legal arguments must be recorded in any discussion of justice at war.

In the division of work between the two brethren, Murphy discussed mainly the substance of the charge against the Japanese general whose troops plundered the islands over which the justice had been high commissioner. Murphy's almost fanatical love for the Philippines was completely buried in his equally strong insistence on fair trials as guaranteed by the 5th amendment to "any person."

Aside from his having been rushed to trial, the main thing that worried Murphy about Yamashita was that he was not even charged with knowledge of the atrocities, much less with having participated in them. The fact, as he saw it, that no precedent for such criminal procedure existed did not concern Murphy so much as the future implications of the case:

"No one in a position of command in an army, from sergeant to general, can escape those implications. Indeed, the fate of some future President of the United States and his chiefs of staff and military advisers may well have been sealed by this decision."

Next, Murphy quoted passages of General George Marshall's report on the war to show how, by our own admission, the United States Army had completely shattered Yamashita's defense in the Philippines, leaving his troops scattered and his command futile. Because it was under those conditions that the atrocities were committed, Murphy felt that Yamashita was actually being accused for failure to maintain the control over his troops which we had made impossible.

The speed of Yamashita's trial was terrific for a major case. On the day he was brought before the military commission he was served with papers alleging sixty-four crimes by his troops. Twenty-one days later he was charged with fifty-nine more of his troops' crimes and denied an adjournment for preparation of a defense against them. Within six weeks he was sentenced to be hanged.

Rutledge was equally concerned about these conditions and complained vigorously against the loaded military commission, especially its charging a man with failure to do something. He pointed out that through we were technically still at war with Japan after VJ-Day there was no danger to the country when Yamashita was tried, no security involved that would justify a military trial. Rutledge then went into a long, documented history of military trials and tried to refute, point by point, the majority contention that this one had been authorized by statutes and international agreements and articles of war.

While details were being arranged for the hanging of Yamashita, stripped of his uniform by a code of disgrace, another Japanese general's case was thrust upon the Court.[6] This time the justices were asked to intervene for Lieutenant General Homma, commander of the bloody campaigns on Corregidor and Bataan. Though Homma was charged chiefly with responsibility for the "death march of Bataan," he was held for forty-seven other specific violations of law.

The Court denied his appeal without an opinion, but Murphy and Rutledge referred to their dissents in the Yamashita case and tossed several more verbal grenades at the military. Murphy deplored the hasty trial and warned: "A procession of judicial lynchings without due process of law may now follow." Rutledge noted that, for the first time, by refusing even to hear the *Homma* case, the Court permitted trial for a capital offense with forced confessions and evidence from previous mass trials.

The same day, February 11, 1946, the military commission finished Homma's trial.

"What did they find me guilty of?" Homma asked, after the sentence had been read. An Army officer handed the defeated general a sealed envelope containing the findings. Homma read the document from beginning to end, then remarked about the penalty of being shot: "Oh, that's good. They're not going to hang me. That (shooting) is an honorable death."

Beyond Homma's jail cell, out in Tokyo, the Murphy-Rutledge dissents pricked the chief United States prosecutor into issuing a denial that "judicial lynchings" will occur in the war criminal trials there. The idea that they would was branded as "offensive, to say the least."

And who was the prosecutor who talked back to a Supreme Court justice? It was Joseph B. Keenan, the man who had done his best in 1937 to get the Senate to pass Roosevelt's plan to get new blood on the Court.

But the final word belonged to General Douglas MacArthur, commenting on his affirmative review of the Homma death sentence. Of the two dissents he said: "No trial could have been fairer. . . . Those who would oppose such an honest method can only be a minority who either advocate arbitrariness of process above actual realism, or who inherently shrink . . . from capital punishment."

Two weeks later the Court handed down a decision that involved some of the same issues but was nearer home and was not supercharged with the advance feeling that the men involved were guilty. The question was whether military tribunals in Hawaii had the power to supersede the civilian courts in dispensing justice to civilians in United States territory during a period of martial law.

A few hours after the sneak attack on Pearl Harbor, the governor of Hawaii proclaimed martial law and suspended the writ of habeas corpus, meaning that no one could appeal to the courts for a jury trial. The law allowed this procedure "in case of rebellion or invasion, or imminent danger thereof, when the public safety requires it." President Roosevelt cabled his approval of the procedure and the romantic island territory became one big military outpost. Justice was thereafter dispensed under the vaguest imaginable safeguards, but quickly.

Eight months after the attack, Harry E. White, a Honolulu stockbroker, was arrested by military police and charged with embezzling stock of another civilian. He was taken before a provost court, refused a civilian jury trial and—five days after his arrest—sentenced to five years in prison, later reduced to four.

Lloyd C. Duncan, a civilian shipfitter, was arrested more than two years after the attack for brawling with two armed Marine sentries at the Navy Yard where he worked. By this time civilian courts had been reopened for some types of cases (but not those involving military personnel), and schools, bars and theaters had been reopened. Over his plea of self-defense, Duncan was sentenced to six months' imprisonment by a provost court. More than four years after the Pearl Harbor attack the two cases were decided by the Supreme Court[7] as a test of the entire procedure in Hawaii. The answer, like that of the lawyer summoned to talk to a man in the local jail: They can't do this to you!

Justice Black, for a six-man majority, cautiously reserved decision on the legality of suspending habeas corpus in the first place, but held that military tribunals should not have replaced regular civilian court trials at the time White and Duncan were jailed. Black had to review the entire subject of martial law to see whether its use in the statute included what he called "this awesome power" to exclude the courts. He found at the outset that no one knew precisely what it meant, but held that it had never been used as it was in Hawaii. He recalled that one of the grievances listed at the time of the Declaration of Independence was that the king had tried to "render the military superior to the civil power," and observed that even in dispatching troops to quell Shay's rebellion, in 1787, and the Whiskey Rebellion, in 1794, authorities had carefully instructed the military to deliver offenders to regular courts for trial. The same principle, Black believed, carried over into congressional authorization for martial law in Hawaii—at least when the court buildings were open and able to do business.

The civilian victory was decisive, but not decisive enough for Murphy. In a separate concurrence he joined with the Court in thinking that military trials in the two cases were unjustified by the congressional act, but added that the first ten amendments also made them illegal. Contrasted to what he termed the "streamlined treatment" given White and Duncan by the military, Murphy insisted that the law plainly allowed the citizens a jury trial. "In short," he wrote, "the Bill of Rights disappeared by military fiat rather than by military necessity."

The argument that juries composed of the many races in Hawaii, particularly of Japanese, might cause trouble angered Murphy. "Especially deplorable," he wrote, "is this use of the iniquitous doctrine of racism to justify the imposition of military trials." He then noted from the record that there had been no acts of sabotage, espionage or fifth column activities by persons of Japanese descent in Hawaii either on or after December 7, 1941.

The dissent, sixteen pages long, was written by the Court freshman, Harold Burton, joined by Frankfurter. Burton first genuflected before the Constitution ("I prefer civil to military control of civilian life. . . ."), then stated that "the controlling facts" in the cases were the "extraordinary conditions" created by the surprise invasion. "The islands were a white hot center of war ready to burst into flames," he wrote, offering quotes from the Army and Navy commanders there to prove his point. In fact, if one did not read the opinion closely he might think the December seventh attack were still in progress. And it was up to the military, Burton and Frankfurter thought, to end martial law when they liked.

The administration took its reversal like a man, dispatching word to Hawaii to start releasing or arranging for the retrial of the thousands of others for whom the White and Duncan cases were good news. The Department of Justice heaved a sigh to have the issue settled, for officials there privately felt that their case was very feeble—so much so that they had trouble finding someone to present it. Only at the War Department was the decision taken hard, and for a good reason: Major General Thomas Green, the Army's judge advocate general, had been, as chief legal officer of the Army's Hawaiian department, responsible for the whole situation.

Laymen, too, saw the far-reaching implications of the Court's forthright decision. The New York *Times*' Washington pundit, Arthur Krock, found himself in agreement with the Court for a change, and the Washington *Post* editorialized: "The court is very tardy in setting the record straight, as courts usually are. Nevertheless, it is heartening to have the constitutional rights of citizens upheld and the rule of law resustained over and above military dictation."

About one block away, across the park that separates Congress from the Supreme Court, the mixture of law and philosophy, of military expediency and enduring liberty, was likewise bothering ninety-six senators and 435 representatives. While the Court was deciding the issues over Yamashita, Homma and the law in Hawaii, Congress was wrestling with compulsory military training, retention of war-won island bases, release of men still in the victorious military force and civilian or military control of atomic energy. And congressional confusion was no worse than the groping tactics of the administration and the bewilderment of the citizenry who stepped into public forums to state their cases.

The Court, presumably confined by what it could find in its library, was by no means able to find a neat formula for resolving the conflict between military and civilian jurisdictions. Nor could it find an easy way out of the problem of punishing war criminals without planting the seeds of hatred which sprout so easily on conquered soil, even before the occupation armies withdraw. The Court had only one advantage: it could state its position by written decisions and cite cases from either side of the fence to justify its decisions. The justices who chose the unpopular side from which to draw their citations chose the hard way out, for which they will undoubtedly be quoted much longer than their brethren of the majority.

The plain truth is that the Court was put on its unenviable spot in these cases because the government was pioneering—breaking ground not only in international relations and treatment of defeated aggressor enemies but also in the law of punishment. No one had remembered to write the new principles into the law books.

However, in the two major cases which involved United States citizens, rather than war criminals, the Court had its choice of two guiding documents: congressional acts and the Constitution. When the Court upheld relocation of citizens and when it ruled in favor of civilian over military rule in Hawaii, it reached opposite conclusions in relation to protecting civil liberties. But it used congressional statutes rather than the Constitution to govern both decisions.

After the specific cases are yellowed with age and the Japanese-Americans have drifted back to wherever they want to go there will be a tendency to forget which way the Court turned in each. However, the underlying principle that congressional laws rather than the Constitution should govern such conflicts is something that will have to be reckoned with later in history, for acts of Congress are usually written in the passion of destroying an enemy. The safeguards of the Constitution, written in the passion of establishing liberty, were used by only a minority of the Court as the enduring guide.

Thus, though the votes in these war cases were not closely divided, giving the appearance of settling issues firmly, another war, another Congress and another Court would revive the issues.

CHAPTER XVI

The Other Justice

WILEY," said the President of the United States, "we had a number of candidates for the Court who were highly qualified, but they didn't have geography—you have that." Attorney General Biddle had brought Wiley Blount Rutledge over to the White House to meet the President that day, early in January of 1943. The well-known Roosevelt charm was turned on, hence the first name technique, and he was having a little joke with the genial judge from the circuit court of appeals for the District of Columbia. However, it wasn't all a joke. On a blank commission form, Roosevelt penned Rutledge's name, inserting after it the geographical designation: Iowa.

The President could just as well have filled in the names of several other states, for Rutledge does have geography. The anecdote illustrates the seriousness with which Presidents try to keep the Court balanced sectionally—this was Roosevelt's eighth appointment—and it illustrates as well how some men achieve the highest place in the nation's judiciary by accident of residence, while others are denied it for the same reason.

Let there be no mistake, however. Rutledge was no fluke. His name was not uppermost on the mythical list which appears like a rash when a vacancy occurs, but it was there. He had been a teacher of the law for many years, with some distinction, and had the advantage most Roosevelt appointees had not; namely, judicial experience. He had been proposed to the White House once before by Iowa's former senator, Guy Gillette, who was then still under the administration's purge cloud for having fought the Court reorganization. The significant thing about Rutledge's past, as of the time he was nominated, is that there was not a vote against his confirmation, yet he holds ideas far different from those of a majority of the Senate.

The importance of his views became apparent the very moment the marshal ushered him to his seat at the chief's far left. A page boy had hardly pushed the heavy black leather swivel chair under him before it was announced that three cases would have to be reargued. Presumably, the departure of Jimmy Byrnes, whose place Rutledge took, had caused a 4-to-4 deadlock, which the freshman would have to break.

The vote he cast in each of them is typical of his record ever since.[1] He joined with Stone, Black, Douglas and Murphy to upset several decisions which had run against the Jehovah's Witnesses; and, with Reed substituted for Stone, he tipped the scales in favor of Communist William Schneiderman, whom the government sought to denaturalize. Also, he voted with the Federal Power Commission against a power company on the borderline of interstate commerce.

Against this preview of his opinions Rutledge's background is not very revealing unless one believes in the existence of a western way of thinking. If there is such a thing and if it includes a "live and let live" philosophy, an open but not aggressive manner and a relaxed approach to great issues, then Rutledge is a product of that culture. Add a dash of southern hospitality, the only trait he carried back from several years below the Mason-Dixon line, mix in a liberal portion of book learning and you have the unpretentious man who rocks comfortably in his swivel chair.

Rutledge began on July 20, 1894, the life which was to take him in and out of towns too small to appear in ordinary lists of population. The town of his birth was Cloverport, Kentucky, where his father was the Baptist minister during Wiley's first six years of life. The peregrinations of this profession took the Rutledge family to Asheville, North Carolina, for three years, then back to a Kentucky farm before settling down in Maryville, Tennessee, for a while to be near better schools. Wiley attended Maryville College, where he majored in the classics that nearly everyone chose in those days. However, he decided to take his last year at the University of Wisconsin, where he shifted to chemistry and received an A.B. degree in 1914.

Times were hard for the Rutledge family and the brand-new college graduate chose the conventional way to lay a little money away for the study of law: schoolteaching. In the next eight years, before finally finishing law, Rutledge taught high school in Bloomington and Connersville, Indiana; Albuquerque, New Mexico; and Boulder, Colorado. In the middle of this pedagogy, however, he contracted tuberculosis and returned to Asheville for a year's rest. It was while teaching at Boulder that Rutledge finished law school, at the University of Colorado. For two years thereafter he engaged in private practice in Boulder, but teaching called him and he joined the Colorado faculty. He stayed only two years but returned to conduct a few courses every summer for many years thereafter. Boulder is still headquarters for annual family vacations, though much of his idle time is spent far up in the Rockies and over on the western slope, where he camps and fishes several miles from any road. His tuberculosis had long since been arrested, but Rutledge is not a picture of health, even though his handsome face is full and he has a small bay window below his belt line.

In 1926 he left Colorado for a bigger job at Washington University in St. Louis, where he taught four years before being made dean of the law school. He is remembered by St. Louis as very much of a public-minded citizen of the city. His merits were heralded there by the newspapers and were even made known in Washington by impressed correspondents. Some, in fact, give a *Post-Dispatch* writer credit for his Court appointment. After five years as dean at St. Louis he was called to the University of Iowa to head that law school, which he did for four years. More people still know him as "dean" than as "judge" or "Mr. Justice"; and Rutledge still regards himself as a teacher of the law. He loved the job of "deaning" because, as his former students testify, it gave him a chance to help young men with personal problems. Each student who worked his way through a Rutledge-run law school knew that the man in the front office was personally concerned about him. Those who merely came in to talk over their futures, as they approached graduation, were given a formula for getting out into the world, though the man who gave it to them has practically no use for formulas. "Decide where you want to live," he would say, "then go after your work. If you want the bright lights, symphonies and advantages of big cities, go there; if you want the small town, take it. For no matter where you go, if you have ability you'll get to the top. However, don't set your heart on any single top place, or you'll be disappointed. Just do your job and play your breaks and you'll get what's coming."

Whatever the merits of this, it worked for Wiley Rutledge. He liked every place he worked, he played his breaks and he was on the top rung at the age of forty-nine.

By 1937, Rutledge was certainly not famous but he was fairly well known and fully respected in his circle. He had been teaching mainly business organization—agency, partnership, etc.—but also torts, conflicts of law, constitutional law and a little of everything else. He had been active in the Association of American Law Schools and the section on legal education of the American Bar Association. He had taken particular interest in his job as a member of the National Conference of Commissioners of Uniform Laws, an adjunct of the ABA which drafts model statutes and otherwise does what its title indicates. One of his main chores for the conference was ironing out the many defects in state "fair trade" legislation, laws passed so fast by many states that even typographical errors in the original were not caught.

When the administration was rounding up witnesses for its Court plan, a high official called Wiley Rutledge. Who could lend more prestige than the dean of a simon-pure Midwestern law school? Slight inquiry would have revealed that Rutledge had been friendly to the administration in what little politics he had uttered. On the Court fight, itself, he had made a few local speeches, taking the stand that the old Court was dead wrong in putting manufacturing and agriculture outside the power of legislative regulation, but he also thought that the plan was trying to accomplish more than its ostensible purpose—to speed up the docket. He favored some system for retirement of justices at the end of their usefulness, even if against their will, but he opposed a mechanical formula based on age for accomplishing the end. Such nonsense would have cut off at their half-way points the careers of Brandeis, Holmes, Marshall and Taney, for example. Rutledge did not appear as a witness.

He had certainly not curried favor with the Department of Justice, as a law dean ambitious of a judgeship would have; but neither did he get himself crossed off the list—real and imaginary—of judicial possibilities for the faithful. Frank Murphy, who had succeeded Cummings as attorney general by 1939, turned up Rutledge in a campaign to recruit from the law schools for the federal bench. Roosevelt appointed him judge on the circuit court of appeals for the District of Columbia in 1939 and he settled down with his wife and children to a life which to most lawyers would be the ultimate. Wiley Rutledge had little reason to think differently, but his solidly progressive background and his satisfactory (though not spectacular) work on the circuit court made him a sound choice for the Byrnes vacancy.

Rutledge's first opinion for the Supreme Court was typical of many to follow, except that there was only one dissent from it. He extended the liability of shipowners to cover accidents to the crew which occur along the way between the ship and the nearest public thoroughfare near the dock. The two crew members involved (one of whom was named David Jones) were not on ship's business but were on authorized leave; the Court ruled that their welfare was covered during that period.[2]

The freshman's first dissent came in a 5-to-3 split whereby the Court declared invalid certain claims for patents on Marconi's wireless radio development.[3] Rutledge is no lover of patents, but he felt that in this case the scientist was being deprived of fruits of genuine invention.

"Until now," wrote Rutledge, "law had united with almost universal repute in acknowledging Marconi as the first to establish wireless telegraphy on a commercial basis. Before his invention, now in issue, etherborne communication traveled some eighty miles. He lengthened the arc to 6,000. Whether or not this was 'inventive' legally, it was a great and beneficial achievement. Today, forty years after the event, the Court's decision reduces it to an electrical mechanic's application of mere skill in the art.

"By present knowledge, it would be no more. School boys and mechanics now could perform what Marconi did in 1900. But before then wizards had tried and failed. . . . The invention was, so to speak, hovering in the general climate of science, momentarily awaiting birth. But just the right releasing touch had not been found. Marconi added it."

The dissent was more illustrative of Rutledge's ability to sprinkle his opinions with kernels of real prose, imbedded in far too many pages of words, than it was of his general attitude toward patents. So much for his first utterances; now for an analysis of his opinions, especially dissents.

On the subject of the federal system Rutledge is by no means doctrinaire, except perhaps that he is among the many who see no legal objection to expanded federal control in that vague area of interstate commerce. He had never been able to reconcile the Court's long-standing inclusion of industry and business within the realm of control for purposes of the antitrust laws with its exclusion of the same segment of the economy from such regulations as those in hours and wages. But there is no longer anything radical about that and Rutledge is merely one of those who call them as they see them.

His opinion of the proper relationship among the executive, legislative and judicial branches of the government was made plain in a dissent when the Court upset an interpretation of the Wage and Hour Administration of the coverage of some agricultural laborers.[4] With Black and Murphy concurring he took a crack at Frankfurter's opinion for the Court which allowed the company retroactive relief.

"The administrative process has increasingly important functions in our legal system. Ordinarily it does enough, if it takes care of today and tomorrow. When it begins to add yesterday, without clear congressional mandate, the burden may become too great. In any event, that has not heretofore generally been considered its task. If that task is to be added, the addition should be made by the body whence administrative power is derived, not by this Court's imaginative resourcefulness."

When the Court got involved in legal niceties presented by three state taxes, one a sales tax, one a use tax and one a tax on gross sales of foreign corporations on the business done within the taxing state—Rutledge protested that he could see no difference among them, except for words.[5] He would have upheld validity of the lot, so long as they were not discriminatory; whereas the Court nullified the sales tax. However, he later drew hard looks from Black, Douglas and Murphy when he wrote the opinion striking down Richmond's $50 annual license fee against solicitors, when applied to interstate transactions.[6]

"The drummer is a figure representative of a by-gone day," Rutledge wrote. "But his modern prototype persists under more euphonious appellations. So endure the basic reasons which brought about his protection from the kind of local favoritism the facts of this case typify."

Rutledge's most scornful comments on the Court's action in a federal system case came in his dissent (joined by Douglas) in the second of the famous Williams divorce cases,[7] whereby it was held that Nevada divorces (or others) could be ignored by another state. Of the folderol about the theory of jurisdiction which underlay the Court's decision Rutledge said:

"Once again the ghost of 'unitary domicil' returns on its perpetual round, in the guise of 'jurisdictional fact,' to upset judgments, marriages, divorces, undermine the relations founded upon them, and make this Court the unwilling and uncertain arbiter between the concededly valid laws and decrees of sister states."

The Court had wandered through a long maze, Rutledge lamented, "only to come out with no settled constitutional policy where one is needed most." He pointed out that the Court had not actually voided the Nevada divorce, had only allowed North Carolina to ignore it if it chose to take action such as bigamy charges against persons holding a Nevada quickie. In fact, he pointed out that one of the divorced spouses was still lawfully wedded in North Carolina and might also be tried for bigamy. Were that to happen, he continued, the jury might conclude that the same Nevada divorce which got the other couple in bigamous trouble at the hands of another jury was perfectly valid. Thus, from the same evidence, two juries could find one graduate from Reno living in sin while the other had done nothing wrong. "Were all judgments (of other states) given the same infirmity," said Rutledge, "the full faith and credit clause would be only a dead constitutional letter."

In the field of labor Rutledge usually goes along with the administrative agency, as opposed to the company being regulated, thus being definitely a prolabor member of the Court. However, there is more than personal sympathy to put him on that side—he believes in the use of experts to do the bulk of the work in this and other fields, backed up by a light-handed judiciary. In the rare instances when he can't go along, however, he lashes right out. When an employer got in trouble with the NLRB for going around a union committee to deal directly with employees, who later repudiated the union, Rutledge dissented.[8]

"The story told by this record," he said, "is not of a dominating or intermeddling employer, interfering with employees in their collective bargaining arrangements or activities. It is rather one which sought to do no more than meet its employees' wishes, freely formed and freely stated; and at the same time to be sure it would do nothing to violate the law governing their relations." And, farther on: "I do not think Congress intended by this legislation, to create rights in unions overriding those of the employees they represent."

Again, in a case involving the well-established labor relations system of the railroad industry, Rutledge took a stand directly contrary to that of organized labor.[9] He wrote the majority (five to four) opinion holding that an individual employee may have judicial review of an award by the Railroad Adjustment Board based on a collective bargaining arrangement in which the employee had not specifically authorized a compromise of his claims. Organized labor came screaming to the Court to demand a reconsideration of this blow to collective bargaining agreements, but a majority turned them back, again through Rutledge.

A labor case from last term in which Rutledge spoke for the Court to enlarge a shipowner's liability for accidents aboard ship is more typical of his attitude toward the flexibility of the law.[10] A shipowner had been for many years liable for damages caused to a crew member by reason of the vessel's not being seaworthy, whether the owner was negligent or not. This time, however, suit was brought by a longshoreman, not a member of the crew but only aboard long enough to unload cargo. However, he was injured by an admitted lack of seaworthiness. Rutledge stepped into the case boldly to extend the owner's liability to the longshoreman, reasoning that in this age of specialized labor the men who unload cargo are covered as much as are the actual crew members, who formerly did the unloading. This is true, the split Court ruled, even though the longshoreman or stevedore is employed by a special firm rather than by the shipowner.

Of the unique law of seamen's injuries he said: "It is essentially a species of liability without fault, analogous to other well-known instances in our law. Derived from and shaped to meet the hazards which performing the service imposes, the liability is neither limited by conceptions of negligence nor contractual in character. It is a form of absolute duty owing to all within the range of its humanitarian policy."

The area of decisions in which Rutledge most often puts in a few words for himself concerns civil liberties. Here his position is closest to that of Murphy, making him co-keeper of the Court's conscience on civil liberties and earning him little current popularity. One of his first separate concurrences, in a denaturalization case, revealed his feelings clearly:[11]

"Immediately we are concerned with only one man, William Schneiderman. Actually, though indirectly, the decision affects millions.

If, seventeen years after a federal court adjudged him entitled to be a citizen, that judgment can be nullified and he can be stripped of this most precious right, by nothing more than re-examination upon the merits of the very facts the judgment established, no naturalized person's citizenship is or can be secure. If this can be done after that length of time, it can be done after thirty or fifty years. If it can be done for Schneiderman, it can be done for thousands or tens of thousands of others. . . .

"No citizen with such a threat hanging over his head could be free. If he belonged to 'off-color' organizations or held too radical or, perhaps, too reactionary views, for some segment of the judicial palate, when his admission took place, he could not open his mouth without fear his words would be held against him. . . . His best course would be silence or hypocrisy. This is not citizenship. Nor is it adjudication."

Similarly, two terms later, when the Court upheld denaturalization of one who was in fact a Nazi at the time he took his citizenship oath, Rutledge wrote about the implications rather than the immediate man in court.[12]

"My concern is not for Paul Knauer," he dissented. "The record discloses that he had no conception of, much less attachment to, basic American principles or institutions. He was a thoroughgoing Nazi, addicted to philosophies altogether hostile to the democratic framework in which we believe and live. . . . If therefore in any case a naturalized citizen's right and status can be revoked . . . it would be in such a case as this. But if one man's citizenship can thus be taken away, so can that of any other. . . . No native-born American's birthright could be stripped from him for such a cause or by such a procedure as has been followed here."

He disagreed with the Court's assertion that it was not making naturalized citizens second-class citizens, adding that "if this means that some or even many disloyal foreign-born citizens cannot be deported, it is better so than to place so many loyal ones in inferior status."

Cases in which defendants have been denied aid of counsel nearly always find Rutledge on the defendant's side. For example, he recently dissented when the Court upheld one of these convictions on the grounds that special features of New York law made the absence not prejudicial in that instance.[13] After analyzing the law Rutledge concluded in behalf of the defendant: "There was no choice but Hobson's."

And in the course of protecting the constitutional ban on unreasonable searches and seizures, Rutledge agreed, in the main, with Frankfurter's long, vitriolic dissent in the gasoline coupons case.[14]

Another Rutledge concern is that no man be convicted under a vague law. When the Court upheld a death sentence for kidnapping, though the law specified that "the sentence of death shall not be imposed by the court if prior to its imposition, the kidnapped person has been liberated unharmed," Rutledge dissented at length, almost lampooning his brethren of the majority.[15] The kidnapped person had been hit twice on the head with an iron bar and her lips abrased and made swollen by application of a tape gag. When she was set free, six weeks later, these wounds were not healed. There was no evidence at the trial, about nine years after the crime, that the injuries were permanent.

Rutledge, with whom Murphy joined, confessed that he didn't know what the phrase "liberated unharmed" meant and that he was unable to see that Congress did. He listed all kinds of things, including mental fear, which might be classed as "harm," then pointed out that a kidnapper might get off easy by holding his victim until the injuries healed. "Is reward thus to be given for prolonging the agony?" he asked rhetorically. Rutledge would have set aside the conviction and tossed the poorly drafted law back to Congress for tightening up rather than have the Court tinker with it by the "judicial legislation," which he felt the majority wrongly engaged in.

Similarly, Rutledge felt compelled to reverse the conviction of the three southern officers who fatally beat their colored, handcuffed suspect.[16] He admittedly wanted to see the men punished for their "gross abuse" of authority, but he felt that the law under which they were prosecuted was too ambiguous to sustain a conviction. Rutledge was in the unique position of having to cast his vote in favor of the officers in order that the badly split Court could have a majority to dispose of the case. His individual opinion explaining the predicament was long, including an extensive history of the law involved, the one that punishes a conspiracy to prevent any citizen from "the free exercise of enjoyment of any right or privilege secured to him by the Constitution or laws of the United States. The history should not require retelling, he admitted. "But the old and established freedoms vanish when history is forgotten." It was an eloquent plea for clarification of the act.

Among Rutledge's majority opinions in protection of individuals, the most famous was that putting four-wheel brakes on the Texas law requiring registration of union organizers.[17] No one on the Court doubted that Texas could regulate unions in a number of ways, but this one—applied to an organizer coming in from out of state expressly to make a speech—could not stand.

"It was not by accident or coincidence that the rights to freedom in speech and press were coupled in a single guaranty with the rights of the people peaceably to assemble and to petition for redress of grievances," he wrote. It is from petty tyrannies that large ones take root and grow, he said, adding: "Seedlings planted in that soil grow great and, growing, break down the foundations of liberty."

He also wrote for the Court an opinion sharply curbing the use of mass trials for conspiracy.[18] The abuse struck down was an attempt to sustain a flock of conspiracies held together only by the slender fact that one man was common to all of them. "Guilt with us," Rutledge wrote for the Court, "remains individual and personal, even as respects conspiracies. It is not a matter of mass application."

Occasionally, however, Rutledge is on the other side of the Court on civil rights. His second majority opinion, upholding a directed verdict against a veteran's claim on the government, was attacked vociferously by the liberals who later were in fairly steady company with him.[19] They felt that the decision by Rutledge was a dangerous departure from the guarantee of a jury trial. Also, he wrote the majority opinion, in a 5-to-4 split, holding that a Massachusetts law banning child labor takes priority over the constitutional freedom of religion, as applied to a youngster of the Jehovah's Witnesses.[20]

It has been in the cases testing war powers that Rutledge's name has most frequently been in the news—always on the unpopular side. If one plotted Rutledge's votes in war cases on a chart he could easily conclude statistically that the justice is both a bitter isolationist and a mossback reactionary worried about the government getting into new functions. Interestingly enough, the exact opposite is true. Rutledge puts his predilections far, far away when he votes on war issues. His public statements prove his support of World War II and it is as easily ascertainable that he loses no sleep over government control of economics.

Nevertheless, he had been (with Murphy) a strong dissenter in a lost-cause way on war cases. In the field of civilian regulations he voted against the validity of the price control legislation on which OPA was based because of its procedural shortcomings, its failure to protect those accused of violations.[21] The perspective against which he viewed these defects was pictured as follows:

"War such as we now fight calls into play the full power of government in extreme emergency. It compels invention of legal, as of martial tools adequate for the Times' necessity. Inevitably some will be strange, if also life-saving, instruments for a people accustomed to peace and the normal working of constitutional limitations. Citizens must surrender or forego exercising rights which in other times could not be impaired. But not all are lost. War expands the nation's power. But it does not suspend the judicial duty to guard whatever liberties will not imperil the paramount national interest."

His worry was that the act allowed the government many avenues of enforcing its regulations, while the individual questioning the validity of a regulation has "one route and that a very narrow one, open only briefly." Of this procedural pattern he protested: "Once approved, it is bound to spawn progeny." Moreover, he thought it unnecessary to effective price control to keep the courts from judging the validity of regulations which it was called on to enforce criminally. In the instance of rent control, however, he felt that the procedural system was adequate enough that he went along with the Court in upholding it.[22]

It was in the cases involving Japanese war criminals that Rutledge really cried outrage. He had gone along with the Court in the Japanese relocation cases but had paused in the Japanese curfew case to light a time fuse in the form of reserving his right to insist on judicial review of certain military decisions. Early in 1946 the blast at the military went off as a dissent in the hurried-up case against General Yamashita.[23]

His extremely long opinion was based mainly on the contention that the military never had jurisdiction to try the defeated general and that, even if they did have, the trial was unfair in a constitutional way. It was too early after V-J-Day, he wrote, for Lincoln's creed to "have wide hold for the treatment of foes"; but he added that "it is not too early, it is never too early, for the nation steadfastly to follow its great constitutional traditions. . . ."

Of the guarantee for due process in trials Rutledge said: "This long-held attachment marks the great divide between our enemies and ourselves. Theirs was a philosophy of universal force. Ours is one of universal law. . . ." His treatise ended with a quotation from Thomas Paine: "He that would make his own liberty secure must guard even his enemy from oppression; for if he violates this duty he establishes a precedent that will reach himself."

Three days later, when the Court turned down a similar appeal from General Homma without doing more than citing the Yamashita case, Rutledge and Murphy dissented again but only briefly. Rutledge merely listed the specific violations of due process which he felt the Court was brushing aside in dismissing both appeals.

These are the opinions of the man who is the least known of the Roosevelt appointees. However, the fact that he may often be thought of as "the other justice," after his seniors have been named accurately, is not to his discredit. It is almost enough to point out that he was the only appointee not elevated from political fields, in which names reach the headlines.

Several factors indicate a better place in the sun to come for Wiley Rutledge. His versatility is an advantage in spite of the age of legal specialization, which accounted in large part, for example, for the rise of William Douglas. Though not a real practitioner of the law before his judicial appointment, Rutledge's background is rich in the advantage that comes to those who teach the law, see its changes indicated or pleaded for in the law journals which practitioners get little chance to read.

It should not be thought, however, that Rutledge was a hothouse product in the sense of sitting in the stacks of a library while others enjoyed life. Though he is not a "joiner," he was active in and enjoyed immensely Iowa City's Rotary Club. To put it tritely, he is a hale fellow well met.

It is doubtful, though, that he would deny having spent considerable time in an ivory tower, thinking of the law as it should be in an ideal society rather than how it will be the next morning in a specific court. His bent for protecting the individual—usually a little fellow—came from no organizational affiliation nor any other source more obvious than a long-time mellowing in his own mind as a quality of justice. Hence he cannot be personally attacked for a hard-hitting but unpopular opinion which would be dismissed by some people as just another radical opinion if expressed by Black, Douglas or Murphy.

He is a New Dealer without having labored in the New Deal vineyard; he is unassailable with conventional stigmas, unless it be that of "college professor." Even that dubious epithet was modified by his four years on the circuit court bench without mishap at the hands of professional bench-watchers.

For these reasons alone Rutledge's career from here on has few limitations on it, few preconceived public notions to curb it. His opinions can pretty well stand on their merits without having innuendoes read into them. They are too verbose to be characterized as classics, even if history should adopt his views of the law, yet there are sparkling places in them reminiscent of former justices who have been acclaimed great. Fortunately, judicial merit is not based alone on literary style, but catchwords passed over lightly today frequently become whole doctrines in the next generation of law, or the one after that.

Throughout the bickering on the Court, Rutledge has kept out of the cross fire. Equally important, he has not been mentioned in the public argument about it. Whether this was due to his determination to remain aloof or was due to the circumstance of his having been brought in from a zone of no politics doesn't matter. His personal prestige is unsullied and he can go right on with his liberal law—without pulling punches.

CHAPTER XVII

Inches and Miles

DOWN in Texas several years ago a Negro by the name of Bob White was accused of raping white Mrs. W. S. Cochran, was tried and sentenced to death. An appeal to the highest court of the state was rejected, as was one to the United States Supreme Court. Three months later the Court rendered its classic opinion in *Chambers* v. *Florida,* striking down a conviction gained through a coerced confession. Immediately, Bob White's lawyers renewed their appeal, pleading that the Negro had confessed raping Mrs. Cochran only because the Texas Rangers took him into the woods for quizzing so many nights that they could not remember exactly how many it was. A few weeks later the Court took the case and reversed the state court's conviction of White.[1]

"Due process of law, preserved for all by our Constitution, commands that no such practice as that disclosed by this record, shall send any accused to his death," declared Black for a unanimous Court, quoting from his *Chambers* opinion.

About one year later, while the jury was being selected for a retrial of Bob White, W. S. Cochran walked up to the prisoner and shot him through the head. The United States Supreme Court had been reversed.

Five years later—on the Fourth of July, 1946, to be exact and ironic—the National Opinion Research Center published results of a poll on civil liberties. Apparently the Supreme Court had been wasting its time in being vigilant toward the Bill of Rights, for one out of three people in the poll opposed freedom of speech even in theory. Asked if people should, in peacetime, be allowed to say anything they want in public, 32 per cent replied "no." Only half believed that Communists should be allowed to talk on the radio and 39 per cent said that Communists should be barred from the air.

But even if the justices read the opinion poll carefully they would probably not take it seriously, for the very nature of civil liberties makes most cases in that category barren of any immediate popularity for the justices. A decision in favor of some lousy character whose rights have technically been denied him is most likely to be greeted on Tuesday morning by an exclamation such as, "Why the hell does that stupid Court waste taxpayers' money on that jerk!" To seek a comment on specific civil rights cases is to get a popular response demonstrative of the very reason that the Constitution gave the ivory-tower Court protection of those rights, rather than giving them to Congress or the President. Not even friends of the New Deal would deny that the Roosevelt administration overreached in a number of its prosecutions. Fortunately, the Court has willingly played backstop for these wild pitches.

Because these cases usually involve colorful people, repulsive as some of them may be, the Court decisions are prominently played in the press. No group of cases got more attention than those involving Jehovah's Witnesses.

The Court's treatment of this small sect started during the great Court fight. Because of this coincidence, the story of the legal scrapes of the belligerent, doorbell-ringing sect illustrates far more about the present Court than merely its attitude toward freedom of religion. The eight years of litigation also reveal the inner scramble of the Nine Young Men to pull together their rugged individualisms.

Justices Black and Reed had hardly donned their robes when the first case came up for argument.[2] The Witnesses ran afoul of a Griffin, Georgia, ordinance which required permission of the city manager before leaflets could be distributed. Chief Justice Hughes, for a unanimous Court, hurled one of his thunderbolts at the city, striking the narrow-minded law with such a flash that the case is now cited as a bulwark not only for religious practitioners but for all pamphleteers.

The Griffin pattern continued for several years, with enough new wrinkles introduced periodically to require the Court's attention now and then. In 1939, an 8-to-1 Court struck down a law requiring a police permit for door-to-door solicitation.[3] The ordinance was ostensibly to prevent, also, littering of the street; but it was voided as applied to religious "literature." Next year the Court protected Witness Newton Cantwell and his two sons from the wrath of the law in New Haven, Connecticut, where they had toured a Catholic district playing a phonograph record attack on the unwilling listeners' church.

"For more than 1,500 years," the record blared, "a great religious system, operating out of Rome, has by means of fraud and deception brought untold sorrow and suffering on the people. It operates the greatest racket ever employed amongst men and robs the people of their money and destroys their peace of mind and freedom of action. . . ."

This vitriol was typical of the rash of doorbell evangelism then current with Jehovah's Witnesses. The Cantwells were arrested for soliciting money without a permit and for breaking the peace. In the Court's chamber the belligerency of the Witnesses' methods evoked a number of interruptions from the bench, the most interesting being that of Justice McReynolds. When he interjected that Jesus stirred up "a good deal of trouble in Jerusalem," the Connecticut attorney general replied: "As I remember my Bible, something was done about that." The Court did not take his suggestion; it voided the law unanimously.[4]

Two weeks later, the luck of the Witnesses changed. Lillian and William Gobitis, aged twelve and ten, had been expelled from the Minersville, Pennsylvania, public schools for refusing to participate in a compulsory flag salute ceremony. Their parents, Witnesses, had taught the youngsters not to salute flags, relying on such Biblical mandates as "Thou shalt have no other gods before me" and "Thou shalt not make unto thee any graven image." Mr. Gobitis was forced to put his children in a private school, as the state law required them to be in some school. Trapped between the Lord and the truant officer, he appealed the case. For eight members of the Court, Frankfurter resolved in favor of the school board what he called a conflict between liberty and conscience and the authority to safeguard the "nation's fellowship."[5] He spoke of the flag as the symbol of national unity; but Stone, in a lone dissent, took a different view of nationalism.

"The law which is thus sustained is unique in the history of Anglo-American legislation," he said. "It does more than suppress freedom of speech and more than prohibit the free exercise of religion. . . . For by this law the State seeks to coerce these children to express a sentiment which, as they interpret it, they do not entertain. . . ."

Then Stone delivered this often-quoted sentence:

"History teaches us that there have been but few infringements of personal liberty by the state which have not been justified, as they are here, in the name of righteousness and the public good, and few which have not been directed, as they are now, at politically helpless minorities."

About an hour before these two opinions were delivered by the Court of Last Resort, a brief drama took place behind the crimson curtains. Frank Murphy, the only Court member whose religion was being called a racket by the Witnesses, rushed in to see Chief Justice Hughes. He wanted to change his vote. Murphy pleaded with the bearded chief, but was dissuaded. The curtains parted for high noon.

But Murphy grew more sure every day that Stone's dissent was correct. The picture of the Gobitis children haunted him, and the same sort of leaven was working on Black and Douglas. More concrete proof that Stone's warning about liberty was right was not long in coming. Immediately after the *Gobitis* decision the West Virginia legislature passed a law requiring all schools to start Americanization courses. The board of education conveniently quoted Frankfurter's opinion in drafting its program setting up a compulsory flag salute.

While young Witnesses were saluting or being expelled in these states, their brethren all over the country were getting into new troubles. Sixty-eight of them in Manchester, New Hampshire, deliberately did not ask for a required city permit before holding a parade on the crowded Saturday night sidewalks. A unanimous Court held that regulation of the time and place for parades, imposed without discrimination, does not violate freedom of religion and sustained the Witnesses' convictions.[6] The same year, the Court upheld the sentence of another Witness who used his legal street-corner position, from which he was distributing pamphlets, to call a heckler "a damned Fascist" and a "damned racketeer." The Court was unable to include such blasphemy, which it called "fighting words," under freedom of religion.[7]

Up to this time the Court had been almost unanimous, though in favor of the Witnesses only about half the time. In June of 1942, two years after the *Gobitis* case, two changes took place in this pattern: The Court split sharply and it slapped the Witnesses down in a major area of operations. In a series of cases headed by *Jones* v. *Opelika*[8] the Court upheld license fees charged the Witnesses for peddling literature in three widely scattered towns. Roosevelt's new blood showed itself in the form of separate opinions in all directions. In as frank a confession of error as one could imagine, Black, Douglas and Murphy announced gratuitously that the whole mess started because the *Gobitis* case had been decided wrongly.

Soon after this shift, Byrnes, who had been one of the 5-to-4 majority against the Witnesses, was replaced on the bench by Rutledge, known to favor the Witnesses. The Court bared its judicial breast and ordered the *Opelika* case returned for reargument. In May of 1943 it not only frankly reversed the decision by a 5-to-4 vote but handed down numerous opinions that governed also some new cases decided the same day and involving similar issues.[9]

In one of them[10] the Witnesses were supported by the General Conference of Seventh-Day Adventists and the American Newspaper Publishers Association—both as "friends of the Court." In another the Court nullified a law against ringing doorbells or otherwise summoning people to the door for leaflets.[11]

To dispose of the two cases and reverse the *Opelika* line, the Justices wrote eight opinions of all kinds and directions; but they weren't done yet. The very next month the Court was called on to decide the fate of the West Virginia law patterned after the *Gobitis* decision. As might have been predicted, the new majority not only negated the new law but frankly reversed the earlier decision, knocking out both copy and model.[12] Jackson wrote the opinion, Roberts and Reed noted laconically that they were standing by the *Gobitis* case, and Frankfurter defended his former opinion with a long dissent.

The majority, which had been aided by briefs from the committee on the Bill of Rights of the American Bar Association and by the American Civil Liberties Union (but opposed by the American Legion), was now set. The same day it threw out a 1922 Mississippi law making it a felony to distribute teachings calculated to bring about refusal to salute the flag and carry on other patriotic doings. This time the Court was unanimous in finding a state without power to punish as a felony the teaching of something which had just been declared lawful.[13]

At the turn of the next year, the Court gave the Witnesses a setback for violating the child labor laws of Massachusetts.[14] The guardian of nine-year-old Betty Simmons, an "ordained" preacher of the sect, was prosecuted for allowing the child to sell literature on the streets, in violation of the minimum age of eighteen for girls. Two years later, in January, 1946, the Court split again on two tough cases in which the Witnesses challenged traditional concepts of the law of private property.[15] In one the sect defied the Alabama Shipbuilding Corporation's ban on soliciting in its company-owned town near Mobile, Alabama. In the other they defied the management of a government-owned housing project in Texas. The Witnesses were upheld in both instances.

Thus, the small but vociferous religious sect has added, by dint of constant heckling, a classic chapter to the law surrounding religious freedom.[16] It scrambled the Court once and forced each justice into at least one essay on the dividing line between religious activity and governmental power to regulate commercial enterprises. The sect also contributed a moral to lawmakers; namely, that unless the first encroachment on liberty is caught it will spread into a general persecution, feeding on itself as it goes along. Nowhere in the law does an inch so surely become a mile.

Another case to be noted in the Court's treatment of the 1st amendment involved the even smaller "I Am" movement, leaders of which were convicted of using the mails to defraud.[17] They promised all kinds of seemingly fantastic divine revelations and spiritual powers. A majority of the Court ruled that the jury had properly been charged by the trial judge to exclude all questions concerning the truth or falsity of the religious beliefs or doctrines of the defendants. Stone, Roberts and Frankfurter felt that the 1st amendment could not protect those who obtained money by fraud; Jackson would have dismissed the entire prosecution.

Probably the greatest impact of the new Court on the day-to-day problems of civil rights is in the area of the criminal trial, an ancient procedure into which the Court has injected itself greatly. The result has been to tighten up the meaning of "fair trial" and "due process of law." If law enforcement officers around the country have protested the Court's decisions, because convictions are harder to obtain, they have been compensated somewhat by receiving specific guideposts for criminal procedure.

In fact, some of the Court's greatest vigilance has been exercised at points *preceding* actual trial by scrutiny of the age-old third degree and its modern, more subtle variations. The *McNabb* case, detailed in Chapter V, had immediate reverberations in the police world. Officers all over the country screamed as they read the opinion and opened jail doors to prisoners who had been coerced into "confessions." Even befor the *McNabb* rule, officers had been put on notice by *Chambers* v. *Florida*, but the *McNabb* case added the element of time. Officers now had to bring their suspects into court speedily, even if they left no marks on the suspects' bodies. The same day, and for the same reasons, the Court threw out the conviction of a group of union members thought to have used dynamite in connection with a strike.[18] They had been questioned for six days without seeing friends or lawyers, all in the atmosphere of a hostile company-owned town. Hardly a year has gone by that the Court hasn't buttressed this principle of going behind the facts of each supposed confession. Most often it has reversed such convictions,[19] but it has also dismissed some as frivolous or merely weighed the evidence and allowed the confession to stand.[20]

A burr under the justices' black silk robes had been the use of evidence obtained from tapping wires. Up to 1942 the new members of the Court held together solidly in interpreting in favor of defendants the federal law against "using" messages intercepted from tapped wires.[21] By that time, however, gum-shoe artists had learned new techniques for invading what Brandeis had developed into "the right of privacy." The modern Court couldn't agree on how to handle the modern methods.

First came the case of a group charged with defrauding insurance companies by presenting false claims for disability benefits.[22] Two of the conspirators, confronted with the evidence gained by tapping their wires, promptly confessed and turned government witnesses against four others. Although the trial court did not allow the tapped evidence to be presented, the four who were put in a corner by their welching colleagues claimed a foul, saying that the illegal conversations had in effect been used against them. A majority of the Court found no foul; they decided that the four had no right to complain, for the reason that their messages were not presented in Court. But Murphy, Stone and Frankfurter could not agree with such a literal interpretation. Writing a strong dissent for them, former Attorney General Murphy said that Congress had set a public policy against the evils of wire tapping and had specifically banned the *use* of such interceptions.

The second case, decided the same day, involved a detectaphone.[23] Law enforcers had broken into an office to install a microphone in the wall, but when it hadn't worked they used a detectaphone instead, taking a stenographic record of numerous conversations, including some into a telephone. The culprits, charged with a racket in bankruptcy proceedings, appealed their convictions.

Climbing on a tight rope the Court majority reasoned that there could be no foul in this case because no wires had been tapped—the police had only overheard the suspects as their messages entered the wires. The unlawful entry did not prejudice the suspects because the microphone planted then didn't work, the Court said; and it refused to overrule the 1928 *Olmstead* case which had held that the Bill of Rights is not violated by wire tapping. Stone and Frankfurter merely stated that they would have been happy to join in overthrowing the old decision, but Murphy wrote of his repulsion toward the idea of letting anyone listen through walls with a detectaphone. He quarreled with the majority logic by pointing out that a casual letter dropped in the mail was protected from disclosure, while personal thoughts so intimate that they couldn't be written even in a diary were left open to wire tapping and detectaphones.

The Court bit another big chunk out of the individual's right to be free from unreasonable search and seizure in the *Davis* case.[24] It upheld the conviction of Davis for having in his possession unlawfully a quantity of gasoline ration coupons. Davis was obviously guilty, but the meat of the case was the method used by OPA officials to get the coupons as evidence. They drove into the filling station, succeeded in getting an attendant to sell them gas illegally, then started putting the heat on Davis to open his locked office for a look at the books. The owner resisted for about an hour, during which time one OPA agent was flashing a light into the back of the office and making motions toward opening a window.

The Court brushed aside precedents concerning *private* papers and set up a category of searching for *public* papers. Also, it said that the place searched was a place of business—another rather novel distinction. Three dissenters went far back into the reasons for protecting individuals from this type of probing and declared, as well, that the

Court was sanctioning a search without a warrant which could not have been made even with one.

After proper arrest and detention, the next guarantee is the right to counsel—a lawyer provided by the court if the defendant can't pay. The Court has split on specific cases brought to it on this score but has contributed great weight to the proposition that no man should be condemned without having a lawyer at his side. Most frequently the Court finds an ignorant defendant who has stumbeld into a position of clear-cut guilt for which he deserves no sympathy. However, the Anglo-Saxon law affords the luxury of a lawyer for even the obvious wrongdoer, and the Supreme Court usually goes to bat for him. In a case involving the death sentence, the Court has even held that counsel must be assigned even though none was requested.[25] More often, however, it merely sends the case back for a retrial with a lawyer on both sides.[26]

Nevertheless, a majority of the Court sometimes finds that no real damage was done the defendant by his lack of counsel. In the *Adams* case the Court went so far as to affirm a sentence resulting from a trial without either counsel or jury.[27] A majority felt that the defendant was well enough educated that his consent to such an arrangement should stand; but Black, Douglas and Murphy dissented. Last year Murphy and Rutledge dissented when the Court sustained a conviction from a trial in which the defendant had pleaded guilty without counsel but was later represented for a day by counsel who could have withdrawn the plea.[28]

Another tightening up of criminal procedure has come from the Court's interpretation of the "impartial jury" guaranteed by the 6th amendment. The most dramatic of these cases have involved Negroes where open abuses and skillful ruses had kept colored defendants from being tried by a jury containing at least a few Negroes. Shortly after Black and Reed had joined the Court it laid down the law to a Kentucky county which always excluded Negroes, solely because of their race.[29] In 1939 and 1940, Black spoke for the Court in even stronger language to Louisiana and Texas.[30] In all three cases the Court declared that exclusion violated the "equal protection of the laws" clause of the Constitution.

The subtleties have sometimes given the Court trouble. In 1942 it decided that a Texas grand jury had discriminated by keeping Negroes from jury duty for sixteen years without investigating the possibility that some might be qualified for service.[31] In 1945 the Court was confronted with the same county's conscious effort to follow that decision.[32] The jury commissioner put one Negro on the panel and he was chosen for the jury. Negroes made up 15½ per cent of the population but the county felt it had done its duty. A majority of the Court agreed that it had met the test; but Stone, Black and Murphy dissented.

Exclusion of Negroes is only one jury abuse struck down by the Court, though the main one. Another came as a surprise to everyone, in 1946, as the result of a suit against a railroad by a newlywed who fell from a train window while suffering delirium tremens. He felt the company owed him $250,000 for letting him fall and not stopping soon enough afterward. The injuries eventually caused the loss of both legs and the use of one arm. But these facts turned out to have nothing to do with the Court's decision; all it was interested in was selection of the jury. It seems that the jury commissioners chose no one for their panels who was employed as a day laborer. Their reason: the judge let them off anyway, because the men couldn't afford to live on the $4.00 per day for jury duty. "To guard against the subtle undermining of the jury system" the Court sent the case back for a new trial before a new jury.[33]

A group of constitutional rights that have given the Court equal trouble but that have become etched deeper and deeper into the law of the land are freedom of speech, assembly and press. The many involvements of free speech in picketing disputes have already been noted; the main remaining contribution of doctrine made by the new Court in this field was authored back in 1919 by Holmes, dissenting from the curbs of wartime feeling against those who differed with the government. That doctrine is known as "the clear and present danger doctrine" and means that a government has the power to curb speech, assembly and press to preserve public safety, but it cannot do so unless there is a clear and present danger to that safety from the activity complained of.

Without mentioning it formally, the old Court used that reasoning in a case decided by a 5-to-4 vote right in the middle of the 1937 fight.[34] By its most narrow division the Court freed Angelo Herndon of a conviction by Georgia for attempting to incite insurrection through a puny organizational drive for the Communist party. The peak of application of the doctrine came in the famous case freeing Harry Bridges and the Los Angeles *Times* of contempt penalties for criticizing a California court.[35] Again, it was a 5-to-4 split, but only Stone and Roberts remained from the old Court. This time the majority came right out with the words "clear and present danger." Interestingly enough, Stone and Roberts dissented, though both had voted for Herndon. Frankfurter, who wrote the dissent, and Byrnes were the other two minority justices.

That was the day after the Pearl Harbor attack. In 1946, after Byrnes, Stone and Roberts were gone from the Court, the doctrine was used in favor of the Miami *Herald*, adjudged to be in contempt of a Florida court which it had criticized at some length.[36] Frankfurter protested against such broad use of the doctrine but went along with the unanimous vote because he felt the editorial attack came after litigation it was aimed at had been decided by the Florida court.

An equally important and more interesting press case arose the same year over the postmaster general's withdrawal of second-class mailing privileges from *Esquire* magazine.[37] What this case lacked in clear and present danger it supplied in sleek long legs, translucent negligees and fullsome curves of the Varga girl. This and other features had been found by the postmaster general to "reflect the smoking-room type of humor, featuring, in the main, sex"—as the Court summed up the charges. The issue was not, however, whether the magazine publishes "information of a public character" or is devoted to "literature" or to the "arts," said the Court. "It is whether the contents are 'good' or 'bad.' To uphold the order of revocation would, therefore, grant the Postmaster General a power of censorship. Such a power is so abhorrent to our traditions that a purpose to grant it should not be easily inferred." Without dissent, the Court upheld the magazine and put its scantily clad art back in the second-class mail.

One of the most widely publicized cases under the 1st amendment was brought by the CIO against Jersey City's Mayor Frank ("I am the law") Hague.[38] The labor organization, and others, sought an injunction to prevent Jersey City from discriminating against them in applying several restrictive ordinances. They had been refused a permit to hire a hall for a public meeting supposedly because they would advocate obstruction of the government or a change of government by other than lawful means. Also, city officials had thrown some of them out of town, had stopped them from distributing leaflets discussing rights under the Wagner Act and had seized some of the pamphlets. The Court, with only Butler and McReynolds dissenting from the substance of the decision, gave Hague's officials a terrific legal slapping, though it modified the injunction decree so as to narrow it down to the specific situation at hand.

The Court has not left cities powerless to stop the littering of streets with handbills; but ordinances to that end must not be administered in such a way as to discriminate against religious literature or public information. When a New York City businessman was stopped from scattering handbills advertising his enterprise and told that he was free to distribute handbills devoted to "information or a public protest," he cannily printed up a batch of dodgers with his ad on one side and a public protest against the city dock department on the other. The Court tersely and unanimously upheld the city, brushing aside the American Civil Liberties Union's argument that a sound distinction between ads and noncommercial handbills was impossible.[39]

Most of these cases result in securing the blessings of liberty, as the framers expressed it, but a category of particular trouble to the Court has been those cases in which a law is put to a use which some justices feel it shouldn't be. Of course, the interpretation of laws is a common job of the Court, but these cases have an added element—a high matter of policy which usually slaps down a prosecutor for trying to snare some unpopular character with an unfair trap.

The best example of this problem came in the *Screws* case, named after one of three Georgia sheriffs who were prosecuted for beating to death a Negro suspect who was handcuffed and being put in jail for allegedly stealing a tire.[40] The United States prosecuted the officers under a little-used statute punishing "whoever, under color of any law . . . willfully subjects . . . any inhabitant . . . to the deprivation of any rights . . . protected by the Constitution and laws of the United States. . . ." A five-man majority of the Court could not agree on the legal grounds but reversed the conviction of the sheriffs. The impact of the opinion was that the statute was too vague to be sound. Were the sheriffs "willfully" depriving the Negro of his constitutional rights? Is so, what rights? Douglas, Stone, Reed and Black wrote that to enforce such a statute would be like sanctioning the practice of Caligula, who "published the law, but it was written in a very small hand, and posted up in a corner, so that no one could make a copy of it."

In the course of the case the Court was asked to abandon its decision in the oddly named *Classic* case, in which the same law had been upheld as used against some Louisiana election officials who deliberately tore up ballots in a primary election.[41] This the Court refused to do, holding that in the earlier case the necessary standard of guilt had been present. The right to vote is specifically granted by the Constitution and the officials very willfully abridged it, the Court reasoned.

In settling the *Classic* case, the Court decided also that primaries are the same as elections, so far as the constitutional rights are concerned, where the primary is an integral part of the state's election machinery or amounts to a final election. The implication was clear: Southern primaries would have to include Negro voters.

Douglas, Black and Murphy agreed with the latter but felt the federal law being used against the election officials was too vague. Thus, in the two cases the Court's liberals appeared to be voting in favor of those who grossly violated civil rights. Certainly they were handicapping federal protectors of civil rights; but their long-range view could hardly be called illiberal, for they wanted no convictions based on vague laws.

Two other arguments over the use of a law involved the Mann White-slave Act, making it unlawful knowingly to "transport or cause to be transported . . . in interstate . . . commerce, or . . . in the District of Columbia, any woman . . . for the purpose of prostitution. . . ." In one case a five-man majority ruled that the act was not violated by the operators of a Grand Island, Nebraska, house of prostitution who took two of their employes on a vacation trip to Salt Lake City, Utah.[42] Upon their return, as the Court put it, the girls "retired to their respective rooms" and resumed their trade. Nothing immoral occurred on the innocent trip, the Court found. However, there were only two dissents when the Court sustained the conviction of an operator who paid the fare and accompanied one of her girls on a four-block taxi ride to a customer's room.[43] Murphy and Black protested that the statute was intended to stop pernicious white slavery, not to apply to that kind of a situation.

A year later the Court unanimously refused to apply the federal kidnapping act to persons who persuaded a fifteen-year-old girl of low mentality, who had contracted a "celestial marriage," to run away in order to live with her celestial husband in another State.[44] There was no physical or mental restraint on the girl, and hence no case against her companions. However, when Earl Browder, while head of the American Communists, complained that he was being victimized by the government's prosecution of him for using a passport fraudulently—pretty obviously not the action the government was really worried about—the Court upheld the conviction without dissent.[45] He was later pardoned in the middle of his prison term without explanation.

In no branch of the law does the Court get more variety of circumstances to fit into lofty principles than in civil rights. The parade of new abuses of individual freedom by indifferent or biased legislatures and administrators is almost endless. One might think, for example, that peonage disappeared from the United States decades ago, yet the Court had to strike down a Georgia statute as recently as 1942 because it conflicted with the constitutional ban on "involuntary servitude."[46] Two years later the Court had to slap Florida authorities and courts down for thinking it could get around the previous decision. A few months before, it interpreted the federal antipeonage statute strictly to uphold the indictment of a Floridian charged with seizing and taking a man with him to work out a debt.[47]

Fewer subtleties are involved in the Jim Crow laws and regulations, but the Court has not had an easy time with them. It is obviously repulsed by racial discrimination, yet it is still aware of the fight to make the Court leave legislatures alone as much as possible. This groping was well illustrated in the Court's nullification last year of a Virginia law making it a misdemeanor to refuse to abide by Jim Crow rules on busses.[48] The law was tested by a Negro passenger on an interstate bus while passing through Virginia. The Court turned the case on burdening of interstate commerce, injecting the rather novel statement that "seating arrangements for the different races in interstate motor travel require a single, uniform rule to promote and protect national travel." Three justices dragged their feet, but the vote was six to one.

A more widely advertised case involved discrimination against Arthur W. Mitchell, former colored congressman from Illinois, who held a first class train ticket but was denied first-class accommodations at the Arkansas line.[49] The Interstate Commerce Commission would do nothing for Mitchell, but the Supreme Court unanimously declared the discrimination to violate both the Interstate Commerce Act and the 14th amendment. Railroads were left with the alternative of letting Negroes into Pullman space with whites or putting on a separate car with equally good places for colored passengers.

The drastic decision was not too much of a surprise, for the Court had reached a similar result in an education case when only Black and Reed, of the present justices, were on the Court.[50] Missouri was, in effect, ordered to allow Negroes to enroll in its state university law school or establish a law course at its college for colored students. It had been paying the tuition of colored students to go to a neighboring state for any course taught in white colleges but not in the colored one.

Among the peacetime alien deportation cases, two are noteworthy. In 1939, in the *Strecker* case, the Court served notice on the government that anyone it wanted to banish as a revolutionist would have to be shown to be a member of some revolutionary group at the time of his arrest. Joseph Strecker had dropped Communist party membership before that time; hence he was freed by the Court, seven to two.[51] The decision jolted the militants in Congress who were daily screaming for the deportation of Reds, especially Harry Bridges. The House was stung into passage of bill singling out the Australian-born CIO leader for export, but the measure died in the Senate after the attorney general warned that it violated good procedure. Congress countered with an amendment to the deportation law by which it clearly and joyfully set aside the *Strecker* decision. The government issued a new warrant for Bridges' deportation under the new law and the attorney general eventually ordered Bridges sent back to Australia. The Court decided the case in 1945 in Bridges' favor, five to three.[52] (Jackson, who had unsuccessfully prosecuted Strecker, did not participate on Bridges.) Review of the long, long record of evidence convinced the majority that although Bridges may have co-operated closely with Communist organizations, he was not "affiliated" with any group seeking to overthrow the government by force and violence. Also, the Court found that the hearing had been unfair.

Another important civil rights decision expressly overruled the proposition that primaries are not part of elections within the meaning of a constitutional guarantee of the right to vote.[53] The Court accepted the case largely in order to clarify doubts left by the *Classic* decision. Its decision was that some primaries, at least, are conducted by political parties as agents of the state, bringing them within the 15th amendment and precluding them from denying Negroes the right to vote in a primary election. It had long been recognized as a practical matter, but it required considerable legal tight-rope walking to merge the law with the reality.

In other miscellaneous actions the Court struck down an Oklahoma law for sterilizing habitual criminals (because its classification of those likely to pass along their criminal traits was hopelessly inadequate) and nullified as a bill of attainder, expressly forbidden by the Constitution, an appropriations rider which denied funds for the salaries of three federal employees suspected of left-wing activities.[54] On the other hand a majority of the Court found nothing wrong with the Illinois supreme court's denial of Clyde Summers' application to practice law in that state after he had refused to take part of an oath which he felt conflicted with his conscientious objection to war.[55] Five justices found no clash with religious freedom, though four dissenters screamed bloody murder.

Except when the Court suffers a lapse, as it did in the previous case, the institution stands as not only the ultimate protector of individual freedom but also the best protector. Congress and the Executive are paled by its vigilance, philosophy and determination. This appears at first blush to be a paradox, the nine justices being so far removed from the people. But this fact is exactly the one that makes the Court able—and willing—to tackle a civil rights problem without fear about community passion, political retaliation or personal welfare.

The Court is not, however, without its share of brickbats from bigots and from frustrated prosecutors. An equally often-heard criticism, though wrapped in padding, is that the Court operates on a double standard—a strict construction favoring individuals brought before it but a loose one for corporations and property owners hailed before its august finality. "Double standard" is an ugly term, implying dishonesty; but the Court would probably not deny its technical accuracy. In fact, it was weakly admitted back in 1938 in a footnote by Stone, writing for the Court in a case upholding a ban on filled milk shipped in interstate commerce.[56]

"There may be narrower scope," wrote Stone, while he was still an associate, "for operation of the presumption of constitutionality when legislation appears on its face to be within a specific prohibition of the Constitution, such as those of the first ten amendments, which are deemed equally specific when held to be embraced within the Fourteenth."

A footnote would be little authority by itself, but the new Court, particularly, does watch the personal guarantees of the nation's basic legal document like nine hawks. The legislatures and administrators may change the nation's economic programs like clothes, but so long as the Constitution stands as it is now written there will be very little cheating on the ground rules for individual freedom.

CHAPTER XVIII

First of a New Series

THE main change that occurred when Harold Burton took the seat of Owen Roberts was one of physical stature. Burton's good friend, Harry Truman, probably wasn't concerned about this difference, but the lack of any more fundamental change he planned.

With the retirement of Roberts, every justice on the Court owed his position to Franklin D. Roosevelt. There was but one Republican left (Stone) and he had been elevated to the chief justiceship by the Democratic President. Moreover, one of Roosevelt's justices (Byrnes) had already resigned. The cry for a Republican appointment, unbased on precedent, had been heard even before Democrat Roosevelt died; now, with Truman in the White House, it was renewed. Truman thought it over carefully and came up with his former colleague, the junior senator from Ohio, a Republican.

By his choice, Truman ended an era. If what Roosevelt had been doing was properly called packing the Court, Truman could easily have gone on doing it. As a senator, himself, during the Court fight Truman had learned what the issue was about and had been on Roosevelt's side, though not actively so. Moreover, in many respects he is more of a party man than Roosevelt was, and there would have been nothing improper about appointing another Democrat to the Court. But the new President was only a mild New Dealer. Where Roosevelt was a crusader, Truman was a fact finder, a fairly neutral observer and a quiet student of public affairs. It may be of some significance that he is not a lawyer, as Roosevelt was. Anyway, Truman's lay judgment was that the Court he had helped kindle a fire under had become too frisky. His decision to end the era was the deliberate one of a relative conservative taking over the situation.

Truman called his friend about five o'clock one rainy Monday night and asked him to come right over to the White House. Burton obliged and the President wasted no words in offering him a justiceship. Burton wasted no more in accepting it, then he hurried to catch a train. Next day, when the public was let in on the appointment, Burton was in the little town of Greenfield, Ohio, doing what he had done in many towns—addressing a luncheon club.

The naming of Burton came as no great surprise, because the advance dope on the appointment had it marked as a Republican inning. However, it was the age of another Republican senator which gave the definite nod to Burton. Warren Austin, of Vermont, had the inside track, but at sixty-eight he could hardly be appointed. Two former Democratic senators also figured high in the speculation, against the chance that Truman would choose from his own party. They were Sherman Minton, of Indiana, a very close friend of Truman's who was by then on the federal bench but suffering from ill health, and Lewis B. Schwellenbach, of Washington, whom Truman had only recently installed as his secretary of labor. A Republican who was not a Truman friend but had a good chance at the job was Robert P. Patterson, former circuit judge who was then undersecretary of war. He was elevated to the secretaryship about the same time Burton went to the Court.

Thus, the era was ended both by a break in party labels and by a change of philosophy when Burton was selected. Truman had many friends in the Senate, but Burton gained his closest confidence. While Truman was chairman of his famous Committee to Investigate the National Defense Program—the job that made him President—he often sought the counsel of fellow member Burton before acting. It was not surprising, then, that the President broke more than 150 years of precedent to go up to the Court to witness his good friend's judicial oath and watch him step around to the relatively hard-backed chair the new justice had selected for himself with a crack that it would help him stay awake. Truman rose with the others when the justices parted the crimson curtains, and he exchanged smiles with each as they settled into their places. It was the last time he would be able to smile—easily—at several of them.

Harold Hitz Burton looked lonely on the bench that first term, starting in October of 1945. It's not that he didn't look judicial, whatever that implies, but between him and the next justice was the empty seat with the name plate of Jackson on its back. Burton's small, perfectly shaped head, sticking up at the right end of the bench by itself, could almost be missed by the public watching the Court in action.

The new justice was lonesome, in terms of what was going on. He didn't pout or make any other signs to indicate that he had little in common with a majority of the justices, but he frequently dissented in an almost subdued way. The few opinions tossed him as a freshman

The general feeling that Justice Burton's appointment might start the pendulum swinging in the other direction was illustrated at the time by Jim Berryman in the Washington *Evening Star*.

to write for the Court were read out firmly, but there was not a tricky phrase in the lot. Whatever hard punches were gotten across that first term by Burton were put across vicariously through the two justices he most often agreed with: Stone and Frankfurter. He replaced Roberts in the general voting line-up, but he was not as vocal or as colorful as Roberts.

Burton wrote dissents in four cases worth noting. The first of these came in the Hawaii military government case, where he protested at length (also for Frankfurter) that the Army had ceased martial law soon enough for constitutional purposes.[1] Also, he came much nearer leaving it up to the military to make that decision of timing than did the majority justices. The opinion which contained more than Burton's usually small amount of good prose, began with a sort of credo:

"With the rest of this Court I subscribe unreservedly to the Bill of Rights. I recognize the importance of the civil courts in protecting individual rights guaranteed by the Constitution. I prefer civil to military control of civilian life and I agree that in war our Constitution contemplates the preservation of the individual rights of all our people. . . ."

However, he thought that the war powers of the Constitution should govern the situation and that the perspective of the Court's decision should be as of the time the military action was taken rather than one of postwar reflection. His long review of the military situation made Hawaii a theater of war much longer than the majority, led by Stone, could agree.

The same day Burton dissented alone from the Court's holding that embezzled money is not subject to income tax because the embezzler does not have it under a claim of right or without obligation to pay it back.[2] Burton thought Congress intended to tax such money as "gains or profits and income derived from any source whatever." Said Burton: "It is difficult to imagine a broader definition."

Near the end of the term Burton boldly stepped up alone to look through the Court's thin legal basis for nullifying Virginia's Jim Crow law on busses.[3] The Court had found an unconstitutional burden on interstate commerce, a fatal lack of uniformity among the states. Burton almost admitted that he would have knocked out the law on some other grounds, but he pointed out that the uniformity argument might apply just as logically against those states which had the opposite type of law—*forbidding* discrimination by race. He thought the record before the Court was inadequate for determining the weight of the burden on commerce, if it insisted on doing that, then brought the law makers into the argument:

"The inaction of Congress is an important indication that, in the opinion of Congress, this issue is better met without nationally uniform affirmative regulation than with it. Legislation raising the issue long has been, and is now, pending before Congress but has not reached the floor of either house. . . . Uniformity of treatment is appropriate where substantial uniformity of conditions exists."

Burton's fourth major dissenting opinion concerned interpretation of a tough wage-hour issue: When does work stop and start?[4] The Court chose the workers' side in a complicated factual situation centering around activities before and after punching the time clock. Again, Burton looked to Congress and got a different answer.

"Workweek," he protested (with Frankfurter), "is a simple term used by Congress in accordance with the common understanding of it. For this Court to include in it items that have been customarily and generally absorbed in the rate of pay but excluded from measured working time is not justified in the absence of affirmative legislative action."

The assertion was the more interesting because one of the authors of the legislation, Hugo Black, voted with the other side. This disquieting coincidence calls attention to justices' use of statutes to find whatever they're looking for. No justice has gone without criticism in some case by at least one of his brethren for misreading congressional intent. The sharpest example might be the *Girouard* case, in which Stone issued his last opinion, to the effect that Congress had not seen fit to change the law so the Court was bound by its earlier decision. Ex-Senator Burton was one of the majority justices who did not feel bound by that inaction of Congress.

It is almost fashionable for dissenters to swear up and down that the majority brethren are either reading something into the statute or reading something out of it. So long as it remains an honest difference of opinion, that is all well and good; but to charge those holding opposite views with legislating by judicial decisions runs squarely into the fact that the Court, by definition, legislates every time it passes on the language of a statute. It is more proper to say that some justices construe statutes liberally (loosely), while others construe them conservatively (strictly). Burton's first-term opinions put him in the latter group.

The freshman's votes with dissenting opinions of other justices his first term put him most often with Stone, Frankfurter and Reed. He voted against the Court when it upheld the right of Jehovah's Witnesses to distribute pamphlets in company towns and government housing projects and when it set aside a conviction because of ambiguous language in the charge to the jury about the burden of proof of guilt.[5] (He was with Black in the latter.) The religious decision was hardly to be expected in view of the fact that Burton held the highest position a layman can attain in his denomination—moderator of the American Unitarian Association.

Burton was in the minority also when the Court held that an employee is entitled to judicial review of the settlement of his claim by collective bargaining under railway mediation machinery; when it ruled that the Anti-Kickback Act does not cover certain collections of fees by the agent of a closed shop union; and when it knocked out an agreement, later repudiated, between an employer and his workers for settlement of back pay due the men under the Fair Labor Standards Act.[6] Also, he voted against the Court when it extended to stevedores the liability of shipowners for unseaworthiness of their vessels.[7]

The phrase, "Mr. Justice Burton delivered the opinion of the Court," naturally did not appear often that term. He straightened out for a unanimous Court the nice question of whether the law of an Indian reservation or of a state governed the trial of an errant minister who had raped an Indian maid.[8] (The state and the maid lost.) He wrote the opinions deciding that a state need not grant a permit before the Federal Power Commission can take jurisdiction and proceed to approve a power project and upholding the antitrust suit against the "Big Three" of tobacco.[9] The latter was mostly a routine recitation of facts which could have been avoided by endorsing the lower court's record, but it was significant because it put Burton on the antitrust side in a case that buttressed the government's drive considerably. The three companies had been convicted, among other things, of monopolizing the market even though competitors admittedly remained.

Burton's analysis of the economics of the industry showed a liberal interpretation of the subtleties of a business grown too large for the spirit—and the letter—of the Sherman Act. "It is not the form of the combination," he wrote, "or the particular means used but the result to be achieved that the statute condemns. . . . Acts done to give effect to the conspiracy may be in themselves wholly innocent acts."

It was a great day for Cleveland when Harold Burton decided to forsake New England and hang his freshly painted shingle in that northern Ohio city. He had been born—on June 22, 1888—in Jamaica Plain, Massachusetts, to the home of the dean of the Massachusetts Institute of Technology. For his own education he chose Bowdoin College, at Brunswick, Maine, where he roomed with Owen Brewster, later Senator from Maine, and where his son later roomed with Brewster's son. Then he studied for a Harvard law degree, which he got in 1912. At Bowdoin he was elected to Phi Beta Kappa, denoting the scholarship he has maintained ever since. A week out of law school he married his school-days sweetheart and started west on a career of law.

After two years of private practice in Cleveland, Burton pulled stakes for Salt Lake City, where he worked for the Utah Power & Light Company and the Utah Light & Traction Company as assistant attorney. Two years later he moved north to Boise, where he spent a little more than a year in similar legal work for the Idaho Power Company and the Boise Valley Traction Company. With about five years of law under his belt Burton entered the Army as a first lieutenant in the 361st Infantry of the "Wild West" 91st Division. During 1918 and 1919 he was in France and Belgium, becoming a captain. By this time he was the outfit's historian, but hardly a headquarters parasite—he was decorated three times, including the Purple Heart and the Belgian *Croix de guerre*. During his last year in uniform, 1919, Burton edited "600 Days' Service—a History of the 361st Infantry Regiment, USA." As a veteran of World War I he retained a reserve commission and joined the American Legion and Veterans of Foreign Wars.

With the restoration of peace, Burton returned to Cleveland for a general law practice. He worked with several different firms from 1919 to 1935, including two in which he was a partner. His firms are not those that Clevelanders think of at the very top of the list, but he was certainly somewhere near there before he was slowly engulfed in public service.

Burton's first public job, significantly, was as a member of the East Cleveland board of education. His friends swear to this day that Burton's entry into politics was one of a man who felt that he, as a citizen, ought to do something about the situation. One public service led to another. At first it was in spite of political organization, then—when he was bigger than political machines—it was with the backing of the Republican party. After two years on the school board (1928-1929) he was made director of law for the city of Cleveland, but before this position had run its course he was made acting mayor for four months. In 1929 he represented Cleveland in the lower house of the Ohio legislature.

By this time the Roosevelt landslide had occurred and the nation was in the pit of the great depression. From 1932 to 1935 Burton knocked around a bit, acting as chairman of the board of education's Committee on Citizenship Training and chairman of the County Charter Commission of the area surrounding Cleveland.

In 1935 this civic work netted him election as mayor. Though he then held nominal membership in the GOP, he was really the coalition candidate. Cleveland liked its new mayor. Since the days of Newton D. Baker it had had only flashes of good administration and those had come under city managers, the system for which Burton worked hard.

The good people of Cleveland showed their gratitude by sending back for a total of three terms the man who returned good government to them in troublesome, messy, depression times.

In 1940 he was nominated United States senator on the Republican ticket, but only after whipping the state party machinery, which then turned about to support the vote-getter. At the turn of 1941 he moved to Washington, a man promoted by voters who liked him personally and liked his administration. He entered the Senate as a man comparatively free of ideology and of politics, but on the conservative side. There were no skeletons in his closet, no ugly stories following him around and nothing about his personality to limit a further rise.

Once inside "the most exclusive club in the world," Burton's friendly manner and work-horse methods started him on the track to a high place of counsel. But a fortunate appointment speeded it enormously when Senator Harry Truman chose him for his carefully selected investigating committee. It was love at first sight. Truman often told friends praiseworthy things about Burton's fair-mindedness, teamwork and conscientious approach to the investigating power. Reporters spotted Burton for his calm but analytical questioning of witnesses in such a way that facts were brought out to the maximum.

However, Burton's association with the man who was to become President should not be allowed to obscure the remainder of his record in the Senate. Though some senators thrive on keeping their necks in, ducking sessions and roll calls and otherwise appearing as neutral as possible, Burton played the opposite game. His attendance record was excellent and he sent summaries of his voting record to constituents twice a year. He read as much mail as any senator, got to work as early and kept well prepared on issues for debate.

Senator Burton will undoubtedly be remembered longest as one of the authors of the Ball-Burton-Hatch-Hill bill to plump the United States for international co-operation before the war was over and for the Ball-Burton-Hatch bill to curb labor activities. The latter, which was first drafted by Washington lawyer Donald Richberg, put Burton in hot water with labor, which claimed it would erase many major gains; but Burton stanchly insisted it was not anti labor.

The foreign policy resolution, which took more courage to propose at the time it was done than might be supposed now, culminated a change in the junior senator from Ohio from a slightly isolationist position, before Pearl Harbor, to an enthusiastic endorsement of the administration's war policy thereafter. On the isolationist side he voted to limit the use of American forces to the Western Hemisphere, to curb the transfer of ships to other nations, to lend money to the British instead of making a Lend-Lease appropriation, against seizing ships of the Axis and against repeal of the Neutrality Act. However, he voted for the passage of Lend-Lease and extension of the Selective Service Act and opposed requiring a year's training for eighteen-and nineteen-year-old draftees. As the war progressed Burton urged the United States to make the peace permanent by pitching into its responsibilities in the family of nations.

A quick summary of Burton's record shows that he voted *against* the following: commodity loans at 100 per cent of parity, requiring Senate confirmation of all government employees paid $4,500 a year or over, the prohibition amendment to the draft law, seating William Langer, including farm-labor costs in the parity formula for farm prices, blanket deferment for farm labor, the St. Lawrence seaway, exempting unions from financial accounting, $1.5 billion for subsidies to control inflation, Senator McKellar's hamstringing of the TVA, shelving the anti-poll tax bill and denying the Fair Employment Practices Committee $500,000.

On the other hand, he voted *in favor* of the following: the Little Steel formula for stabilizing wages, repealing the $25,000 salary limitation proposed as part of the stabilization program, the Ruml tax plan, continuance of the National Resources Planning Board, extension of reciprocal trade, the Smith-Connally antistrike bill, freezing social security taxes, the antisubsidy bill (vetoed), closure on poll tax debate, and the program of federal aid to education.

It takes more than a divining rod to make a partisan Republican record out of this list of votes, and in labeling it conservative one must add the modifier, "fairly." There is yet no reason to think that Burton will go down as a bitter reactionary, as four of the Nine Old Men will.

In fact, it is unlikely that Burton will go down for much of anything as a justice. That is not meant to be derogatory, though it may be unflattering. It merely means that Burton appears to have no dominant trait which will make him or his law stand out. That might be as good as it might be bad, depending on how one looks at the Court. Burton is paradoxically as personally popular as he is unprovocative of anecdotes and color items. His friends have to pause a long time before coming up with something like the time that the senator arrived for a speaking engagement without his tuxedo or the time he had all of his tuxedo except the tie and was taken off the spot by the hotel manager, who rounded up a selection of ties from his waiters. Then there's the fact that Burton went over to the Court building shortly after his appointment to see what kind of gymnasium facilities it had and decided to maintain his frequent workouts at the Senate Office Building—by special permission.

People just don't go around talking about Harold Burton's life. But there is one private conversation to which Burton was a party that is both interesting and portentous enough to report at the end of any chapter on Burton. That rainy evening at the White House, Burton's old friend Harry Truman said, in effect: "Harold, I want you to go on the Court and tell what the law is—and put a stop to this *making* the law up there."

CHAPTER XIX

In Passing

THE eighty-six men who have served on the United States Supreme Court since the first session, in 1790, have been as varied as the United States itself. Some have been political sharpsters, like Samuel Chase, who missed impeachment by one vote for attacking the administration from the bench. Others, like Horace Gray, have been scholars. Individually they have been either colorful men, like the inimitable Oliver Wendell Holmes, or "mummies," as William Howard Taft once called them collectively.

The Civil War Court found it necessary to appoint a committee of its members to tell Robert C. Grier what his best friends would not—that he was senile and had overstayed his service on the bench. A later Court occasionally had its attention to oral arguments interrupted by a justice at one end of the bench sending word to a brother at the other end that he had forgotten his chewing tobacco. The borrowed chaw was dutifully passed along.

The dignity of the secret conference has been kept by some and shattered by others, both by levity and by bitterness. The struggle around 1937 reacted on McReynolds to the point of causing him to refuse to eat in the justices' private dining room. His retirement, early in 1941, not only assuaged group relations but lifted the ban on smoking and on crimson drapes. Conferences have been brightened by stories, saddened by acrimony and have wound up with a bit of a tipple in one of the brethren's office. Usually the justices have become fast friends.

The good-natured differences of opinion which often mark exchanges among the justices are illustrated by a story told by an eyewitness to their emergence from conference one Saturday evening. The Court was then meeting in the Capitol; the conference was late in breaking up. The tall, slender Holmes came out, talking earnestly to the huge Chief Justice Taft. As they reached their cars, Holmes spoke.

"Mr. Chief Justice," he said, "as Chief Justice of the Supreme Court I respect you. As former President of the United States I honor you. But as a lawyer you are no damn good."

Then there was the time that the justices were sharply split over the law that should govern Jehovah's Witnesses who invaded privacy by ringing doorbells and by blaring phonographs from front porches. The sect's right to operate on the streets had been settled, but the front-door zone was giving the justices plenty of trouble in a Saturday conference. A majority was set to vote that laws could not be used to ban this type of activity, explaining that persons who didn't want Witnesses around could post signs on their homes. One of the minority justices was puzzled.

"What kind of a sign," he asked his brethren, "could one put on his door to keep religious zealots away?" Then he suggested this one: "Keep off this property, for Christ's sake."

The conference table and the Court's method of operating is also a leveler of personalities. For example, each new justice must sit beside the chief at the big table and act as messenger for his eight seniors. The justices see more of each other than Cabinet members do, for example, and they have a common bond in their love for the law. The old custom of shaking hands before each session was started as a symbol of recognition that these nine men have to live together and have to subordinate emotions to public welfare in the form of objective decisions. The justices now view this custom dimly, rightly considering it only a superficial gesture no better than the feelings underlying it; but the justices still must work extremely closely together. The picture of Jackson walking past Black's door on his way to the Court room and conference chamber without observing social amenities is almost incomprehensible. Their personal feud (*their's* only if one assumes that the silent Black feels the way Jackson does) is a terrific exception to the decorum of the Court.

Were it not for one institution, the dissenting opinion, anyone who accepted appointment to the Court would almost immediately lose his individual identity, except for what he could retain in Washington society or during summer vacations. If justices wrote only majority opinions, blended to fit the views of five or more justices, the name on the opinion would mean little and the Court would become as impersonal as a big bank. But through dissents justices have asserted their personal views. Thus, each justice can build a reputation even after arriving on the Court, in addition, of course, to shaping future law by protesting that of the present.

Each justice is, therefore, important to the record of the Court as a whole. This book, being concerned with the present crop of justices, cannot give departed justices, even recent ones, their due. However, these men of the past cannot be brushed aside completely, for in law and in personality they have become interwoven with the new men. This is true of Brandeis, Cardozo, Byrnes, Hughes, Roberts and Stone. The impacts of Van Devanter, Sutherland, Butler and McReynolds, however, were so negative after 1936 as to be subjects for archaeologists rather than for students of current history. This is not to say that Van Devanter, Sutherland, Butler and McReynolds contributed nothing to the national government—conceivably history may still prove them right. It is only to say that, in the march of time, for ten years they have been dropped by the wayside.

Louis Dembitz Brandeis could not be left behind in the history of the new deal in justice because he was, in many ways, the first New Dealer. He had been fighting against economic royalists and for wage-and-hour legislation many years bofore the term "New Deal" was coined. His book, *Other People's Money*, was a primer for New Dealers. One of the chief weapons in the Roosevelt administration's arsenal was forged by Brandeis—his famous system of preparing legal briefs, or arguments. For example, of the one hundred pages in his brief supporting validity of an Oregon law fixing a ten-hour day for women workers, three pages analyzed the legal issues and ninety-seven diagnosed factory conditions and their impact on workers and on public health. Small wonder that a howl went up when President Wilson nominated this radical to the Supreme Court in 1916.

Brandeis was born in 1856 at Louisville, Kentucky, to parents who had only recently come to the United States from Europe, though not in the traditional steerage. After public schools, he studied two years in Dresden, then—without a college degree—entered Harvard Law School at the age of eighteen. The panic of 1873 had made it necessary for him to work his way through; in 1877 he was given a law degree, the age requirement having been waived, partly because of his phenomenal grades.

Brandeis was a highly successful combination of academician and practicing lawyer. He helped found the *Harvard Law Review*, first such periodical, and he built a lucrative practice. But mostly he became connected with causes, crusades which needed smart legal handling. He established an evaluation system for public utilities, the Massachusetts savings bank insurance plan and the impartial arbiter in the garment trades. The chief economic principle he espoused was that business should be kept small; the legal principle most closely linked with his name, because he pioneered it, is the right of privacy.

In his twenty-three years on the Court, Brandeis wrote 528 opinions.

His political belief in letting legislatures have their say, plus his economic belief in making little businesses out of big ones, would seem obviously to put him in the Roosevelt camp during the Court fight. His decisions were on Roosevelt's side, all right, but his view of the way to change the Court was quite opposite. Being eighty-one at the time, he could hardly agree on the age factor. Moreover, he joined Van Devanter in endorsing the Hughes letter to Senator Wheeler which refuted the President's argument about the Court's being behind in its work and demolished the entire plan for reorganization.

Brandeis' great fluffy shock of white hair was practically a tourist sight in the mid-thirties. His name was magic to the generation which had by that time caught up to his legal ground-breaking. Even before he died, on October 5, 1941—indeed before he retired, in 1939—his unusual name had been carved deep in the noncorrosive tablets of the law. It was inevitable that both sides of the Court would quote him in defense of their differing positions.

Just ahead of Brandeis, chronologically, is the name of Benjamin Nathan Cardozo, whose career on the Court was cut short by death at the age of sixty-eight but still embraced enough great philosophy to make it revered wherever lawyers gather. Cardozo was one of the few justices in modern times to be appointed as a promotion from lower courts. His break came in 1932 after Hoover had been turned down by the Senate on his choice of Circuit Judge John Parker, branded as antilabor because of a decision upholding a yellow-dog contract against union membership. Opponents have since regretted much of that incident, for Parker was, in general, a liberal judge; but the appointment of Cardozo easily quieted the tempest which was raised at the time.

Cardozo's eminence had long been acclaimed, partly from two books which have become classics of the law: *The Nature of the Judicial Process* and *The Growth of the Law*. His judicial career started in 1914 on the supreme court of New York, where he served until 1927. Then he was elevated to chief judge of the court of appeals, the highest court of that state. This record, plus his scholarship in behalf of an expanding concept of the law, made him an appropriate successor to the seat of Holmes. Oddly enough, the naming of Cardozo to that seat put Hoover in the position of having appointed a justice who would go along with the new-fangled laws of the New Deal.

Hoover's appointments in 1930 of Charles Evans Hughes as chief justice and Owen Josephus Roberts as associate were more orthodox. Both were known to the public as conformists of their profession. Hughes had served on the Court from 1910 to 1916 as an associate justice by the appointment of Taft, then had resigned to run for President against Woodrow Wilson. Roberts had been a Philadelphia lawyer in at least the lucrative sense of the term and had earned public attention as investigator for President Coolidge of the great Tea Pot Dome scandal—an appointment suggested to Coolidge by Stone.

Besides their conservative (but not reactionary) approaches to the law Roberts and Hughes shared another note—they were the last of the targets to leave Roosevelt's shooting gallery. Hughes retired in 1941; Roberts left in 1945. The two made bench marks, literally, for appraising how far to the left the Nine Young Men moved the Court around the pivot position occupied by both in the mid-thirties.

The most immediate surface change was that Hughes and Roberts replaced Brandeis, Stone and Cardozo as the great dissenters. In Hughes' last term (1940) he dissented twenty-four times, second only to the thirty-one times of Roberts. During Roberts' last term he dissented fifty-seven times.[1]

The last five of Hughes' eleven years as chief justice were years of moderation. His long white mustache majestically parted the bench and his beard punctuated the balance. Also, in his written opinions he was tractable enough to stay in the center of the Court. What balancing could not be attributed to tractability could be laid to self-restraint, which he practiced more than many justices did and which he sometimes preached. Hughes' most quotable quote about the Court came not while he was on the Court but while he was governor of New York: "The Constitution is what the judges say it is." The phrase was hurled back at Hughes and his Court with impish delight when the battle was on, though it is only a simple little truism which should be obvious to anyone.

As presiding officer Hughes was a master strategist. His quickly drafted letter to Wheeler, though the senator was not even a member of the Judiciary Committee which was studying the packing plan, knocked into a cocked hat the charges that his Court was behind in cases. He is generally thought to have talked Van Devanter into resigning at the height of the battle, one of the most strategic retreats in nonmilitary history. Certainly he did not discourage Roberts from shifting ground on the constitutionality of wage-hour legislation, thus breaking the log jam which had been furnishing the pressure for Roosevelt's campaign. Hughes' contribution in that stormy time was considerable, but it was not as great as was his contribution to the institutionalism of the Supreme Court. His opinion for the Court in the 5-to-4 decision which legalized the Wagner Act was a contribution to the law, it is true, but it paled beside his moves as presiding justice.

Hughes had lectured at several law schools, had developed a top law practice in New York City, had been counsel to investigations of such things as insurance for the New York legislature, had rejected the Republican nomination for mayor, had been twice elected governor of New York and had run for the presidency. He was an elder statesman, to put it tritely, before he became chief justice. The temptation to refer to him as Jovian or as a Zeus hurling judicial thunderbolts was irresistible.

Roberts left the Court with a considerably different reputation. He had come to it with a background of teaching at the University of Pennsylvania, his alma mater; but teaching was only a sideline. Roberts' main identification tags were the names of big corporations which he represented in his Philadelphia practice. In addition to his investigation of Tea Pot Dome, in 1924, he had prosecuted local espionage cases during World War I. His fact-finding ability, garnished with a Republican point of view placed him in charge of the inquiry into the military debacle at Pearl Harbor. His report was hailed as fair, though it was necessarily—at that time—short on military facts.

Roberts will always be remembered as the "swing" man on the Court, whose "switch in time saved nine" from the fate for which Roosevelt was preparing them. Roberts may have been wishy-washy, but he was not reactionary, hard shelled or inflexible. The opinions after 1936 in which Roberts joined the majority of the Court show little more than a conservative attitude. Often this was directed at conserving civil liberties, perhaps partly because of his very high place in the Episcopalian laity. His dissents from the Court were of all kinds, but the noteworthy ones were warnings that the Court was getting off the track, was substituting emotions for cold, legal logic.

One of the best examples of his attitude came in a dissent in which Hughes joined, delivered exactly five years after announcement of the Court plan. Seven justices, in the *Hutcheson* case, decided that certain restraining practices of the carpenters union were exempt from the Sherman Act because of language used later by Congress in amending that law.[2] It was the ugly jurisdictional dispute over installation of brewery machinery; the administration's trust-busters were eager to crack down on the union. The process of construction used by the majority to turn the prosecution aside was branded by Roberts and Hughes as never used before by the Court.

"I venture to say," wrote Roberts, "that no court has ever undertaken so radically to legislate where Congress has refused to do so." The result, he added, "seems to me a usurpation by the courts of the function of the Congress not only novel but fraught, as well, with the most serious dangers to our constitutional system of division of powers."

It was a harsh warning. The other side would say, of course, that either way one voted he would be "legislating." It is always possible, of course, that Roberts and Hughes will be proved right in their misgivings about the new majority. In this particular case Congress need only amend its laws to reverse the Court, so not much damage could have been done. However, if the unexpected happens and the Court swings too far in the direction Hughes and Roberts felt it was going toward "legislating," then the heroes of the Supreme Court will turn out to be Roberts and Hughes—or even Van Devanter, Sutherland, McReynolds and Butler—rather than such justices as Brandeis, Black and Douglas. The liberals are not worried about that chance. In answer to the charge that they "legislated" in favor of labor in the *Hutcheson* case they can readily point out that they voted against the prolabor administration which brought the prosecution.

Anyway, it is not difficult to imagine what position was urged on President Truman by Hughes and Roberts when the two men, then in retirement, were called to the White House for confidential advice after the death of Stone. If the two elders spoke bluntly what their dissents carried in legalese, Harry Truman got an earful.

James Francis Byrnes was quite a different animal from any of these four justices. Far from being a so-called "pure scholar of the law," Byrnes first hooked onto the law as a way of buying groceries, then mixed it successfully with politics. He began his law career as a court reporter, taking precedents down in shorthand, rather than as an honor student in a big university, poring over the law as the masters wrote it. In fact he didn't go to college.

Jimmy Byrnes was born in 1879 at the wrong end of a Charleston, South Carolina, street and had to go to work very early in life to help support his widowed mother, a seamstress. Like Vinson, Byrnes got his first political education by hanging around the courtroom. By 1903 he had read enough law on the side, in the old-fashioned way, to be admitted to the bar; but he kept at his court reporting for another five years. In addition he was editor of the Aiken *Journal and Review* during four of those years.

In 1910 the voters sent their politically wise young lawyer to the United States House of Representatives, where he served fourteen years. Then, from 1925 to 1931, he engaged in a general law practice in Spartansburg. In the inner politics of the Democratic party that year, Byrnes was for Roosevelt before the Chicago Convention and was elected to the United States Senate.

In a few years he belonged to a handful of Democrats who ran the Senate—and ran it about as Roosevelt wanted it run. Only a few times did Byrnes vote against his President. He revolted on a couple of spending measures and he introduced a resolution condemning sit-down strikes at a time when the administration was tolerating them. But Jimmy's ability to design and build compromises most often made him an administration crutch in Congress. His ability to tell local stories and to subordinate both his personal dislikes and his personal ambitions eventually made him the real leader of the Senate.

It was, therefore, not surprising that Byrnes was rewarded with an appointment to the Court, even though he was then sixty-two. Nor was it surprising that Roosevelt remarked during the swearing-in ceremony that he wished he were Solomon and could halve Jimmy Byrnes, keeping one half in the Senate and the other half on the Court. At that moment he was losing the smoothest, most effective worker he ever had in the Senate, at the same time acquiring an unknown quantity for the Court. Unknown? Yes, because Byrnes had remained as close to old mossbacks like Carter Glass as he had to the New Dealers.

Byrnes had been a good lawmaker in the sense of technical ability to draft legislation. For example, he once got disgusted with the haphazard method of cluttering up the legislative hopper with dozens of road bills, so he called the major authors together, discarded more than forty of the individual measures and drafted one coherent bill which was also pleasing to everyone concerned.

Byrnes was on the Court only one year before Roosevelt "drafted" him for wartime administrative work around the White House, but the year was long enough to mark him as a conservative justice. At first it was hard to tell. His first opinion for the Court was both liberal and unanimous, but it drew several separate concurrences. Byrnes spoke for the Court in striking down the California ban on Okies, declaring it to be a barrier to interstate commerce.[3] Others agreed with the result but thought the case should turn on rights of citizenship rather than on commerce. Then he voted with Frankfurter, Stone and Roberts in dissent from the Court's release of Harry Bridges from a contempt of court conviction.

Almost never did Byrnes vote with his former Senate colleague from the South, Hugo Black, or with Douglas or Murphy. He was with them in a few important decisions, but not many. Those few included a unanimous opinion Byrnes wrote nullifying a Georgia law which the Court felt violated the federal ban on peonage[4] and another opinion which will probably be connected with his name longer than any other—the almost unanimous opinion upholding New York teamsters against prosecution under the federal Anti-Kickback law.[5] The latter law exempted from its scope "the payment of wages from a bona fide employer to a bona fide employee." The teamsters had been forcing truckers to hire an additional employee upon entering New York or pay an equivalent sum if they rejected union help. Byrnes found that the teamsters had always been willing to perform the job they asked money for and that the history of the law showed that it did not purport to outlaw this kind of labor activity. Nevertheless, a great hue and cry was raised that Byrnes (and the Court) had placed some kind of moral approval on the practice involved.

It was the last important decision in which he sided with labor. For example, he later wrote a 5-to-4 opinion upholding the Southern Steamship Company against an NLRB order of reinstatement for merchant seamen who struck while their ship was away from home port.[6] The men and the board insisted that the company's unfair labor practices had caused the strike; the Court ruled it was mutiny, even though the ship was not at sea. Another 5-to-4 opinion by Byrnes ruled against workers in a dispute over calculating wages of employees having very irregular hours of work.[7] Organized labor protested both decisions vociferously; Reed, Black, Douglas and Murphy did likewise. Except for Reed, the same people screamed at Byrnes' vote against redcaps in the tipping case.[8]

In civil rights cases Byrnes usually voted against the individuals. His votes in the Okie and peonage cases were sharply offset by his votes (*a*) against a defendant unable to get the trial court to appoint counsel for him, (*b*) against the Jehovah's Witnesses in three cases of soliciting converts, (*c*) upholding the use of a tapped telephone message against a third person and (*d*) upholding use of a detectaphone.[9]

It may be unfair to appraise anyonc's career on the basis of his first term on the Court, but organized labor and Jehovah's Witnesses were glad to see Byrnes leave the Court, just before the October term began in 1942. The President was equally glad to get his old friend to take the newly created position of director of economic stabilization, from which Byrnes moved to director of war mobilization, where he was promptly and accurately dubbed "assistant president." Thereafter he narrowly missed being nominated vice-president and soon became secretary of state for the man who beat him out, Harry Truman. He will be remembered as the postwar secretary of state longer than he will be recalled as associate justice.

The reason that Harlan Fiske Stone, a Coolidge appointee, was chosen by Roosevelt to preside over the Court when Hughes retired is well illustrated by a remark scribbled on the examination paper of one of Stone's students at Columbia Law School: "Interesting; of course no court in the land would agree with you." The grade was A.

The quality which made it possible for Stone to bridge a span on the Court from 1924 to 1946 with distinction was summarized shortly before Stone died by Walton Hamilton, professor of law at Yale and close student of the Court. Hamilton, writing in *Mercury*, noted that Stone was a legacy from the conservative Coolidge to the liberal Roosevelt, then explained: "Not that any one of the three intended it; for Coolidge would never have passed on anything New Dealish; Roosevelt would never have turned to Calvin the Cool for a good thing; and Stone would never have sought to become a human bridge between the two eras. Accident conspired with merit to catapult Stone into the high office of Chief Justice."

Stone had started out to be a scientific farmer, but was bounced from Massachusetts "Aggies" over a chapel incident. He then moved across town to enroll at Amherst College, where he ran off with all the honors, including that of being one of Amherst's all-time great football players. He was preparing for a medical career and was a good scholar. But attention to his books didn't keep him from hiding a class mascot or from heading a committee of students which drew up a report that led to the ousting of the college president.

"The great thing Stone learned at Amherst," concluded Hamilton, after researching school records, "was not to abandon hell-raising but to subdue it to due process of law." The class of '94 voted him most likely to succeed.

Stone left Amherst and medicine for Columbia, where he worked his way through a law degree and was grabbed off by a big Wall Street law factory belonging partly to J. P. Morgan's son-in-law. He combined a few years at this firm with lecturing at Columbia and in a comparatively short time was made dean of the law school. However, when President Nicholas Murray Butler violated an agreement to make no appointments without approval of the faculty, Stone resigned. He returned only when the arrangement was reinstated. Though Stone was teaching technical courses such as mortgages, personal property and equity rather than broad subjects like constitutional law, he developed a broad approach to the law which, to the conservatives, tagged him as a radical. The radicals, on the other hand, thought of him along with high-buttoned shoes. As dean he lived with both groups and led Columbia to new heights of legal education.

Stone had early become interested in religious freedom—at Amherst he could not reconcile it with compulsory chapel—and he was chosen during World War I to serve on a board of inquiry into cases of conscientious objectors. Among other things, he recommended liberty of conscience for CO's who had no particular religious background.

In 1923, after thirteen years as dean, Stone left teaching for full time with corporate practice, but he had been there only a few months when Coolidge, harassed by Cabinet scandals inherited from Harding, turned to Stone, who had been a class ahead of him at Amherst, for a cleanup job as attorney general. Within a year, Stone had brought the Department of Justice up to date, fired the infamous group of volunteer snoopers then operating, put J. Edgar Hoover in charge of the FBI and halted the irresponsible Red raids started by A. Mitchell Palmer. Also, he started using the antitrust laws.

When Coolidge stood for re-election in 1924, Stone went into the hinterland to speak for the President, a highlight of his tour being an attack on the elder Robert LaFollette's plan to amend the Constitution so as to allow Congress to repass laws invalidated by the Supreme Court. "Only one branch of government would remain supreme," said Stone, "the one which responds most speedily to temporary and often fleeting changes in public opinion."

Coolidge then appointed his attorney general to the Supreme Court. Some said it was a "kick upstairs" for a tough guy, but the most vocal attacked the appointment as putting a tool of Wall Street on the highest tribunal. The onslaught was led by liberal Senators Tom Walsh and George Norris, both of whom later changed their minds.

The change in attitude toward Stone came, not because he did a flip-flop, but because his philosophy of law was a creed for all times—Republican, New Deal, war or whatever. When he joined the Court his approach to the law was similar to that of Holmes, but he soon found himself in a bloc also with Brandeis, with whom he had very little in common up to that time. The flaming crusades of Brandeis were not for Stone, but he arrived at the same conclusion by a process of inquiring into the facts and merits, then applying a light-handedness with legislative experiments.

Stone's best-known opinion, a scathing dissent, fits exactly into this pattern. Six justices, led by Roberts, struck down the AAA; Stone protested both the result and the majority's exercise of its power.[10] Considering Stone's background and the fact that the dissent was delivered one year before Roosevelt announced his Court plan, the opinion is most revealing of Stone's judicial philosophy. He referred to the majority ruling as a "tortured" construction, adding that "while unconstitutional exercise of power by the executive and legislative branches of the government is subject to judicial restraint, the only check upon our own exercise of power is our own sense of self-restraint."

His undoubted feeling that the decision was more political than judicial was summed up in the next sentence: "For the removal of unwise laws from the statute books appeal lies not to the courts but to the ballot and to the processes of democratic government." And, later on: "Courts are not the only agency of government that must be assumed to have capacity to govern."

Three years later the principle of the AAA decision was abandoned by the Court in upholding an amended law, again with Roberts as spokesman for the majority. Stone's carefully measured lecture had apparently had results. In any event, it had results on Stone's own life. Because of this line of reasoning Roosevelt appointed him chief justice a few years later. Everyone was satisfied. The choice allayed some of the talk about Roosevelt's appointments of rubber stamps, yet it accomplished for Roosevelt as much as he could expect from any appointment.

In fact, much of the bitter rubber-stamp criticism is based on decisions of the new Court which merely followed earlier dissents of Stone. Two examples in addition to the AAA case are the Court's reversals of decisions invalidating minimum wage and railroad pension legislation.

Another of Stone's well-known opinions was his solitary dissent in the flag salute case, a dissent which he read softly, in near embarrassment, then lived to see adopted by the majority in an outright flip-flop by three liberal justices. Stone probably had no more love for the Jehovah's Witnesses than he had for the AAA, but his sense of freedom was repulsed—perhaps in the same way it had been many years before by compulsory college chapel.

Yet Stone was not dogmatic or doctrinaire in his civil rights votes. His vote was often unpredictable. For example, he helped slap down Mayor Frank Hague, of Jersey City, for violating the constitutional rights of the CIO, yet he dissented when the Court halted the deportation proceeding against Harry Bridges. To him, who had helped build up the administrative process against rebuffs by the judiciary, the Bridges situation was one in which the administrative procedure had run its course and the decision should stand. He protested the Court's original upholding of wire tapping and he was against the Court when it sustained an antitrust suit against the Associated Press. He crossed the line down the center of the Court many times, but rarely was he accused of basing his official, legal opinion on his personal predilection.

So much was this true that a fiery New Dealer, Maury Maverick, wrote in 1939: "An ideal Court would be composed of men of the general stamp of Justice Stone—men who did not allow their personal views and prejudices to influence the opinions they wrote."[11]

It is a little-known fact that Stone narrowly missed being elevated to chief justice in 1930 to replace William Howard Taft. Hoover's secretary told reporters to get out their files on Stone, who had frequently fished with Hoover and was a member of his "medicine ball cabinet." Reporters were caught by surprise when Hoover announced that very day the appointment of Hughes. As pieced together later, the story seems to be that several prominent Republican lawyers had urged Hoover to offer the job to Hughes as a generous gesture, believing that Hughes would turn it down if for no other reason than that his son would have to resign as solicitor general if he accepted. Somewhere the signals were crossed, for Hughes accepted. Stone served the next eleven years under Hughes, then presided over the Court another five.

As a presiding officer, Stone will go down as one who could neither get an agreement among his colleagues nor limit debate. The first criticism is based on a naïve idea of how the Court operates. The chief has little but his own prestige with which to get harmony from his fellows and Stone never lacked the quality of prestige. That he could not limit debate is troubling only to those who want their decisions cut and dried. As one observer remarked, after reviewing Stone's role as one of the great dissenters: "Who was Harlan Stone to be cutting off debate—even if he could?"

One of his dissents which will be remembered longest was delivered on April 22, 1946, a few hours before the chief justice died. The majority had bluntly reversed three old decisions to rule that an alien, seeking naturalization, need not promise to bear arms for the United States.[12] Stone had dissented in two of the three precedents for reasons which the new Court adopted as grounds for overruling them. However, he felt bound that day to go along with the former result, though admittedly wrong, for the reason that Congress had refused to adopt the old dissents by changing the law they interpreted.

Stone's stand was courageous, to say the least. It became dramatic, as well, a few minutes later, when he started to read another opinion incoherently and was helped from the bench by the associates next to him. Only a couple of people knew, when the crimson curtains closed behind Stone's huge frame, that it would be for the last time.

At least one justice thinks that had Stone chosen a valedictory he would have chosen that very dissent as an exit. Others feel that Stone is being martyred on the basis of his protest that the will of Congress was not being followed. While that argument goes on one less controversial observation about Stone's career is possible—he changed very little. Like a block of New England granite he stayed in place while the Court shifted around him.

CHAPTER XX

On Second Thought

THE strongest words ever delivered from the Court," is the way one justice privately described the dissenting blast by Owen Roberts when, in January of 1944, the Court disapproved part of an obscure admiralty case decided sixteen years before. Seven justices, led by Stone, believed that the old opinion conformed to decisions handed down neither before nor after it. Roberts disagreed with this interpretation, then launched a lengthy attack on all of his colleagues except Frankfurter who joined in his dissent.[1]

"The evil resulting from overruling earlier considered decisions must be evident," said Roberts. If litigants cannot follow old decisions, he feared, "the law becomes not a chart to govern conduct but a game of chance." Moreover, "the administration of justice will fall into disrepute. Respects for tribunals must fall when the bar and the public come to understand that nothing that has been said in prior adjudication has force in a current controversy."

Roberts denied being a slave to precedent wherever new conditions call for growing law, but he felt that this was not such an instance.

"The tendency to disregard precedents in the decision of cases like the present," he said, "has become so strong in this court of late as, in my view, to shake confidence in the consistency of decision and leave the courts below on an uncharted sea of doubt and difficulty without any confidence that what was said yesterday will hold good tomorrow. . . ."

The dissent was plastered over front pages all over the country, fanning a dispute which predated the case by many years. Oversimplified, the issue is: Should the Court reverse previous decisions which it feels were wrong, or should it plow right along in the old furrow for the sake of consistency and predictability?

Every justice has, at some time or another, expressed his reluctance to depart from *stare decisis*, the maxim that the decision should stand. Nevertheless, practically every justice has participated in the overthrow of some precedent. In 1940, the argument for casting off outmoded decisions was made as follows:[2] "We recognize that stare decisis embodies an important social policy. It represents an element of continuity in law, and is rooted in the psychologic need to satisfy reasonable expectations. But stare decisis is a principle of policy and not a mechanical formula of adherence to the latest decision, however recent and questionable, when such adherence involves collision with a prior doctrine more embracing in its scope, intrinsically sounder, and verified by experience. . . . This Court, unlike the House of Lords, has from the beginning rejected a doctrine of disability at self-correction."

The writer was Felix Frankfurter. Roberts dissented with McReynolds that "if there ever was an instance in which the doctrine of stare decisis should govern, this is it."

It is confusing that Frankfurter should be the champion of change in one case, while joining in a bitter attack on change just four years later. But it is no more confusing than the fact that Roberts was the man who, by shifting his position in 1937, contributed as much as any justice to the abandonment of old-fashioned judicial interpretation. It was hardly for him to cast stones. Incidentally, the Court overruled two precedents in the four years between the two Roberts dissents just mentioned without protest from Roberts.[3]

Several years before, the organized bar had become concerned about this tendency of the Court. Frank Hogan, urbane president of the American Bar Association, told a meeting of that group after the 1938 terms of the Court that confusion reigned.

"Again and again," complained the lawyers' spokesman, "the Court turned aside from what had long been looked upon as 'established' principles of constitutional law which, to use the Court's own reiterated phrase, had been 'settled by repeated decision of this court.' And there was no subtlety about it. . . . 'Established' principles, which we had come to regard as part of the warp and woof of the nation's fundamental law, were liquidated so effectively that, as the Court said, 'they cannot survive.' "

Hogan had other complaints to interlace with his reverence for *stare decisis*. Some of the changes "were in fact the most devastating destruction of constitutional limitations upon federal power, and the most unprecedented expansion of that power over the every-day affairs of individual citizens witnessed in the century and a half of the existence of the United States. . . ."

Hogan was speaking only a year after the Court fight and was speaking to the group which rallied against the President's plan. It was natural that he would call upon *stare decisis* to help damn the social-legal changes which the ABA had been unable to stop. However, Hogan is no exception. Nearly everyone who enters the debate over *stare decisis* purposely confuses two things: the principle of adhering to precedent and the merits of the case under consideration. If the result of a specific case overthrowing a precedent is pleasing, then the principle is quite all right. Or, at least, the advocate of the result keeps quiet about *stare decisis*. If the result is bad, then the whole nation is represented as being on the brink of ruination because precedents are not being followed.

This process is intellectually dishonest, but judged even on the basis of results in each case there is little reason for expecting ruination. By isolating the cases, nearly a score of them, in which the Court has recently overruled precedents a fairer perspective of the issue can be obtained. At least it will be easier for one to form his own opinion of any damage done to the law. In the following list, the statement of each decision will be that of the Court's most recent opinion. Each overruled a contrary conclusion.

Congress has power to regulate maximum hours and minimum wages, upholding the Fair Labor Standards Act.[4]

States may regulate maximum hours and minimum wages.[5]

A state licensing system for travel agents is a valid exercise of the police power and not an undue burden on commerce when applied to an out-of-state agent.[6]

As a general proposition, federal courts must apply the decisions of state courts in interpreting the common law.[7]

States may tax the income of federal employees.[8]

An income tax on the salary of a federal judge does not violate constitutional protection of the judiciary.[9]

States may tax out-of-state bank accounts of individuals at a higher rate than they tax those within the state, providing the difference is justified in costs of administration.[10]

States may impose a sales tax on goods purchased for use on a "cost-plus-fixed-fee" contract for the federal government, notwithstanding the historic immunity of federal "instrumentalities" from state taxation.[11]

A state must recognize the validity of a divorce decree obtained in another state by a spouse who acquired bona fide domicile there, when the spouse who remained behind did not contest the proceedings.[12] (A subsequent case added the important consideration that the orginal state may attack and upset the facts of domicile in the divorcing state, thus showing it not to be bona fide.)

A state may tax intangible property, even though another state taxes the same property.[13]

A state cannot compel students to participate in a flag salute exercise; to do so violates freedom of religion.[14]

An ordinance is unconstitutional, for the same reason, which imposes a flat license tax on canvassers and solicitors engaged in distributing religious literature.[15]

A political party, acting as agent of a state in conducting primary elections, must allow Negroes to vote.[16]

States may regulate the compensation received by employment agencies.[17]

States may not exclude persons from entry on the grounds that they are paupers.[18]

Unwillingness to bear arms in the country's defense does not preclude admission to citizenship.[19]

Of less interest and more complexity, the Court recently overruled three other cases involving injuries to seamen and the incidence of taxes.[20]

The technique of reversal was by no means invented by the new Court. As long ago as 1932, Brandeis listed in an often-cited footnote the many times when the Supreme Court reversed itself.[21] Interestingly enough, the dissenting position he was there advocating was later adopted in one of the reversals enumerated above. And it was done through Chief Justice Hughes, at a time when there was only one Roosevelt appointee on the Court, and with the support of Roberts.

As spokesman for the Court in junking the old and unrealistic decision that primary elections are not protected by constitutional guarantees, Reed inserted a few sentences on the Court's rationale in reversing precedents.

"In constitutional questions," he wrote for seven justices, "where correction depends upon amendment and not upon legislative action this Court throughout its history has freely exercised its power to reexamine the basis of its constitutional decisions. . . . This is particularly true when the decision believed erroneous is the application of a constitutional principle rather than an interpretation of the Constitution to extract the principle itself."

Lawyers generally complain that the Court does not exercise even this much restraint, that its reversals are more fundamentally upsetting than Reed would have one believe. Roberts protested in this case that such overruling "tends to bring adjudications of this tribunal into the same class as a restricted railroad ticket, good for this day and train only."

However, several of the justices, if not all of them, are cognizant of the value of leaving the broad principles unchanged wherever they have been adjudicated by the Court in a clear-cut case. Reed's big words for the distinction the Court tries to keep in mind are at least as sincere as lawyers' complaints that the law should be predictable so that they can advise their clients whether it will be necessary to sue.

Another type of attack on the Court's refusal to let *stare decisis* be a dead hand on the law is illustrated by a dissent by Butler from Frankfurter's opinion for the Court that federal judges must pay income taxes. It was, indirectly, a rejection of any new-fangled ideas brought to the Court by outsiders.

"The opinion also cites . . ," Butler said, "selected gainsaying writings of professors—some are lawyers and some are not—but without specification of or reference to the reasons upon which their views rest, and in addition it cites notes published in law reviews, some signed and some not; presumably the latter were prepared by law students."

This narrow thinking recalls the legendary farmer who withdrew his daughter from college when he learned that the boys and girls matriculated together. One can practically plot the course of eventual reversals by observing attacks on landmark decisions by law review writers and others operating under the opprobrium of "professor." These ivory-tower workers don't have to wait for a concrete case to come before them, whereas the Court usually waits years for an issue on which it has spoken to return for a second crack. By the scheme of things, cases usually cannot be accepted for the Court's consideration if their issue has already been directly decided.

It should be noted in passing that the Court has refused to overrule a few important decisions, though strongly urged to do so. Black, Douglas and Murphy—dissenting as a team—have made onslaughts on two particularly noteworthy precedents. They would overrule *Eisner* v. *Macomber*, which stands for the proposition that stock devidends cannot be taxed because the income is not really separated from the investment, and the "paper bag" doctrine, greatly protecting a patent owner who deliberately holds his patented article off the market.[22] There is room for thinking that the two more votes needed to make a majority for this view will be obtained from more recent appointees —Rutledge, Burton or Vinson.

There is one great exception to the principle that the system of accepting cases for decision naturally stacks the cards against reversals. When the personnel of the Court has changed enough that it is mathematically possible for a different result to be obtained from the new justices, the issue will be raised and a reversal sought. The institution of dissenting opinions then comes into full play and the law reaches its ultimate in adaptation to changing events and the arrival of new generations. The effort in this country has always been for "a government of laws, not of men," but no one believes that the human factor will be gone by merely commanding it to be absent.

So long as this process of human evolution is kept within reasonable bounds the Supreme Court continues to be the stability of the United States government—not a static, unmoving pillar, but a stable, *relatively* unmoving force which has administrations and Congresses blowing hot and cold around it. At this point a phenomenon in the recent history of the Court enters the picture—the death or retirement of enough justices in a few years' time to enable nine appointments to be made in less than nine years, eight of them by one man. In both medical and political terms, this is enough of an influx of new blood into the Court to cause shock.

It did cause shock and is still causing it. Nevertheless, the cases reversed by the young Court do not add up to anything more dangerous than a little shock. Most of them expand civil liberties or stand for a more liberal grant of power to legislatures to raise money by taxation. If the nation is endangered by that change, then it will take more than any kind of a Supreme Court to pull the nation through trouble ahead.

Moreover, the departure from precedent has not always been disliked by the conservatives on the Court. Reversal of the *Adkins* case, in March of 1937, made possible by Roberts' shift, took the conservatives off an untenable spot. Chief Justice Hughes, delivering the new position, said flatly of Chief Justice Taft's dissent in the old case: "We think that the views thus expressed are sound and that the decision in the *Adkins* case was a departure from the true application of the principles governing the regulation by the State of the relation of employer and employed."

Jackson, in his book, aptly referred to this period as "a retreat to the Constitution." There is much room, in the analysis of each case which reversed another in the early months of the new Court, for finding a return to the Constitution.[23] Certainly—and ironically—there was as much turning back as there was going off on a tangent away from the document.

But supposing that the current Court wreaks no havoc by its reversals. The phenomenon will still recur in another fifteen to twenty-five years, when the Nine Young Men will have hardened arteries, literally, if not figuratively, and another President will have the power to appoint a new majority, perhaps a whole new Court.

The chronological situation arose through no one's special fault, but it does make for some reversals which might otherwise have been accomplished by mutation rather than by outright reversal. A new Court surely has some right to dispose of the antiques left it by the old order. It is not necessarily casting aspersions on a deceased ancestor to move some of her furniture out after she is properly buried and bring in something more modern or merely better liked. It would be sheer mysticism to think that justices never make mistakes. As one of them explained privately after frankly reversing his own vote in the flag salute argument, "an honest confession is as good for a Supreme Court member's soul as for anyone else's."

Like any other woman, the Goddess of Justice seems entitled to the privilege of changing her mind.

CHAPTER XXI

Number Thirteen

FREDERICK MOORE VINSON was born, January 19, 1890, in a Kentucky jail and has been close to the law ever since—practicing it, making it, administering it or judging disputes over it. His father was the jailer, at the town of Louisa, a post which, being political, symbolically started the future congressman on his long career in politics.

Vinson, who is a master storyteller, likes to tell people about his inauspicious birth and about the sign over the door of his father's combination jail and home: "$10 fine for talking to prisoners." Young Fred played on the lawn of the Lawrence County courthouse, romped in and out of the judge's chambers and sat lazily in the courtroom window on hot summer days listening to lawyers matching skill. He soon started playing baseball, a game in which he excelled; he sold a weekly journal called the *Pennsylvania Grit*; and studied his books on the living-room floor, flat on his belly.

In the fall of 1908, Vinson enrolled at Centre College, in Danville, Kentucky, to finish the limited schooling available at Louisa, and immediately took over the campus. He is remembered for his political leadership and for being captain and shortstop of the ball team; but his main fame was his scholastic record. Unless some prodigy has come along recently his marks are still the highest ever carried away from Centre. At least one of his college cronies remembers him also for having confided in 1909 that he intended to represent his district someday in Congress. Fifteen years later he did.

Before the political side of his interests matured, however, Vinson jumped into a home-town law practice. His first year he was appointed city attorney, but his practice continued to be general until 1923, when he won his first political race—for commonwealth attorney—and took over the county's criminal prosecutions. He is remembered in that role as aggressive, though fair, and always well prepared. In 1928, he moved to Ashland, where there were more clients, and formed a partnership which thrived until 1938, even though Vinson was in Congress most of that time. In that year he was appointed by President Roosevelt to a lifetime job on the important circuit court of appeals for the District of Columbia. A little later, when Congress created the emergency court of appeals for litigation arising from price control, Vinson was named to head it.

There he acquired the title of "judge," which he dearly loves, but he indicated no ability to set the world on fire. His opinions had two strikes on them—mostly technical cases went through those courts and his style is heavy, if not sleep producing—but the bar will recall him as a popular judge of solid judicial bent. The term "solid" is not as flattering as it might seem, for it is sometimes used when nothing more precise can be thought of. Certainly, however, there was nothing flighty about his decisions of that period.

The supersober Arthur Krock, probing into these opinions, came up with four which he thought tentatively proved that Vinson was a judge who "has a passion for facts, is not disposed to torture them or set them aside to accommodate precedents or general principles, and who believes that courts of high appeals should not upset judgments based on present-day standards because of a preference for those of the past or a desire to accelerate the arrival of new ones." Of the four cases cited, one showed Vinson to believe that administrative procedure must be followed to the end before someone affected adversely can run to the courts for help. Another showed that he would hold a reign on administrators cutting statutory corners.[1] If these revealed little that was exciting, another afforded a look at Vinson's approach on a knotty legal problem: banning books. A lower court had ordered destroyed a shipment of imported, illustrated books about a nudist colony. The circuit court reversed that decision, but Vinson dissented.[2]

"It is settled," he wrote, "that whether a book is obscene presents a question of fact, if reasonable men could differ on that question. From this it follows that, where there has been a jury verdict . . . that a book is obscene, an Appellate court cannot disturb that determination unless it is prepared to say that no reasonable man could have found as did the jury. . . .

"Accepting the premise: that 'time marches on,' I am nevertheless unable to agree that we have here and now 'progressed' to a point where a publication of this character is beyond the possibility of reasonable difference of opinion to the community. . . . This case calls, not for the individual judge's personal opinion, but for a gauging of the present community sentiment. . . . A court should rarely attempt that task as a matter of law."

Freedom of the press has many times been set back by just such community determination, but the decision displayed a certain simple consistency which marks other phases of Vinson's thinking. He is more at home in economics, the "progress" of which he has witnessed while courts fumbled to keep apace. His last decision—and last dissent—on the circuit bench gave him a chance to lay out his attitude toward what constitutes a public utility in this day and age.[3] A warehouse company was arguing that it was a public utility and hence came under the exemption from price control in the act administered by OPA. A majority of the court held against the warehouse, noting especially that it was regulated by a state commission.

"I do not regard a public utility as having any tangible existence," Vinson said; "it is like a corporation in that respect. The concept 'public utility' is, as I see it, merely a bundle of attributes or characteristics, and our problem, here, simply stated is first to consider some of the fundamental attributes which compromise that bundle. . . .

"To say that a business is clothed with a public interest is not to import that the public may take over its entire management and run it at the expense of the owner.

"I feel that it has been demonstrated that complainant's public warehouse is a business which is (1) affected with public interest, and (2) bears an intimate connection with the processes of transportation and distribution, and (3) is under an obligation to afford its facilities to the public generally, upon demand, at fair and non-discriminatory rates, and (4) enjoys in a large measure an independence and freedom from economic competition brought about by the grant of a franchise from the state placing it in this position."

Vinson is proud of the fact that the Supreme Court upheld his minority view; it may be significant that those who voted to do so were Jackson, Roberts, Stone, Reed, Rutledge and Frankfurter. The high court's dissenters felt that the Vinson position placed "an unwarranted burden on those who are waging the present war against inflation."

One more of Vinson's opinions deserves a glimpse, if for no other reason than that he has been known to single it out, along with that just mentioned, as one he's proud of.[4] The complicated situation of the case, one on wills, is not essential to excerpts from his reasoning: "Posthumous avarice leading to disherison is bad. Living greediness is bad, too. We are told that this will is a carry over from feudal days and diametrically opposed to the principles of democracy. We presume that is because this trust is a large estate, a modern security-landed gentry. Yet the whole system of inheriting is a carry over from the past. That does not necessarily make it good or bad. It is contended that balance between security and frontier resourcefulness is needed. Today we do not feel the omniscience to promulgate the balance that will make us a race of supermen." He upheld the terms of the will.

An analysis of how Vinson's circuit opinions fared on appeal to the Supreme Court, prepared by Lewis Wood, veteran New York *Times* reporter, showed Vinson's record to be good. Of his twenty-four opinions which were appealed, the Court refused to hear twenty of them, letting his decision stand; it reversed three and upheld one. The most interesting of these was the reversal of Vinson's opinion in favor of George Sylvester Viereck, the German agent. Vinson said that Viereck's contentions could be disposed of in short order, that his main contention was "euphemious, but not meritorious." However, that was the case in which the Supreme Court, through Chief Justice Stone, used strong words in letting Viereck out from under the charges and in criticizing the prosecuting attorney. Of the latter, Vinson had written that some of his statements were "improper" but did not cause reversible error.

There are two significant things about Vinson's circuit court experience. First, immediately after his appointment as chief justice was announced, Vinson's lawyer friends—and there are many of them —were at a loss to help newsmen find opinions worth citing. Second, that didn't matter, for Vinson was not appointed because of being an outstanding judge. The most unique distribution of his opinions was back in Kentucky, during the summer recesses, when Vinson would drop in on main street to pass the time of day and hand copies to his old cronies.

The latter is not a facetious observation. Vinson was appointed mainly because of his political eminence, using the term in its technical sense; and politics, according to Fred Vinson, "is folks." Vinson never removed himself far from the folks who started sending him to Congress in 1924. When those folks put him on the shelf for two years because he chose to support Catholic Al Smith in 1928 (he was Smith's Kentucky manager), Vinson took the occasion to move to Ashland; but he soon sunk his roots as deeply there as he had sunk them in Louisa. Though he has maintained a spacious old home in Ashland, he seldom misses a chance to visit in Louisa and practically has two hometowns. The folks sent him back after the Smith intermission four more times and it has always been thought that the state of Kentucky would have sent him to the Senate had he chosen to make a fight which would have involved good friends already there.

Vinson's brand of politics was realistic but not at all lowdown. He tells a story of one incident which his friends say actually happened to him in 1928. He was soliciting the vote of a courthouse character in Louisa.

"I can't vote for you this time," the friend told him.

"Why not?" asked Vinson. "Didn't I send you free seeds last spring? Didn't I get that pension for your mother-in-law? Didn't I get your brother out of trouble when they caught him operating a still? And didn't I get your daughter a job in the post office?"

"Yep," replied the character, "but you ain't done nothing for me lately."

Vinson's record in Congress has been acclaimed as at least very good by partisans of both sides, though his phenomenal handling of tax legislation has somewhat obscured other features. The three terms he served during Republican administrations gave him a chance to work up some seniority from which to be quite effective when the tables turned in 1932. As labels go, he was a New Dealer; but he broke with Roosevelt over two early, important measures. He opposed the first economy slash and, after Roosevelt had vetoed one of his veterans' bonus measures, he fought tooth and nail to get another passed. (He was once very active in the American Legion, though the war ended when he was little more than out of officers training.)

Vinson was rated as a good parliamentarian, but his maneuvers were aided more by the fact that he got along famously with majority leaders. His management of Sam Rayburn's successful campaign for speaker of the House left him a strong friend who was able many times thereafter to propose him at the White House for top jobs in the administration.

In 1936 his almost unbelievable knack with tax bills and his prodigious memory for figures put across the administration's hotly fought undistributed profits tax. All in all, Vinson participated in ten tax bills, pushing seven of them through as chairman of the tax subcommittee of the Ways and Means Committee. When his last bill was passing the House (after he had been confirmed for the circuit bench), the opposition joined in tributes to its departing expert. Said Harold Knutson, bitter Republican opponent of Vinson's tax bills: "The gentleman from Kentucky is the greatest authority on taxation that has served in this House in the 21 years I have been a member of this body."

The Kentuckian's approach to taxes was sometimes as human as it was most times almost superhuman—he consistently opposed higher taxes on tobacco and his own income tax is made out by Paul Kelley, his assistant for a dozen years.

Though it correctly summarizes Vinson's legislative record to list it as New Deal, there is one Vinson measure that deserves special consideration because of his latest job. That is the Guffey-Vinson bill, authored by him in the House but always referred to, for some reason, by the name of its author in the Senate. It was the measure by which the New Deal sought to bail out the gasping old coal industry, and it was one of those that made the Nine Old Men especially furious. By a vote of six to three, the Court knocked it into a cocked hat both as too much delegation of legislative authority and as an attempt to regulate a local industry, coal mining.

Congressman Vinson went back to his books, redrafted the law to avoid its proclaimed pitfalls, and helped get a new version passed. In May, 1940, the Supreme Court decided that the new act was constitutional, that Congress had remedied its defects.[5] Only McReynolds dissented. Naturally, the change in Court personnel helped in the change, but the congressman who was to become chief justice deserves —in the parlance of his favorite game—credit for an assist.

Between these two bits of judicial history, Vinson was figuring in a minor way in more important history: the Court fight. Though the House of Representatives never got a real crack at the Roosevelt plan, the gentleman from Kentucky was counted on by the White House for leadership on that side of Congress.

One year after he was spared any battle scars by the Senate's defeat of the plan, Vinson left Congress to become a judge, freely explaining to his friends that the extra $2,500 in yearly salary was needed to make ends meet for his family. Sometimes thereafter he would lunch at Congress to hash over politics; as often he would drop in at Sam Rayburn's apartment for a quiet game of ten-cent bet and twenty-five-cent-limit poker.

After exactly five years of passing on legal disputes, Vinson was "drafted" by the President to pass on the myriad economic disputes of a nation at war. Jimmy Byrnes was being elevated to director of War Mobilization, "Assistant President," and Vinson was taking his place as director of Economic Stabilization. Here, instead of dealing with lawyers arguing with briefs, Vinson had to choose a course from among the more devious arguments of government officials and lobbyists. With both he was more successful than was thought possible. He had been used to pressure as a tax bill drafter, so he was able to take a substantially philosophic attitude toward lobbyists.

"They remind me," he once told an assistant, "of an old uncle of mine who was married to a good woman who objected to his love for good bourbon. She kept a little in the house for medicinal purposes, but it was always locked up. My uncle used to wait around until it rained, then go out and get himself wringing wet, just so he could come in and get some medicine. That's what pressure groups remind me of."

Vinson accomplished his dispatch of stabilization problems with somewhat of a record for a small staff. Besides Paul Kelley, his chief assistants were for some time Paul Porter, later price administrator, and Edward F. Prichard, son of an old Kentucky friend of Vinson's and formerly clerk to Frankfurter. Later he added economist Robert Nathan to his brilliant but small stable. Like as not, on the day of a World Series baseball game, visitors to Vinson's quarters in the immaculate Federal Reserve building would find the judge listening to a small radio, thrashing out the fine points of the game with his associates.

It should never be thought, however, that Vinson handled this job fliply. On the contrary, he took on the oil industry, backed by Texan Sam Rayburn and even Secretary of Interior Ickes; the railroad industry; and all of organized labor that tried to crack the Little Steel formula. (A senator from Missouri, named Truman, tried to upset Vinson's rail decision by specific legislation.) He umpired food-price disputes most often in favor of OPA and against the Department of Agriculture, and earned a reputation as a tough man from whom to wangle an economic favor.

Not long before President Roosevelt died, Vinson quite naturally was moved into the shoes left vacant by Byrnes, when the latter went home. Vinson had been over in the west wing of the White House only a few days when VE-Day made possible the stroke for which he will probably be remembered longest in his role of director of War Mobilization and Reconversion. A few hours after word of the European victory he called a press conference and announced the discard of Byrnes' ban on horse racing, curfew on night spots and curtailment of electric lighting.

Vinson's next move around the executive branch came as a result of the refusal of Congress to give Henry Wallace both the secretary of commerce post and the federal loan administrator's job which had gone with it until Jesse Jones broke with the administration. Rayburn suggested to the right ears that Wallace might be acceptable if Vinson were put in charge of the money bags. The idea clicked and Vinson moved across Lafayette Park to become the nation's largest lender.

This lasted all of a month before the new President picked Vinson for his Cabinet, in the Treasury position. The administration could well say of Vinson, as a college baseball teammate once did: "Fred covered the whole infield." As a matter of fact, he started covering part of the outfield—international finance and economics—before he came to the Treasury. As vice-chairman of the United States delegation to Bretton Woods and chairman of the steering committee, he was not expected to contribute much. Immediately, however, his associates there started testifying how well he had boned up on global finance and how well he handled the mixed problems of diplomacy and parliamentary procedure. Much of this good beginning was dissipated later at Wilmington Island, when Secretary Vinson headed the United States delegation to start the world bank and fund functioning. He alienated several countries, mainly by high-handed tactics as presiding officer and his determination to keep the bank within sight of the United States Treasury, and alienated the press by his tight-lip policy.

As secretary of the treasury one of his toughest jobs was negotiating with Lord Keynes the money part of the controversial British loan. Also, because he was automatically chairman of the National Advisory Council, a misleading name for the inter-agency committee on foreign loan policy,Vinson actively directed much of the liberal United States postwar attitude toward monetary rehabilitation of foreign countries.

It was assumed that the new secretary of the treasury would be the top man available for drawing up administration tax programs, but his other duties never received much chance for appraisal. He was criticized for running a bond drive after the war was over, the proceeds of which would merely go to pay off the public debt, part of which they would simultaneously create; but he was praised for moving toward a balanced budget. For the most part, his pronouncements on domestic fiscal policy were so glib as to defy appraisal. He kept on his desk his pet "worry bird," a gadget of bits of wood and a pine cone which is supposed to be unable to look ahead at trouble because it always flies backward. A few days before taking the oath as chief justice, Vinson called in the press for a farewell handshake and a few bits of the good-natured chatting for which he's famous around Washington. At the other end of his dark blue office hung the portrait of Salmon P. Chase; at his right that of Roger B. Taney, the other secretaries of the treasury to be made chief justices.

On Monday, June 24, 1946, Fred Vinson was sworn in as number thirteen. His good friend Harry Truman, had arranged a unique ceremony. Around the south portico of the White House he had called congressmen, his Cabinet, other high officials and a number of Vinson's old pals. A military band added full dress to the occasion and the President of the United States added a few complimentary remarks. The new chief justice walked down the lawn, heartily kissed his talented wife for the photographers and started on a summer of preparation for the biggest of many big jobs he had tackled. His new colleagues were scattered from the mountains of Oregon to the beaches of New England, badly in need of vacations.

The setting for a new chief justice was capable of being called either auspicious or ominous. Few, if any, editorials on the appointment of Vinson failed to emphasize a hope that he would be able to bring "harmony" to the Court. Of even more significance, most of them chose to fill their contents with that hope rather than express a firm stand pro or con Vinson himself. There was double reason for the superficial demand for harmony. Chief Justice Stone had died on April twenty-second, almost literally reading an opinion critical of the Court's majority. After national homage had been paid to Stone's outstanding work as a justice, it was asserted that he had been a failure as a presider, accentuating the supposed need for a new chief of vague qualities which would enable him to pull the Court together.

However, the more harmony was urged, the more talk of disharmony crept into gossip. Black and another justice—some thought Murphy—were rumored to have sent word to Truman that they would resign if Jackson were appointed chief, as the best dope had him about to do. The rumors made spicy stories. Meanwhile the President called in the venerable Charles Evans Hughes for advice. Some say he even asked the old man (eighty-four) to step back into the job, but it will probably be many years before that private talk is recorded, if it ever is. Truman likewise called in Roberts for two private talks. It is assumed that if either gentleman spoke frankly to the President he either recommended bringing in a chief from outside or recommended Jackson. It is almost sure that neither man said kind words about a justice from the left side of the Court. Certainly no observers thought that Harry Truman would choose someone to the left of Reed because of his own political color. At the same time, it was pretty well known that Truman admired Jackson. After an obvious struggle, Truman gave a press conference his answer on June 6, 1946.

But at least one person, Bob Jackson, had taken the rumors of Black's secret maneuverings seriously. Four days later his white-hot blast from Nuremberg hit the Washington wires and the ugly word "impeachment" was bandied about. Vinson had not yet been confirmed and further delay in the process was caused by a feeling for several days that the Senate Judiciary Committee might order an investigation of Jackson's charges. However, after a brief flurry of oratory the charges were formally put aside and Vinson was easily confirmed.

The appointment was historically significant for several reasons: Truman turned his back on a Republican choice; he chose a middle-of-the-roader for the center of the bench; his nominee had lower court experience; his choice was not a distinguished national lawyer in the

The popular idea of what faced the new chief justice in settling the Black-Jackson feud was captured in this cartoon by Jim Berryman in the Washington *Evening Star*.

American Bar Association sense; and the new chief came from outside the Court.

No one predicted that Vinson would be a really great judge, but he did seem to have the qualities for bringing the associate justices closer together. Vinson's versatility in the administration left him with a high reputation for being able to listen to diverse opinions, then settle down to work out an acceptable program which would also be workable and constructive. Like Byrnes, he had been a compromising trouble shooter; but, unlike Byrnes, he worked at a technical level rather than at a more superficial level. He could run his big hands through a problem, pore over it and come up with a written solution. By that time he would know the subject matter thoroughly, without glossing over it. Thus it was predicted that he would accomplish more teamwork on the Court than would a professional "glad-hander."

It was even more certain that Court relations would have been even further ruptured if the President had chosen to send it a driving, iron-handed chief. The new Court not only had individually high I.Q.'s—probably the highest in history—but its passions ran high. It could not be driven nor cajoled. There was an outside chance, though, that it would respond to the earthy, conscientious and friendly efforts of a man like Vinson to weld it together. Vinson was not expected to lead the Court; the man with the face of a tired sheep or Saint Bernard would be much more of a catalyst.

But while he was carrying on this subtle presiding function, how would Vinson vote? Three of his associates who have been closer students of the Court than Vinson have had no trouble placing the new chief very near the center of the Court. One thought he'd go along more often with the liberals than with the conservatives; another gave the conservatives the best chance of capturing the Vinson vote more often; and the third placed him squarely in the center. A more penetrating analysis, however, is by subject matter of cases. In civil liberties, Vinson has had practically no chance to reveal his stand, but friends point out that "he was born on the other side of the tracks" and is likely to stand up for the little fellow. He most assuredly will go along with major government programs for regulation of interstate commerce. He believes in the administrative process and he believes in letting the legislature have its say. But he is expected to be a strict constructionist of what that say is. Moreover, it must be noted that the area in which he probably will agree with a majority of the Court is an area which is no longer in controversy. True, there are refinements to be sketched in, but the basic principles have been settled.

One of Vinson's greatest contributions to the Court can come from his unique experience of having served in a major way in all three branches of the government, for the Court is the umpire from whom there is no appeal on the separation of powers. Vinson, for one, will not be acting in a vacuum when he irons out some kink in that part of our government.

The most frequent comment heard on the choice of Vinson was "It was not a great appointment," but for some strange reason there was almost no analysis of how the new man would vote, or whether it is possible for any chief justice to obtain harmony, even if he is the original personality kid or the legal Zeus. The cold fact was that Truman could have gotten a degree of harmony only by appointing someone who would join the liberals. That was due to the line-up. If the new man voted liberal he would likely make a five-man majority and probably pull one or two over from the other side of the bench. But if he voted conservative he could not count on enough votes with him each time to make a majority. The liberal bloc is more definite in its voting than is the conservative one.

Unless the new chief justice exhibits extraordinary judicial capacities, where they have been no more than good so far, his best chance of a high pedestal in history is to become known as the man who brought stability to the Supreme Court in a troubled time. There are as many reasons as there are associate justices why he will probably not achieve that place.

CHAPTER XXII

Mercury and Comfits

IF YOU'RE going to pack a court at all you've got to really pack it," Jackson is supposed to have told the strategists of the Court fight at a time when compromise was being talked. For a number of reasons, this view did not prevail and a compromise was accepted as better than nothing. But Jackson was right. The present Court personnel has proved, if new proof was needed, that it is hard to make a Court stay packed. Nothing gives a justice a better laugh than to hear himself and his colleagues branded as "rubber stamps."

Neither the brand nor the laugh are true gauges of who won the great battle of the judiciary. Underlying the many separate concurrences and dissents from the young justices is a body of majority opinions which clinched the New Deal's legislative program. Assuming that Roosevelt sent his appointees up to the Court to accomplish that goal, he won his battle. That, however, was only the immediate objective. To herald the ultimate winner, the collateral issues must be laid out against some bench mark.

Taking the measurements from F.D.R. himself, the bench mark of victory would include a reduction in the age of justices, an increase in the speed of handling cases, a decrease in the cost of litigation and a return of the justices to their rightful function of keeping only a very light hand on the legislators.

The Senate Judiciary Committee, in June of 1937, declared that the original plan would not achieve these purposes. Whatever may have been the senators' real motives for rejecting the plan, their official explanation was blunt:

"It would not banish age from the bench nor abolish divided decisions. It would not affect the power of any court to hold laws unconstitutional. . . . It would not reduce the expense of litigation nor speed the decision of cases. It is a proposal without precedent and without justification."

Of course the plan could not "banish" age from the Court, but even the compromise helped reduce the age by *allowing* retirement at full pay upon reaching seventy. Added to Roosevelt's penchant for appointing young men to replace the oldsters this system worked well. As late as 1945, when Burton took Roberts' place, the average age was only fifty-seven, contrasted with an average of seventy-two during the Court battle.

Almost nothing was done to change the cost or speed of litigation. The man who can get a case up the hierarchy and through the nation's highest tribunal in two years is lucky. Probably the quickest appeal job on record was accomplished in behalf of the eight Nazis who came ashore one night for sabotage. The Court even broke up its vacation to have a full hearing of that case and shattered years and years of precedent to give a yes-or-no answer the next day, being satisfied to release its long opinion a few months later. Yet when a major case was brought to challenge the validity of the 1946 Illinois primary the Court stewed over it for weeks, finally deciding it after the primary. The case could easily have been answered sooner, had the justices wanted to change custom and do so before writing their opinions.

An interesting footnote to the history of trying to speed up the Court was provided by Jackson in his Nuremberg attack on Black. While opinions were being prepared in the *Jewell Ridge* case, he charged, it was suggested by someone that the decision be handed down without waiting for opinions. It apparently shocked Jackson that this would be proposed at a time when a strike and negotiations for settling it were going on, yet Jackson was one of the chief pleaders in 1937 for speeding justice.

Undoubtedly the greatest objective won by the Court fight was in getting the Court to refrain from declaring laws unconstitutional. The rash of nullification of state legislation was headed off in 1938, though the Court kept a close watch over the criminal statutes which its liberals had always scrutinized carefully. But the new Court let states experiment with social legislation while it sat independently by. The new vogue of self-restraint went so far, in fact, that states built up a number of new walls against their sisters which might result in damage to the federal system more important than that formerly done by striking down state laws.

Federal laws fared even better than state laws in the young hands. In fact, congressional acts nullified since 1937 can be counted on two fingers, and few people would be able to name the two laws. The first was the Federal Firearms Act of 1938, which offended the Court by presuming that a gun found on someone convicted of a crime or who was a fugitive from justice had been received in violation of the act. There was no dissent from the Court's discard of the statute as an unconstitutional curb on fair trials.[1] The other offensive law concerned the three federal employees whom Congress decided were too radical to stay on the pay roll. An appropriations bill rider banned payment of their salaries, but the Court declared the measure to be a bill of attainder, banned by the Constitution.[2]

For the first eighty years of the Court's life it averaged one nullification of a congressional law each ten years. Then, for fifty years, it averaged seven each decade. In the ten years up to 1930, however, the court struck down nineteen federal laws. From 1930 to 1936 it negated sixteen laws. That it cut the figure down to two nullifications in the ten years since then proves that the Court heeded the admonition of the President, the public and its own dissenting justices to keep hands off the voters' will.

The single largest stumbling block for legislation had been a legal fiction built around due process of law. The 5th amendment provides, among other things, that "no person shall . . . be deprived of life, liberty, or property, without due process of law." For many years this meant little more than that everyone is entitled to a fair trial. After the Civil War the clause was written into the 14th amendment, supposedly to keep the states from abusing fair procedure; but by 1890 lawyers had succeeded in getting the Court to use the clause to keep state legislatures from regulating the business of their clients. By 1936 use of the due process clause for purposes never intended for it had become a racket.

A number of scholars predicted long ago that overuse of the device would have to stop. In April of 1941, for a unanimous Court, young Bill Douglas applied the brakes.[3] Black had already declared war on the phony use of the clause, but the case in which Douglas spoke for the entire Court deserves attention as the best single one for demonstrating that it was indeed a new and victorious Court.

The state of Nebraska had passed a law fixing the maximum fee which employment agencies might collect from a job-seeker for landing him a job. A private agency fought the measure as depriving him of property without due process of law. The Nebraska supreme court relied on the 1928 *Ribnik* decision of the nation's highest tribunal to declare the law unconstitutional. The authority could hardly seem clearer —the precedent was well known as holding that states have no power to regulate the rates of employment agencies. But Douglas minced no words in changing course: "The drift away from Ribnik v. McBride has been so great that it can no longer be deemed a controlling authority."

Moreover, the standard used in that case, borrowed from the earlier

Tyson case, was swept into a corner. The *Tyson* doctrine was that business "affected with the public interest" could be regulated by legislation fixing rates. That test had been labeled by Holmes in a dissent as "little more than a fiction" and had been disapproved even before the Court fight. Douglas threw dirt on its grave, then he led the bar through a useful review of the Court's chronology in pulling away from the *Ribnik* case: In 1930 the Court upheld federal regulation of commission rates in interstate stockyards; the following year it upheld a New Jersey law limiting commissions of fire insurance agents; and in 1934 it approved the New York law for fixing retail prices of milk.

Then, in the crucial swing year of 1937, the Court upheld the Washington state law for fixing minimum wages for women and minors—overruling the famous *Adkins* case in doing so—and went on to uphold a Georgia statute fixing maximum charges in warehouses dealing with leaf tobacco.

Two years later (with Roosevelt's appointees having tipped the scales) the Court upheld the congressional power to fix minimum prices for milk; the next year the price-fixing features of the Bituminous Coal Act were sustained. Then, in 1941, the Court upheld sweeping federal power over minimum wages and maximum hours covered by the Fair Labor Standards Act.

"These cases," Douglas commented, "represent more than scattered examples of constitutionally permissible price-fixing schemes. They represent in large measure a basic departure from the philosophy and approach of the majority in the Ribnik case."

There was one more punch at the old Court in Douglas' opinion. The Nebraska employment agencies had insisted that they catered only to professional, executive and technical job-seekers rather than to the common labor for whose protection such legislation was originally passed. Douglas' answer went to the root of Roosevelt's ostensible reason for wanting to get rid of the Court's reactionaries, whom he felt were wrongfully injecting their opinions of the wisdom of the legislation. Said the new justice: "We are not concerned, however, with the wisdom, need, or appropriateness of the legislation. Differences of opinion on that score suggest a choice which 'should be left where . . . it was left by the Constitution—to the States and to Congress,' " He was quoting the Holmes-Brandeis-Stone dissent in the *Ribnik* case.

A shackling doctrine of law in the area of property rights versus human rights had been cleared away—and without a dissenting voice, not even a protest from Hughes or Roberts. McReynolds had retired two months before. An old score was settled, at least for a while.

It is all very well for the new justices to say that the wisdom of the legislation under review is none of their affair, but the Nine

Old Men said the same thing. Men like Black, Douglas and Murphy could disclaim interest in the object of the legislation the rest of their lives without convincing their critics that their minds are that neatly compartmentalized or disciplined. The suspicion will always prevail that the Court's New Dealers personally like laws such as that regulating employment agencies, so they vote to uphold them. The law, according to the skeptics, comes second to the result. Some legal justification can always be called up from the books.

But those who attacked the old Court for its "government by judiciary" were not unaware of the fact that a justice's personal opinions would always have to be reckoned with. Their argument, in fact, was that this situation, being unbeatable, should be turned to advantage by appointing justices whose personal views were in tune with the times. Kicking the seventy-year-olds off the bench was only a means to this end. Perfection in self-restraint could not be expected, so the Court was made current and it wouldn't matter much if the new personnel fell for the human temptation to stick their fingers in the merits of the laws before them. The justices who were brought in deny that they use this "realistic" system of deciding cases, but even if they do use it, the results have been what were wanted by those who remade the Court.

The next question becomes: Isn't this dangerous to the stability of our government—won't these justices someday be out of tune with the times? Put more harshly, the question can well be phrased: "Doesn't this give the nation a government of men rather than a government of laws? What was Roosevelt's meat may be another administration's poison.

The answers to both posers would be quite clearly "no," if the personnel of the Court rotated at regular intervals. For example, if a vacancy occurred every other year, justices could be appointed at the age of fifty-two and retire at the age of seventy. Stability would be supplied as well as a mechanical formula could supply it, and half the justices at any given time would have served no more than about nine years.

However, appointments became so bunched from 1937 to 1945 that it will probably be several generations before chances for making appointments to the Court are scattered out. Until that time comes there may be several crises like that which Roosevelt found himself facing. Avoidance can best be accomplished by the type of self-control expressed by Douglas in the employment agency decision.

There is another restraint on any Court from running away with itself and the country, a restraint demonstrated by the present Court. That is the way in which new Courts split. This phenomenon already has been compared with the love life of the amoeba; another description was used privately in 1942 by one of the Justices—"Trying to classify these justices is like trying to pick up mercury." The accuracy of either figure of speech is a bulwark against the Court's ever being stampeded too far in one ruinous direction. Let it never be forgotten by those who fear Court packing that Wilson appointed both the tory McReynolds and the liberal Brandeis, that Hoover appointed both the conservative Roberts and the liberal Cardozo.

Nor was Franklin D. Roosevelt the first President to find himself at odds with the Court inherited from his predecessors. As Attorney General Jackson put it in his book: "Another generation may find itself fighting what is essentially the same conflict that we, under Roosevelt, and our fathers under Theodore Roosevelt and Wilson, and our grandfathers under Lincoln, and our great-grandfathers under Jackson, and our great-great-grandfathers under Jefferson, fought before them." To this, gladiator Jackson added ominously that "the truce between judicial authority and popular will may, or may not, ripen into a permanent peace."

History certainly gives little reason for a contrary belief. In fact, the relations among the Supreme Court, Congress and the President are remindful of the "caucus race" which Lewis Carroll invented for *Alice in Wonderland*. Lawyers should be familiar with the entire book, but the great caucus race was a running contest in which each entry started when he felt like it and stopped when he felt like it. This made it difficult to determine the winner, but it didn't matter because each contestant won a comfit—a confection. The Supreme Court issue mills around just as interminably; so far there have been enough prizes to go around.

It was too seldom realized, during the fight of 1937, that there were alternatives much uglier than the age juggling which Roosevelt finally chose as his plan of battle. There might have been impeachment, such as was brought against Justice Samuel Chase after he attacked the Jeffersonians; or there might have been open defiance of the type used by Lincoln during the Civil War. The *Dredd Scott* decision that Congress had no power to regulate slavery in the territories was reversed by a civil war; the Court's refusal to uphold the legality of the paper money which financed that war was overcome by Grant's appointment of two new justices assigned to that specific mission. The Court's narrow view of the legality of income taxes forced resort to the cumbersome process of amending the Constitution.

Amendment is, of course, the soundest way to get around the Court and the way planned by the founders. There would not have been time, Roosevelt reasonably felt, to do this in the crisis of the mid-thirties; but there was nothing to prevent its being started at the time of the Court fight so as to insure that no relapse occurs. The liberals, who rightfully have been able to claim credit for anticipating such crises and trotting out a program they feel will head them off, remained fairly silent about the broader issues of the 1937 fight. By going along with the Roosevelt expedient, instead of getting into the deeper considerations, they made it possible for one of their number, Jackson, to write four years later: "The struggle did little to clarify the underlying issues of Judicial Supremacy, for both sides evaded it."

But on the issue which *was* presented, Jackson was able to report victory in a masterpiece of summation: "In politics the black-robed reactionary Justices had won over the master liberal politician of our day. In law the President defeated the recalcitrant Justices in their own Court." The statement epitomizes one of the greatest national struggles of all times, a struggle which seems well enough settled now but which succeeding generations are likely to have to continue. To cite one tiny reason, the due process clause is still in the Constitution for another crop of justices to interpret as it wishes.

The temporary nature of the victory was nowhere better stated than in a brief exchange during the Senate Judiciary Committee hearings on the Roosevelt plan for the Court. Senator O'Mahoney was quizzing Attorney General Cummings.

"Do you recognize," asked O'Mahoney, "that this does not afford a permanent remedy for the situation of which you complain?"

Cummings smiled. "There is nothing permanent in this world, Senator."

Citations

CHAPTER II

1. Marbury v. Madison, 1 Cranch 137, 1803.
2. Scott v. Sandford, 19 Howard 393, 1857.
3. Hepburn v. Griswold, 8 Wall 603, 1850.
4. Legal Tender Cases, 12 Wall 457, 1871.
5. Pollock v. Farmers' Loan & Trust Co., 158 US 601, 1895.
6. Panama Refining Co. et al. v. Ryan et al., 293 US 388, 1935.
7. Perry v. United States, 294 US 330, 1935.
8. Railroad Retirement Board v. Alton Railroad et al., 295 US 330, 1936.
9. Carter v. Carter Coal Co., 298 US 238, 1936.
10. Louisville Joint Stock Land Bank v. Radford, 295 US 555, 1935.
11. Schecter Poultry Corp. v. United States, 295 US 495, 1935.
12. Morehead v. New York, ex rel., Tipaldo, 298 US 587, 1936.
13. Adkins v. Children's Hospital, 261 US 525, 1923.
14. United States v. Butler, 297 US 1, 1936.

CHAPTER III

1. Ashwander v. TVA, 297 US 288, 1936.
2. West Coast Hotel Company v. Parrish, 300 US 379, 1937.
3. Virginian Railway Company v. System Federation No. 40, Railway Employees Department of the A.F. of L., 300 US 515, 1937.
4. Wright v. Mountain Trust Bank, 300 US 440, 1937.
5. National Labor Relations Board v. Jones & Laughlin Steel Company, 301 US 1; The Associated Press v. N.L.R.B., 301 US 103; and Washington, Virginia & Maryland Coach Company v. N.L.R.B., 301, US 142, 1937.
6. Carmichael v. Southern Coal and Coke Company, 301 US 495, 1937.

CHAPTER IV

1. For a helpful study of Black's Senate record see "Black—A Study in Modern Liberalism," a thesis submitted by Horace J. Bresler

to the department of government, Harvard University, March 17, 1941.

2. New York Life Insurance Co. v. Gamer, 303 US 161, 1938.
3. Erie Railroad Co. v. Tompkins, 304 US 64, 1938.
4. Connecticut General Life Insurance Co. v. Johnson, 303 US 77, 1938.
5. An appendix in Felix Frankfurter's book, *Mr. Justice Holmes and the Supreme Court,* Harvard University Press, 1939, lists 232 Supreme Court decisions holding state action invalid under the 14th amendment—most of them under the due process clause.
6. Bogardus v. Commissioner of Internal Revenue, 302 US 34, 1937.
7. McCart v. Indianapolis Water Co., 302 US 419, 1938.
8. Indiana ex rel Anderson v. Brand, 303 US 95, 1938.
9. Calmar Steamship Co. v. Taylor, 303 US 525, 1938.
10. Crown Cork and Seal Co. v. Guttman, 304 US 159, 1938; and General Talking Pictures Corp. v. Western Electric Co., 304 US 175, 1938.
11. Johnson v. Zerbst, 304 US 458, 1938.
12. Helvering v. Gerhardt, 304 US 405, 1938; and Allen v. Regents of the University System of Georgia, 304 US 439, 1938.
13. United States v. Carolene Products Co., 304 US 144, 1938.
14. Lovell v. Griffin, 303 US 444, 1938; New Negro Alliance v. Sanitary Grocery Company, 303 US 552, 1938; and Hale v. Kentucky, 303 US 613, 1938, respectively.
15. Polk Company v. Glover, 305 US 5, 1938; McCarroll v. Dixie Greyhound Lines, 309 US 176, 1940; and Southern Pacific Company v. Arizona, 325 US 761, 1945, respectively.
16. Morgan v. Virginia, No. 704, 1945 term.
17. Texas v. Florida, 309 US 398, 1939.
18. Hines v. Davidowitz, 312 US 52, 1941.
19. Williams v. North Carolina, 325 US 226, 1945.
20. New York v. United States, No. 5, October 1945 term.
21. Pierre v. Louisiana, 306 US 354, 1939; and Smith v. Texas, 311 US 128, 1940, respectively.
22. Galloway v. United States, 319 US 372, 1943.
23. Chambers v. Florida, 309 US 227, 1940.
24. Hysler v. Florida, 315 US 411, 1942; Lisenba v. California, 314 US 219, 1941; and Feldman v. United States, 322 US 487, 1944.
25. Smith v. O'Grady, 312 US 329, 1941.
26. Avery v. Alabama, 308 US 444, 1940; and Betts v. Brady, 316 US 455, 1942, respectively.
27. Bridges v. California, 314 US 252, 1941.
28. Hague v. Committee for Industrial Organization, 307 US 496, 1939.
29. Jamison v. Texas, 318 US 413, 1943; and Martin v. Struthers, 319 US 141, 1943.
30. Marsh v. Alabama, No. 114; and Tucker v. Texas, No. 87, October 1945 term.

31. West Virginia State Board of Education v. Barnette, 319 US 624, 1943.
32. Re Summers, 325 US 561, 1945.
33. Sibbach v. Wilson, 312 US 1, 1941.
34. United States v. Lovett, Nos. 809-11, October 1945 term.
35. United States v. Classic, 313 US 299, 1941.
36. Screws v. United States, 325 US 91, 1945.
37. See, for example, his opinion for the Court in Davis v. Department of Labor of Washington, 317 US 249, 1942; and his dissent in Marshall v. Pletz, 317 US 383, 1943.
38. Herb v. Pitcairn, 324 US 117, 1945.
39. De Zon v. American President Lines, 318 US 660, 1943; Brady v. Southern Railway Company, 320 US 476, 1943; and Stewart v. Southern Railway Company, 315 US 283, 1942.
40. Union Joint Stock Land Bank of Detroit v. Byerly, 310 US 1, 1940; and Wood v. Lovett, 313 US 362, 1941.
41. Federal Power Commission v. Natural Gas Pipeline Company, 315 US 575, 1942. See also his dissent in Federal Power Commission v. Hope Natural Gas Co., 320 US 591, 1944; and in Public Utilities Commission of Ohio v. United Fuel Gas Co., 317 US 456, 1943.
42. Interstate Commerce Commission v. Inland Waterways Corporation, 319 US 671, 1943.
43. United States v. South-Eastern Underwriters Association, 322 US 533, 1944; Associated Press v. United States, 326 US 1, 1945; and Fashion Originators' Guild of America v. Federal Trade Commission, 312 US 457, 1941, respectively.
44. Gibbs v. Buck, 307 US 66, 1939. See also Watson v. Buck, 313 US 387, 1941.
45. United States v. Cooper Corporation, 312 US 600, 1941.
46. Federal Trade Commission v. Bunte Brothers, 312 US 349, 1941.
47. Goodyear Tire & Rubber Co. v. Ray-O-Vac Co., 321 US 275, 1944.
48. See, for example, Exhibit Supply Company v. Ace Patents Corporation, 315 US 126, 1942; and Williams Manufacturing Company v. United Shoe Machinery Corporation, 316 US 364, 1942.
49. General Talking Pictures Corp. v. Western Electric Co., 305 US 124, 1938 (rehearing).
50. Washingtonian Publishing Co. v. Pearson, 306 US 30, 1939; and Fisher Music Co. v. Witmark & Sons, 318 US 643, 1943.
51. National Labor Relations Board v. Fansteel Metal Corp., 306 US 240, 1939; and National Labor Relations Board v. Columbian Enameling & Stamping Company, 306 US 292, 1939.
52. National Labor Relations Board v. Indiana & Michigan Electric Company, 318 US 9, 1943.
53. Milk Wagon Drivers' Union v. Lake Valley Farm Products, 311 US 91, 1940; and Milk Wagon Drivers Union v. Meadowmoor Dairies, 312 US 287, 1941, respectively.

54. Carpenters & Joiners Union v. Ritter's Cafe, 315 US 722, 1942.
55. Allen Bradley Company v. International Brotherhood of Electrical Workers, 325 US 797, 1945; and Hunt v. Crumboch, 325 US 821, 1945, respectively.
56. Williams v. Jacksonville Terminal Company, 315 US 386, 1942.
57. Viereck v. United States, 318 US 236, 1943; and Cramer v. United States, 325 US 1, 1945, respectively.
58. Falbo v. United States, 320 US 549, 1944; and Korematsu v. United States, 323 US 214, 1944, respectively.
59. Ex parte Kawato, 317 US 69, 1942; Keegan v. United States, 325 US 478, 1945; and Baumgartner v. United States, 322 US 665, 1944, respectively.
60. Duncan v. White, Nos. 14 and 15, October 1945 term.
61. C. J. Hendry Co. v. Moore, 318 US 133, 1943.
62. Colegrove v. Green, No. 804, October 1945 term.
63. Creek Nation v. United States, 318 US 629, 1943; County of Mahnomen v. United States, 319 US 474, 1943; and Oklahoma Tax Commission v. United States, 319 US 598, 1943.
64. McDonald v. Commissioner of Internal Revenue, 323 US 57, 1944.

CHAPTER V

1. Betts v. Brady, 316 US 455, 1942.
2. Securities and Exchange Commission v. Chenery Corporation, 318 US 80, 1943.
3. McNabb v. United States, 318 US 332, 1943. See also Anderson v. United States, 318 US 350, decided the same day.
4. Elgin, Joliet & Eastern Railway Co. v. Burley, 325 US 711, 1945 (first decision); 325 US 711, 1946 (second decision).
5. Schneiderman v. United States, 320 US 118, 1943.
6. Malinski v. New York, 324 US 401.
7. Northwestern Bands of Shoshone Indians v. United States, 324 US 335, 1945.

CHAPTER VI

1. Gray v. Powell, 314 US 402, 1941.
2. Switchmen's Union v. National Mediation Board, 320 US 297, 1943.
3. Stark v. Wickard, 321 US 288, 1944.
4. United States v. Rock Royal Co-operative, Inc., 307 US 533, 1939.
5. Social Security Board v. Nierotko, No. 318, October 1945 term.
6. Mayo v. United States, 319 US 441.
7. Browder v. United States, 312 US 335, 1941.
8. Jones v. Opelika, 316 US 584, 1942. See Chapter XVII for the history of these and other Jehovah's Witnesses cases.

9. In re Clyde Simmers, 325 US 561, 1945.
10. McNabb v. United States, 318 US 332, 1943.
11. Smith v. Allwright, 321 US 649, 1944.
12. Girouard v. United States, No. 572; and United States v. Lovett, Nos. 809-11, October 1945 term.
13. Pennekamp v. Florida, No. 473, October 1945 term; and Morgan v. Virginia, No. 704, October 1945 term.

CHAPTER VII

1. National Broadcasting Company v. United States, 319 US 190, 1943.
2. United States v. Socony-Vacuum Oil Co., 310 US 150, 1940.
3. American Tobacco Co., et al. v. United States, Nos. 18-20, October 1945 term.
4. American Medical Association v. United States, 317 US 519, 1943.
5. United States v. South-Eastern Underwriters Association, 322 US 533, 1944.
6. Associated Press v. United States, 326 US 1, 1945.
7. Ethyl Gasoline Corporation v. United States, 309 US 436, 1940.
8. United States v. Univis Lens Company, 316 US 241.
9. Hartford-Empire Co. v. United States, 323 US 386; and 324 US 570, 1945.
10. Interstate Circuit, Inc., v. United States, 306 US 208.
11. United States v. Borden Company, 308 US 188, 1939.
12. U.S. Alkali Export Association v. United States, 325 US 196, 1945.
13. United States v. Bausch & Lomb Optical Company. 321 US 707, 1944.
14. United States v. Frankfort Distilleries, Inc., 324 US 293, 1945.
15. United States v. Masonite Corporation, et al, 316 US 265, 1942.
16. United States v. Crescent Amusement Company, 323 US 173, 1944.
17. Bigelow v. RKO Radio Pictures, Inc., No. 444, October 1945 term.
18. Fashion Originators' Guild of America v. Federal Trade Commission, 312 US 457, 1941. Millinery Creators' Guild v. Federal Trade Commission, 312 US 469, 1941 halted the same system in the women's hat business.
19. Corn Products Refining Co. v. Federal Trade Commission and Federal Trade Commission v. A. E. Staley Manufacturing Company, 324 US 726, 1945.
20. Georgia v. Pennsylvania Railroad, 324 US 439, 1945.
21. Southwestern Bell Telephone Co. v. Public Service Commission of Missouri, 262 US 276.
22. Driscoll v. Edison Light & Power Company, 307 US 104.
23. Federal Power Commission v. Natural Gas Pipeline Company 315 US 575, 1942.
24. Federal Power Commission v. Hope Natural Gas Company, 320 US 591, 1943.

25. North American Company v. Securities and Exchange Commission, No. 1, October 1945 term.

CHAPTER VIII

1. Hearings before a Subcommittee of the Committee on the Judiciary, 76th Congress, 1st Session; January 7 to 12, 1939.
2. Graves v. New York ex rel O'Keefe, 306 US 466.
3. O'Malley v. Woodrough, 307 US 277.
4. Bruno v. United States, 308 US 287.
5. Minersville School District v. Gobitis, 310 US 586.
6. Puerto Rico v. Hermanos, 309 US 543.
7. Osborn v. Ozlin, 310 US 53.
8. United States v. Hutcheson, 312 US 219.
9. Sibbach v. Wilson & Company, 312 US 1.
10. Milk Wagon Drivers Union of Chicago v. Meadowmoor Dairies, 312 US 287.
11. Federal Trade Commission v. Bunte Brothers, 312 US 349.
12. Phelps Dodge Corporation v. NLRB, 313 US 177.
13. Bridges v. California, 314 US 252.
14. Glasser v. United States, 315 US 60.
15. Hysler v. Florida, 315 US 411, 1942.
16. Carpenters & Joiners Union v. Ritters' Cafe, 315 US 722.
17. Goldstein v. United States, 316 US 114.
18. Goldman v. United States, 316 US 129, 1942.
19. United States v. Bethlehem Steel Corporation, 315 US 289.
20. Cloverleaf Butter Company v. Patterson, 315 US 148.
21. West Virginia v. Barnette, 319 US 624.
22. Jones v. Opelika, 319 US 103, and Murdock v. Pennsylvania, 319 US 105, decided together.
23. Martin v. Struthers, 319 US 141.
24. Adams v. United States, 317 US 269.
25. Schneiderman v. United States, 320 US 118.
26. McNabb v. United States, 318 US 332.
27. Anderson v. United States, 318 US 350.
28. National Broadcasting Company v. United States, 319 US 190.
29. Williams v. North Carolina, 317 US 287, 1942; and same, 325 US 226, 1945.
30. Federal Power Commission v. Hope Natural Gas Company, 320 US 591.
31. Mercoid Corporation v. Mid-Continent Investment Company, 320 US 661.
32. Mahnich v. Southern Steamship Company, 321 US 96.
33. Northwest Airlines v. Minnestota, 322 US 292.
34. United States v. South-Eastern Underwriters Association, 322 US 533.
35. Ashcraft v. Tennessee, 322 US 143.

36. Feldman v. United States, 322 US 487.
37. Baumgartner v. United States, 322 US 665.
38. Hartzel v. United States, 322 US 680.
39. Singer v. United States, 323 US 338.
40. Keegan v. United States, 325 US 478.
41. Korematsu v. United States, 323 US 214.
42. Williams v. Kaiser, 323 US 471 and Rice v. Olson, 324 US 786.
43. Railway Mail Association v. Corsi, 326 US 88.
44. Thomas v. Collins, 323 US 516.
45. Hill v. Florida, 325 US 538.
46. 10 East 40th Street Building, Inc. v. Callus, 325 US 578.
47. Associated Press v. United States, 326 US 1.
48. Elgin, Joliet & Eastern Railway Company v. Burley, 325 US 711.
49. McDonald v. Commissioner, 323 US 57.
50. New York v. United States, No. 5, October 1945 term.
51. Colegrove v. Green, No. 804, October 1945 term.
52. United States v. Carbone, No. 474, October 1945 term.
53. D. A. Schulte, Inc. v. Gangi, No. 517, October 1945 term.
54. Davis v. United States, No. 404, October 1945 term.
55. Fisher v. United States, No. 122, October 1945 term.
56. Marsh v. Alabama, No. 114; and Tucker v. Texas, No. 87 of the October 1945 term, respectively.
57. Duncan v. Kahanamoku, Nos. 14 and 15; and Girouard v. United States, No. 572, October 1945 term, respectively.
58. Thiel v. Southern Pacific Co., No. 349, October 1945 term.
59. United States v. Lovett, Nos. 809-11, October 1945 term.
60. *Mr. Justice Holmes and the Supreme Court*, by Felix Frankfurter, Harvard University Press, 1939; Chapter III.
61. Ex Parte Peru, 318 US 578, 1943.

CHAPTER IX

1. Hammer v. Dagenhart, 247 US 251, 1918.
2. United States v. Darby, 312 US 100, 1941.
3. Gibbons v. Ogden, 9 Wheaton 1.
4. United States v. E. C. Knight Co., 156 US 1, 1894.
5. Paul v. Virginia, 8 Wall 168, 1869.
6. Bernard C. Gavit, *The Commerce Clause of the U. S. Constitution*; Principia Press, Bloomington, Indiana; page 134.
7. International Text-Book Co. v. Pigg, 217 US 91, 1910.
8. United States v. South-Eastern Underwriters Association, 322 US 533, 1944.
9. Apex Hosiery Company v. Leader, 310 US 469, 1940.
10. Consolidated Edison Company v. National Labor Relations Board, 305 US 197, 1938.
11. Kirschbaum v. Walling, 316 US 517, 1942; and Borden Company v. Borella, 325 US 679, 1945.

12. Mabee v. White Plains Publishing Co., No. 57, 1946.
13. Currin v. Wallace, 306 US 1, 1939.
14. Mulford v. Smith, 307 US 38, 1939.
15. United States v. Rock Royal Cooperative, 307 US 533, 1939.
16. Nebbia v. New York, 291 US 502, 1934.
17. Wickard v. Filburn, 317 US 111, 1942.
18. Clason v. Indiana, 306 US 439, 1939.
19. Eicholz v. Public Service Commission, 306 US 268, 1939.
20. Hale v. Bimco Trading, Inc., 306 US 375, 1939.
21. Clark v. Paul Gray, Inc., 306 US 583, 1939; and Maurer v. Hamilton, 309 US 598, 1940.
22. Terminal Railroad Association of St. Louis v. Brotherhood of Railroad Trainmen, 318 US 1, 1943.
23. McCarroll v. Dixie Greyhound Lines, Inc., 309 US 176, 1940.
24. Southern Pacific Company v. Arizona, 325 US 761, 1945.
25. Morgan v. Virginia, No. 704, October 1945 term.
26. McLeod v. Dilworth, 322 US 327; General Trading Company v. Iowa, 322 US 335; and International Harvester Co. v. Indiana, 322 US 340, respectively.
27. McGoldrick v. Berwind-White Coal Mining Co., 309 US 33, 1940.
28. Nippert v. Richmond, No. 72, October 1945 term.
29. Northwest Airlines v. Minnesota, 322 US 292, 1944.
30. Williams v. North Carolina, 317 US 287, 1942; and (second case) 325 US 226, 1945.
31. Graves v. New York, 306 US 466, 1939.
32. New York v. United States, No. 5, October 1945 term.
33. Helvering v. Gerhardt, 304 US 405, 1938.
34. United States v. County of Allegheny, 322 US 174, 1944.
35. Hooven & Allison Co. v. Evatt, 324 US 652, 1945.
36. Hines v. Davidowitz, 312 US 52, 1941.
37. Federal Trade Commission v. Bunte Bros., 312 US 349, 1941.
38. United States v. Wrightwood Dairy Co., 315 US 110, 1942.
39. United States v. Appalachian Electric Power Company, 311 US 377, 1940.
40. State of Oklahoma v. Guy F. Atkinson Co., 313 US 508, 1941.
41. Edwards v. California, 314 US 160, 1941.

CHAPTER X

1. Case v. Los Angeles Lumber Products Company, 308 US 106, 1939.
2. American United Mutual Life Insurance Company v. City of Avon Park, Florida, 311 US 138, 1940.
3. Consolidated Rock Products Co. v. E. Blois Du Bois, 312 US 510, 1941.
4. Group of Institutional Investors v. Chicago, Milwaukee, St. Paul & Pacific Railroad, 318 US 522, 1943.

5. Federal Power Commission v. Natural Gas Pipeline Company, 315 US 575.
6. Federal Power Commission v. Hope Natural Gas Company, 320 US 591.
7. United States v. Powelson, 319 US 266, 1943.
8. Cuno Engineering Corporation v. Automatic Devices Corporation, 314 US 84.
9. United States v. Masonite Corporation et al, 316 US 265.
10. United States v. Crescent Amusement Company, 323 US 173, 1944.
11. Georgia v. Pennsylvania Railroad Company, 324 US 439, 1945.
12. Olsen v. State of Nebraska, 313 US 236, 1941.
13. Southern Pacific Co. v. Arizona, 325 US 761, 1945; and Nippert v. Richmond, No. 72, October 1945 term.
14. Morgan v. Virginia, No. 704, October 1945 term.
15. State Tax Commission of Utah v. Aldrich, 316 US 174.
16. Helvering v. Griffiths, 318 US 371.
17. Skinner v. Oklahoma, 316 US 535, 1942.
18. Williams v. Kaiser, 323 US 471, 1945.
19. Malinski v. New York, 324 US 401, 1945.
20. Bridges v. Wixon, 326 US 135, 1945.
21. Hannegan v. Esquire, No. 399, 1945 term.
22. Adams v. United States, 317 US 269, 1943.
23. Cramer v. United States, 325 US 1, 1945.
24. Girouard v. United States, No. 572, October 1945 term.
25. Davis v. United States, No. 404, October 1945 term.

CHAPTER XI

1. National Labor Relations Board v. Jones & Laughlin Steel Corp., 301 US 1, 1937 (See Chapter III); Darby v. United States, 312 US 100, 1941 (See Chapter IX); and West Coast Hotel Co. v. Parrish, 300 US 379, 1937 (See Chapter III).
2. Tennessee Coal, Iron & Railroad Co. v. Muscoda Local No. 123, 321 US 590, 1944.
3. Jewell Ridge Coal Corp. v. Local No. 6167, 325 US 161, 1945.
4. Williams v. Jacksonville Terminal Co., 315 US 386, 1942.
5. Western Union Telegraph Co. v. Lenroot, 323 US 490, 1945.
6. United States v. White, 322 US 694, 1944.
7. Senn v. Tile Layers Protective Union, 301 US 468, 1937.
8. Thornhill v. Alabama, 310 US 88, 1940. See also, Carlson v. California, 310 US 106, decided the same day.
9. Milk Wagon Drivers Union v. Meadowmoor Dairies, 312 US 287, 1941.
10. Carpenters & Joiners Union v. Ritter's Café, 315 US 722, 1942.
11. American Federation of Labor v. Swing, 312 US 321, 1941.
12. Cafeteria Employees Union v. Angelos, 320 US 293, 1943.

13. See in general "Majority Rule in Collective Bargaining," XLV *Columbia Law Review* 556 (July, 1945) by Ruth Weyand.
14. J. I. Case Co. v. National Labor Relations Board, 321 US 332, 1944. See also Order of Railroad Telegraphers v. Railway Express Agency, 321 US 342, 1944, for a similar result under railway legislation.
15. Medo Photo Supply Corp. v. National Labor Relations Board, 321 US 678, 1944.
16. May Department Stores v. National Labor Relations Board, No. 39, October 1945 term.
17. Hill v. Florida, 325 US 538, 1945.
18. Steele v. Louisville & Nashville Railroad Co., 323 US 192, 1944.
19. Railway Mail Association v. Corsi, 326 US 88, 1945.
20. Wallace Corporation v. National Labor Relations Board, 323 US 248, 1944.
21. National Labor Relations Board v. Fansteel Metal Corp., 306 US 240, 1939.
22. Southern Steamship Co. v. National Labor Relations Board, 316 US 31, 1942.
23. Apex Hosiery Company v. William Leader, 310 US 469, 1940.
24. United States v. Hutcheson, 312 US 219, 1941.
25. United States v. Building & Construction Trades Council, 313 US 539, 1941, and two other cases reported there.
26. Allen Bradley Co. v. Local Union No. 3, International Brotherhood of Electrical Workers, 325 US 797, 1945.
27. Hunt v. Crumboch, 325 US 821, 1945.
28. United States v. Local 807 of International Brotherhood of Teamsters, 315 US 521, 1942.
29. United States v. Laudani, 320 US 543, 1944.
30. United States v. Carbone, No. 474, October 1945 term.

CHAPTER XII

1. Minersville School District v. Gobitis, 310 US 586.
2. West Virginia State Board of Education v. Barnette, 319 US 624.
3. Martin v. City of Struthers, 319 US 141, 1943.
4. Prince v. Massachusetts, 321 US 158.
5. Falbo v. United States, 320 US 549.
6. Lyons v. Oklahoma, 322 US 596.
7. Malinski v. New York, 324 US 401.
8. Screws v. New York, 325 US 91.
9. Atkins v. Texas, 325 US 398.
10. Thornhill v. Alabama, 310 US 88.
11. Tennessee Coal, Iron & Railroad Co. v. Muscoda Local No. 123, 321 US 590, 1944; Jewell Ridge Coal Corp. v. Local No. 6197, 325 US 161; and Anderson v. Mt. Clemens Pottery Co., No. 342, October 1945 term.

12. United States v. White, 322 US 694.
13. Steele v. Louisville & Nashville Railroad Co., 323 US 192, 1944.
14. Baumgartner v. United States, 322 US 665.
15. Bridges v. Wixon, 326 US 135.
16. Schneiderman v. United States, 320 US 118, 1943.
17. Korematsu v. United States, 323 US 214.
18. Ex parte Endo, 323 US 283.
19. In re Yamashita, Nos. 61 and 672, October 1945 term.
20. In re Homma, Nos. 93 and 818, October 1945 term.
21. Duncan v. Kahanamoku, Nos. 14 and 15, October 1945 term.
22. Bridges v. State of California, 314 US 252, 1941.
23. Associated Press v. United States, 326 US 1.
24. National Broadcasting Co. v. United States, 319 US 190.
25. Endicott Johnson Corporation v. Perkins, 317 US 501.
26. United States v. Beach, 324 US 193.
27. Mortensen v. United States, 322 US 369.
28. Goldstein v. United States, 316 US 114; and Goldman v. United States, 316 US 129, 1942.

CHAPTER XIII

1. Abrams v. United States, 250 US 616, 1919.
2. Gilbert v. United States, 254, US 325, 1920.
3. United States, ex rel. Milwaukee Social Democratic Publishing Co. v. Burleson, 255 US 407, 1921.
4. Gitlow v. New York, 268 US 652, 1925.
5. Viereck v. United States, 318 US 236.
6. Hartzel v. United States, 322 US 680.
7. Cramer v. United States, 325 US 1, 1945.
8. Baumgartner v. United States, 322 US 665.
9. Yakus v. United States, 321 US 414.
10. Bowles v. Willingham, 321 US 503.
11. Davies Warehouse Company v. Bowles, 321 US 144.
12. Vinson v. Washington Gas Light Company, 321 US 489.
13. Bowles v. United States, 319 US 33.
14. Falbo v. United States, 320 US 549.
15. Billings v. Truesdell, 321 US 542.
16. Bartchy v. United States, 319 US 484.
17. Singer v. United States, 323 US 338, 1945.
18. Keegan v. United States, 325 US 478, 1945.
19. Girouard v. United States, No. 572, October 1945 term.
20. Knauer v. United States, No. 510, October 1945 term.

CHAPTER XIV

1. New York, C. and St. L. Railroad Co. v. Frank, 314 US 360, 1941.
2. Duckworth v. Arkansas, 314 US 390, 1941.

3. Edwards v. California, 314 US 160, 1941.
4. Skinner v. Oklahoma, 316 US 535, 1942.
5. Tax Commission v. Aldrich, 316 US 174, 1942.
6. National Labor Relations Board v. Indiana & Michigan Electric Co., 318 US 9, 1943.
7. De Zon v. American President Lines, 318 US 660, 1943.
8. Helvering v. Griffiths, 318 US 371, 1943.
9. Interstate Commerce Commission v. Inland Waterways Corp., 319 US 671, 1943.
10. Wickard v. Filburn, 317 US 111, 1942; and West Virginia State Board of Education v. Barnette, 319 US 624, 1943.
11. Douglas v. Jeanette, 319 US 157, 1943.
12. Bowles v. United States, 319 US 33, 1943.
13. Williams v. North Carolina, 317 US 287, 1942 (first case).
14. Marcus v. Hess, 317 US 537, 1943.
15. Federal Power Commission v. Hope Natural Gas Co., 320 US 591, 1944.
16. Mercoid Corp. v. Mid-Continent Investment Co., 320 US 661, 1944.
17. United States v. South-Eastern Underwriters Assn., 322 US 533, 1944.
18. J. I. Case Co. v. National Labor Relations Board, 321 US 332, 1944.
19. Tennessee Coal, Iron and Railroad Co. v. Muscoda Local, 321 US 590, 1944.
20. Pollock v. Williams, 322 US 4, 1944.
21. United States v. Ballard, 322 US 78, 1944.
22. Ashcraft v. Tennessee, 322 US 143, 1944.
23. Prince v. Massachusetts, 321 US 158, 1944.
24. Magnolia Petroleum Co. v. Hunt, 320 US 430, 1944.
25. Northwest Airlines v. Minnesota, 322 US 292, 1944.
26. General Trading Company v. State Tax Commission, 322 US 335, 1944.
27. Cramer v. United States, 325 US 1, 1945.
28. Wallace Corporation v. National Labor Relations Board, 323 US 248, 1944.
29. Western Union Telegraph Co. v. Lenroot, 323 US 490, 1945.
30. Thomas v. Collins, 323 US 516, 1945.
31. Hunt v. Crumboch, 325 US 821, 1945.
32. Jewell Ridge Coal Corp. v. Local No. 6167, United Mine Workers, 325 US 161, 1945.

CHAPTER XV

1. Ex Parte Quirin, et al, v. 317 US 1.
2. Korematsu v. United States, 323 US 214.
3. Hirabayashi v. United States, 320 US 114, 1943.
4. Ex Parte Endo, 323 US 283.

5. Yamashita v. Styer, Nos. 61 and 672, 1945 term.
6. Re Homma, Nos 93 and 818, 1945 term.
7. Duncan v. Kahanamoku, Nos. 14 and 15, 1945 term.

CHAPTER XVI

1. Jones v. Opelika, 319 US 103, 1943; Schneiderman v. United States, 320 US 118, 1943; and Jersey Central Power & Light Co. v. Federal Power Commission, 319 US 61, 1943.
2. Aguilar v. Standard Oil Company of New Jersey, 318 US 724, 1943.
3. Marconi Wireless Telegraph Co. of America v. United States, 320 US 1, 1943.
4. Addison v. Holly Hill Fruit Products, 322 US 607, 1944.
5. International Harvester Co. v. Department of Treasury, 322 US 340, 1944.
6. Nippert v. Richmond, No. 72, October 1945 term.
7. Williams v. North Carolina, 325 US 226, 1945.
8. Medo Photo Supply Corp. v. National Labor Relations Board, 321 US 678, 1944.
9. Elgin, Joliet & Eastern Railway Co. v. Burley, 325 US 711, 1945; reaffirmed in No. 160 of the October 1945 term.
10. Seas Shipping Company v. Sieracki, No. 365, October 1945 term.
11. The *Schneiderman* case, supra.
12. Knauer v. United States, No. 510, October 1945 term.
13. Canizio v. New York, No. 152, October 1945 term.
14. Davis v. United States, No. 404, October 1945 term.
15. Robinson v. United States, 324 US 282, 1945.
16. Screws v. United States, 325 US 91, 1945.
17. Thomas v. Collins, 323 US 516, 1945.
18. Kotteakos v. United States, Nos. 457 and 458, October 1945 term.
19. Galloway v. United States, 319 US 372, 1943.
20. Prince v. Massachusetts, 321 US 158, 1944.
21. United States v. Yakus, 321 US 414, 1944.
22. Bowles v. Willingham, 321 US 503, 1944.
23. Re Yamashita; Nos. 61, Miscellaneous and 672; October 1945 term.

CHAPTER XVII

1. White v. Texas, 310 US 530, 1940.
2. Lovell v. Griffin, 303 US 444.
3. Schneider v. Irvington, 308 US 147.
4. Cantwell v. Connecticut, 310 US 396.
5. Minersville School District v. Gobitis, 310 US 586, 1940.
6. Cox v. New Hampshire, 312 US 569.
7. Chaplinsky v. New Hampshire, 315 US 568, 1942.

8. Jones v. Opelika, 316 US 584, 1942.
9. Jones v. Opelika (Second case), 319 US 103, 1943.
10. Murdock v. Pennsylvania, 319 US 105.
11. Martin v. City of Struthers, Ohio, 319 US 141.
12. West Virginia State Board of Education v. Barnette, 319 US 624.
13. Taylor v. Mississippi, 319 US 583, 1943.
14. Prince v. Massachusetts, 321 US 158, 1944.
15. Marsh v. Alabama, No. 114; and Tucker v. Texas, No. 87, October 1945 term, respectively.
16. For a broad treatment of the subject see "The Debt of Constitutional Law to Jehovah's Witnesses." 28 *Minnesota Law Review* 209 (March 1944) by Edward F. Waite, a retired federal judge. Also, "Recent Restrictions on Religious Liberty," XXXVI *American Political Science Review* No. 6 (December 1942), by V. W. Rotnem and F. G. Folsom.
17. United States v. Ballard, 322 US 78, 1944.
18. Anderson v. United States, 318 US 350, 1943.
19. Ward v. Texas, 316 US 547, 1942; and Ashcraft v. Tennessee, 322 US 143, 1944, and No. 381, October 1945 term (second case).
20. Lisenba v. California, 314 US 219, 1941; and United States v. Mitchell, 322 US 65, 1944; and Lyons v. Oklahoma, 322 US 596, 1944.
21. Weiss v. United States, 308 US 321; and Nardone v. United States, 308 US 338, 1939.
22. Goldstein v. United States, 316 US 114.
23. Goldman v. United States, 316 US 129.
24. Davis v. United States, No. 404, October 1946 term.
25. Tomkins v. Missouri, 323 US 485, 1945.
26. Williams v. Kaiser, 323 US 471, 1945; and House v. Mayo, 324 US 42, 1945.
27. Adams v. United States, 317 US 269, 1942.
28. Canizio v. New York, No. 152, October 1945 term.
29. Hale v. Kentucky, 303 US 613, 1938.
30. Pierre v. Louisiana, 306 US 384; and Smith v. Texas, 311 US 128, respectively.
31. Hill v. Texas, 316 US 400, 1942.
32. Akins v. Texas, 325 US 398.
33. Thiel v. Southern Pacific Co., No. 349, October 1945 term.
34. Herndon v. Lowry, 301 US 242, 1937.
35. Bridges v. California, 314 US 252, 1941.
36. Pennekamp et al. v. Florida, No. 473, October 1945 term.
37. Hannegan v. Esquire, No. 399, October 1945 term.
38. Hague v. Committee for Industrial Organization et al, 307 US 496, 1939.
39. Valentine v. Chrestensen, 316 US 52, 1942.
40. Screws v. United States, 325 US 91, 1945.
41. United States v. Classic, 313 US 299, 1941.

42. Mortensen v. United States, 322 US 369, 1944.
43. United States v. Beach, 324 US 193, 1945.
44. Chatwin v. United States, Nos. 31-33, October 1945 term.
45. Browder v. United States, 312 US 335, 1941.
46. Taylor v. Georgia, 315 US 25, 1942; and Pollock v. Williams, 322 US 4, 1944.
47. United States v. Gaskin, 320 US 527, 1944.
48. Morgan v. Virginia, No. 704, October 1945 term.
49. Mitchell v. United States, 313 US 80, 1941.
50. Missouri ex rel. Gaines v. Canada, 305 US 337, 1938.
51. Kessler v. Strecker, 307 US 22, 1939.
52. Bridges v. Wixon, 326 US 135, 1945.
53. Smith v. Allwright, 321 US 649, 1944.
54. Skinner v. Oklahoma, 316 US 535, 1942; and United States v. Lovett, Nos. 809-811, October 1945 term, respectively.
55. Re Summers, 325 US 561, 1945.
56. United States v. Carolene Products Co., 304 US 144, 1938.

CHAPTER XVIII

1. Duncan v. Kahanamoku, Nos. 14 and 15, October 1945 term.
2. Commissioner of Internal Revenue v. Wilcox, No. 163, October 1945 term.
3. Morgan v. Virginia, No. 704, October 1945 term.
4. Anderson v. Mt. Clemens Pottery Co., No. 342, October 1945 term.
5. Marsh v. Alabama, No. 114; Tucker v. Texas, No. 87; and Bihn v. United States, No. 675, October 1945 term, respectively.
6. Elgin, Joliet & Eastern Railway Co. v. Burley, No. 160; United States v. Carbone, No. 474; and D. A. Schulte v. Gangi, No. 517, October 1945 term, respectively.
7. Seas Shipping Co. v. Sieracki, No. 365, October 1945 term.
8. Williams v. United States, No. 123, October 1945 term.
9. First Iowa Hydro-Electric Cooperative v. Federal Power Commission, No. 603, October 1945 term; and The American Tobacco Co. v. United States, Nos. 18-20, October 1945 term, respectively.

CHAPTER XIX

1. "The Divided Supreme Court," by C. Herman Pritchett; 44 *Michigan Law Review* 427.
2. United States v. Hutcheson, 312 US 219, 1941.
3. Edwards v. California, 314 US 252, 1941.
4. Taylor v. Georgia, 315 US 25, 1942.
5. Local 807 v. United States, 315 US 521, 1942.
6. Southern Steamship Co. v. National Labor Relations Board, 316 US 31, 1942.

7. Walling v. A. B. Belo Corp., 316 US 624, 1942.
8. Williams v. Jacksonville Terminal Co., 315 US 386, 1942.
9. Betts v. Brady, 316 US 455; Jones v. Opelika (first case), 316 US 584; Goldstein v. United States, 316 US 114; and Goldman v. United States, 316 US 129, respectively, 1942.
10. United States v. Butler, 297 US 1, 1936.
11. *In Blood and Ink*, by Maury Maverick, page 141.
12. Girouard v. United States, No. 572, October 1945 term.

CHAPTER XX

1. Mahnich v. Southern Steamship Co. 321 US 96, 1944.
2. Helvering v. Hallock, 309 US 106, 1940.
3. California v. Thompson, 313 US 109, 1941; and Alabama v. King & Boozer, 314 US 1, 1941.
4. United States v. Darby, 312 US 100, 1941.
5. West Coast Hotel Co. v. Parrish, 300 US 379, 1937.
6. California v. Thompson, 313 US 109, 1941.
7. Erie Railroad Co. v. Tompkins, 304 US 64, 1938.
8. Graves v. New York, 306 US 466, 1939.
9. O'Malley v. Woodrough, 307 US 277, 1939.
10. Madden v. Kentucky, 309 US 83, 1940.
11. Alabama v. King & Boozer, 314 US 1, 1941.
12. Williams v. North Carolina, 317 US 287, 1942.
13. Tax Commission v. Aldrich, 316 US 174, 1942.
14. West Virginia v. Barnette, 319 US 624, 1943.
15. Murdock v. Pennsylvania, 319 US 105, 1943.
16. Smith v. Allwright, 321 US 649, 1944.
17. Olsen v. Nebraska, 313 US 236, 1941.
18. Edwards v. California, 314 US 160, 1941.
19. Girouard v. United States, No. 572, October 1945 term.
20. Mahnich v. Southern Steamship Co., 321 US 96, 1944; Helvering v. Producers Corp., 303 US 376, 1938; and Helvering v. Hallock, 309 US 106, 1940.
21. Burnet v. Coronado Oil & Gas Co., 285 US 393, 1932.
22. See Helvering v. Griffiths, 318 US 371, 1943; and Special Equipment Co. v. Coe, 324 US 370, 1945.
23. See for example, "The Return to the Constitution," by Henry Weihofen, in *Dicta*, October, 1941.

CHAPTER XXI

1. Black River Valley Broadcasts v. Federal Communications Commission, 69 App. D. C. 311; and Tumulty v. District of Columbia, 69 App. D. C. 390, respectively.
2. Parmelee v. United States, 113 F(2d) 729.

3. Davies Warehouse v. Brown, 137 F(2d) 201.
4. Gertman v. Burdick, 75 App. D. C. 48.
5. Sunshine Anthracite Coal Co. v. Adkins, 310 US 381, 1940.

CHAPTER XXII

1. Tot v. United States, 319 US 463, 1943.
2. United States v. Lovett, Nos. 309-11, October 1945 term.
3. Olsen v. Nebraska, 313 US 236, 1941.

Index

Set in Linotype Electra
Format by A .W. Rushmore
Manufactured by The Haddon Craftsmen
Published by HARPER & BROTHERS
New York and London

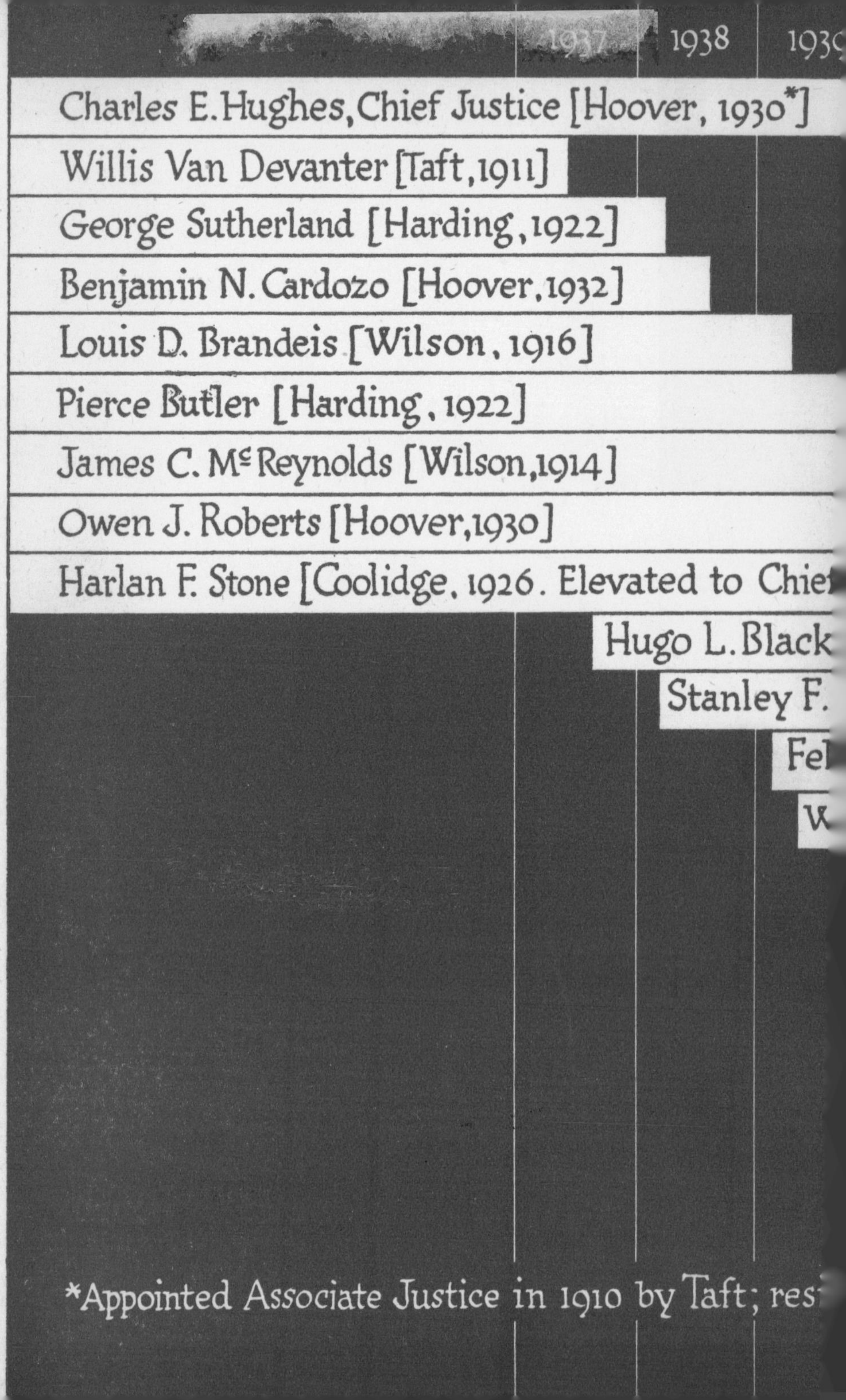

1937 | 1938 | 1939

Charles E. Hughes, Chief Justice [Hoover, 1930*]

Willis Van Devanter [Taft, 1911]

George Sutherland [Harding, 1922]

Benjamin N. Cardozo [Hoover, 1932]

Louis D. Brandeis [Wilson, 1916]

Pierce Butler [Harding, 1922]

James C. McReynolds [Wilson, 1914]

Owen J. Roberts [Hoover, 1930]

Harlan F. Stone [Coolidge, 1926. Elevated to Chie

Hugo L. Black

Stanley F.

Fe

W

*Appointed Associate Justice in 1910 by Taft; res